# Alligators in the Arctic and How to Avoid Them

Climate change is a matter of extreme urgency. Integrating science and economics, this book demonstrates the need for measures to put a strict lid on cumulative carbon emissions and shows how to implement them. Using the carbon budget framework, it reveals the shortcomings of current policies and the debates around them, such as the popular enthusiasm for individual solutions and the fruitless search for 'optimal' regulation by economists and other specialists. On the political front, it explains why business opposition to the policies we need goes well beyond the fossil fuel industry requiring a more radical rebalancing of power. This wide-ranging study goes against the most prevalent approaches in mainstream economics, which argue that we can tackle climate change while causing minimal disruption to the global economy. The author argues that this view is not only impossible, but also dangerously complacent.

**Peter Dorman** is Professor Emeritus of Political Economy at the Evergreen State College in Olympia, Washington

# Alligators in the Arctic and How to Avoid Them

## Science, Economics and the Challenge of Catastrophic Climate Change

**Peter Dorman**
Evergreen State College

CAMBRIDGE
UNIVERSITY PRESS

# CAMBRIDGE
## UNIVERSITY PRESS

University Printing House, Cambridge CB2 8BS, United Kingdom

One Liberty Plaza, 20th Floor, New York, NY 10006, USA

477 Williamstown Road, Port Melbourne, VIC 3207, Australia

314–321, 3rd Floor, Plot 3, Splendor Forum, Jasola District Centre,
New Delhi – 110025, India

103 Penang Road, #05-06/07, Visioncrest Commercial, Singapore 238467

Cambridge University Press is part of the University of Cambridge.

It furthers the University's mission by disseminating knowledge in the pursuit of
education, learning, and research at the highest international levels of excellence.

www.cambridge.org
Information on this title: www.cambridge.org/9781316516270
DOI: 10.1017/9781009029582

First published 2022

A *catalogue record for this publication is available from the British Library.*

*Library of Congress Cataloging-in-Publication Data*
NAMES: Dorman, Peter, author.
TITLE: Alligators in the Arctic and how to avoid them : science, economics and the
    challenge of catastrophic climate change / Peter Dorman, Evergreen State College
    (Washington State).
DESCRIPTION: Cambridge, United Kingdom ; New York, NY : Cambridge University
    Press, 2022. | Includes bibliographical references and index.
IDENTIFIERS: LCCN 2021050502 (print) | LCCN 2021050503 (ebook) | ISBN
    9781316516270 (hardback) | ISBN 9781009014731 (paperback) | ISBN
    9781009029582 (epub)
SUBJECTS: LCSH: Climatic changes–Economic aspects. | Fossil fuels–Environmental
    aspects. | Carbon dioxide mitigation.
CLASSIFICATION: LCC GE195 .D675 2022 (print) | LCC GE195 (ebook) |
    DDC 333.72–dc23/eng/20211217
LC record available at https://lccn.loc.gov/2021050502
LC ebook record available at https://lccn.loc.gov/2021050503

ISBN 978-1-316-51627-0 Hardback

To Bill Steel (1916–2017), who set the course.

# CONTENTS

# FIGURES, MAPS AND TABLES

## Map

## Figures

## Tables

# PREFACE

This book has its origins in a graduate course on climate change I co-taught with a climate scientist and a global justice specialist in 2015 and again in 2016. Prior to this I had been involved for over a decade in the economics of climate policy, but combining my background with that of my two teaching colleagues changed my perspective. It was in this course, for example, that I first learned about the Paleocene–Eocene Thermal Maximum, whose peripatetic alligators have been adopted as the book's mascots. More importantly, as I expanded my understanding of the biogeochemical basis of the carbon cycle, I saw more clearly how dubious were many of the assumptions underlying the usual discussion of climate issues.

The precipitating event, however, was the release of the Fifth Assessment Report in 2014 by the Intergovernmental Panel on Climate Change (IPCC). The centerpiece of this massive work was the promulgation of a clear target, limiting global warming to 2°C above the preindustrial level, and a means for achieving it, a fixed cumulative limit on all emissions over the coming century. This yardstick, a carbon budget, established a framework for the more elaborate policy analysis that filled out the report.

Immediately, a vast gap had opened up between the most authoritative scientific body concerned with climate change and not only the policies already in place, but nearly all the reforms on the table as well. The ideas of political leaders, environmental advocacy groups, journalists and just about everyone else with an opinion about what needed to be done were out of sync with the IPCC and its participating scientists. While the proposals they put forward might be steps in the right direction, the crucial element of a fixed emission budget was missing. In particular, my own tribe, professional economists, was preoccupied with complex calculations of the optimal amount of carbon emissions, unaware or unimpressed that climate scientists had already made the call.

In this context, there was an obvious need for a book that would point out the chasm between the worlds of science and policy, and I set out to write it. I would lay out the scientific perspective for lay readers with the goal of explaining why the IPCC had decided on the necessity of its carbon budget and explain how the "solutions" put forward by governments, corporations and activists alike were often inconsistent with the budget imperative. Then I would sketch what a budget-adhering approach would look like. Finally, drawing on my own background in economics and political economy, I would explain why economists in particular have been so resistant to a more scientifically informed approach, and why government policy has been so delayed and inadequate.

By the middle of 2017, after outside reviews and revisions to respond to them, I had drafted the book in roughly its current form. Alas, *Alligators* then encountered stiff headwinds. Putting aside the ups and downs, what transpired was a delay of more than four years. Of course, most any manuscript will benefit from so many additional years of tinkering, and I am sure the current version of this one is stronger for it. The problem with this hiatus, however, is that important developments were undermining the simple message I originally intended to convey.

Some had to do with the IPCC carbon budget itself. New information had altered estimates of historical carbon emissions and the climate's sensitivity to them, increasing budget recommendations a bit. But new research findings also showed that "moderate" climate change was more dangerous than previously thought, so the IPCC created a second, lower warming target, 1.5°C, introducing a new source of ambiguity that hasn't been resolved. This meant I couldn't just pull a single number of an IPCC report and present it as the consensus yardstick. Like the IPCC, I would have to juggle two targets and greater budgetary uncertainty.

Meanwhile, the idea that the whole of climate policy could be summed up in a single limit on remaining emissions depended on converting all other greenhouse gases to their carbon dioxide "equiva-lent." This was codified in a table of global warming effect ratios, that is, how much of one gas had the same effect as how much of another. Beginning with the publication of the Fifth Assessment Report, how-ever, a number of researchers challenged the IPCC's methodology. Their arguments were persuasive, and before long a consensus emerged that a single budget number couldn't fold together qualitatively differ-ent gases. There was still support for a carbon dioxide emission budget, but not as an all-encompassing solution to mitigating climate change.

And there were still other developments. The IPCC was giving increasing attention to policies that didn't directly control carbon emis-sions but made it easier to do so; this was reflected in the methodology of "shared socioeconomic pathways." The existence of this new research framework expanded policy discussion beyond the simple mandate of setting and adhering to a carbon budget.

All of these developments qualified and complicated the core theme of the book I had set out to write, applying an ostensibly settled IPCC position on carbon budgets to a policy world that hadn't yet grasped it. Further revision was needed to incorporate the new wrinkles by adjusting the core message.

As all this was happening, policy fashions were changing as well. The focus of *Alligators* had been on strategies ostensibly aimed at controlling carbon emissions directly, like emission caps and taxes, but these were losing some of their luster. The United States under Trump had tried to suspend climate policy altogether, of course, but even more activist US states, the European Union and other jurisdictions had increasingly begun to see such controls as secondary measures whose purpose was to clean up the odds and ends left over from their preferred policy kit, investment. The new emphasis of governments and critics alike was on spending large sums of money for renewable energy sources, infrastructure, energy efficiency and research into advanced carbon-removing technologies. To all appearances, the world was drifting away from the types of policies the IPCC had foregrounded with its 2014 carbon budget and around which I had organized my book.

Adapting *Alligators* to this new context was challenging but feasible, and the book you have in your hands, or on your screen, is the outcome. I won't go through all the adjustments that had to be made, but if you are looking for them they will be easy to spot. In the end, this rethinking and the more nuanced argument it produced resulted in a stronger book. Of course, if the current draft were delayed for another four years, there would be new findings, new policy trends and new complexities to incorporate. That too might yield a deeper study, but the climate clock is ticking, and the best argument is the one that can be made today.

Writing this book benefited from the various research topics I had explored previously; I was fortunate they also proved relevant to climate policy. Even so, one area in which my background was spotty was the natural science basis on which the entire topic rests. Here I have to acknowledge the immense benefit I received from interdisciplinary teaching at Evergreen State College. My classroom colleagues included geologists, biologists, chemists, physicists, geographers, energy policy experts and many others. I doubt I could have written a book of this scope without some of their expertise rubbing off on me. My first acknowledgment, then, goes not to any single individual but the philosophy and practice of interdisciplinary inquiry embodied in the Evergreen approach. Of course, it also goes to these dedicated and inquisitive colleagues themselves. If I haven't thanked them enough in our end-of-course wrap-ups, I hope they will feel warmly thanked now.

Outside Evergreen I am grateful for the stimulation I received from Peter Barnes, who pulled me into climate policy many years ago when I was preoccupied by other issues, Jim Boyce, who has helped clarify my thinking on the economics and politics of carbon pricing, and the reviewers who took apart earlier versions of this book in a spirit of constructive criticism. When it came to scrubbing out errors of scientific understanding and interpretation, I received timely, invaluable help from Jerry Dickens, Joost Frieling and Joeri Rogelj, although of course any residual mistakes are mine alone. Tom Athanasiou provided feedback on one of the chapters. Particular recognition should be given to Phil Good of Cambridge University Press, who supported *Alligators* when it was most needed and made important stylistic recommendations. Above all, the support, understanding and insight of Saumya Comer was the final, crucial ingredient – especially the encouragement I needed when the future of the project was in doubt and I needed again to make it across the finish line.

# INTRODUCTION
## When Alligators Go North

### A Warning from the Past

Ellesmere Island is in the very far north of Canada, above the Arctic Circle. It lies just to the west of Greenland, and like its bigger neighbor it is almost entirely glaciated. If you are on your way to the North Pole by way of Canada, this will probably be your last stop (see Map I.1). Few scientists had made their way to Ellesmere when Mary Dawson, a paleontologist at the Carnegie Museum of Natural History, launched her first expedition there in 1973. Dawson, forty-two at the time, was fascinated by the possibility that there had once been a land bridge between North America and Europe, and she hoped to find evidence that terrestrial species had migrated across it millions of years ago. Accompanied by a coworker, she hauled her gear to a remote camp and began scouring the desolate, frozen territory for fossil remains.[1]

Her initial efforts met with little success, but on a return visit in 1975 she struck paydirt. One after another, she found fossils of ancient mammals, turtles, plants – and alligators. *Alligators.* By analyzing the oxygen isotopes embedded in bone material, Dawson and her colleagues were able to estimate the temperature conditions that made semi-tropical life possible hundreds of miles north of the Arctic Circle. They found that, during the time of the alligators, summer temperature on Ellesmere averaged a balmy 68°F (20°C), and even average winter temperatures didn't dip below freezing. Was this because the island was further south back then? No: ancient

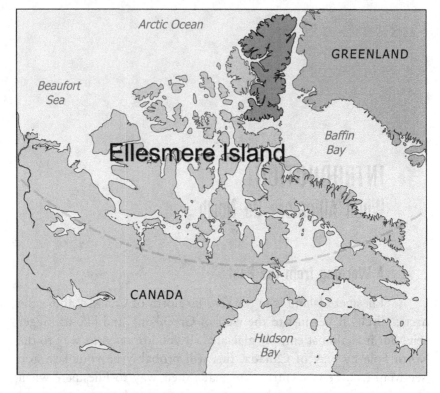

**Map I.1**  Map of Ellesmere Island.
*Source*: New World Encyclopedia.

Ellesmere was a few degrees south of its current position, but still well above the Arctic Circle. Somehow the far north had roughly the same climate then as the southeastern United States has today, with cypress swamps where you might find not only large reptiles but also hippopotamus-like mammals wading in to gnaw on aquatic plants. If you find this stunning, imagine the surprise of Dawson's team when they stumbled upon the fossil evidence.

They kept coming back to Ellesmere and nearby islands, working under challenging conditions and deepening our understanding of an extraordinary period in Earth history. (Dawson herself fought off a wolf attack in 1977.[2]) Her last visit was in 2002 – she's now an emeritus Curator of Vertebrate Paleontology at the Carnegie Museum – but a team from the University of Colorado headed by Jaelyn Eberle has continued where she left off.[3] There is another astonishing fact to reveal, but first we need to put Ellesmere's alligators in context.

Arctic lushness dates from an unusual episode in the geological record, the Paleocene–Eocene Thermal Maximum (PETM). This occurred approximately 56 million years ago, when temperatures soared for about 170,000 years, a long time from a human perspective but just a brief moment in Earth history.[4] Just how and why this happened is a matter of dispute, but decades of research have progressively culled the list of possible explanations and are narrowing the differences in estimated temperatures and environmental conditions.[5] One reason it is taking time to reach consensus is that the geological brevity of 170,000 years means there are relatively few traces for today's researchers to locate and analyze, and different remains require different methods and modeling frameworks.

How warm did it get during the PETM? Temperatures rose 5–8°C from a previously warm epoch, making the average temperature at the PETM peak 12 to 18°C warmer than today.[6] When alligators roamed the north, sea-level temperatures at the North Pole averaged between 14 and 19°C year-round,[7] which of course meant not only that there was no sea ice in the Arctic but that humans, if they had existed, would have enjoyed comfortable summer swimming conditions at their polar getaways. Balmy weather at the pole meant torrid conditions in the tropics, however. A recent analysis of a site in Tanzania, which at the time of the PETM was 70 kilometers offshore, found that surface water temperatures were as high as 36–43°C, or 97–109°F, suggesting that inland temperatures were even steamier.[8] As we will see later, conditions of this sort would render a significant portion of the globe uninhabitable by humans, at least if they are not enclosed in a technological cocoon.

There is little doubt the temperature extremes of the PETM were primarily the result of large emissions of greenhouse gases, carbon dioxide ($CO_2$) and methane ($CH_4$), into the atmosphere. Several explanations exist for its cause. For a time there was speculation that a cyclic change in the Earth's orbit around the sun might have played a significant role, but as measurement of the timing of the event and the composition of atmospheric carbon has become more precise, other explanations have gained ground.[9] A plausible hypothesis, for instance, is that the triggering event was the separation of the North American and European landmasses east of present-day Greenland, which might have resulted in a period of intense volcanic releases of greenhouse gases into the atmosphere. The initial warming resulting from this cataclysmic process may then have led to further releases of carbon previously sequestered in soils or very cold, deep marine deposits, although this is currently a matter of considerable dispute.[10] This is our first hint that *feedback mechanisms* may play an important role in historic, and future, climate fluctuations, a topic we will return to shortly.

Of critical importance to modern-day humans is the question of how much additional carbon dioxide did it take to turn the Earth into a PETM planetary sauna and how close are we today to replicating it? Of course, the amount of carbon dioxide in the atmosphere millions of years ago is not directly measurable today, so researchers have to find indicators that point to it indirectly.

A (relatively) convenient approach takes advantage of the fact that chemical elements are not uniform in nature. They can differ in the number of protons and electrons they contain, and the term "isotope" is used to designate a specific combination. Carbon-13 (written as $^{13}$C) is one such isotope, whose six protons and seven neutrons sum to thirteen, and it is associated with a particular molecular history, especially methane; by measuring the proportion of the carbon preserved from an earlier period that shows up as carbon-13 it is possible to estimate how much of it originated from various methane-generating sources like decaying plant matter and magma releases. The point is that, on release, this methane would have found its way into the atmosphere, where, as we will see in the next chapter, it would have been transformed into carbon dioxide, augmenting the greenhouse trapping of solar radiation. Even after this additional carbon dioxide leaves the atmosphere many thousands of years later to be incorporated in carbon-bearing sediments, fossils or rocks, its telltale $^{13}$C isotope records its sojourn as methane and then atmospheric carbon dioxide.

Once the quantity of prehistoric methane releases can be estimated, the next step is to determine how much of this additional carbon would have accumulated in the atmosphere and for how long. This can be estimated using models of the global carbon balance (stable relationships between the amounts of carbon in the atmosphere, soils, ocean and living organisms). Because different research sites and carbon-bearing substances yield different isotopic proportions, and different climate models perform this conversion into estimates of atmospheric carbon dioxide somewhat differently, there is a range of estimates of how carbon-saturated the PETM atmosphere was when alligators dipped into waters that sport polar bears today. The latest research gives us a lower bound of about 1,200 parts per million (ppm) carbon dioxide and an upper of about 2,000 ppm.[11] Note these are estimates of *peak* carbon dioxide concentrations; as we will see, it is possible that less than this is needed to set the process of extreme climate change in motion.

So, if the PETM was triggered by unusual releases of greenhouse gases and produced a global heat wave that lasted for over 100,000 years, how did it end? Why didn't the planet just stay hot? As you would expect, this is another matter of dispute, since the record that has come down to us is so fragmentary. One possibility is increased weathering, where carbon is stripped from soils or precipitated into rock formations and buried beyond the reach of the Earth surface carbon cycle. It is increasingly agreed, however, that a significant role was played by a profusion of living organisms, which pulled carbon from the atmosphere and redirected some of it to deep sea or deep earth burial.

What does that mean specifically? Here is where a remarkable fact about the PETM comes into play. Recall the far north experienced near-tropical conditions for many thousands of years. The Arctic Ocean was not only free of ice, it was a welcoming habitat for plants and animals usually found far to the south. One such new inhabitant was *Azolla*, a fern that floats freely on open waters with moderate temperatures and limited salinity. With the Arctic sea accepting massive inflows of freshwater from north-flowing rivers in Canada and Siberia – a reflection of altered precipitation patterns – and enjoying alligator-friendly temperatures, it was eventually covered with a mat of this sea fern.[12] Tangles of ferns, not ice, would have obstructed your trip to the North Pole. *Azolla* serves as a poster child for the explosion of biological growth during the PETM, although even more carbon would have been funneled into increased growth of marine plankton invisible to the naked eye. While most of the carbon pulled out of the atmosphere by this "biological pump" would have returned through transpiration and decay, some small amount each year would have migrated down into the sea floor, no longer available for greenhouse service. After tens of thousands of years, enough carbon would be withdrawn in this fashion to help bring atmospheric carbon dioxide concentrations down to a more normal level.[13]

## A Warning from the Future

And so, from alligators to *Azolla*, this completes our first exposure to the disturbing topic of catastrophic climate change. What we know is that, spurred by singular natural processes, like the pulling apart of tectonic plates – processes unlikely to be repeated for many millennia to come – much of the Earth became uninhabitable for organisms like modern-day humans. But the truly frightening prospect is that human beings, through their own actions, could bring about a similar result. Instead of volcanoes we have coal, oil and natural gas companies drawing long-buried carbon from the earth and sending it into the atmosphere. Where are we on the road to the PETM? Consider the most recent data posted by the US Environmental Protection Agency (EPA), shown in Figure I.1. This time path considers only carbon dioxide, the main form that carbon appears in the atmosphere. Carbon also shows up in methane, whose heat-trapping effects are far greater but whose life span is also much shorter. Carbon dioxide, however, is a stable gas, and its carbon exits the atmosphere only as a result of the flows between air, land and water we will look at in the next chapter, while methane reacts with oxygen, resulting in the separation of its hydrogen and the formation of new carbon dioxide. This process is complete in a few decades, so measuring just carbon dioxide over a timescale like that in Figure I.1,

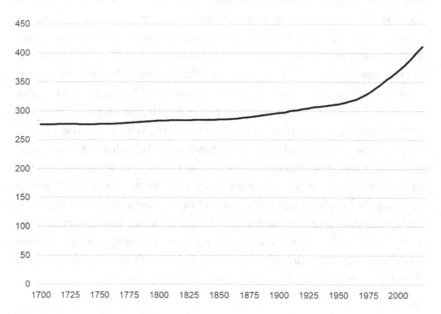

**Figure I.1** Atmospheric $CO_2$ accumulation since 1700 in parts per million (ppm). The carbon concentration in the atmosphere has increased from about 275 ppm in 1700 to over 400 ppm today. Multiple measurements in a given year are reported as arithmetic averages. Direct measurement began in 1959.
*Source*: US EPA (2021).

with its global carbon dioxide concentrations over the past 300-plus years, captures most of the "older" methane as well. (There are also other, highly potent greenhouse gases with intermediate life spans like nitrous oxide, but we will set them aside for now.)

For many tens of thousands of years, the carbon dioxide concentration has fluctuated between 180 and 280 ppm, as ice ages came and went. For the past thousand years it remained stable at around 275 ppm – until the late eighteenth century, when it slowly began to rise. The rate of increase gradually picked up as the industrial revolution took hold, and fossil fuel use became widespread. For the past half-century it has taken off at a full gallop, and each year brings us into new, unexplored territory.

The most recent annual average is 410 ppm, nearly a 50% increase over the preindustrial level. Extraordinary as this is, however, it still leaves us well short of the 1,200 ppm that can serve as a guess of likely carbon dioxide concentrations during the PETM, but there are two more factors that need to be considered. First, carbon dioxide concentrations in the atmosphere continue to grow year by year, as people extract, burn and release carbon in various forms. Because carbon dioxide (and some other) greenhouse gases are very long-lived, in the absence of any further large-scale human intervention annual net additions of atmospheric carbon are effectively permanent.[14] While there have been slight ups and downs, during the past decade the rate of growth in carbon dioxide concentrations was a bit over 0.5% (0.00575) per year – until, of course, the global economic slump triggered by the coronavirus.

Let's extrapolate this trend. Taking 410 ppm as our starting point in 2019 and 0.575% as our growth rate, unless we change course we will hit 437 ppm in 2030, 490 ppm in 2050 and 652 ppm by 2100. But what about the economic slowdown due to the pandemic? We will return to that question later, but for now, let's assume that the growth in atmospheric carbon dioxide falls by 25% as the world struggles with the coronavirus, and that this phase lasts for five years, after which growth returns to its 0.575% trajectory.[15] Making that adjustment gives us 434 ppm in 2030, 486 ppm in 2050 and 648 in 2100 – just a minor reduction. These numbers would be alarming, but not enough in themselves to cause us to worry about wandering alligators.

But there is a second factor that casts an even darker shadow over all our thinking on this topic. It is likely that the very high atmospheric carbon dioxide concentration of the PETM was not the result of a single triggering event and nothing more. Suppose the process that set it in motion began, as many think, with an upsurge of volcanic releases as two giant tectonic plates in the North Atlantic tore apart. That would have caused a big influx of carbon, previously sequestered within the Earth, into the atmosphere–ocean–biosphere carbon cycle, leading in short order to higher temperatures. But higher temperatures, in turn, would likely have caused further releases of stored carbon, as methane was released from soils, peats and underwater deposits. The benchmark against which we should measure our own "progress" in achieving higher atmospheric carbon dioxide is not the final peak realized during the PETM, whether this was 1,200 ppm or some other level, but the concentration resulting from the initial trigger that was sufficient to bring about *further* releases, creating a self-feeding process that stopped only when a much hotter planet struck a new balance.

To put numbers on it, suppose the peak was 1,200 ppm and the trigger alone brought the atmosphere to 600 ppm, after which the initial warming released the rest of the carbon that contributed the other 600. This should be taken with many grains of salt, since there may have been multiple triggers operating at different times and coexisting with many feedback mechanisms, and of course the numbers we are using are strictly hypothetical. The logic, however, is essential: it tells us that, if this example were true, the level of atmospheric carbon dioxide with "thou shalt not pass" written on it would not be 1,200 but 600 ppm. If we were to allow ourselves to exceed this limit, we would run a very high risk of initiating the same feedback processes that fueled the PETM.

What makes the situation so uncomfortable, however, is that, rather than a line, what we face is a slippery slope of increasingly dangerous and unforeseeable feedback risk. There is no perfectly safe level of atmospheric carbon dioxide we can still plateau at given past and unavoidable future emissions. Perhaps there are particular carbon dioxide concentrations we might regard as tipping points, and if we had perfect knowledge of the Earth's carbon system in prehistoric times as well as the present we could possibly identify them. But the system is extraordinarily complicated. We have models of it, but they embody assumptions that can't be fully tested because we don't have enough data, especially as we begin to alter the Earth's climate in ways it hasn't experienced in millions of years. We know only that peak atmospheric carbon dioxide during the PETM was somewhere between 1,200 and

2,000 ppm. That's not nothing, but it leaves a lot of uncertainty for what to expect in the coming century.

A frightening thought: Could we have already passed key tipping levels of carbon dioxide that make a full-on climate catastrophe unavoidable? Very unlikely. What if we add to the current level the near-future emissions that are baked in irrespective of policy? Still unlikely. But this is the wrong question. What we do know, even with our still-emerging knowledge of complex Earth systems, is that the longer we allow greenhouse gases to be emitted, the greater is the risk that we *could* trigger feedback responses that make runaway climate change a dire threat. Even intermediate scenarios, with feedbacks that intensify climate change but not on a PETM scale, involve taking unknown risks with unfathomable consequences. It is the premise of this book that it is simply unacceptable to continue blindly on the current course and let these risks mount year after year.

To be specific: I will argue for the position that climate change needs to be minimized as a matter of extreme urgency, and that this entails, above all, adhering to a carbon emissions budget that would steadily reduce the use of fossil fuels each year until they are largely phased out in just a few decades. The pace of this phaseout needs to be set by the necessity of keeping warming to a minimum, not by economic convenience. This will not be easy; in fact, it will be highly disruptive to the institutions, technologies and habits we have come to depend on – and which have brought us to this point. I am convinced it can be done, that we have the economic tools we need to extricate ourselves from a carbon nightmare, but there is little room for delay, obfuscation, magical thinking or compromise. I wish the message could be friendly and encouraging, but instead it's hard and offers little wiggle room. Perhaps there was a time, decades ago, when easier, more relaxed methods might have done the job, but not now.

## Mapping a New Economics and Politics

Why begin with a tale of wandering alligators and hothouse temperatures 56 million years ago? This is not a treatise on paleoclimatology or Arctic environments. What I hope this story gives you, however, is a feeling for the scale of the crisis we face and its extraordinary implications in light of Earth history. The difficult part will be holding onto this frame when we wade, as we must, into the morass of economic and policy detail.

Many books have been published putting contemporary climate change into a planetary and geological perspective. (One of these, *Laboratory Earth: The Planetary Gamble We Can't Afford to Lose* by the late Stephen Schneider, was the book that first convinced me of the centrality of this issue.[16]) I have little to add to them. The problem, however, is that they don't draw out the economic and political implications of this perspective, while the much greater number of policy-oriented books on climate change, although inspired in a general way by the science, put the constraints of economics and politics first. What would it mean to consider today's policy debates through the lens of Earth history and global environmental processes – the same lens through which we viewed the PETM? That's what the rest of the book is about.

In particular, I will focus on the strange dual role of economics, an indispensable tool for formulating and evaluating policies, yet also a primary source of misunderstanding. Carbon emissions are produced, every bit as much, and often in the same moment, as automobiles, restaurant meals and bank loans. Economics is the branch of knowledge that best explains how and why these things are produced and therefore also how to produce them differently or not at all. In addition, the economy is intricately interconnected, so that changes in some products or industries typically have ramifications throughout the system. This too is the province of economics.

But economics, at least in its dominant versions, brings a perspective to climate change that competes with the Earth history view. Consider the interesting case of William (Bill) Nordhaus of Yale University, winner of the 2018 Economics Prize "in honor" of Alfred Nobel.[17] This award was based on decades of work during which Nordhaus developed methods that have come to be standard for most researchers. As we will see in more detail later, his innovation was to marry models of economic "general equilibrium" with other equations representing the impacts of human activity on global warming. You would think this was exactly the integration of scientific understanding and human production systems we need in order to avoid the recurrence of PETM-like conditions.

The purpose of Nordhaus' modeling, however, was not to minimize the risk of a catastrophe but to ascertain the "optimal" level of global warming, the one that ideally balances, in his view, the costs of not taking enough action with the costs of taking too much. His recommended target has changed over the years as he has continued to revise his model and the data it feeds on; at first he advocated only the most minimal effort to tamp down carbon emissions, while now he is willing to go further. Even so, he still advocates policies that would result in a 3.5°C global temperature increase, far above the 1.5–2.0° ceiling proposed by the UN's Intergovernmental Panel on Climate Change (IPCC) and endorsed, at least on paper, by the Paris Climate Agreement.[18]

To be as clear as possible, the situation is this: the economist who has received the highest honors for his research on climate change and has been the most influential in guiding the work of his peers thinks the upper limit on allowable warming should be twice as high as the one set by the world's leading climate scientists – an accommodation, we will see, that carries with it a substantial risk of uncontrollable further warming with even more catastrophic implications. How is this possible?

The short answer is that economics has two faces. One describes and forecasts, telling us how effective different policies are likely to be in controlling carbon emissions and what impacts on different groups in society will result. The other assigns value; it treats every outcome as if it were a consumption good and asks how we can maximize the benefit we get from the total basket. In the pages to come we will have a lot more to say about both faces – how we aren't using enough of the first but instead too much of the second. Even as regiments of economists are enlisted to second-guess science and compute "optimal" levels of warming, immensely consequential aspects of regulations to control carbon emissions are barely considered. The questions not asked about the economics of climate change will be surprising and disturbing.

Insisting on an honest, clear-eyed view of the economics of forestalling a climate catastrophe is one way of being realistic, but there is another version of realism that currently dominates policy debates. According to this other view, we should begin with measures that are politically popular, or can readily be sold to the public, and not too costly economically. Once modest climate policy gets a foothold we can gradually ramp it up, and if we are fortunate the process will go quickly enough that we might be able to avoid the worst climate outcomes. This

approach is realistic, which is to say not too demanding, in its economics and politics but crosses its fingers about climate tipping points. The
way this book interprets realism, however, is to begin with climate
imperatives and commit to ways to adhere to them even if the economics and politics are difficult. Just how difficult they might be is one of the
core themes of the pages to come, and what we will learn will not be
comforting. Nevertheless, if looking at the challenge we face through
the lens of Earth history and its peripatetic alligators means anything,
it's that climate realism has to come first.

## Defogging

Meanwhile, as we have drifted through decades of obfuscation
and delay, a number of misconceptions have grown up around how to
think about climate action. In some cases, this is because people brought
their prior mental frameworks to this new area of concern, not stopping
to reflect on whether they still made sense. In others it was a matter of
expedience: it was simply more convenient to believe that a climate
disaster could be prevented by simple, low-cost, politically popular
measures even if the reality were otherwise. In order to clear space for
an economics and politics fitted to the climate challenge it will be
necessary to dispel these sources of confusion.

Here is a list of specific misconceptions that future chapters will
examine:

1. False symmetry: *Action against climate change is just another case
   of economic balancing, weighing the costs of climate alteration
   against the costs of limiting it.* Yes, these commentators say, the
   accumulation of greenhouse gases is a problem, but it isn't fundamentally different from other problems we cope with every day. We
   shouldn't do too little about it, but we shouldn't do too much
   either. The trick is to recognize that climate change is simply an
   economic problem, costly in the same way regulation to counter it
   will be. This allows us to measure the combined costs at each level
   of global warming, so we can turn the policy dial to the precise
   point where their sum is minimized.
2. Wishful thinking: *Combating climate change will not be difficult.* It's
   just a matter of getting past the diehard denialists. We will create lots
   of green jobs, and we won't even have to put a climate label on it.

People will support our program for all the economic opportunity it creates. And government revenue from carbon caps or taxes is a wonderful resource for new public services, since only the corporate polluters will pay it.[19]

3. Ideological preconceptions: *Climate change is not primarily about geology and chemistry; it's a sign of a deep flaw in human nature or ideology or modern ways of life.* Climate change may superficially look different, but it is just another result of the same deep flaw responsible for all modern problems. Depending on who you ask, this flaw is (a) overpopulation, (b) the desire for economic growth, (c) money and markets, (d) living in cities, cut off from deep experience of nature, (e) racism and sexism or (f) all of the above. Unless we fix the root cause, policy actions focused directly on reducing carbon emissions will only reinforce the system that gave us climate change in the first place. In fact, policies that zero in on fossil fuels without getting to the "true" causes are illusory and should be opposed.[20]

4. The individualist illusion: *We can solve the climate problem by changing behavior one person/company/community at a time.* Each of us can calculate our own carbon footprint and then take measures to become carbon neutral. Once our carbon audits show we've all brought our net emissions down to zero the problem is solved. In the end, climate change is about personal responsibility.

Each of these misconceptions, in its own way, is well-intentioned; the people who hold them understand we face a serious problem and want to do something about it. Nevertheless, usually without much reflection, they have imported assumptions that make effective action less rather than more likely.

Economists and policy wonks espousing a false symmetry between the costs of planetary destabilization and those of combating it want to fit climate change into a well-known mold, a sort of business-reform-as-usual that would minimize uncertainty and inconvenience. Those are reasonable goals under many circumstances, but climate change is not one of them; its threat is existential and the economic problem is how to minimize it with the least disruption to our quality of life. Of course, there are still trade-offs, yet the metaphor that comes to mind is not balancing but navigation. As we will see, difficult choices lie ahead, especially when we confront the tension between decarbonization and the need for low-income countries to develop their economies to meet other human needs. Rejecting the false symmetry between the demands of the natural world and the economy we erect on it forces us to think more deeply about the paths open to us.

The soft-pedaling of climate action summarized in claim (2) is often motivated by the desire to sidestep potential political obstacles. It's a bit like being told by a doctor that a needed medical procedure won't hurt very much, as a way to convince you to go through with it. No doubt, it will be easier to take the first steps toward addressing the climate crisis if the public thinks the economic costs will be minimal or that there won't even be costs at all. But what if the claim isn't true? Unraveling the likely costs entailed in drastically reducing carbon emissions is complex, especially as some of the most troublesome economic aspects have barely been considered – but the evidence isn't encouraging. When we examine the perils of wishful thinking close up it will become clear why downplaying cost is bad politics, and also why understanding what forms these costs will take and who will bear them reveals what a more effective politics will look like.

Just as some people downplay the climate crisis for purposes of political convenience, others, in thrall to ideological preconceptions, try to exploit its epic seriousness to pursue other, largely unrelated goals. The problem is not necessarily the ideologies themselves, but the tendency to apply them to climate change whether they fit or not – especially when they are made the basis of a politics of all-or-nothing. Although the claim we can meet the climate challenge only by addressing some other "deeper" cause is often advertised as radical, we will find that directly curtailing carbon emissions on the timescale required by climate science is itself a radical, even transformative undertaking, although not in ways most standard ideologies would predict.

If ideological preconceptions appeal to all-encompassing social theories, the individualist illusion lies at the opposite extreme, lacking any theory to explain why society is more than just an aggregation of individuals. This illusion operates on two levels. One is the adding-up approach to limiting carbon emissions, according to which the social objective of meeting a climate target can be broken down to each person's or organization's individual share. It is not too difficult to show, on the contrary, that serious action needs to be collective, since many of the necessary changes can be made only at scale. The more surprising illusion, however, is more fundamental, that we can know what our individual contributions to global emissions are at all. As we will see, even the most scrupulous of carbon audits depend on assumptions and arbitrary accounting boundaries that leave the bottom line uncertain – and there is no way to avoid this.

One of the reasons the misconceptions sketched above have taken hold is that existing measures to curtail the use of fossil fuels have been so inadequate: with the path of direct public action to shut down emissions discredited, those who care about the problem have been attracted by other paths, however wayward. Part of the project of dispelling false leads in climate policy has to be explaining why it has been so difficult to make progress at keeping fossil fuels in the ground; unless we can do this the science-based realism I advocate will turn out to be just another form of magical thinking.

Here we come to a crucial point in the story, the *political economy* of climate change. Our economies have evolved over centuries in which fossil fuels played a central role but their impact on the global carbon cycle was overlooked. Where we live, how we travel, the work we do and the goods we consume all reflect this evolution. This has obvious implications for the livelihoods that millions of people have devoted their lives to and depend on. These people vote, and technocratic policy strategies haven't given enough thought to making solutions to the climate crisis work for them too, at least tolerably.

But we also can't overlook the significance of living in a capitalist world. Wealth derives its value from the revenues generated by carbon-dependent production and consumption networks, and a large portion of it would be at risk if we were to implement tough policies against fossil fuels. Although the vulnerability of the fossil fuel sector itself has been studied, not enough attention has been given to the wider impacts of decarbonization on wealth – a topic we will take up later. As we will see, there is a deep conflict between the no-loss-of-wealth constraint that usually binds political life and the no-loss-of-planet constraint imposed by the need to forestall catastrophic climate change. Understanding the basis for this conflict and what it implies for future economic and political agendas is central to any hope of making meaningful progress.

The rest of the book will weave together these different strands: the implacable demands of the climate challenge, the misconceptions that continue to obstruct progress even apart from the efforts of the outright climate deniers, the dismal record of existing policies and programs despite the feasibility of measures that would actually ensure a livable planet, and finally the conundrums of politics and power that have to be overcome nationally and internationally. It's an immense set of topics, but each bears on the others. To examine them responsibly means taking account of a wide range of research and the uncertainties of still-evolving fields of study. Fortunately, there will be a stream of surprising discoveries along the way and at least the faint glimpse of a possible happy ending.

# 1 CARBON ACCOUNTING FOR PLANET EARTH

On March 21, 2017, officials from the Idaho National Laboratory of the US Department of Energy (DOE), en route to a destination in San Antonio, Texas, stopped for the night at a Marriott hotel. Rather carelessly, they left a suitcase on the back seat of their rental car in the hotel's parking lot containing small bits of radioactive plutonium and cesium they intended to use the next day. They woke up to find the car broken into and the suitcase gone (Malone and Smith, 2018).

This event required new entries into the DOE's plutonium accounting system. The agency records inventories of this most dangerous of substances in federal laboratories and weapons facilities as well as nongovernmental outfits that borrow small amounts for their own use. One of the accounting categories is "materials unaccounted for"; the San Antonio theft meant that the Idaho National Laboratory would have to be debited a few grams, which would be designated as missing. At the time of its last public report back in 2012, the DOE reported about six tons of missing plutonium. Most of it is presumably secure but disappeared from the accounting system – residues lodged in equipment, for instance – but even so, the amount is troubling given that only seven pounds of plutonium is enough to produce a usable nuclear explosive (Malone and Smith, 2018).

The purpose of bringing up this unpleasant subject is to illustrate the observation that a wide variety of accounting systems plays a crucial role in modern life. We are accustomed to thinking about accounting in financial terms, but accounts can be drawn up for units of time, grams of plutonium or – and this is our subject now – for the storage and flows of carbon across, and even within, the entire planet. All an accounting system needs is something measurable it can keep track of, and carbon qualifies easily.

But why carbon? It is significant for each component of the Earth system: it can appear in the form of a rock like limestone (calcium carbonate), as a gas in the atmosphere (carbon dioxide), as a component of the chemistry of the ocean and, crucially, as an irreplaceable element in living organisms. The same carbon atoms can be all of these in sequence, as we will see shortly. Keeping track of carbon as it transits from one substance and location to another is why we need a special system of accounts. Before plunging into the accounting framework itself, however, we will pause to take a closer look at the critical role this element has played in Earth history – a detour that will illuminate why the burning of fossil fuels on an industrial scale is the most consequential action ever undertaken by human beings.

## Carbon and Life over Geological Time

If you happen to be an animal, a plant or a fungus, carbon is in your every cell.[1] Along with oxygen, nitrogen and other elements, carbon forms molecular chains that are the basis of organic chemistry; depending on what other atoms hook onto them and where they position themselves, you can end up with proteins, plant tissue or petroleum. There may be other forms of life in the universe that are not based on carbon, but life on this planet is a set of intricate variations on a carbon theme.

Carbon is ever on the move, and a particularly important flow is photosynthesis. Green plants have the capacity to convert carbon dioxide, water, nitrogen, phosphorus and other nutrients, with an energy boost from solar radiation, into sugars to feed themselves and grow. When this happens, carbon dioxide is being withdrawn from the atmosphere and biologically stored carbon in the form of plant tissue is increasing. Plants that use carbon this way are referred to as primary producers; all other organisms, including us, get our food directly or indirectly from them. Of course, there are reverse processes that take carbon from plants and animals and return it to the atmosphere. The most important is simply the death of the organism: with decomposition carbon is released and made available to be transported through air and water. The movement of carbon from the inorganic environment (air, water and minerals) into the tissue of organisms and then back to the environment, and then back to organisms and so on is the *carbon cycle* – or, more precisely, the Earth surface carbon cycle. (We will get to the deep Earth cycle later.) At any moment in time you could measure the amount of carbon in each location, but start the clock and the carbon will be flowing in every direction. The movement of carbon from one place, like the atmosphere or storage in organisms, to another is called carbon exchange. It is a fundamental component of our world, happening everywhere and always; human beings couldn't hope to stop or contain it even if they wanted to.

Changes in the carbon cycle have played a key role – in some ways *the* key role – in Earth's history. Let's take a quick tour.

The Earth is about 4.5 billion years old; the most ancient rocks identified by geologists are zircon crystals found in Australia that date to about 4.4 billion years ago.[2] We don't know when life first appeared, but complex, multicellular life leaves its first records "only" 600 million years ago.[3] To put this in perspective, consider that the earliest humans showed up just 2 million years ago, and that heavy use of fossil fuels occurred within only the past 130 years. But we are getting ahead of the story.

Let's spend a moment thinking about what the Earth was like more than half a billion years ago when living cells first began to work in tandem. There was a lot more carbon in the atmosphere back then – about twenty-five times more than in the modern era. There was also a lot less oxygen, perhaps 40% less.[4] The sun was also weaker in those days, emitting about 2.5% less radiation. Nevertheless, largely because of the immense concentrations of atmospheric carbon the Earth was a very toasty place.[5]

This is an appropriate moment for saying something about the greenhouse effect. Without an atmosphere, hardly any of the sun's radiation would remain to warm the planet; it would all be radiated back into space, as the Moon's is. Our atmosphere traps some of this radiation, letting it in but preventing it from leaving. The reason this is possible is that radiation can occupy different portions of the electro-magnetic spectrum, where visible light is situated at higher frequencies than heat. Since solar radiation comes to us primarily as light and is re-radiated primarily as heat, the greenhouse effect works by selectively blocking out the lower portions of the spectrum. Carbon dioxide is effective at this, so the more of it there is in the atmosphere, the more heat trapping occurs. There are other gases that do this even more efficiently, but we'll postpone considering them until later.

So now we have the Earth at the dawn of complex life: an atmosphere rich in carbon, a somewhat cooler sun, but extremely high temperatures down on the ground. Why didn't it stay this way? An important reason is that atmospheric carbon reacted with silicate-rich rocks as they were weathered over long time spans. Carbon bonds readily with silicon compounds, and the resulting minerals were slowly incorporated into the mantle of the earth. That would explain a gradual steady reduction of atmospheric carbon – but that's not what the historical record appears to show.

We will bypass the complex theory that lies behind reconstructions of ancient atmospheric conditions. There is a lot of uncertainty in the exact numbers, but different approaches yield roughly comparable pictures. The one we will use comes via Robert Berner, perhaps the foremost name in the study of long-term carbon cycling; Berner was a professor of geology at Yale who died in early 2015. His GEOCARB model, which is roughly corroborated by other modeling strategies, estimates the bumpy ride shown in Figure 1.1.

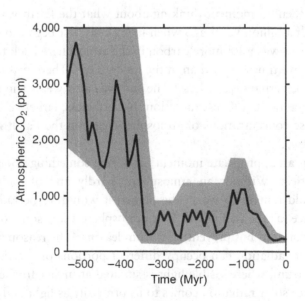

Figure 1.1 Atmospheric carbon dioxide over the past 500 million years. *Source*: Royer (2014). Adapted from Berner (2003).

In the figure, the shaded area represents a band of uncertainty around the model's central estimates. Several things stand out. First, there is a dramatic long-term reduction in atmospheric carbon dioxide, from about 3,700 ppm down to about 200. Second, over the "shorter" run of 50 million years or so there were periods when carbon dioxide increased. Third, the biggest plunge was 300–400 million years ago when some planetary change shifted the Earth's atmosphere from fluctuation at high carbon dioxide concentrations to lower ones. Finally, the last 40 million years or so have seen a relatively low concentration, fluctuating in the vicinity of 200 ppm. In addition, although you can't see it on this graphic because it was rather short-lived, there was the large and very rapid upward spike about 56 million years ago, the Paleocene–Eocene Thermal Maximum (PETM), which gave us alligators on Ellesmere Island and aquatic ferns at the North Pole.

One of the sources of the ups and downs in atmospheric climate is vulcanism: when volcanos erupt they send large amounts of carbon, formerly buried in the deep earth, back into circulation above ground. For various reasons there appear to be periods in which plate movements instigate a higher rate of vulcanism. (If you are old enough, you may remember the "Rite of Spring" episode in Walt Disney's remarkable animation *Fantasia*: after a titanic battle between prey and predator dinosaurs, lots of volcanos erupt, it suddenly gets hot, and swamps turn into deserts, through which the giant reptiles march toward their doom. This was based on 1940s science – not the current wisdom on dinosaur extinction but not entirely wrong either.)

For our purposes, the really important piece in this puzzle is the switch from a generally carbon-rich atmosphere during early Earth history to a generally carbon-poor atmosphere later on. The key is recognizing that the period of transition begins about 400 million years ago with the emergence of terrestrial plants; life evolved from protozoa pools to bogs and forests. Now there was someplace for carbon to go without waiting for the slow process of silicate weathering: it could be stored in plant tissue and the soils that plants and the first small animals were creating as a matrix for yet more life. Even more, runoff from terrestrial ecosystems could be transported by water to the oceans, where it provided nutrients for marine life, another large, expanding carbon sink.

Now comes the interesting part. While most of the carbon that had made its way from the atmosphere to terrestrial and marine life kept circulating between air, land and water, a little bit of it would, like our mysterious plutonium, "disappear." This was a minute portion of any year's carbon flow, but over the expanse of geological time it added up. Some of the carbon from decomposing organisms sank to the bottom of lakes or swamps and eventually got incorporated into sedimentary rock formations. Other carbon, lodged in marine plants and animals, ended up on the ocean floor where it was similarly excluded from the endless recycling process higher up. Subduction, when one tectonic plate pushes underneath another, drove many of these carbon caches deeper into the earth.

One result of this process is limestone, which is made out of the remains of shell material from generations upon generations of ocean life. To look out on a large limestone formation is to realize how massive this process was and over how long a span of time it occurred. But another is the formation of fossil fuels – coal, oil and natural gas. The carbon in carbon fuels is none other than what had been extracted through photosynthesis eons ago by living organisms, deposited in soils or sands, and then taken into the earth. Under immense pressure the carbon was concentrated, which is exactly what makes these minerals and gases so valuable as energy sources. The Carboniferous Period, during which luxuriant plant growth was ultimately converted into coal beds, occurred approximately 300–350 million years ago. It is worth remembering that fossil fuels make available to people living today the accumulated energy of hundreds of millions of years of life.

Figure 1.2 shows us the amount of organic carbon that was removed from the Earth's surface during the past half-billion years, taken from a publication by Robert Berner. The scale is in quadrillion moles of carbon per million years, about the same as 12 million metric tonnes per year. (A metric tonne equals 1,000 kilograms and is about 10% larger than a nonmetric ton. We will measure in tonnes throughout this book.) One can see the increase in carbon burial as complex life takes hold and then at its peak in Carboniferous times. But this is not only a feature of Earth history long past; it continues right up to the present.

There is one more escape route for carbon, the trapping of methane in long-lived soil or marine deposits. Methane ($CH_4$) is created by the labors of microorganisms (think of smelly swamps) and is normally released so it can find its way back into the atmosphere. But some methane is cut off from air channels and can be encapsulated

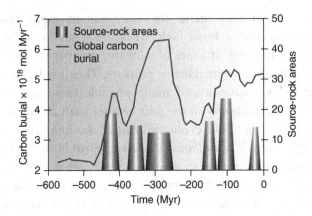

**Figure 1.2** Long-term carbon burial.
*Source*: Berner (2003).

in stable containment. For instance, about 500 billion tonnes of methane are trapped beneath permafrost soils in Arctic regions, possibly as much as the world's combined natural gas reserves.[6] (Gas reserves may turn out to be twice as great – we don't know.) Far more methane may be encased in frozen "bubbles" beneath lakes and along continental shelves; these bubbles take the form of crystals and are referred to as methyl hydrates, or simply hydrates. (They are also called clathrates.) Estimates of how much methane lies trapped in this manner vary wildly, from as low as a few hundred billion tonnes (or gigatonnes, Gt) to 20,000 or more. Moreover, several hundred more gigatonnes may be biding their time at greater marine depths in dissolved or suspended form.[7]

But remember that the movement of carbon is two-way: we have tracked long-term sequestration in carbon-bearing rocks, fossil fuels and hydrates, but carbon is also returned to the Earth's surface through volcanic eruptions. While volcanic activity varies from year to year, a reasonable annual average during the current period is the return of about 33 million metric tonnes. This is about half the rate of organic carbon burial indicated in Figure 1.2, but considering the immense forces at work independently in both directions, that's fairly close. As we'll see, there are also indications that there have been significant hydrate releases from time to time. Very roughly, flows of carbon from the surface to the inner Earth and back to the surface, a process we termed the deep carbon cycle, have been balanced over the past 40 million years ago or so – until recently.

Now we can understand the extraordinary importance of humanity's exploitation of fossil fuels. They are a gift from the ages, the distillation of millions of years of sunlight, photosynthesis, burial and concentration under unimaginable pressure. Their use has powered several industrial revolutions and made possible more advances in human comfort and longevity in the past century than in the previous two million years of hominid evolution. *But at the same time we are partly undoing hundreds of millions of years of earth history – hunting down, extracting and returning to the atmosphere carbon that had been buried over geological time spans in the space of a few human generations.* Should we be surprised that doing this might have serious consequences?

## The Earth Surface Carbon Cycle

With this overview of carbon flows over deep time, we are ready to look at what happens in the course of a calendar year. It is helpful to think of the surface carbon cycle as a system of pipes and reservoirs – channels through which carbon is exchanged between one location and another, and places of temporary storage. In formal language, this is about flows and stocks, fluxes and sinks.

Consider financial accounting for a moment. Every business needs two systems of accounts, a profit or loss accounting for flows within a specified time period like a year, and a balance statement as of a moment in time like the end of a financial or calendar year. The first records flows of money into the organization, income, and flows out of it, such as payroll and materials expenses, interest payments and taxes. For analytical as well as legal purposes, it is important that the main sources and destinations of these funds all be itemized. The second documents the organization's assets and liabilities, whose dimensions are largely the result of all those inflows and outflows.

The key insight underlying the system of carbon accounts is that it combines both of these functions.[8] It registers the amount of carbon stored in all the planet's repositories at a moment in time, and it also keeps track of the flows of carbon between them on (conventionally) an annual basis. This points to a crucial difference between financial and earth system accounting. The financial stock and flow accounts are connected, but not tightly. The firm's assets are credited by revenues and debited by expenses, but the possibility of capital gains and losses – changes in valuation due to changes in market assessments – drives a wedge between them. No such fluctuations are possible in the chemistry of the earth; the carbon stored in any form or location is strictly the product of carbon inflows and outflows. The whole system has to balance at any moment in time. This way we can use measurable changes in carbon stocks to infer otherwise invisible flows between them and measurable flows to infer changes in stocks. We can also trace how changes in one flow reverberate to alter other flows and the distribution of carbon among the various sinks. It is a powerful framework.

To be specific, let's lay out the most important items in the consolidated carbon accounts. Storage types are called "sinks," and flows between them are referred to as exchanges, since they are generally two-way (but inevitably net in one direction or the other). Table 1.1 sums them up. The first five rows roughly make up the Earth surface carbon cycle, the last four the deep (or slow) cycle. Whether surface exchanges balance depends on whether exchanges between the surface and deep cycles also balance. This is a crucial point, since stability of the sinks depends on balanced inflow and outflow of carbon between them; if the whole cycle is unbalanced, the sinks have to pick up the difference. Since climate change is about progressive accumulation of carbon in the atmospheric sink, diagnosing and responding to it requires an understanding of the range of imbalances in the surface

Table 1.1. Carbon sinks and exchanges

| Sinks | Exchanges |
| --- | --- |
| Atmosphere | Atmosphere – biota |
| Biota | Biota – soils |
| Soils | Soils – water leachate |
| Rocks | Atmosphere – rocks |
| Oceans (surface, intermediate, deep) | Soils/biota – rocks |
| Terrestrial methane storage (peats) | Biota/soils – terrestrial storage |
| Marine methane storage (hydrates) | Ocean/biota – marine storage |
| Deep Earth storage | Rocks – deep Earth |
| | Deep Earth – atmosphere |

carbon cycle and their cascading effects on the whole system of sinks and exchanges. As we will see, this system-aware perspective undermines many widely held beliefs and policy "solutions," even some embraced by ardent climate activists.

Figure 1.3, excerpted from the 2013 IPCC Synthesis Report, gives us a visual sense of how the carbon cycle fits together, along with estimates of several sinks and exchanges. It leaves out a crucial piece of the puzzle, one that may play a significant role in our understanding of the risk we face, but we will put that aside temporarily. One nice thing about this illustration is that it gives us the data for both flows and stocks, where the physical unit PgC translates to petagrams of carbon, and a petagram (Pg) is a billion metric tonnes, or a gigatonne (Gt).[9] Darker arrows indicate flows that predate human intervention, while slightly lighter ones indicate flows that modern humans have added to the mix.

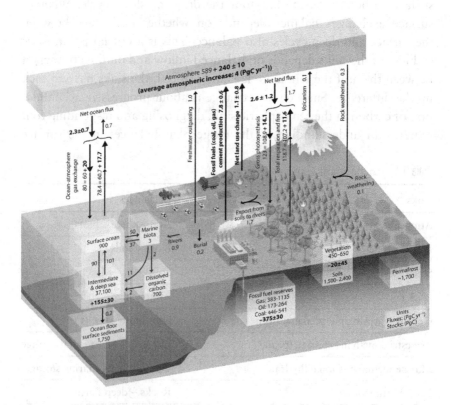

**Figure 1.3** A summary of the carbon cycle.
*Source*: IPCC Working Group I (2013).

Perhaps the place to start is the exchange between the surface carbon cycle, taken as a whole, and the deep Earth. Before humans began interfering, 0.2 Pg were being withdrawn per year due to burial, and another 0.2 made its way to the deep ocean in the form of sediments, carbon no longer available to circulate through the surface cycle. Meanwhile, about 0.1 Pg was returning each year from the deep Earth to the atmosphere as a result of volcanic activity. The upshot was a very small annual reduction of carbon in active circulation, minuscule in relation to the key stocks.

But now consider the human-induced flows. Burial and sedimentation are unaffected, but humans are responsible for transferring 8–10 Pg of carbon from subterranean storage to the atmosphere; most of this is due to the excavation and burning of fossil fuels, with a lesser amount due to the manufacture of cement (which reverses the flow of carbon from atmosphere to rock). This represents an enormous infusion of additional carbon into the surface cycle. It goes immediately into the atmosphere, but then some of it exchanges with other parts of the system, adding to the carbon circulating throughout. This means some of it will return to the atmosphere over time as the interlocking network of carbon exchange takes its course. The process can stabilize only when it reaches a new equilibrium between sinks (where inflows and outflows balance), but as long as we keep transferring long-sequestered carbon from the deep to the surface system any such equilibrium is postponed.

So now let's take a close look at the bottom line of climate change, the quantity of carbon stored as atmospheric gases. The diagram says that the preindustrial level was about 589 Gt, and that by 2013 this had risen to about 829 Gt, with a continuing annual increase of 4 Gt per year once concurrent exchanges between the atmosphere and other sinks are taken into account. Translated into percentage terms, this means atmospheric carbon had increased by 40% due to human activity with each year adding another two-thirds of a percent to this total.

But it's important to place changes in the carbon sink in the context of all the other interconnected sinks and exchanges – the whole system of carbon accounts. By injecting extra carbon into the atmosphere, humans are also accelerating the movement of carbon from atmosphere to organisms, and every other destination it could go to.

To begin, notice that carbon exchange between the atmosphere and ocean would approximately net out except for the influence of modern human economies. Because of the increase in atmospheric carbon due to fossil fuel burning, more carbon now flows from air to water – but an increasingly carbon-rich ocean sends more carbon back to the atmosphere. On balance the inflow to the ocean slightly exceeds the outflow from it, meaning that the ocean plays a role in slowing down the accumulation of greenhouse gases, while undergoing its own process of carbon enrichment. This may sound like a fortuitous benefit, but we will see in the next chapter it also poses a grave threat.

A similar process is at work in the world's vegetation, which holds roughly the same amount of carbon as the atmosphere. Note in this case, however, that the ratio of flows to stock – the proportion of carbon exchange relative to carbon storage – is very high, over 20% per year. Plants are working overtime to convert carbon to biomass through photosynthesis, and the reverse processes, releasing carbon back to the atmosphere, are nearly in balance. As with the ocean, the overall increase of atmospheric carbon is slightly diminished as vegetation fixes a bit more than it releases, but as we will soon see, this assistance is vulnerable to disruption.

They don't always get the attention they deserve, but soils store three to four times the amount of carbon as vegetation; they constitute an important sink. However, the movement of carbon in and out of the soil is very slow. This is a problem from a human point of view, since it means that natural processes don't significantly alter this form of carbon storage over a meaningful time frame. Carbon runoff, for instance, is about 1.7 petagrams per year, and of course its immediate effect is to increase the carbon concentration of rivers and ultimately the ocean, where it then undergoes the slow process of carbon exchange with the atmosphere.

A special case is the permafrost found in Arctic latitudes. The amount of carbon it sequesters is immense, about three times the amount in the atmosphere. We should hope it stays there.

Digging deeper, we see there is considerable uncertainty regarding fossil fuel reserves, but the amount of carbon we humans are potentially capable of extracting and burning is on the order of 1,000–2,000 petagrams. This is enough to further double or triple the atmospheric carbon load, depending also on what happens with flows into and out of other sinks. As we will soon see, it is *imperative* that most of this carbon remain right where it is, underground and beyond the reach of the surface carbon cycle.

Finally, note that the marine methane deposits itemized in Table 1.1 are *not* included in the diagram. Above all, this is because we don't know if there is routine carbon exchange between them and the surrounding ocean environment. There may be a steady process of new hydrate formation and simultaneously a release of methane from existing formations. Or there may not. In the absence of sufficient evidence to draw flow arrows, the IPCC excluded this sink altogether. That also means that the vigorous debate over the size of the marine methane inventory, a topic we will return to later, does not impinge on this consensus graphic.

## Feedback

Direct estimates of how much carbon migrates from any one location to another, such as from fossil fuel reserves to the atmosphere, fail to take into account the other elements of the carbon cycle. As we've already seen, the web of carbon exchange between air, land and water is complex. Any change in an initial carbon flux, such as more fossil fuel use, will trigger further changes in how much carbon goes to land and water, to and from living organisms, and ultimately from these repositories back to the atmosphere. Secondary effects like these are sources of feedbacks, and so also are qualitative changes within these systems – ocean currents, cloud patterns, environmental impacts on forest and other biotic communities, ice melt – that can alter the amount of climate change we can expect to get from burning carbon.

Feedbacks can be positive or negative: they can amplify the effect of the initial carbon jolt or dampen it. The language can be a bit confusing, since a positive feedback is one that amplifies the original impulse, but that constitutes *bad* news for us humans if it's in response to a burst of carbon emissions. We would prefer our feedbacks to be negative, but we don't have as much choice as we'd like.

Broadly speaking, feedback mechanisms fall into two categories, those that adjust the amount of carbon in the atmosphere due to the operation of the rest of the cycle, and those that alter the climate in other ways. They need to be considered together, however, not only because their effects combine but also because they are interdependent: a change in one form of feedback will likely change the other.

Let's begin with the interplay between air and sea. Atmospheric carbon exchanges with the ocean through chemical bonding. Carbon atoms readily attach themselves to other elements, and this is the vehicle by which carbon moves from atmosphere to ocean and back again. If the concentration of carbon increases in the atmosphere, there will be an increase in the net flow to the ocean, at least until a new equilibrium is reached, an effect that currently diverts about 30% of the carbon we burn that would otherwise accumulate in the atmosphere. In other words, this is currently a negative feedback.

Of course, atmospheric carbon also exchanges with terrestrial vegetation. Insofar as a more carbon-rich atmosphere encourages plant growth, this can lead to an increase in the amount of terrestrial carbon storage. In fact, about a third of the carbon emitted by fossil fuel use finds its way to this (temporary) destination. That might not be the case in the future, however, because climate change will alter weather patterns, and existing plant communities may not be able to adapt quickly enough. For instance, it is likely that a warmer climate with different precipitation patterns will result in the replacement of portions of the world's tropical and temperate forests by savanna or even completely unforested biomes like grasslands and deserts.[10] These biomes store a lot less carbon, so this would imply a net release of carbon from land to air – a positive feedback to offset the initial negative one.

In addition to its indirect effect through plant growth, environmental change can feed back directly through alteration of the earth's albedo. "Albedo" refers to the reflectivity of the earth's surface; a darker surface absorbs more heat, and climate change is likely to result in a darker planet. While many changes in the Earth's albedo are possible, the main culprit is likely to be the loss of polar ice cover, especially in the Northern Hemisphere where dark waters will take in solar radiation that the former ice cap had reflected back into space.[11] There has also been recent speculation that high-altitude light-reflecting clouds will diminish beyond some tipping point of atmospheric carbon accumulation.[12]

Perhaps the most serious potential feedback is the release of stored methane, and it is strictly positive. A lot of methane is stored in the permafrost and in crystallized form under pressure in cold bodies of water. As long as it stays there, it is mostly removed from the carbon exchange that passes between terrestrial and marine ecosystems and the global atmosphere. But an increase in local temperatures can cause a release. For permafrost, this is about the thawing and disruption of previously frozen soils that encase the methane.[13] For hydrates it is about the warming of adjacent water to the point at which the crystal-line structure can no longer hold, and methane is released as a gas. Nearly all of it would be oxidized as it made its way to the surface, turning into tiny bubbles of carbon dioxide.[14] This process can be seen in a recent video study of a pair of cold seeps (marine methane release sites without geothermal heat) in the South China Sea, which recorded roughly five to twenty-five bubbles per second, with the median bubble diameter fluctuating between 2.5 and 6 millimeters.[15] What does that mean in everyday terms? Methane releases produce slightly less rapid effervescence but much larger bubbles than you'd see in a freshly uncorked bottle of Champagne.[16]

There are three things to pay attention to regarding methane feedbacks. First, if those who think global methane deposits are large and susceptible to being mobilized are right, there is potential for immense, catastrophic effects. Look again at the amount of carbon stored in permafrost in Figure 1.3 and add to it estimates of 10,000–20,000 Gt of carbon stored in hydrates; together they vastly exceed the highest estimates for recoverable fossil fuels, and even a partial release could propel us past the 1,200-ppm carbon dioxide mark that sets the lower bound for PETM-like catastrophes.

Second, there is some evidence that such releases have occurred in the prehistoric past on a large scale, and over relatively brief time periods to boot. We have already seen that this is a candidate explanation for at least a portion of the extraordinary increase in atmospheric carbon during the PETM. Even more disturbing, paleoclimatologists think there is a good chance that the wild temperature swings during the most recent phase of ice ages alternating with interglacial warming – which are ultimately attributable to oscillations in the Earth's orbit around the sun – have been exacerbated by methane feedbacks, even over time frames as short as a century or so.[17] In other words, if human carelessness induces a large-scale permafrost or hydrate methane release, it won't be the first time rapid climate change has occurred this way.

Finally, given the multiplicity of potential feedback mechan-isms, there is no rule that says methane has to be the sole threat. On the contrary, as a recent, much publicized warning pointed out, we are at risk above all from cascading feedbacks instigating and reinforcing each other: permafrost and hydrate releases, albedo effects and forest diebacks, initiated by fossil fuel emissions but then taking on a life of their own – the path to a hothouse earth.[18]

Although we are learning more about them, these feedbacks are still speculative. They make perfect sense in theory, although the proxy data used to identify them for periods of abrupt climate change in the Earth's past leave room for uncertainty over which mechanisms operated when and to what extent. This makes it difficult to forecast future effects, and especially the specific conditions that might trigger them, on the basis of the historical record. All we can say at this point is that, by moving atmospheric carbon concentration outside the range that has persisted for hundreds of thousands of years, we are taking a frightening chance. And if positive feedbacks begin to kick in, especially permafrost and hydrate releases, there may be little to be done but watch in horror. The processes at work are simply too large and too ubiquitous for humans to intervene in a meaningful way.[19] Are there tipping points that, if crossed, will initiate an uncontrollable feedback loop? Maybe, and we don't know that either. With each year's increase in greenhouse gas levels, we increase the unknown odds of a cataclysm by an unknown amount.

## Carbon and Climate

So far we have been talking exclusively of carbon, its circulation through atmosphere, land and ocean and its central role in the very long story of Earth history. Although we have paused to take note of the greenhouse effect and the physics behind it, we haven't considered the relationship between changes in the atmosphere and changes in climate in any systematic way. But that, of course, is what this issue is ultimately about.

The greenhouse effect changes the Earth's heat balance, but how that heat is distributed is a complicated topic. The second law of thermodynamics (the one about entropy) tells us that energy will flow from hotter substances to cooler ones – conduction – reducing the energy difference between them. If additional heat is introduced to one part of a system, some of it will dissipate, and the process will continue until a new equilibrium is reached.

Much of the heat captured by the greenhouse effect will be absorbed by the ocean. In fact, "ocean" is something of an oversimplification, since the air will transfer heat to the ocean surface, and then the surface will transfer heat to deeper layers beneath it. The amount and speed of heat dissipation depends on the size of the initial discrepancy between atmosphere and ocean and the extent of upwelling that inter-mixes water from different ocean layers. There is obviously a lot of uncertainty involved in making a prediction, and different models of the global system give different results. In the most widely cited survey, each of several models was given the same scenario: 100 Gt of carbon dioxide is emitted into the atmosphere, and then emissions abruptly stop. How long would it take before peak warming of the Earth's surface takes place? Most of the delays fell within the range of six and a half to thirty years, and the median was just above ten.[20]

This is just one scenario, of course, and not a particularly realistic one at that. A different pair of researchers used the same approach, but using just a single model, comparing a 100-Gt emissions burst to 1,000 Gt. They found that, while the smaller quantity of carbon dioxide took eleven years to reach peak temperature, the larger took thirty-one years. A lag that long between emissions and consequences could introduce a further complication to the politics of climate change, although even in the 1,000-Gt case, 93% of the warming occurs during the first decade.[21] Of course, this is a long time from the standpoint of climate policy; having delayed for so long we can hardly afford to wait ten years to see how much additional heat our current emissions have caused.

Meanwhile, other aspects of the carbon-and-climate system will continue to evolve even after human-originated carbon emissions are brought down to near zero. Methane in the atmosphere will convert to $CO_2$, a process that will be largely completed in about a decade; this will effectively reduce warming. Carbon in the atmosphere will be out of equilibrium with the carbon balances in the ocean and on land, leading to a steady reduction in atmospheric carbon to restore them, another cooling influence. Of course, the feedback mechanisms we briefly considered will also play a role; for instance, even after weather patterns change and some regions become drier than before, it will take many fire seasons to convert a forest biome into an arid savannah, releasing some of the carbon formerly stored in trees and soils.

Much of this is uncertain taken individually, but combining all of them into a comprehensive forecast is especially daunting. Barring truly calamitous feedbacks, it is likely that further warming would be modest for the century following a cessation of carbon emissions, giving way to gradual cooling, but if that condition doesn't hold, all bets are off. At the least, it would be useful to have a clearer sense of what after-the-end-of-emissions-with-limited-feedback warming would look like as a baseline for considering worse outcomes, and this is an important area for ongoing research.[22]

There are other gaps that introduce a delay between greenhouse gas accumulation and the outcomes people care about. The most important is probably the potential for melting the great terrestrial ice sheets of Greenland and Antarctica, which in turn will determine how much sea level rise ultimately occurs. Very simply, there are two factors that govern the volume of water on Earth. One is the temperature of this water, since it expands when heated. Most near-term (i.e., twenty-first-century) projections of sea level rise, such as those promulgated by the IPCC during its last synthesis report, have been based solely on this factor. That's because thermal expansion is instantaneous: as soon as the ocean warms, it gets bigger. The exact amount of sea level rise we can expect from this process depends, of course, on how much warming occurs, but even in the most extreme scenario it should be less than one meter by 2100.

The other factor is the melting of terrestrial glaciers, with the result that vast quantities of water stored in the form of ice are released, adding to the volume of the ocean. Only terrestrial glaciers matter for this process, not sea ice, since sea ice already displaces water, whereas land-based ice, when it melts, adds new water to the oceans. Really catastrophic sea level rise of several meters or more – enough to fully inundate the world's coasts – can occur only as a result of this glacial melting. But the melting process is likely to be slow. While we can observe initial melting taking place today, dramatic reductions in glaciation will probably not begin to occur before the end of the century. However, it is not only possible but even probable that today's warming is setting in motion forces that will inexorably lead to massive loss of ice cover and extremely destructive sea level rise over the course of the next three millennia.[23]

Over intermediate time scales are the lags we can expect to govern many of the feedback mechanisms sketched above. While albedo responds quickly, the other processes may be slow. Reductions in terrestrial carbon storage due to forest loss, if they occur, will play out over many decades. It is believed that plausible methane release timetables could be even slower, operating over centuries, although the entire topic is shrouded in uncertainty.

For any other effect of interest – for instance, loss of biodiversity – there are corresponding lags. Essentially nothing of importance happens in the realm of climate impacts immediately; the effects we experience today are the result of greenhouse gas accumulations going back into the past. This poses a deep problem for the politics of addressing this crisis. As severe as some climate impacts have already become, societies will somehow need to mobilize to deal with far greater threats that are decades, centuries or millennia in the future, even though they are being caused by what we are doing today. There is no precedent for this in human history, and we have not evolved as a species to generate and act on this kind of foresight. I can't provide answers for how to do this, but, if nothing else, it should be clear that a political strategy that depends on the motivating force of current climate impacts to propel a demand for action is destined to be weaker than it should be.

## The Carbon Conundrum

Fossil fuels are extraordinary. They compress the energy of eons into dense, easily transportable packages, ready to meet our needs for power, warmth, cooling and motion. The exploitation of fossil fuels is central to the industrial revolution and its transformative impact on living standards and the development of civilization. If you measure human flourishing by life expectancy, for instance, you find that hardly any increases occurred anywhere in the world until well into the eighteenth century, and the spread of longevity coincides geographically and through time with the spread of technologies based on energy-dense carbon fuels.[24]

*There is nothing corrupt or unwarranted about humanity's attachment to coal, gas and oil.* We seek to use these fuels because they do their jobs so phenomenally well, and our societies have benefited enormously from their services to us. If it were not for the problem we are exploring in this chapter, we could still indulge this desire for cheap, convenient power for centuries to come. It is mean of nature to play this trick on us, tempting us with fuels whose continued use poses a catastrophic threat to our planetary home. Yet this is how it is, and once we understand the causes of climate change we can see that the process that concentrates solar energy into fossil fuels makes it inevitable that burning them much longer is out of the question: we will be returning long-sequestered carbon to the sinks and exchanges of the planet's surface, resurrecting the Earth of millions of years ago whose conditions were not suitable for the evolution of our species.

Given the inconvenience of abjuring the use of fossil fuels, people inevitably seize on alternative "solutions" to the climate crisis. Perhaps we could burn more carbon fuels if we also plant more trees. Or perhaps we can find a way to capture all that carbon dioxide before it makes its way to the atmosphere, and redirect it to a safe, well-contained place of storage. But the technology to extract carbon from the combustion process and sequester it for centuries to come at the scale we need is far too expensive – even more expensive than forgoing the fuels altogether – and likely to remain that way.[25] Trying to tweak the carbon cycle by increasing the quantity of biomass acting as a sink might provide some breathing space for carrying out an energy transition, but its effects are uncertain; we don't know how long higher levels of vegetation can be sustained as the climate change we can no longer avoid begins to alter life on the planet. (We will return to reforestation, the great green hope, in Chapter 4.)

We face no reasonable alternative to decarbonizing the world's energy system with all deliberate speed. This will be a massive, difficult, even wrenching undertaking. It will complicate most of the other goals a fair-minded society should set, above all making higher standards of living available to all the world's people. (A discussion of climate mitigation and economic development awaits us in Chapter 7.) And there is very little time left for trial and error. To adjust to the constraints of a livable climate while minimizing the cost to our well-being is the unavoidable challenge of our time.

# 2 THE RISKS OF CLIMATE CHANGE, OR WHY CARBON BUDGETS NEED TO BE BINDING

In the 1999 movie *Being John Malkovich*, a hapless puppeteer accidentally discovers a portal to the mind of the somewhat-well-known actor. Once inside, he can see the world through Malkovich's eyes, control his movements and speech and generally operate him as a human puppet. This power is only temporary, however; after a few minutes he is ejected and finds himself alongside a highway in New Jersey. On paper this probably comes across as senselessly random, but seeing it acted out on the screen – well, it's still pretty random.

Anyway, John Malkovich himself eventually discovers there's an external entryway into his consciousness and makes his way through it. What happens when his sensory awareness reenters his mind from the outside? In the film, everything he sees is John Malkovich. He finds himself at a restaurant where all the other diners are him, and so is the waitstaff; on the menu every item for order is "John Malkovich." It is pure solipsism projected onto the external world.

Economics functions a bit similarly. It is as if the field has discovered a portal to its own vantage point, and everything it sees is economics. Critics of the discipline sometimes claim that economics places its own concerns above competing ones, but that's not quite right. What economics does is to fold nearly all other concerns into itself, so that, instead of competing, these other aspects of life show up as line items in its own system of accounts. In other words, it dominates by inclusion.

Consider that economics recognizes the prices people pay for goods they buy in the marketplace and the price they receive for their own labor, but it traffics just as readily in prices for many things we might not think of as "economic": $9.5 million for the cost of premature death due to increased risk from a cause like pollution, $160,000–$480,000 for the cost of being subjected to rape in prison ($675,000 if the victim is a juvenile) and so on for nearly every event you could imagine.[1] Economists don't argue that health, safety and other values should be set aside in favor of financial priorities; rather, they translate *all* values into monetary ones so they can be entered into a common formula. Of course, the critics are also right insofar as such a translation will always leave something out.[2]

This chapter takes aim at the framework of economic balancing applied to climate change, a "false symmetry" identified in the Introduction as one of the key misconceptions undermining effective action. Balancing is predicated on the notion that all significant outcomes of planetary warming can be assigned a monetary value, so comparison of the costs and benefits of taking action can be apples-to-apples. It is then just a short step to arguments for middle-of-the-road policies that supposedly strike the right balance between doing too little and doing too much. While the specifics of such arguments depend on methodological choices used in assigning prices, the deeper problem is that the framework itself doesn't fit. It's not an all–John Malkovich world, nor an all-economics one either.

Before delving into this issue, however, we first need to survey the costs of global warming in all their dimensions, including not only the economic but also ecological, health, cultural and other aspects. We will begin with the best-known and most immediate impacts and then segue to the more speculative possibilities. After this we can look more closely at the economic balancing act with critical, informed eyes. (For an examination of the economic approach and its shortcomings that wades into the technical details, see the Appendix.)

## A Spectrum of Risks

We can begin with the effects of climate change that are likely to be familiar and gradual: impacts we have enough experience with and which will materialize at a slow enough pace that we can devise protective countermeasures.[3]

*Sea level rise.* This has become the poster child for climate risk, perhaps because it is easy to visualize and its effects are straightforward.

As briefly discussed in the previous chapter, there are two processes that will give rise to retreating coastlines: thermal expansion of the ocean due simply to its heating and the melting of large, land-based ice systems. The first is immediate, occurring as heat is transferred from the atmosphere to the ocean, while the second will take decades and probably centuries to unfold. Thermal expansion is easy enough to calculate given our fairly precise estimates of the total volume of the global ocean, but its future is uncertain because we don't know how much warming human activity will cause. Glacial melting is trickier because it depends not only on the extent of local warming but also on changes in the climate system (including precipitation) and the structural dynamics of the ice sheets themselves, a topic we are only beginning to understand. For instance, the recent discovery that glaciers can have water tables at their base might lead to the possibility of much more rapid breakup as temperatures rise, or it might not.

The costs of sea level rise are both economically uncomplicated and culturally ineffable. Expensive coastal infrastructure will have to be reinforced or abandoned; indeed, much of the world's stock of housing, transportation networks and other built capital could be inundated. River deltas often play an important role in agriculture, but they will be at ever greater risk of flooding and salinization. Eventually, new coastlines and new deltas will form, but this could take many thousands of years. Whole countries, small island nations like those in the Pacific and Indian Oceans, could disappear. We can estimate the financial costs of these impacts by assessing the values of the assets at risk or the new investments, like seawalls, that would have to be made to protect them. Flooding will also cause loss of life, which has significance far beyond its calculable economic effects.

The cultural importance of the world's coastal regions should not be overlooked, however. For thousands of years our ancestors have sought out sites with access to marine shipping for their homes, temples, monuments and workshops. Much of the cultural patrimony of the human race will be obliterated as the oceans expand and the land retreats. Putting a monetary price on these losses is beside the point: nothing money can buy can replace the historical continuity we may lose to inundation.

*Extreme weather.* The scientific understanding of the connection between a stronger greenhouse effect and more frequent and violent storms is rapidly evolving; it seems to get less speculative with each passing year. At the same time, the factors governing storm formation are highly specific to each storm and sensitive to small changes in local conditions and their timing, so one can never attribute them *solely* to climate change – but the same can be said for smoking and lung cancer or just about any statistical risk. It is virtually certain that we face a stormier future because of elevated atmospheric carbon.[4]

The damage from storms can be minimized by proper planning and investment in storm-resistant buildings and infrastructure. It should come as no surprise that the greatest losses of life and livelihood have occurred in developing countries, where the level of preparation is generally lower. Florida, for example, is repeatedly struck by hurricanes, some with terrifying force, yet it manages to carry on, while similar storms in the Philippines are vastly more destructive.[5] And the exception proves the rule: the vulnerability of New Orleans to Hurricane Katrina was seen as an outrage because it showed that "first world" standards for flood control and emergency planning had not been applied. Levees were in disrepair, coastal wetlands had been stripped, and the infrastructure to resist the ravages of the storm and facilitate evacuation was inadequate. Of course, if this state of affairs was unacceptable in New Orleans, it should also be unacceptable in Manila or Port-au-Prince. Wealthy countries who have profited from decades of carbon emissions should shoulder their responsibility to help those at greatest risk from extreme weather.

*Drought and other effects on agriculture.* For a period of time it was thought that a more carbon-rich atmosphere would be beneficial for plants in general, including the ones humans grow for food. Carbon, after all, is a key element – *the* key element – in photosynthesis. Perhaps the future would see vegetables bigger than the refrigerators we now use to store them, as in the Woody Allen movie *Sleeper*. And so the first generation of economic models assessing the cost of climate change often assigned a benefit to agriculture: more carbon, more food.[6]

Today we don't see it the same way. Carbon is not a limiting factor in agriculture (other nutrients, like nitrogen and potassium, play this role), and field experiments show limited growth responsiveness to its availability. Meanwhile, rapid changes in temperature and precipitation challenge farmers to switch methods and cultivars quickly enough to keep abreast. Their ability to do this, especially in drier regions, is a big unknown.[7] If the impacts are severe enough, as in the recent string of droughts and heat waves in Australia, it is difficult to see how agriculture can adjust. Where farmers depend on seasonal rainfall, like the monsoons off the Indian Ocean, or spring and summer runoff from mountain snowpacks, as in the Andes and Himalayas, alterations in precipitation could be catastrophic.[8] Concern over long-term climate system changes due to the weakening of the North Atlantic "conveyor belt" have returned with recent measurements suggesting that ice melt from Greenland may play a role.[9] This is a highly speculative impact, but has the potential to lead to substantial changes in temperature and precipitation patterns, particularly in Europe, over the coming centuries. Another concern is that higher atmospheric carbon concentrations, in themselves and without considering their impacts on climate, could result in nutritional losses for many common cultivars.[10]

As with other impacts, the economic and human costs depend partly on how the climate evolves and partly on how much societies invest in order to adapt. The outlook for food supplies in wealthier countries is unfavorable, but to some extent expensive technology can substitute for temperature and precipitation changes, and research is under way to discover more drought- and heat-resistant cultivars. It is especially in the poorer countries, where agriculture often fails even under current climatic conditions, that the greatest potential for crisis lies.[11]

*Loss of biodiversity.* Evolution is a perpetual contest between the destabilizing pressure of environmental change and the adaptive force of natural selection. The extent of biodiversity depends on adaptation keeping up with change, so that species that become extinct are counterbalanced by new evolutionary branching. Over most of the Earth's history this is how it has been, although there have been exceptional periods of mass extinction and biodiversity loss associated with sudden, cataclysmic alterations in the Earth's environment.

We are entering such a period now. The cause is human-induced change, especially the widespread destruction of habitat to provide more land for farming, ranching and commercial plantations (like palm). Even without climate change we would be facing a rate of extinction not seen in tens of millions of years.[12]

Climate change will make the situation more desperate because the environment will change much faster than it has in a very long time. Considerable swaths of forest will turn into savannah; for instance, the dry northeast region of Brazil is expected to encroach upon the Amazonian rainforest, and there is little humans can do to forestall this.[13] Similarly, the forests in the central and eastern Cascades of the

Pacific Northwest will die back, and the agent of change will be forest fires; larger and more frequent fires have already begun to affect the region.[14] In theory, if they were good at packing and moving, most of the plant and animal species could migrate north or to higher elevations, but the speed of the transition makes this unlikely. Estimates vary, but it is not unreasonable to think that a majority of the world's species could vanish in the next few centuries.[15]

The biggest question is what this means for us. In a few cases the consequences are easy to see and substantial. For instance, recent research suggests that as atmospheric carbon dioxide levels increase, the protein content in pollen that bees depend on for their nutrition falls, leaving them weakened and more vulnerable to the other threats implicated in the ongoing wave of die-offs.[16] Realistically, however, we know little about most of the species we are about to lose, nor do we normally see them, much less make economic use of them. This pretty much exhausts all the channels used by economists to attach a monetary value to nonhuman life. The effects are likely to be indirect, as changes in species composition alter the functioning of whole ecosystems. Species that help propagate desirable plants, for instance, may become unviable because they lose their food source, or they may fall victim to predators that have lost their other food sources or that used to be something else's prey but no longer are. These are all speculative propositions because there is no precedent within the range of human experience for what is about to take place, no data to draw on. It's a giant experiment, and we will simply have to wait to find out.

*Ocean acidification.* When we think of species loss, we usually have in mind fields and forests, because we are a terrestrial species, but the greatest risks are faced by marine life. The problem is less the direct warming of the ocean than the lowering of its pH, or ocean acidification. The process begins with the encounter between atmospheric carbon dioxide and water:

$$CO_2 + H_2O \rightarrow H_2CO_3$$

The right-hand term is carbonic acid, which then undergoes further transformation due to the instability of hydrogen and the acid's interaction with other substances. Free hydrogen ions released from acids constitute acidity as measured on the pH scale; they bond with and dissolve other compounds including calcium carbonate, the basis for shell and skeletal formation in marine life.

The acidity of ocean water has increased about 30% compared with preindustrial times, entirely due to the changing carbon dioxide content of the atmosphere.[17] This already appears to exceed the tolerance of important species in a variety of locations, such as sea coral in the tropics, mussels in temperate waters, and pteropods, tiny mollusks at the base of the marine food chain, in the cooler waters of the Southern Hemisphere. But acidification will only intensify. It may double or triple by the end of the century, threatening a collapse of much or perhaps most marine life. In fact, the latest research suggests that large dead zones for pteropods could appear as early as 2030.[18] This could have devastating effects on communities dependent on protein from fish and seafood, and it could trigger ecological ramifications we can barely imagine at this stage in our knowledge of natural processes.

*Health impacts.* Two main consequences of climate change for human health are of interest to researchers in this area. One is that it will get a lot hotter, especially close to the equator. While high temperatures can be uncomfortable and lead to lower work productivity, the combination of *very* high temperatures and humid conditions can be life-threatening. In recent years there have been several high-profile heat waves resulting in hundreds or even thousands of excess deaths, but this is just a warm-up (sorry) for the main event. One recent study, focusing on the Persian Gulf region, summarized the findings of several climate models under two business-as-usual (no carbon emissions control) scenarios over the period between now and 2100.[19] Using past and predicted weather data from reporting stations in Iran, Saudi Arabia, Qatar, and United Arab Emirates, it estimated that temperatures in the range of 50°C (122°F) will become normal during the summer, with readings rising periodically to 60°C (140°F). Heat events of this magnitude are almost beyond our ability to imagine.

But it's worse, since humidity also has to be taken into account. One way to gauge the combined effect of heat and humidity is the "wet bulb" temperature, or TW. To understand this measurement, consider what happens when a moist object is placed in a hot, humid environment. If the temperature outside the object is lower than the inside, the object will cool down. Also, evaporation from the object's surface will have a cooling effect; this is why we sweat. TW is the temperature this object would arrive at if it has a damp surface that produces evaporation. It's higher when the external temperature is hotter but also when the air is more humid, since that limits evaporation. Now suppose the object is a human being. If TW is below the normal human body temperature, some form of insulation, like putting on clothes, is necessary. If TW is above it, however, human beings are out of luck; evaporation will not prevent overheating, and sustained exposure will result in loss of life. This critical level of TW is about 35°C (95°F).[20]

In fact, a recent heat wave in Iran came close to the 35°C threshold. Over several days in late July and early August 2015, ambient temperatures repeatedly spiked in the mid-40s at Bandar Mahshahr, a reporting station at the north end of the Persian Gulf. At the most extreme point, reached on July 31, it was 46° (about 115°F) and relative humidity was 49%, yielding a TW only fractionally below 35°. In other words, today, without any further climate change, there are places on the planet that are skirting the edge of at least temporary unsurvivability. But atmospheric carbon concentrations will continue to rise, and the lag between heat-trapping and terrestrial temperatures will continue to play out, making peak events even more extreme. Climate models indicate that large portions of the Persian Gulf region will indeed exceed the 35°C threshold repeatedly as the century wears on, and a similar risk applies to northeastern India and Bangladesh.[21] Even these dire projections may be too conservative, since they overlook the potential for momentary spikes in TW that can still be deadly.[22] Either the entire population of regions at risk will need to be outfitted with air conditioning or areas of settlement will have to be given up.[23]

What is most important about this analysis is that it does *not* represent catastrophic climate change. It is business as usual, without the compounding feedback effects we will consider later in this chapter. The actual future could turn out to be a lot worse.

The second health risk is from disease. Climate change will effectively transform large portions of the globe from temperate to tropical, at least insofar as pathogens are concerned. This means malaria, dengue fever and similar mosquito-borne illnesses will threaten regions where they were previously unknown or eradicated. Coping is not an impossible task, of course, because intensive efforts have shown that infectious tropical diseases can be controlled even in their existing range, but the cost and the residual background risk need to be considered.[24] Moreover, it's not only human beings who face increasing disease risk, as we'll see; it's a problem for other species, including the trees that some policy analysts depend on to reach their carbon targets, a topic we'll return to in Chapter 4.

It's important to recognize that these risks – rising seas, mega-storms, drought, threats to health – are not walled off from each other. Occurring simultaneously, their effects will likely be intensified. Moreover, some may make others more likely; for instance, the melting of the Greenland ice sheet will impact ocean circulation in the North Atlantic, which would likely affect rainfall in South America, with consequences for the Amazon rainforest and, with it, further acceleration of global warming. These potential interactive processes are well grounded in theory but not understood to the extent they can be quantified.[25]

All of this adds up to considerable climate risk. As we will see, the costs of rising seas, extreme weather, widespread extinction and other predictable consequences of a warming planet defy the logic of balancing to which many economists are attached. But we have saved the worst for last: a runaway, self-feeding climate meltdown whose consequences are so extreme they defy any cost analysis at all: this is the problem of alligators in the Arctic.

## Beyond Calculation: The Threat of a Climate Catastrophe

Alligators basked in the swamps of what is now Ellesmere Island during the Paleocene–Eocene Thermal Maximum (PETM), which as we have seen was an extraordinary period in Earth history. The Arctic was lush, but what life was like in the former temperate and tropical regions to the south we can hardly imagine. The PETM lasted for about 200,000 years, a blip in geological time, but vast in human terms; take the elapsed time from Julius Caesar to the present and multiply by 100. (Of course, there were no people nor any mammals remotely suggestive of humans during the PETM.) Despite the rather substantial fluctuations in atmospheric carbon and global temperatures associated with the ice ages of more recent vintage, they do not begin to compare with the radical alterations of the PETM.[26]

In the previous chapter we speculated on the forms a catastrophic feedback process might take. It could come through changes in the Earth's albedo through glacial and sea ice melting, or from the loss of forest cover due to rapid environmental change, or decreased high altitude cloud formation, or the progressive release of ever more marine and terrestrial stored methane. For instance, recent research suggests we may have underestimated how rapidly carbon in permafrost deposits can be released into the atmosphere: warmer temperatures not only melt the frozen soils containing trapped methane but also break them up by destabilizing soil structure, and the result is likely to be a much larger and more rapid feedback effect.[27] Most likely a feedback crisis would appear as a combination of some or all of these individual mechanisms. In the first stage humans would blunder across a carbon cycle or climate system tipping point; in the second massive processes would take over to produce a climate nightmare.

It's worth thinking for a moment about what it would be like to live through such a train of events. At first we would begin to see signs of unmistakable feedback responses, like measured increases in atmospheric carbon concentrations that can't be tied to fossil fuel emissions, or increases in forest fires whose carbon releases rival those from other anthropogenic sources.[28] There would probably be a period of debate: Are these responses the beginning of runaway climate change, or just a temporary blip in a chaotic world with no overall trajectory? If they are actually the feedbacks we fear, they will continue to intensify, and scientific modeling will converge on an understanding of what they portend. At this point most people would understand they had entered a new and terrifying phase of history.

Beyond this we can only speculate. I suspect there would be panicked, last-ditch efforts to curtail the use of fossil fuels or reengineer the chemistry of the atmosphere or oceans. These measures, too long delayed or too speculative, would likely fail and might create new problems at a monumental scale, political as well as environmental. Both draconian economic controls and major interventions in the Earth's natural systems would likely depend on or result in the collapse of democratic institutions; rebellion and war are not out of the question.

My purpose in having you pause to visualize this horrific possibility is not to scare or depress you, but simply to establish the nature of the problem we face, so we can separate what makes sense and contributes to a solution from what is a distraction or just a feel-good palliative. *The goal is to achieve the most rapid feasible reduction in carbon emissions in order to minimize the likelihood of a climate catastrophe.* By doing this, we will also be working to minimize the other, less terrifying – but still daunting – risks described above. Of course, there are better and worse ways to do it, and much of the rest of this book will be about trying to keep alligators out of the Arctic with the least cost to human living standards, but the challenge of climate change is fundamentally about averting catastrophe.

## The Economic Problem

The problem of climate change is *produced*. We human beings have manufactured it through our wizardry at locating, extracting and burning fossil fuels. It is a byproduct of how our economies have operated since the large-scale development of coal and oil took off in the late nineteenth century, and addressing it means changing the way we produce and consume.

Of course, we face many other economic problems. Some are urgent, like reducing poverty and providing everyone access to food, health care and the other necessities of life. Others are less pressing but hardly unimportant: art and leisure, more satisfying and less taxing work, and in general an improved quality of life. Is climate change just one more economic problem – another reason to spend a little more here and a little less there – or is it qualitatively different, more existential?

One point of view we could take is that, while the specifics of the climate challenge are different from other problems, in the end it's all about consumption – and this is the view of most academic economists. When we go to a supermarket we have to decide how much money to spend on fruits and vegetables and how much on household cleaning products, and climate change presents us with the same choices, only at a social level. If we do nothing about it and expose ourselves to more sea level rise, extreme weather and other impacts, we experience costs. These costs, to continue the logic, can be given a monetary value: a storm or a heat wave will result in economic losses that can be calculated in advance. If so, policies to prevent these outcomes, to cut down on the use of fossil fuels and reduce the buildup of greenhouse gases, have the monetary value of the losses they prevent. And once we figure out what this value is, we can put them on society's version of the supermarket shelf alongside other programs, "buying" the amount of climate mitigation that justifies its cost – no less and no more.

Suppose, for instance, we thought that unconstrained climate change will cost the world $2 trillion. That's a lot of money, but the world economy is much larger still: about $87.5 trillion at current market prices.[29] The people inhabiting this planet spend money on all sorts of things, and reducing fossil fuel use would be one more option. How much should they spend? The climate-change-as-lost-consumption argument would be anything less than $2 trillion but nothing more. If it costs, say, $3 trillion to keep the alligators in their current environs, that's too much, since the benefit is only $2 trillion. If you agree with this perspective, the most important task policy researchers face is doing the math, figuring out the monetary cost of global warming so the rest of us know how much protection against it to "buy."

I will argue vehemently that this is the wrong way to look at the issue, but first I will consider what doing the math actually entails in the face of global climate uncertainties.

The first step is to identify all the potential impacts of climate change, along with the probability they will occur. Some of these are rather obvious because they are already taking place: the oceans have gradually begun to rise, weather patterns are shifting and extreme events, like droughts and mega-storms, are becoming more frequent. Others are still in the category of "perhaps" – logically implied by models of the climate response to global warming but not yet apparent. The most important task is to be complete, not leaving out any impact that might occur.

The second step is to estimate the likelihood of impacts of various severity with and without a given quantity of additional carbon emissions, like an extra gigatonne of carbon dioxide. This can take the form of either a greater chance of a specific impact, such as a hurricane that delivers as much rainfall as Harvey (the scourge of Houston in 2017), or the expectation of a more intense impact, such as an extra few centimeters of sea level rise. These marginal effects of greenhouse gas emissions, so-called because they pertain to the additional ("marginal") contribution of an extra input of atmospheric carbon rather than the total accumulation, are derived from complex models of the carbon cycle and climate sensitivity to changes in it. Together, these two steps give us vital information, albeit wrapped in immense uncertainty. As we have seen, the greatest unknown is the effect that an extra gigatonne of carbon dioxide emissions is likely to have on subsequent feedback processes, a multiplier effect that can take us from uncomfortable but manageable impacts to utterly unmanageable ones. Even if we know little about these tipping points, however, it is helpful to know as much as possible about the full range of consequences.

The third step, however, is where the economic calculation becomes dicey: the biophysical risks identified in the first two steps have to be expressed in terms of prices. If climate protection is to sit on our policy supermarket shelf next to the other uses for our money, with costs measured against benefits, the benefits – reduced risk – have to be measured monetarily. So an extra dollop of sea level rise has to be valued according to the economic cost of increased coastal inundation; additional exposure to heat waves, with their effects on human health, have to be measured according to the financial price we put on better health and longer life; and the various species that face greater risk of extinction each has to be assigned a price tag as well.

In fact, this is exactly what economists working on the "social cost of carbon" do for a living; they devise clever ways to derive prices for all these things.[30] Their primary tool is an "integrated assessment model" (IAM), which has interlinked equations for physical processes like the carbon cycle and the climate response to atmospheric and oceanic warming, as well as the interplay between all of this and the economy that generates additional greenhouse gases. A few of these IAMs have been further embellished with modules that convert physical climate impacts into monetary ones, based on prior studies.[31]

There are two types of problems which bedevil this attempt to make climate change a "normal" economic concern: the technical question of how to deal with scale in assessing impacts, and the philosophical one of whether consumer choices in the everyday marketplace provide the appropriate benchmark for thinking about what "value" means in the era of global environmental change.

The scale problem is obvious once you think about it: the price consumers put on goods today in a state of relative abundance may not reflect how much they will value them in a future of climate-induced scarcity. An extra kilo of rice today is one thing, an extra kilo in circumstances of widespread agricultural disruption is another. Of course, no one can know just how large a difference this will prove to be, but this uncertainty casts a dark shadow over the calculations of the IAM jockeys. The standard response among modelers is to build in a cost escalation factor; for instance, the most widely respected model, William Nordhaus' Dynamic Integrated Model of Climate and the Economy (DICE), makes the assumption that a doubling of atmospheric warming adds a squared term to equations for the cost of impacts.[32]

On a slightly more formal level, the key to understanding this issue is the distinction between total and marginal costs (or benefits). The total cost of an action is just that, the entire cost the action engenders. The marginal cost is the additional cost that arises because an additional bit of action is undertaken. An example is the effect of erecting a dam on fish habitat in a river that is no longer free-flowing.

The total cost of such dams would be the effect of all the dams in the world on all the rivers and all the fish. That's a big toll, but in practice we don't make a single decision on all these dams at once, so it doesn't matter. Instead, we decide one dam at a time, and the relevant consideration is the marginal cost of that dam: How much fish habitat, and fish, do we lose by building just this one?[33] Ultimately, this is a question of scale, and in normal times the scale is a single project and its incremental costs and benefits. Economists are so habituated to doing this that they have tended to not notice when the scale shifts dramatically – as it does for climate change. Here we are literally talking not about a few fish more or less but all the fish in the ocean, which is what we may lose if carbon lowers the ocean's pH below the level the bottom of the marine food chain can tolerate. In such cases the marginal cost of a little bit of damage (a few fish plus or minus) is a poor guide to the total cost of a drastic alteration of the Earth's environment.

Marginal thinking is built into the methodology of standard economic tools like the IAM. The value of goods and services, including natural resources like fish stocks, is taken from their market prices if they have them. This is justified by the argument that value is ultimately in the eye of the beholder, and the market tells us the price that reflects the valuation of the marginal beholders whose choices nudge the equilibrium one way or the other. The problem is that this is a marginal measurement, and its relevance depends on scale. If we are evaluating actions that have a small impact on the environment and the goods and services we derive from it, it may make sense to use market prices. Thus, if we lose one more bluefin tuna because of a climate impact, we can establish its value by using the price this fish commands in the market. But if we lose whole stocks of fish, or if in fact we lose the entire marine food resource, the current market price is a useless indicator. IAM methods rely extensively on market prices to ascertain values, but climate change is so sweeping in its potential impacts that prices established under current conditions tell us almost nothing. Pointing this out is not the same as suggesting a solution, however. If markets are not the answer, how do we value all the fish in the sea? It is difficult to come up with the justification for any alternative method, which suggests the whole enterprise may be ill-conceived.[34]

And that brings us to the deeper problem, whether consumer behavior is the right basis for thinking about the effects of large-scale climate alteration. There are important reasons for thinking otherwise.

First, the consumer is not always right. Behavioral economics, once a renegade field of study but now a respected branch of the discipline, is rife with examples of decision-making that fail to adhere to the ironclad rationality of *Homo economicus*, the economist's model citizen.[35] Market prices reflect the choices people actually make, not the choices they would have made if they always acted in their best interests. For instance, the price of a pound of fish relative to a pound of sugar reflects the dietary choices made by the public. Are we so sure that food decisions are free of emotional distortion, addictive behavior, or problems of unawareness or miscalculation?

And then there are all the goods that don't have market prices. Sea level rise, for example, will obliterate a large portion of the world's cultural and historic structures and places. What price should we place on the coastal heritage of China, India, Europe and the Americas? Economists pursue this by estimating the willingness of people to pay to preserve such things, either in practice or in response to hypothetical questions on surveys. But if consumers are unreliable decision-makers in contexts they have everyday experience in, how much credence should we give their views on events for which they have no experience at all and are almost impossible to visualize?

An even more fundamental problem is that consumer choice is just one context in which people put values on things and make decisions about them; it has virtues for some purposes but is a poor guide to others. If the question is what flavors should be used in toothpaste, the consumer is, or should be, king. If the people want mint, let them have mint, and let those who prefer cinnamon or anise have that instead. The market is the most appropriate guide, and there is little more to be said about it. But we make many other choices in our roles as citizens that we would be loath to leave to market forces. What would you think, for example, of a jury that made a decision about a defendant's innocence or guilt on the basis of how much its each of its members was willing to pay to convict or acquit? Questions of right and wrong are not best left to the market, where choices are made by individuals largely in isolation and don't have to be justified to others. To the extent that the value dimension of climate change – how much we value the losses of human life, environmental disruption and other consequences of letting emissions continue unabated – is about judgments of right and wrong, which is to say *political* values, it should rely on a process that resembles jury deliberation more than supermarket browsing.

Climate change, by its extreme implications, indicates the limits of market-oriented value systems. In the marketplace we select choices among a mostly given set of opportunities. We do this one individual or organization at a time, taking also as given the choices made or likely to be made by everyone else. Our purpose is primarily that of advancing our self-interest in a world in which others are looking out for theirs. There is a vast array of problems that are relatively well-addressed in this system.

But there are other problems we can't afford to leave to markets or market-based decision methods, such as using market prices to assign a monetary value to climate protection. As we will see in great detail in later chapters, action to forestall a climate catastrophe is not reducible to a number of measures we might take as private individuals; it demands collective action on as large a scale as possible. It is the sort of goal people must accomplish simultaneously and together; it can't succeed any other way. Moreover, in its impacts on humans and the natural world, a climate disaster that makes much of the planet uninhabitable is not simply a question of greater or lesser consumer satisfaction. It isn't worth so many pizzas or tropical vacations. It requires us to move from "me" to "we," to consider what actions we are obligated to take according to our ethical standards. Finally, scientific understanding of what climate alteration entails has to be a crucial part of the process. For all these reasons, it is not to the world of prices that we should turn at a time of extreme ecological risk, but to that of ethical values and scientific constraints.[36]

The conclusion I propose, which animates the remainder of this book, is that we should look to climate science for the goals and timetables of carbon policy. Economics is crucial, but as a guide to means, not ends. Economics, as we will see, has much to say about how to achieve climate goals as efficiently as possible, and we can use it to advance social justice as well. In fact, as we will see, ignorance of economics has been nearly as costly as ignorance of the natural science basis for climate change by fostering confusion and denial.

Note: For those who want to delve deeper into the misapplication of economics to climate policy, see the Appendix.

# 3 MEASUREMENT
## Myths and Distractions

Since forestalling catastrophic climate change will be a voyage into uncharted waters, it may be useful to think about earlier times when boats set forth across great expanses of water without any clear indication of where they were or where they were headed.

Earth positioning is a matter of latitude and longitude, the first measured in degrees north and south, the second east and west. Since ancient times mariners had astronomical methods for calculating latitude, but longitude was a tougher puzzle, because the reference points – especially the sun's zenith – depended on a highly accurate measurement of time. During the long centuries in which Chinese, Norse, Basque and other sailors ventured into the open ocean with an ability to measure how far north they were but not how far to the east or west, navigation was as much a matter of luck as skill and experience.

In 1714 the British Parliament offered prizes, enormous for their time, to inventors who could solve the problem of measuring longitude. The story of the eventual winner, John Harrison, a carpenter who tinkered alone in a rural workshop for forty years, has been well told in *Longitude: The True Story of a Lone Genius Who Solved the Greatest Scientific Problem of His Time* by Dava Sobel.[1] Initially denied the recognition he had earned, Harrison took his case to court and won. More important was the result of his labors for global colonization and trade: with an accurate timepiece that could withstand the rigors of an ocean voyage, the transcontinental movement of people and goods quickly became safer and more reliable. More than any other innovation in boat design or construction, measurement of position gave us a smaller world.

And proper measurement will be equally crucial to the task of decarbonizing the twenty-first-century world during the space of just a few decades. Where do we stand as we begin the task? How will we gauge our progress? How can we tell whether governments are living up to their promises or just kicking the can down the road? Avoiding a climate catastrophe is above all a matter of numbers: yearly carbon emissions, the accumulation of carbon in the atmosphere, the trans-formation of that carbon into degrees of planetary warming. Without the ability to measure these things well enough, we are truly at sea.

The premise of this chapter is that measurement is currently a mess – not so much at the scientific level, although there are technical complexities and uncertainties that remain to be sorted out, but above all in the domains of politics, policy design and popular culture. Current programs of carbon regulation and the targets they are supposed to reach are based on measurement systems so inappropriate and opaque it is nearly impossible to tell what contribution they might make to safeguarding the planet, defeating any meaningful notion of account-ability. Meanwhile, in a well-intentioned but misconceived effort to parcel out responsibility to individuals, corporations and other entities, millions of us are made to worry about our carbon footprints – even though their measurement is all but impossible.

Measurement that connects the policies we implement to cli-mate outcomes is the place to begin. By the end of the chapter it will be clear what this means: exactly what we need to know in order to take effective action and assess how well it's working.

## The Footprint Fetish

During the summer of 2020, while the coronavirus pandemic was clamping down on all forms of travel, readers of the *New York Times* were presented with a quiz on carbon footprints containing this question: "You have a midsize car and you're environmentally con-scious, so you set yourself a strict limit of 100 miles per week. If you switched to a hybrid car, how many miles could you drive while still producing the same amount of greenhouse gases?"[2]

It's a complex problem; to answer correctly we would need a plethora of information that would change from time to time and place to place. (We will see this in greater detail later.) Being a climate hero isn't easy! But this is what each of us is supposed to be able to figure out, right?

Overall, what's your carbon footprint? Surely, this isn't the first time you've been asked this question; you've probably asked it of yourself. Go through all your possessions, the size and insulation of your house, how much you drive and whether you take frequent airplane trips. There are online calculators to help you condense your hundreds of lifestyle choices into a single number, your personal contribution to the climate problem.[3]

For many environmentalists, personal footprints are a measure of moral virtue. They see the world divided into the solid citizens, the ones who are always looking to shed a few ounces of carbon guilt, and the villains who shirk personal sacrifice. The virtuous drive Priuses, while the evildoers can be found in big SUVs, pickups and other incarnations of fossil fuel profligacy.[4] Carbon moralism in this sense has two faces: the warm glow the green-minded get from actions that shrink their footprint, and the opprobrium they assign to the unenlightened.

As we will see, carbon footprints have almost no meaning at the level of a single individual and their personal choices, so the moralism is without foundation. Even if this weren't the case, however, it should be obvious that virtue-environmentalism is a political disaster. Rather than reaching out to new constituencies and building broader alliances, many environmentalists prefer to demonize everyone who isn't already engaged, as if the public sphere were a morality tournament rather than an arena for collective action. It's entirely possible, however, that many of those who trumpet their carbon virtue are bigger contributors than those they disdain.

Meanwhile, an entire industry of carbon auditing has established itself at the institutional level, where corporations, universities, municipalities and other organizations pay for a reckoning of "their" carbon emissions. The goal is carbon neutrality or even negativity, where one's very existence somehow reduces emissions that would otherwise occur. In the absence of meaningful action at the national and international levels, this is the form that carbon activism has taken. It gives those who take part in it the feeling that they are doing their share to address the problem, and of course its public relations value is not overlooked.

Take the case of Microsoft. In a series of public statements and reports issued during 2020 it outlined its carbon goals, which includes achieving carbon negativity by 2030 and even removing by 2050 all the carbon it has emitted since its founding in 1975. How is this possible? They have instituted an internal carbon fee of $15 per metric tonne that units will have to pay for their direct emissions, purchases of noncarbon energy from local electricity companies and payments to businesses engaged in carbon removal by forestation, soil enhancement and other approaches.[5]

While I will have critical things to say about programs like Microsoft's, I don't mean to suggest its staff who work on carbon emissions are anything less than honest and competent. They would certainly defend themselves on the grounds that something is better than nothing, and they may well be right. What needs to be considered, however, is how much we should rely on corporate and other institutional policies and whether the measurements they offer for how much carbon they are responsible for and mitigate can be believed. Exactly what is being measured – or should be measured – by estimates of emissions at the level of individuals and organizations?

## Economic Complexity and the Limits to Measurement

If historical eras are remembered for the questions they ask, ours might go down as the age of paper-or-plastic. That is, which kind of shopping bag is better for the environment and, in particular, has the least embedded carbon emissions, and how do they both compare with cotton?

A nice summary of the current state of confusion is provided by Ben Adler, writing on the popular environmental site Grist.[6] How much energy, for instance, does it take to produce a paper bag compared to a plastic one? In general, more, but the carbon impacts depend on how the energy itself is produced. Transportation is also somewhat more demanding for paper because it's heavier, but a big uncertainty is reuse. Will the paper bag be used once and then tossed? What about the plastic bag? Or will either bag be used to replace another bag at home after its shopping duties are fulfilled? Meanwhile, cotton bags, which would certainly win the reusability contest, are sourced from a crop with an exceptionally high environmental impact. One point the article doesn't get to is the energy expended in cleaning reusable bags if they acquire food residues: Is the carbon footprint of the hot water rinse bigger or smaller than that of just getting a new bag? Adler makes it clear there are no general answers to these questions; it depends, and a consumer would need to be a full-time bag researcher to know the precise comparison for any two kinds of bags under all potential circumstances. And bags are simple compared to other products – not to mention the entire production operations that are the subject of carbon audits.

This illustrates a fundamental difficulty with measurement tasks like carbon footprints; the web of direct and indirect inputs into production is intricate to the point of incalculability. But a second type of complexity is even more disconcerting: the impact of any particular choice we make as individuals or organizations depends on what choices we and others would have made otherwise, since the world is interdependent socially and economically as well as technologically. If a business executive employed by Microsoft decides to forgo a plane trip to meet with a client, that saves the carbon that would have been emitted otherwise. (True, an airplane that carries one traveler more or less might emit almost the same carbon dioxide, but over a large enough number of business travelers an extra trip per year will lead to more flights being scheduled.) Yet the decision to not travel will have other consequences. Would the client come to Microsoft instead? That might completely negate Microsoft's carbon savings. Would Microsoft's business go to some other company? And would that loss of a client have a carbon impact in some way, positive or negative? For instance, perhaps a representative of a different company will end up making the same trip and getting the account Microsoft passed on. How can these consequences be tallied by Microsoft's carbon auditors?

Sometimes the trail from cause to effect is short enough that the absurdity of carbon footprint measurement is unmistakable. One of the ways Microsoft claims to be reducing its emissions is by buying electricity from a local public utility that operates three hydroelectric dams. The idea is that by paying a premium for this power, Microsoft can book it as "their" electricity even though it comes off the same grid as everyone else's.[7] But no new hydropower is being generated, which means that other customers on Microsoft's grid will now need to be designated as buyers of more of its nonrenewable power – by simple arithmetic their carbon footprint must go up by the same amount Microsoft's goes down. This maneuver looks fine on Microsoft's Corporate Social Responsibility Report but does nothing for combating climate change. Later on, when we survey the existing state of carbon policy, we will find this dodge is nearly universal.

Stepping back for a moment, it helps to think about just what we mean, or should mean, by "carbon footprint." In everyday use, it seems to denote the additional carbon I or my organization is responsible for by making a given decision or carrying out a particular operation. If my company sends twenty managers to a conference in another city, its footprint is the carbon that's emitted in the course of their travel. The carbon footprint of a building, according to this view, consists of the emissions from its construction, maintenance and operation. The key notion that does the heavy work in the background is "responsible": I am responsible for what I do, and the building is responsible for what it does. Other consequences may ensue, but we are not responsible for them.[8]

But there's another way to think of it. We can compare two different states of the world – parallel universes, if you will. In one, I have taken one action, like traveling to a conference or paying a surcharge for renewable energy from the grid; in the other I've taken a different one, like not traveling or paying the same electric rate as everyone else. In each world there is a total amount of carbon emissions, so the effect of my choice on the accumulation of carbon in the atmosphere is simply the difference, the first minus the second. Of course, World no. 2 may differ from World no. 1 in many ways that reflect ripple effects, the way my choice affects someone else's, which affects someone else's and so on. These ramifications occur because we are interconnected with one another, and what we choose to do is influenced by our family and friends, coworkers and competitors – really just about everyone in a world without social or economic borders.

Which should it be, the first sort of footprint or the second – what we think we're responsible for or what results from our actions? It depends on what we want to calculate. If the question is one of morality or virtue, the first has merit. I should be judged on what I myself do, and if your actions change because of what I've done, that's on your moral account. The problem with that definition, however, is that adding it up for each one of us doesn't sum to the social outcome. We can add up the effects of my choice holding yours constant and yours holding mine constant, but the combined outcome, where we each react on the choices of the other, is seldom the same. To put it differently, what actually occurs is not just what gets chalked up to me on a moral scorecard but everything that results from my choice, whether I am held "responsible" for it or not. To truly estimate the carbon consequences of a personal or business decision, I should adopt the second footprint definition and take into account all the ripple effects, seen and unseen. But is it doable?

The challenge of mitigating climate change is relatively new, but the dream of capturing the "real," physical substance behind the world of money and markets is older. At least as early as the middle of the nineteenth century, radical economic reformers organizing under the banners of socialism, communism and anarchism proposed we could dispense with markets altogether and create a planned, rational economy that better served human needs. What they had in mind was a system in which public servants would calculate the amount of each good, like wheat or steel, needed directly or indirectly for the production of an agreed-on list of consumer goods. These amounts would be communicated, and the "community of producers" would see to it that all quotas were filled.

Markets already do this in their own way. "Needs" are determined by what consumers are willing and able to buy, and the materials and intermediate goods required to produce these end products are supplied in other markets. If consumers seek to buy more cars, requiring more steel to feed the assembly lines turning them out, car producers add to their steel purchases, stimulating supply. There is a lot to question about the values that do and do not get expressed in this process, but the ability of the system to coordinate the flows of millions of raw materials and intermediate and final goods under normal circumstances is not in question.

For radicals the issue was whether such coordination could be achieved directly by calculating the needed amounts of all these items and allocating them to their uses. The topic was debated for decades, and although there are holdouts who still believe in an economy based on physical planning, most economists think the matter has been resolved in favor of markets. A modern economy is simply too complex to be organized by explicit calculations of how all its goods and services interact.[9]

Carbon accounting at the product or organizational level is exactly the sort of calculation that economists felt they had refuted. Consider again the eternal question of paper or plastic. The relative carbon footprint depends on the materials used to make them, how the forest that produced the pulp is managed (if paper) or what feedstock was used for the plastic, what kind of energy is used in their production processes, how the bags are transported, how often consumers reuse them, and so on. And this is just one production choice in a world that faces literally millions of them. Worse, the choices are interdependent: the carbon footprint of a stack of paper bags, for instance, depends on where people choose to live (transportation), how much energy they use for other purposes (how much load is placed on renewable energy sources that might be available to produce bags instead), what products they buy when they shop, how those products are packaged (which affects reuse), and so on. Any one calculation could be performed holding everything else constant, so it's possible – with enough research! – to figure out the carbon footprint of a given bag assuming the rest of the economy remains exactly as it was at a certain moment in time, but of course nothing is constant. And the paper or plastic dilemma is infinitesimal compared with the challenge facing Microsoft in its effort to calculate the direct and indirect carbon emissions resulting from their operations.

This doesn't mean, of course, that there aren't real direct and indirect carbon emissions in everything we produce and consume, only that their full extent is beyond calculation. But if we ever take the necessary step of placing a meaningful price on carbon, one substantial enough to dramatically alter the choices we face in economic life, we will *find out* what our carbon footprints actually are; linkages between goods, materials and the decisions we make about them will be revealed by the way price effects ricochet through the system. The things we won't be able to afford to make or do any more, once carbon emissions are sufficiently costly and people have adjusted to them, will be the ones whose true footprints turned out to be the largest.

But maybe these abstract economic arguments aren't convincing yet. In that case, we should consider more examples taken from the practical world of carbon audits.

## Taking Carbon Measurement on the Road

Consider the problem of the automobile, now and in the future. It hardly needs to be emphasized that automobility is central to the decarbonization of modern economies, whether we ultimately succeed or fail. Can the use of fossil fuels, particularly petroleum, be phased out without massive disruption to transportation systems and the geographic patterns based on them? Or will the grip of the automobile prove to be more tenacious, defeating serious action on the climate? It's likely that the answer depends on the prospects for a transition to electric vehicles: not only the economic feasibility of this transition but its outcome for actual carbon emissions.

Not surprisingly, there has been an immense outpouring of studies comparing electric vehicles, vehicles with internal combustion engines and hybrids of various types in recent years. A good review article that summarizes most of them is by Nordelöf et al., which emphasizes the role of life cycle analysis; another is by Delucchi et al.[10] It is far beyond the scope of this book to delve into the intricacies of this literature, but here is the essence of what we know today:

- In general, electric and hybrid vehicles have lower carbon emissions than conventional vehicles, but nowhere near zero.
- There are other aspects of vehicle design, especially size, that play an important independent role. A small, fuel-efficient conventional car tends to have fewer life cycle carbon emissions than a monster electric or hybrid competitor.
- But it all depends! The variability of comparative emissions is enormous: there are larger differences between different scenarios that depend on factors other than vehicle type than between the vehicle types themselves.

So let's take a look at the variability. It can be sorted into three broad categories:

1. *The electrical grid.* Since cars that derive some or all of their power from electricity will draw on whatever grid is in place, this is a crucial consideration. In coal-dominated electrical systems such as China's (today), electric vehicles have little if anything to offer in the way of decarbonization. Moreover, it isn't the average composition of the grid that matters, but the source of any marginal increase.[11] If 50% of a region's electricity comes from renewables but 90% of any additional demand has to be met by coal, then coal's carbon footprint will dominate a proper calculation of the carbon cost of electric vehicles. Not only the feedstock matters, incidentally; losses in generation and transmission can be a third or more of the ultimate energy use of the network, so how the grid is set up and where the

vehicle recharging takes place can also make a difference. Moreover, as Graff Ziven and his coauthors pointed out, the time of day when recharging takes place can also be important. In the absence of inexpensive storage options, evening will draw less on solar and wind and more on fossil fuels; this can actually double the indirect carbon emissions of electric vehicles.

2. *Life cycle factors.* Due mainly to their batteries, electric vehicles have substantially more carbon embodied in their production – but this depends on the specifics of vehicle design, where their materials are sourced and what power sources are available in the regions where their parts are manufactured. Moreover, a critical point raised by Nordelöf et al. is that, to determine the complete life cycle impact of an electric vehicle in use today, we need to know how fully it will be recycled at the end of its useful life. Much of the carbon cost of producing an electric battery, for instance, can be reduced if materials recycling is adhered to, but how can we know how assiduously this program will be followed?

3. *Use factors.* Here is where all attempts at precise estimation collapse. How much will each kind of car be driven? Electric vehicles are better adapted for shorter trips and conventional cars lose mileage in stop-and-start driving, so travel patterns are important. But this in turn depends on the evolution of geography: Will urban density increase in coming years if carbon policy makes driving more expensive? That will increase the advantage of electric vehicles. But an ironic feature of switching to cars without internal combustion engines is that, by reducing the demand for petroleum, they lower its price, which can then result in *more* demand for this fuel elsewhere – a rebound effect.[12] Also, whether and how much electric cars have a carbon edge depends on how long they are used. Hawkins et al. found that if cars are replaced after 150,000 kilometers, electrics have a 10–24% carbon advantage over conventional vehicles under the current European power mix, but this falls to 9–14% if they are swapped out after just 100,000 kilometers.[13]

To sum up, the sort of uncertainties that came to light in the twentieth-century debate over economic calculation can be identified in this one, relatively well circumscribed problem. (1) Everything depends on everything. The carbon footprint of an electric car depends on the electrical grid; the manufacturing base; the location of residences, jobs and commercial areas; and the rest of the global demand for fossil fuels of various types. Each will be changing over the coming years, and their changes will depend on how all the other factors evolve. Quantitative planning is as much guesswork as science. (2) Many of the factors that govern relative carbon footprints are intrinsically unknowable in advance. How will consumers *want* to drive their cars? This is irreducibly subjective, and we will learn only through trial and error. How will technology develop? Where will cars be manufactured and how?

At a personal level, many readers of this book may be alarmed at the prospect of catastrophic climate change and eager to do their share. They may sincerely question their next car purchase: Should they go with a less expensive conventional model, or a hybrid of some sort, or should they invest in a fully electric plug-in? What they probably don't want to hear, but in all honesty I have to report, is that the best research doesn't give them much to go on. There are many local factors that need to be considered in this decision, and they are likely to change unpredictably in the years ahead. Sorry; the skeptics about economic calculation in physical units were right.

## Auditing the Carbon Audit

Let's try a different set of issues posed by carbon auditing. I used to teach at Evergreen State College, which, like many other academic institutions around the country and the world, wants to display its green credentials; it last produced a Greenhouse Gas Emissions Inventory for fiscal year 2014–2015.[14] In it you can find that total emissions had continued their downward trend for the fourth consecutive year, with the two biggest items being heating and travel (including commuting). Electricity is largely carbon-free, it says, because the college purchased renewable energy credits (RECs) roughly equal to its power usage.

Since carbon auditing is standard in higher education, schools employ off-the-shelf tools. Evergreen used the Campus Carbon Calculator developed by the University of New Hampshire, documented in their User Guide.[15] This is an elaborate spreadsheet; college staff fill in the cells for a wide range of activities, from heating and electricity use to student commuting and travel, and the spreadsheet model converts them to greenhouse gas equivalents. Of course, being a standardized tool, the Calculator can't take account of the full range of local circumstances, but it does offer the opportunity for colleges to specify a number of technology factors that affect their footprints.

One of the issues that immediately presents itself is electricity: How should an institution determine the emissions it's responsible for due to its use of electrical power? Evergreen reports that this accounts for almost 36% of its total carbon footprint – and then it nets out almost all of it due to its purchase of RECs for the entire amount. This is exactly the same approach that we saw Microsoft using to reclassify its electricity consumption as "carbon neutral": even though the amount of carbon-free electricity coursing through the grid is unchanged, an entity like Evergreen or Microsoft can claim *their* electricity is guilt-free because they purchased credits. Does this sound a bit like the medieval practice of buying indulgence? It does to me. Even though no one's carbon-emitting behavior has changed, the REC buyer can claim to have wiped the carbon stain from its accounts. Even better, the RECs can be resold on a secondary market, which wasn't possible with indulgences. (I've decided my immortal soul isn't so valuable after all, so I'll trade you this ticket to heaven for 1,000 florins.)

To be fair, defenders of the REC system claim that, by paying a premium to electricity producers for the renewable portion of their output, buyers of credits are creating an incentive for new energy investments to be greener. It could be true, but is it? As it happens, the empirical evidence suggests the purchase of RECs has little if any effect on renewable energy investments.[16] This is because there is little demand for credits beyond the current level of supply, and prices are too low to have a material impact. Even if it were otherwise, however, the true decarbonizing effect of a given REC would be difficult to pin down and would be constantly changing in light of economic and technical conditions, since the demand for credits relative to their supply depends on a wide array of variables, including the evolution of aggregate energy demand and the cost components of different technologies.

But back to Evergreen – what about the rest of its carbon footprint, the 64% that isn't electricity? The accounting problems are most severe where the carbon impact of the college's choices depends on the carbon embodied in goods and services produced elsewhere, which then depend on goods and services produced somewhere else, and so on – the conundrum of a complex, interdependent production system. In fact, it's common for institutions to simply take a pass on most of these sorts of emissions, a sensible decision under the circumstances. But the items in Evergreen's greenhouse gas inventory run up against a different problem: identifying the counterfactual. Consider one element, commuting, especially student commuting, which accounts for about a quarter of all emissions. When instruction isn't mostly virtual, as it has been during the pandemic, many students need to commute because there is limited on-campus housing. This is the justification for ascribing the resulting carbon emissions to the college and not some external group (like the students themselves). But suppose, as a thought experiment, that the college were to go out of business – perhaps the state of Washington suddenly pulls the plug.[17] The students wouldn't just disappear; they would find something else to do. Many would attend a different college or university; others would look for a job. In any case, they wouldn't reduce their travel and its carbon footprint to zero. The college's impact on emissions from student travel depends on the *extra* travel they do because of the college's operations. For instance, the college shouldn't be held responsible if some of its students fly sunward during spring break to get away from Puget Sound's spring diet of constant rain. But the college's impact does depends on how much students would travel, and in what modes, if the college didn't demand their attendance.

And now consider the reliance on virtual instruction during the pandemic. Most students have not needed to travel to campus from other parts of the state or country, and of course the daily commuting of even local students has fallen off dramatically. How much should the college credit itself for these reduced carbon emissions? This is actually an important question, since, once the viral threat has passed, decisions will have to be made about how much virtual instruction to retain. The true answer is almost impossible to guess, since it depends on what remotely based students are doing instead of attending classes in person. If they are using the opportunity to earn more income, they may be commuting to work. Or maybe they are sheltering in place, staring at professors on their computer screen and emitting no carbon at all. We can survey them and get an approximation, but it would capture just the period in which the survey is being answered; today's responses may be a poor predictor of what the carbon consequences might be a year or five in the future.

But what's *really* odd about the Evergreen example is that its largest potential impact on greenhouse gas accumulation is missing entirely from the inventory: the effect it has, as an educational institution, on future climate policy. Every year hundreds of students take courses (called "programs" at Evergreen) that examine climate change from multiple angles, including natural science, political economy, ethics and the arts. They take pH measurements in Puget Sound, analyze policy alternatives, debate the meaning of climate justice, and try their hand at environmental art and literature. If all this learning and exploration speeds up the adoption of significant national carbon legislation by just a single day, it will completely offset all the emissions in the college's inventory. This is not an argument for ignoring opportunities to shrink the footprint of doing business, but it reminds us that the biggest impacts often come from what we do and not just how much carbon we burn doing it.

Others too have noted the mismatch between the effort organizations put into auditing their small increment to carbon emissions and their inattention to the much larger impact they potentially have on carbon policy.[18] Consider the case of Microsoft again. It's great if this company can increase its energy efficiency or use more decarbonized inputs into its production process. Again, I admire the work of employees who have dedicated themselves to this, as I admire the carbon beancounters at Evergreen. But this pales to insignificance compared with the *political* footprint of Microsoft as a funder of politicians, parties and policies in the United States and elsewhere. If Microsoft supports politicians who deny the very existence of anthropogenic climate change and put up every possible barrier to action on that front – and it does – this has vastly greater effect on future climate scenarios than whether or not a solar array is installed on an office building.

There is a lot of dark, unreported money in American politics about which we should assume the worst, but even Microsoft's publicly reported political donations are troubling. Its bias is strongly Republican: in ten of the twelve national election cycles since its significant donations began in 1998, contributions to Republicans exceeded those to Democrats. In the 2019–2020 cycle, Republicans took in 56% of Microsoft's donations in House elections and 57.4% for the Senate.[19] Of course, many Democrats are also foot-draggers on climate policy, but the Republican party has become completely intransigent on this issue. We would be much better off as a country and world if corporations like Microsoft spent less money on installing rooftop solar collectors (or buying renewable energy credits) and funneled it instead to politicians and organizations committed or at least open to taking decisive action for decarbonization.

Confronting the political dimension leads us to the deepest problem with personal and organizational carbon audits: they struggle to find answers to the wrong questions. A careful accounting of your individual consumption or business operations makes sense if the question is, "How can we address climate change through the separate choices we make as individuals and enterprises?" If the road to climate salvation is through changing light bulbs, driving fewer miles per week, or installing double-paned glass, accounting, aside from the difficulties we've cataloged, could possibly tell us what we need to know. The reality, however, is that while a bit of progress is possible at the individual and enterprise levels, the battle will be won or lost depending on whether we make the changes at a society-wide level that shift our economy to a decarbonized trajectory.

There are two reasons for this. The first is that, as separate decision-makers we can choose only among the options currently available to us. I can drive my car more or less. I can ride a bike, but only on roads as they are designed and maintained in my area. A company can introduce an incentive program to get more of its employees out of their cars and onto public transit, but the transit system itself, not to mention the urban geography it is embedded in, is beyond their control. All of us depend on the electrical grid, but as separate consumers we have little input into how adaptable the infrastructure is to intermittent renewable generation. But collectively, through policies that reshape governments and markets, we can do all this and more. The carbon metrics that matter are on the economy-wide level; they tell us what needs to be done and how much progress we're making toward doing it. In a few paragraphs I will switch to that crucial topic, but for now the point is that the intense demand for personal and institutional carbon inventories suggests that something has gone very wrong.

The second reason is that decarbonization is what social scientists refer to as a collective action problem.[20] If I make sacrifices to reduce my carbon footprint but few others do, I have the worst of both worlds, personal hardship and a climate apocalypse. On the other hand, if I forgo sacrifices but most others undertake them, I get the best of both worlds, convenience and a livable planet. Under such circumstances it is virtually impossible to achieve widespread participation. The problem is not so great if the sacrifices we're being asked to make are small – and many symbolic measures that signal our climate goodwill are in fact widely adopted – but really biting the bullet is another matter.

Consider again the issue of corporate travel or academic travel for a college like Evergreen. If there are only modest benefits to flying your personnel or students around the world it's not too difficult to cut back. As we've learned during the pandemic, some meetings can be held through teleconferencing, or perhaps one official could travel instead of two or three. Such measures can be taken voluntarily; they even save money. (The drive for a smaller carbon footprint could be an excuse for an organization to do something it wants to do anyway.)

But what happens if travel is valuable – and *competitive*? I raised this issue earlier when thinking about a company that organizes a trip to woo a client. If your business is unwilling to allow managers to do this but your competitor has no such scruples, you may be out of luck. Similarly, suppose a college unilaterally decides to forgo allowing its students to travel for field trips or study abroad; not only does this reduce their educational opportunities, it also puts the college at a disadvantage compared with others that permit and even encourage these options. It's one thing if everyone is cutting back on activities that burn carbon, another if you're doing it alone.

As we will soon see, difficult decisions await us on the road to forestalling a climate catastrophe. Some conveniences we have become used to will need to be given up, and it is unlikely this can be done one individual or business at a time – which is why politics is crucial. To get the job done we need to think less as consumers or employees carrying out the policies of organizations and a lot more as citizens.

## Global Carbon Measurement: From Targets to Budgets

On December 12, 2015, after literally decades of frustrating negotiations, a partial breakthrough was achieved when the final text of the COP21 "Paris" Agreement was hammered out. For the first time most of the world's countries committed themselves to specific reductions in carbon emissions. Each was free to specify its own targets, but, on paper at least, they were commitments and not just pious wishes. The agreement was hailed around the world as the biggest step ever taken toward forestalling catastrophic climate change.

Table 3.1. Selected intended nationally determined contributions to carbon mitigation

| Country/Region | Commitment |
| --- | --- |
| Brazil | Reduction of greenhouse gas emissions by 37% below 2005 levels in 2025 |
| China | Peak carbon emissions in 2030, with reduction of emissions per unit of GDP by 60–65% from the 2005 level |
| European Union | At least 40% domestic reduction of greenhouse gas emissions by 2030 compared with 1990 |
| India | Reduction of the emissions intensity of GDP by 33–35% by 2030 from 2005 level |
| Japan | 26% reduction of emissions by 2030 compared with 2013 (approximately 1.042 billion t-$CO_2$ equivalent as 2030 emissions) |
| Korea | Reduction of emissions by 37% from the business-as-usual scenario (850.6 MtCO2eq) by 2030 |
| Russia | Reduction of emissions to 70–75% of 1990 levels by the year 2030 |
| United States[a] | Reduction of emissions by 26–28% below its 2005 level in 2025 |

Source: UNFCCC (2016b).
[a] The United States, following the election of Donald Trump, withdrew from the accord, but it reenlisted under Joe Biden.

So what did these countries pledge? So far, 189 have submitted their goals, and it would be an unnecessary complication to list them all here – you can read them for yourself at the United Nations Framework Convention on Climate Change (UNFCCC) website – but Table 3.1 lists some of the most prominent players.

A quick question: Which of these countries has offered the most ambitious commitment? If you are mystified as you stare at this table, you aren't alone. Countries are using different metrics for their targets (absolute emissions versus emissions per unit of economic output), different baselines against which to compare progress and different target years. It was difficult enough to get them to agree on the concept of mitigation commitments in the first place, and negotiators apparently didn't feel like staying in Paris for an extra month getting everyone on board with a common set of mitigation parameters. (They also failed to agree on a framework for holding countries to their pledges, a topic we'll return to later.)

But the problem with these mitigation targets goes well beyond their lack of standardization. In fact, they are only loosely informative about the effect they would have on the accumulation of carbon in the atmosphere, and they offer hardly any guidance for setting and evaluating policy. Rather, they demonstrate just how damaging faulty measurement can be.[21]

Let's go back to the core science of greenhouse warming.[22] The amount of carbon in Earth's atmosphere largely determines the extent to which the sun's radiation is trapped and heats up the planet. Individual molecules come and go, but a portion of the carbon released from burning fossil fuels, mostly in the form of carbon dioxide, remains in the atmosphere for centuries. From the point of view of human lifetimes, the carbon people send up into the atmosphere is effectively permanent.

The relevant arithmetic is not about *levels* of carbon emissions but about their *sums*. In the year 2030, the target date for most of the countries that signed the Paris Agreement, the amount of carbon dioxide and other greenhouse gases in the atmosphere will be the amount that's there today, plus the amount we add next year, plus the year after next, the year after that – until 2030 actually arrives. The amount emitted in 2030 or any other individual year is not the point; the total accumulation is what matters.[23]

This is why the IPCC has proposed a carbon budget, a fixed amount of emissions we should adhere to over the coming decades, rather than a target we might arrive at some number of years into the future. It's obvious to them, and should be to us, that a target aims at an emission level in a given year but doesn't keep total accumulated emissions within a budget.

If this isn't immediately clear, imagine a recreational gambler at a casino. He realizes he might risk his family's savings at the gaming table, so he purchases a certain number of chips and promises to play only those and no more. This budget-setting approach can work. Win or lose, when the chips are gone, the gambling adventure is over and it is time to go home with finances still intact. But suppose that instead of holding himself to a fixed number of chips, the gambler tells himself he will not bet more than twenty chips during the period from midnight to 1 a.m. That promise could have some significance, but it is not nearly as effective as simply setting a firm total of chips to be spent, no matter when. In fact, if the gambler runs up large losses when the night is still young, by midnight his noble promise may not make any difference at all.

This is exactly how it is with global carbon emissions. Every tonne emitted this year, next year and so on counts the same as a tonne emitted in an eventual target year.[24] Postponing effective policies until the last moment and then going on a crash diet leads to virtually the same atmospheric carbon concentrations as having no policies at all. Pledges to cut back to a certain emissions level at some future time do not mean very much.

Realistically, the situation is even worse. If countries merely promise to hit particular levels for carbon emissions in a given year or string of years, exceeding such limits signifies a mere "oops" – a disappointment not consequential for meeting further targets down the road. On the other hand, if countries – alone or together – promise to stay within a total budget for future carbon emissions, each tonne emitted above the intended level in a given year has to be offset by one less future tonne. In our casino analogy, if the gambler loses too many chips between 11 p.m. and midnight, he has that many fewer to risk between midnight and 1 a.m. Since climate-related pledges to cut back carbon emissions may be even more difficult to live up to than gamblers' resolutions – and similarly lack real enforcement mechanisms – slippage on targets is likely to be the rule.

And setting targets rather than budgets has an additional consequence for enforceability. A target for 2030 or some other year is met or missed only in that year. Governments might argue they are "on track" to achieve a target, but there is no precise meaning to this. They could claim they are on track because they've made investments that are "poised" to yield results in the near future, or they have raised public awareness, or, by some initial emissions cuts, they have made a "down payment" on future, more stringent measures. The language is familiar, because governments often pledge to achieve goals many years in the future (after the current crop of politicians has retired) and typically fall short of achieving them. Verbal foggery is serviceable because it dodges a quantitative test that would allow critics to show that promises are not being kept. It's exactly this testing that a proper measurement framework for carbon emissions ought to provide.

A carbon budget is more transparent in that respect. If a cap on all future emissions is proposed, like those put forward by the IPCC, an emissions monitoring system can tell you how much has been used and how much is left. It's straightforward to calculate how many years of emissions at the current rate will exhaust the budget, or to generate reduction scenarios that permit a soft landing when the budget limit is reached. While there are challenges with this methodology as well, it offers the most logical approach, and we will use it in future chapters as we explore its implications for the speed with which we need to wean ourselves from fossil fuels and the costs we'll face as we do this.

On a very practical level, carbon budgets simplify the task of adding up mitigation commitments; they are stackable. The pledges in Table 3.1 are not easily combined, and the UNFCCC had to analyze them in detail to arrive at a composite picture; even so, they could provide only a rough indication of how far the commitments in the aggregate go toward meeting global goals. Budgets, on the other hand, can be added directly, just as a group of players in a casino can pool together their chips. Real international coordination, rather than the parallel play exemplified by the Paris agreement, requires a shift from targets to budgets.

From now on in this book, when we consider the constraints that climate science places on human economies, we'll represent them through the use of a carbon budget, using annual emission reductions only as a way to convey an average effect of the budget constraint on progress toward decarbonization.

## Global Carbon Budgeting: Difficult but Possible

The central idea of this book is the urgent need to adopt and religiously stick to a carbon budget crafted to keep the alligators in their place. Up to now I have referred to this approach as if it were a straightforward matter of arithmetic, a fixed quantity of cumulative emissions to ensure us a known margin of safety. But budget calculations, like everything else in the complex world of carbon and climate, are anything but clear. There are deep disputes about how to construct such budgets and even whether they are useful guides to policy.

The very first question to ask is, What should be the target? We can give ourselves an ample, easy-to-satisfy budget if we're willing to allow a high level of warming over the coming century. In fact, we currently adhere to no carbon budget at all, so the implied complacency is immense. But once we take up the issue seriously, how ambitious should we decide to be?

There is no scientifically established line that separates safe from sorry in carbon emissions. In political debate one sometimes hears that if a particular fossil fuel project goes forward or emissions exceed some specific level it will be "game over," but what we actually face are fine gradations of risk with little basis for establishing a firm cutoff anywhere. Nevertheless, and perhaps exactly because of this, the global political and scientific structure established through intergovernmental negotiations and spearheaded by the IPCC has established two bright lines intended to guide policy. The initial choice was a warming target of 2°C, with a bias toward a budget that would result in a two-thirds chance of not exceeding this level.[25] The probability target is nearly as meaningful as the warming one, since, as we will see, quite a bit of uncertainty surrounds forecasts of the impact of carbon emissions on warming; a lower probability, such as a third or a half, would give us substantially more budget space.[26] Responding to political pressure from nongovernmental organizations and a few governments, however, a second target was drawn up several years later, 1.5°C, with a similar array of one-third, one half and two-thirds probabilities for restricting warming to this even lower level.

In its special report on the 1.5° target, the IPCC made a compelling case that impacts would be much less at that level than at 2°.[27] I agree. But without a deluge of negative emissions – unlikely, as we will see subsequently – it is already too late. Decades of delay have put the more ambitious target out of reach. Reluctantly, I think 2° warming is likely to be the best we can do, and even this will be difficult. The most optimistic course that stays within the bounds of realism is a two-tiered approach in which a strict carbon budget is adopted to keep warming within 2°, while other less certain measures like forestation and the development of carbon removal technologies are also taken to retain a glimmer of 1.5° hope. Of course, this judgment, like others I will make concerning carbon budgets, could well be altered by future developments, but it would not change the overall analysis of this book very much to raise or lower the warming target by a modest amount.

With a warming target in hand, we can now confront the difficult task of tying it to a specific carbon budget. Recall that the underlying idea is that, at least for carbon dioxide, once a new quantity finds its way to the atmosphere it will stay there for centuries. Because of this, it is the cumulative emission over a time horizon and not annual emissions that matter for climate change; annual emissions may be going down, but as long as they are positive the atmospheric concentration of carbon dioxide will keep going up. That said, it is not easy to determine just how much carbon accumulation translates to a given amount of warming.

A first hurdle is determining how responsive the climate system is to the greenhouse effect as carbon emissions are taking place, which scientists refer to as the transient climate response. Much of the warming initially takes place in the ocean rather than on land, and cloud cover as well as water and air currents also have to be taken into account. Fortunately (or unfortunately depending on how you think about it), we now have many decades of evidence to draw on: greenhouse gas emissions coupled with an array of marine and atmospheric temperature measurements. There is still uncertainty, since with each new round of emissions we enter further into unknown territory, but it is possible to at least quantify the potential for the future climate response to differ from what it has been in the past.[28]

A related but different problem is posed by the likelihood of lagged responses: warming that continues even after the budget has been exhausted and carbon emissions have ended. As was pointed out earlier, the extent of this zero emissions commitment has been controversial, with most estimates envisioning about a decade of post-emission warming but a few extending to hundreds of years – although the level of additional warming is generally believed to be under 0.5 °C.[29]

Overlapping the question of zero commitment is the potential for positive (or negative) feedback mechanisms, such as those we noted in the previous chapter. The warming that ultimately occurs will be the result of our carbon emissions plus the feedback effects they induce, so we need to incorporate both when drawing up a budget. As we saw, however, the likelihood and strength of these feedbacks are difficult to ascertain, especially since the conditions we will experience in the coming decades have not been seen for millions of years. As a practical matter, the scientists affiliated with the IPCC have used a fixed feedback estimate of 100 Gt in their own budget estimates.[30] This of course excludes the small but crucial risk of cascading, catastrophic feedbacks that would send the alligators on their way.[31]

Among climate modelers perhaps the most controversial problem currently is how, or even whether, to combine the warming effects of carbon dioxide and other gases that remain in the atmosphere for centuries with those of methane and others of its ilk whose effects diminish quickly over the course of a few years. While many short-lived gases play a measurable role in climate change, the one that matters most is methane.[32] During its residence in the atmosphere, molecule for molecule, it is more than 100 times as potent a greenhouse gas as carbon dioxide, but about a tenth of its carbon is converted to carbon dioxide each year, so after a decade its "superpowers" have mostly dissipated. How best to incorporate both methane's potency and transience in a combined carbon-dioxide-and-methane budget?

At one extreme we could take the instantaneous greenhouse effect and give each molecule of methane the warming equivalent of a hundred molecules of carbon dioxide. At the other we could compare them a few decades after emissions of methane have ended, which would give an equivalence of one to one, since all the carbon in the methane would have turned into carbon dioxide. In its reports up to this point, the IPCC has adopted a framework in which the relative potencies of the two gases are averaged over a century: in the first year it would be 100 to 1, and then it would go down as methane dissipated, asymptotically approaching 1 to 1 long before century's end, averaging overall 28 to 1.[33]

Critics were not appeased. Isn't the effect of methane emissions grossly overrated? they asked. If the extra warming impact lasts only ten years, why aren't only emissions during the final decade of the budget horizon counted? Indeed, if methane emissions are falling from their initial level in the present to some lower level in the future, doesn't this mean the greenhouse effect will be going down? If so, methane works in exactly the opposite way from carbon dioxide, in that it is the change in emissions rather than their cumulative total that matters.[34]

The quantitative stakes are noticeable. The concentration of carbon dioxide in the atmosphere in 2018 reached a seasonally adjusted level of about 410 ppm.[35] Meanwhile, the corresponding concentration of methane in the same year was 1.87 ppm.[36] At a methane-to-carbon-dioxide equivalence ratio of 28:1 these two gasses would give us the same warming effect as about 462 ppm carbon dioxide alone, almost a 13% increase. If short-term warming doesn't matter much, however, this same methane might be assessed at the same effect it will have when it oxidizes into carbon dioxide – in other words, at a ratio of 1:1. In that case the combined equivalence will be just under 412 ppm, a bit less than an extra year's worth of carbon dioxide accumulation. Clearly, how we incorporate methane and other short-lived gases matters significantly for carbon budgeting.

What have ensued are suggested alterations to the IPCC's greenhouse equivalence framework. Some have argued for a reduced equivalence between methane and carbon dioxide, others for a much more complex approach in which equivalence varies over time according to the specifics of the emissions scenario. Still others suggest that the budget template be restricted to only carbon dioxide and other long-lived gases, while methane and its evanescent cousins are accounted separately. This final position strikes me as the most logical, since it recognizes that the budget concept strictly applies only to gases that affect the climate cumulatively, while short-lived gases demand a treatment that corresponds to their specific potency and stability properties. That's the approach I will take for the remainder of this book, where budget calculations will apply to emissions of carbon dioxide only.

Now on to applying actual data.

## The Climate Challenge in Numbers

To provide a benchmark for gauging the stringency of climate policy, let's look at a few numbers. First, what should we take as the total remaining carbon dioxide we can emit over the remaining decades of the twenty-first century if we want to retain a two-thirds chance of keeping warming below 2°? In an analysis from 2019, a leading team of climate scenario modelers proposed 1,070 Gt.[37] Deduct from that the 71.5 Gt emitted in 2019–2020 to bring us to the beginning of 2021, and then deduct a further 108 Gt assuming policy doesn't take hold until the beginning of 2024, while emissions over that period average 36 Gt per year. This will give us a budget of 890.5 Gt to work with, bearing in mind that, since it is calculated separately from projections of methane and other emissions, it might have to be adjusted up or down depending on what happens on those other fronts.

The next assumption is unrealistic but very useful: let's imagine global carbon dioxide emissions will be cut at an equal rate, year after year, not only staying within the budget over the course of a century but also leaving us with no less a margin of safety at the end than we have now. By margin of safety, I'm thinking of the number of years we could continue to emit at the current rate, without any cuts at all, until the budget is fully used up. In our hypothetical scenario, that would be a little less than 25 years (2023's remaining budget of 926.5 Gt divided by 2023's emission of 36) at the outset of 2024, so we would want approximately the same ratio 10 years into the program, 50, or 100, meaning that emissions would be going down at the same rate as the remaining budget. This is much more prudent than selecting a rate of emissions reduction that completely wipes out our budget by the end of the planning period, putting us in a potentially disastrous position at that point. The notion of maintaining an equal number of budget-consuming emission-years throughout the planning horizon strikes me as a plausible definition of "sustainability" in this context.

Based on all these assumptions, a continuing annual reduction of 3.9% would meet our criteria. The program would begin in 2024 with a reduced annual emission of 34.6 Gt, and cuts would continue at this percentage rate from then on. By midcentury, to pick one checkpoint at random, we would have only a bit more than a third of our budget left, but emissions would have also fallen by the same amount, leaving us still the same number of years to exhaustion. By century's end, only about 5% of our budget would be left, but our emissions would be about 5% of what they were at the start as well. Conclusion: one possible emissions path for the world to remain within a 2°C budget constraint is one that reduces them at a constant rate of 3.9% per year.

Now for the caveats: (1) This depends on agreement that, while less would be better, 2°C is a tolerable level of global warming to permit. (2) It depends on estimates of the relationship between atmospheric carbon dioxide accumulation and likely warming, which are likely to change. (3) It depends on concomitant reductions in greenhouse gases other than carbon dioxide, which could turn out to be more or less. (4) As a global budget, it is based on the improbable assumption that a worldwide policy of planned emissions reductions will be in place at the outset of 2024. (5) It doesn't take account of the possible feedback mechanisms we looked at in the previous chapter, such as accelerated carbon releases from melting permafrost. The latest round of studies is finding that incorporating a wider range of feedback and other risks significantly reduces the estimated remaining carbon budget.[38]

Finally, we ought to think a bit more about what it means to hold ourselves to a constant rate of emissions reduction. As a practical matter it has little to be said for it. It's worth noting that the integrated assessment models we survey in Chapter 5 are programmed to generate lowest-cost emission paths, and they feature large percentage reductions in the near future followed by drawn-out mitigation in later years. This pattern hasn't been a topic of discussion, but I suspect the higher intensity of near-term effort has the effect of buying time for the harder job of removing stubborn emission sources like air travel and the last (and most variable) portion of electrical power generation.[39]

In any event, there is an unlimited number of year-by-year emission pathways consistent with any carbon budget and no firm rules for selecting one over another. The reason for picking a constant rate is not that it's a good choice but that it serves to index – summarize in a single number – the stringency of cuts we face. Remember that if a 3.9% annual reduction pathway would get us to our goal, years of emissions above that path have to be counterbalanced by years of greater reductions later on. The goal of 3.9% is not a plan of action but a simple yet meaningful way to summarize the challenge ahead. If the budget is recalculated upward, so would this rate, and the same for a downward revision. It's a benchmark that conveys how rapidly on average we have to decarbonize.

One further point: it is extremely important to stress that this is a *global* benchmark and not a national one. Should each individual country agree to cut its emissions at the same rate? In Chapter 7 I will make the case that this would be profoundly unfair as well as politically impossible. Wealthier countries should expect to have to make larger cuts; to pick a number out of the air, a plausible baseline might be 50% above the global average, placing them around 6% per year. No particular authority attaches to this number, of course – I just made it up – but I think it conveys a rough sense of what a likely policy framework would require of us. For the remainder of the book I will use 6% annual emissions cuts as a stand-in for the decarbonization stringency that ought to be faced by more developed countries.

But 3.9% and 6% are just numbers; what do they mean in human terms? How difficult would they be to achieve? Who would the costs fall on, and what impact would they have on the plans and priorities of businesses and governments? To answer these questions we have to take stock of our economies and the role carbon plays in them – the realm of economics, politics and political economy. This is where we are headed next.

(Note: those interested in more detail on the method this chapter uses to translate carbon budgets into average annual emission reductions can consult the Addendum posted on the book's website.)

# 4 IT'S ABOUT FOSSIL FUELS

One of Monty Python's best loved skits has Greek and German philosophers facing off in a football (soccer) match. The Greeks, with stars like Aristotle, Plato, Socrates and Archimedes, are dressed in togas; the Germans feature the likes of Kant, Hegel, Nietzsche and Wittgenstein dressed according to their era. The players practice; the referee, Confucius, blows his whistle; and then – nothing. The great thinkers amble about lost in thought while the ball sits abandoned at midfield. And so it goes, on and on and on – all thought and no play. Shortly before the end of regulation the Germans make a substitution to get their offense going: Karl Marx takes the place of Wittgenstein. At first it looks like he's a bundle of energy, but as soon as he takes to the field he starts wandering around immersed in thought like everyone else. Then, with seconds to go, Archimedes shouts, "Eureka!" He just came to the realization that this is a football match, not a philosophical academy. He launches an attack, and while the Germans look on in confusion the Greeks score with a cross and a header; the match is theirs.

You can find this bit on the internet, and if you haven't seen it you really should. What makes it funny, of course, is the absurdity of philosophical immersion when the task at hand is to score a goal. Substitute "ending carbon emissions" for putting the ball in the net, and you have the gist of much of the chapter that follows.

As we've seen, the central task in forestalling catastrophic climate change is very simple: barring the very rapid adoption of trans-formative technologies that don't exist yet, we need to leave most of the known coal, oil and gas reserves in the ground. How to do that without causing an economic – and social and political – cataclysm is complicated, but the climate objective isn't.

But many of our present-day thinkers resist this simplicity. Having long dedicated themselves to abstruse speculation about the nature of our economic and cultural systems, they insist that the climate crisis is not *really* about carbon emissions but a deeper, more far-reaching flaw in our civilization. Like Monty Python's philosophers, they may indeed be profound, but not in the game they, and all of us, are actually playing.

A much-advertised claim, for instance, is that the true cause of the climate crisis is economic growth, and unless it is ended and even put into reverse ("degrowth") we are all doomed. Or perhaps the "real" cause is population growth, or capitalism, or global inequality. Others point to the global flows of the carbon cycle and argue that planting trees or bulking up other terrestrial carbon sinks will allow us to burn fossil fuels a little longer. And there is widespread misunderstanding of the relationship between carbon and renewable energy, that the latter somehow makes the former disappear. To be very clear, I am not saying that economic growth is unrelated to carbon emissions, nor that inequality and economic dysfunction can be ignored, nor that forests aren't an important part of the story, nor that a crash program to expand the supply of renewable energy isn't necessary. Climate change touches everything. But it's crucial to keep cause and effect clearly in mind and not get distracted from the primary mission of curtailing the use of fossil fuels. This chapter is about keeping our eye, and our foot, on the ball.

Recall the graphic depiction of the carbon cycle(s) from Chapter 1. Carbon serves two crucial roles simultaneously, the key component of the atmosphere that traps solar radiation and allows the Earth to maintain a toasty temperature suitable for life (unlike our moon, which reflects all the radiation back into space), and the building block of life – the stuff all animals and plants are made of. These functions operate in tandem and support each other. By warming and stabilizing the earth's temperature, atmospheric carbon has created the conditions under which life could flourish. And life recirculates carbon, absorbing it from the atmosphere, fixing it on land and in the oceans as living tissue and releasing it again to make its way back to the atmosphere. These flows were approximately in balance and kept the system in a rough equilibrium for eons.

But there is a slower carbon cycle at work as well. Some of the terrestrial and marine carbon leaves the surface cycle as mineral deposits or organic matter that gets pulled down into places, like ocean and lake beds, that are outside the regular flows, and some of this trickle is drawn further into the Earth's mantle by the activity of tectonic plates. In any given year these amounts are minuscule, but over geologic time they add up to very large withdrawals. Meanwhile, some of this carbon leaves long-term subterranean storage and reenters the circulation of atmosphere and life through venting, as with volcanoes. This slow carbon cycle is also roughly balanced over long time periods. The instigator of climate fluctuations over the past several hundred thousand years, the ice ages and interglacial periods, has been variation in the amount of solar radiation received by Earth (due to orbital wobbles), not autonomous changes in carbon flows. The last big climate event caused by imbalances in the deep, slow carbon cycle – unusually large releases of carbon from beneath the earth that vastly exceeded carbon deposition and withdrawal – was probably the Paleocene–Eocene Thermal Maximum that gave us alligators in the Arctic.[1]

The reason we are facing a climate crisis today is that human beings are mimicking this giant uptick in volcanic carbon releases, only at a pace much faster than the one 56 million years ago. The carbon in fossil fuels is, like the name suggests, the residue of ancient life, concentrated under pressure and buried in the Earth. If we had just left it there, the surface and deep carbon cycles would have continued to remain in approximate balance, and climate change would not be an issue. But drawn to the extraordinary energy density of these fuels, humans, with great ingenuity, have been finding them, bringing them back to the Earth's surface and sending their carbon up into the atmosphere through combustion. The withdrawal phase of the deep carbon cycle is still as slow as it always was, but the release phase is in hyper-acceleration. Whatever else it entails, the solution requires us to stop using fossil fuels as soon as possible, leaving them in the Earth where they can bide their time for millions of years to come.

How could we not understand this basic point? The rest of this chapter shows that human ingenuity is at work on this front too.

## The Crusade against Economic Growth

On the political left it is now common to hear that the root cause of climate change is an economy addicted to growth. Burning fossil fuels is just a symptom, they say, and we won't exit our predicament until we dig beneath this superficial approach and tackle economic growth directly. Perhaps the origins of this antagonism can be found in the writings of Nicholas Georgescu-Roegen, the author of *The Entropy Law and the Economic Process,* and Herman Daly, whose breakthrough was the book *Toward a Steady-State Economy.*[2] The "degrowth" philosophy was a minor current until recently, but the urgency of action on climate change has elevated it to a litmus test in some circles of whether you are a "corporate" or "radical" proponent of carbon policy.[3]

Actually, there are two versions of anti-growth ideology. One upholds actual degrowth as a matter of urgent necessity; its bumper sticker version is "You can't have unlimited growth on a finite planet," which, of course, is quite true. And even if future advances in space travel allow us to inhabit other planets and even galaxies, it is also true that unlimited growth must some day come to an end in a finite universe. A relevant question is, Is this relevant? That is, are we so close to hitting this wall that we have to start backing up right now? The degrowth rejoinder is that we are, and that the peril of climate change is the proof.

The second version is not about the actual rate of growth, positive or negative, but our thinking about it. Its proponents oppose what they regard as the modern obsession with economic growth, which, depending on the source, is itself rooted in the fundamental nature of capitalism, or neoliberal ideology, or Keynesian macroeconomic policy or the use of gross domestic product (GDP) as a tool of economic measurement. It is this intellectual commitment, they say, that has prevented us from acting to limit carbon emissions because doing so would limit growth. According to them, our survival depends on dethroning economic growth from the all-powerful place it occupies in our culture.

I think both are mostly wrong and serve only to distract us from what needs to be done. In fact, their errors and omissions are so glaring I have to wonder how such ideas can be taken seriously.[4] Why are we even having this debate? Let's consider them one at a time, beginning with that apparent truism, "You can't have unlimited growth on a finite planet."

The first problem lies in misunderstanding what "economic growth" means. You certainly can't have unlimited increases in the use of resources on a finite planet, but the size of the economy isn't the same as the amount of "stuff" it uses. The standard measure of economic growth is growth in GDP, and GDP measures the number of goods and services we produce, each multiplied by its value.[5] And what is value? It's what people are willing to pay for, and "stuff" is not the only or even necessarily the most important aspect. A $30 restaurant meal is "bigger" than two $10 meals in economic terms, and a $500 music system is bigger than two $100 systems, with resource use often smaller for the higher-priced item. When you pay for the more expensive meal, ideally you are compensating the services of more skillful kitchen staff, and the more costly music system rewards engineers for their knowledge and skill.

The rejoinder is that, while my objection is correct, in practice economic growth has not "decoupled" from carbon emissions anywhere. From this it is deduced that such decoupling is impossible, but that logical leap overlooks a critical fact: no country has yet begun to take the measures required for decarbonization. Without such policies in place and implemented, we shouldn't be surprised that business as usual is eating up our carbon budget year after year. As we will see in a moment, *any* size of our economy, even one much smaller than what we currently have, is incompatible with meeting the climate challenge unless we make fundamental changes in what and how we produce. Those changes are the objective of climate policy.[6]

To illustrate how public policies can foster growth in the skill component of value without spewing out more carbon emissions, consider the example of Finland. This tiny country of somewhat more than five million people decided many years ago to make music a central part of its public life. Its music policies include programs in the schools and support for live concerts and broadcasts, but also a network of specialized music academies in every region. As of 2007, Finland had ninety-nine such academies, one for approximately every 53,000 citizens. There students of all ages can get heavily subsidized instruction in every type of musical performance – rock, folk, jazz and classical. That year about 60,000 students were enrolled, instructed by 3,500 teachers.[7] To visualize what this means, suppose the United States in this same year had proportional numbers in its own system of music academies; that would mean almost three and a half million students and about 200,000 teachers. By comparison, employment in all aspects of the US coal industry, white and blue collar alike, was somewhat less than 70,000 in 2015.[8] Not surprisingly, Finland, despite its small size, is a major force in many varieties of music, especially classical where it accounts for a disproportionate share of the leading conductors and composers – names like Esa-Pekka Salonen and Kaija Saariaho. But beneath the headlines you can find plenty of interesting live music in every Finnish town.

The point is not to promote Finnish music, but to see why it's important that economic growth doesn't have to mean growth in "stuff." Finland's music sector is every bit as much a part of its economy as Nokia or its pulp and paper mills – a more stable, reliable sector in recent years. The money paid to music teachers is real money, just as real as money paid to other workers for the goods and services they provide. Music is a component of the GDP of Finland, as it is anywhere else people pay for it. By collecting taxes to support music instruction, Finland is redirecting consumption from other uses to the spread of culture, while at the same time reducing carbon emissions. Of course, people can't live on music alone – they still need food and heat and produced goods of many types – but societies can enlarge their economies by choosing to promote knowledge, culture, and discovery and not just more "stuff." The first problem with the degrowthers is that they greatly underestimate the potential for economies to grow in ways that have nothing to do with burning fossil fuels.

The second problem is that arithmetic is against them; no reasonable amount of economic shrinkage will make more than a tiny dent in our carbon dilemma. We have evidence for this. As the second millennium CE gave way to the third, global carbon emissions continued their upward trend, growing by more than 2% per year. There was a hiccup in 2009, however, when carbon dioxide emissions actually declined, falling by 0.45% relative to their 2008 level.[9] Why was this? The cause was the financial crisis of 2008, which struck economies all across the world. While the biggest impacts were in the developed countries with the largest financial sectors, the global economy as a whole slipped by about 0.3% in 2009 – the so-called Great Recession.[10] With the resumption in economic growth the following year, emissions resumed growth as well.

Here is where the arithmetic comes in. As we saw in the previous chapter, a benchmark global carbon dioxide emissions pathway that gives us a reasonable chance to hold warming to 2°C requires a 3.9% reduction every year for generations. Now combine this with the 2009 experience, where a 0.3% decline in the global economy gave us a 0.45% decline in emissions. That yields an economic-degrowth-to-emissions-reduction ratio of 0.64, just under two-thirds. So to get a 3.9% reduction in $CO_2$ emissions in a given year, we'd have to have an economic contraction of 0.64 × 3.9%, or about 2.5%. Now for some common sense. A 2.5% hit to the global economy is over *eight times* what the world went through in the financial crisis of 2009. And to stay within our carbon budget according to our benchmark we would have to do this *every year* for decades. It's absurd. *A full-on policy of economic shrinkage, if we chose to implement it, would have an insignificant effect on meeting our carbon goals.* Obviously, carbon policy will have to be about what's in our economic pie and how we bake it, not the size of the pie per se.

And yet degrowth proponents are not altogether wrong. There is one way in which our economy could shrink to some extent while leaving most of us better off, and this shrinkage could play a supportive role in climate policy if the other, more important measures (to be discussed in Chapter 6) are also in effect. The issue is hours of work.

Over time economies generally become more productive, measured in economic output (GDP again) divided by the amount of labor it takes to produce it. The benefit of this process can be captured either by continuing to work as much as before and increasing consumption or by working less (or some combination of the two). There is plenty of scope in some countries, particularly the United States, to shift from the first approach to the second, from the rat race to something like a squirrel lifestyle: working hard for a while and then enjoying fourteen hours per day of refreshing sleep.[11] (This is how squirrels do it; people could sleep less and play more.)

As an example, consider work hours in the United States compared with Germany. On average, in 2015 Germans worked 23% fewer hours per year.[12] The reasons are many: the United States has a lower rate of part-time work and no laws mandating paid vacation time; in Germany all workers are guaranteed a minimum of four weeks of paid leave per year, and those covered under nationwide union bargaining get six weeks.[13] The statutory work week is also shorter for full-time workers in Germany, although standards there as elsewhere in Europe are set by a complicated combination of general legislation, sectoral norms and collective bargaining agreements.[14]

Let's return to the arithmetic about economic shrinkage and carbon dioxide emissions in the Great Recession. Suppose the United States were to reduce its labor hours to the German standard with a proportional effect on the size of its economy, and that the same ratio, 0.64, we saw between economic degrowth and reduced emissions in 2009 is applied to this new effort at planned shrinkage. This would give the United States 36% fewer carbon emissions, a meaningful contribution to needed decarbonization, the equivalent of nearly seven years of 6% cuts. I regard this as a substantial overestimate, however, since modern experience around the world with planned reduction in work hours indicates the consequences for economic growth are far less than commensurate.[15] But it's still worth doing.

Now let's move to the second version of the critique of growth. Since actual economic shrinkage runs up against an arithmetic problem – not to mention its political toxicity – more sophisticated degrowthers tell us that what they meant all along was to attack not economic growth as such but the ideology centered on it. By prioritizing growth above all else, they say, "growthism" has frustrated climate action. As for who holds these pernicious ideas, some versions of this story pin the blame on ruling elites, while others denounce economics professors in thrall to neoliberalism.

In reality, this argument is easily punctured. First, political elites are hardly wedded to a philosophy of maximizing economic growth, whatever they may say to justify their actions. All too often they opt for austerity instead, despite its destructive effects on economies and living standards.[16] Arguably, China is the only country that has consistently organized its policies around economic growth since the advent of the twenty-first century.[17]

Second, mainstream political and intellectual figures regularly invoke the desirability of economic growth as the motive for demanding action to *forestall* climate change. They rightly recognize that overheating the planet with all its attendant impacts will cause immense economic harm; in fact, the harm is already being felt. The opening fusillade of high-level climate concern was the Stern Review of 2006, a massive study of the economics of climate change commissioned by

the British government and led by Nicholas Stern, former chief economist of the World Bank. Stern's group concluded that the economic
costs of business as usual far exceeded those of curtailing carbon
emissions, and it was a turning point for public debate in the English-
speaking world.[18] Since then, each year has seen several further studies
by intergovernmental bodies, most of them concurring with Stern.[19] In
straightforward language they explain why uncontrolled climate change
would be economically disastrous. In the previous chapter, I argued that
the conventional economic argument is flawed, but not because I think
it conceptualizes economic growth in a manner that erases the effects of
global warming on it.

Third, the claim one sometimes hears that economic growth is
without value is indefensible in a world of massive poverty and deprivation. Yes, we surely need redistribution when the gap between the
richest and billions of the worst off is so immense, but even if we
confiscated every "unnecessary" possession of the haves, we wouldn't
have enough to give the have-nots the necessities and comforts they
rightfully demand. The world may need less of some things, but it needs
a lot more of others. Even within the wealthier societies and the wealthier regions and populations within them, we will need massive investments for decarbonization, and investment is a component of the
economy and its growth. It is entirely reasonable to search for solutions
to the climate challenge that minimize impacts on economic growth and
poverty alleviation.

Finally, there is a more general point to be made about the
role of political and economic values. When degrowthers say economic growth should not be given a priority over all other objectives, they are on solid ground, but this is true of *any* value and not
just economic ones. Consider freedom. Freedom is a value all of us
would surely endorse, but not to the exclusion of all else. Sometimes
it is necessary to restrict it for purposes of public health, fairness,
preservation of the environment, animal welfare or other goals.
Similarly, I would count myself an egalitarian; I would like to live
in a world that is far more equal than this one, but I would hardly
set aside all other values in order to eliminate every last vestige of
inequality. The same applies to protecting the environment, advancing cultural and intellectual progress, and every other conceivable
ideal; no value is so all-encompassing that it can be sensibly pursued
without regard to all the others. This is why it doesn't break new

ground to acknowledge that economic growth is generally desirable, but not at the expense of a livable planet. If recognizing the need to balance competing objectives is what is meant by degrowth, we can also embrace de-freedom, de-equality, de-culture and de-every-other-single-value.

To set this topic to rest, I want to emphasize that causation runs from climate action to diminished growth, not the other way around. As we will see at length in the following chapter, making the transition to an economy devoid of fossil fuels within the span of a few decades will be a daunting challenge. It is difficult to foresee how much disruption it will entail, but there will almost certainly be periods in which adherence to climate policy interferes with economic growth. With well-designed policies we can keep those periods to a minimum. To think, on the other hand, that stopping growth or even devaluing it will fix the climate crisis, however, is like thinking that living on the street solves the problem of not being able to pay the rent.

## A Choice of Crusades

Long before climate change emerged as a critical issue humanity needed to address, groups had arisen to combat a wide range of other ills. For those campaigning on some other front, it seemed natural to enlist the climate crisis as one more reason why their issue was the "true" challenge facing society. Carbon emissions, we are often told, are only a symptom, and unless we join some additional crusade we are doomed – third in the parade of misconceptions previewed in the Introduction to this book. In reality, while many of the causes promoted in this way merit our support, it is not because they have much to do with the climate, and claiming they do distracts us from the measures we actually need to take. While the list of these purported "deeper" causes is long, here we will consider just a few of them to see how little basis there is for such claims.

Let's begin with the original Malthusianism, the claim that "unchecked" population growth is the true source of our carbon problems.[20] There is a long history to debates over this issue which I will avoid entirely.[21] As far as climate change in particular is concerned, it is obviously true that both carbon emissions and global population have risen during recent decades, but this doesn't mean that the first trend has caused the second. Indeed, if human population were to suddenly level off at its current level, our carbon predicament would be essentially unchanged.

The arithmetic is, if anything, even more unfavorable to the population argument than it was to economic degrowth. While population has continued to grow, its rate has gradually declined from 1.31% in 2000 to 1.05% in 2020, to take the most recent decades.[22] For population to actually decline, this rate has to be brought below zero, and even if this were to happen (it has already happened for some upper-income countries) it would be a long time before the number of people would be significantly less than it is at present. For example, suppose our approximate 1% growth rate were to instantly become −1% – impossible, of course, especially considering the inertia caused by past growth's effect on the age distribution, but this is just an illustration. Global population in 2020 was about 7.8 billion. This immediate and continuing 2% change would, after forty years, still leave us with about 5.2 billion fellow humans, or two-thirds of our current number. To repeat, this scenario is inconceivable without some sort of catastrophe in the background, and even so it yields a human population whose demands on the planet's resources would be only moderately less. If we are still emitting two-thirds of today's carbon emissions per year after four decades, the alligators will be firmly on top.

Simple arithmetic demonstrates that, to be environmentally meaningful within the time frame the climate crisis has bequeathed to us, any reduction in human population must entail a mortality apocalypse of Black Death proportions, and even then our carbon budget will still be on a path to rapid exhaustion. This should not be taken as complacency on my part with humanity's abundance or claim on the planet's living space. I would be happier with fewer of us, and any environmental problem will be easier to solve if people are taking up less room. Nevertheless, the pace and scale of any plausible population reduction is nearly irrelevant to preventing a climate catastrophe.

While concern over rising population has a long history, other putative "true" causes of the climate crisis are more recent. Among them is the belief that globalization is the true enemy, and the solution is to greatly cut back on international trade, producing as locally as possible. Examined closely, this turns out to be a mood, not an argument. First, "international" is not the same as "far away." A large portion of international trade is between countries that border each other, like the United States and Canada or Mexico, or the member nations of the European Union.[23] For geographically large countries like the United States and Russia, trade within their borders can often cover longer distances than trade with neighbors. Moreover, from a carbon point of view, the issue is not how far a good travels but how much carbon it uses to get there. Consider an item, like a carton of consumer electronics, that first travels by container ship from China to a US port in Seattle or Long Beach and then goes by truck to a warehouse in St. Louis. It will certainly be responsible for far more carbon emissions in the second leg of its journey than the first. In fact, if it goes by train to St. Louis and then by truck to its final destination a few miles away, that last truck ride may still be the largest contributor. Carbon distance is not spatial distance. Finally, all maritime shipping combined was responsible for about 2.2% of global $CO_2$ emissions in 2014. This is not trivial, but it is not a major factor either. Improved methods have the potential to reduce this amount further, even without a reduction in the volume of trade.[24] The bottom line is that you may have a preference for locally produced goods for some other reason, but this does not translate into any particular position on international trade, nor is it likely to make much of a difference in global carbon emissions.[25]

Another recent trope has it that the underlying cause of our predicament is psychological, the separation of people from nature and the awareness they would then have of their carbon-burning lifestyle. Cities are mental dead zones; we should flee them for the fields and forests that nurtured societies wiser than ours; only then will we be able to pull back from the apocalypse.[26] I suppose it makes intuitive sense to those who expound this view, but there is no evidence that living closer to nature leads to a less exploitive relationship to it. On the contrary, consider a fascinating graphic essay, "The True Colors of America's Political Spectrum Are Gray and Green," which appeared in the *New York Times* prior to the national election of 2020.[27] Seen from the air, precincts can be placed on a color spectrum from gray (asphalt and buildings) to green (vegetation). As they show, the greener a neighborhood, the more likely its inhabitants were to vote for Donald Trump rather than Hillary Clinton in 2016. While Clinton was hardly a hawk on climate matters, she was certainly more supportive of curtailing carbon emissions than Trump, who campaigned in favor of rescuing the coal industry. It's as if trees, food crops and other green things were transmitting chemical signals urging nearby humans to maximize their pollution.

The irony in the back-to-nature argument is that one of the greatest successes enjoyed by environmentalists is in the field of education. It is now common for children to be exposed to ecological knowledge and principles from an early age, and this has likely played a role in sensitizing them to the need for protecting natural systems; presumably, the Clinton supporters have internalized this learning better than the followers of Trump. But environmental education, even though it may entail occasional field trips to greener places, is a product of our industrialized, urbanized world – scientific research, expertly produced books and films, and skilled, professionally trained schoolteachers. Good programs can be found in schools everywhere, and they prosper in communities that support education in general. The lesson is that climate activism and acumen are, above all, products of knowledge and understanding, and not so much the epiphanies that arise spontaneously from leaning against a tree or fishing a trout stream. It's good to get out into nature, of course, but voting patterns show it's even more important to get into schools and libraries. In any case, to the extent that nature deprivation is a factor in humanity's poor response to the climate challenge, remedying it matters for this issue only insofar as it leads us to adopt the policies required to keep fossil fuels in the ground.

It's understandable that people should care about things other than limiting planetary warming, and it is not the message of this book that we should drop everything and devote ourselves only to adhering to a carbon budget. When it comes to mitigating climate change, however, our success will depend on whether we can bring about the rapid curtailment of fossil fuel use; it doesn't help to overload this difficult task with unrelated demands. Other crusades are worthwhile only if they are recognized as additional goals we should strive for while we struggle to decarbonize.

## Salvation through Silviculture?

Deforestation was not the instigator of modern climate change, but many look to reforestation as an essential part of the solution. Models of future anthropogenic impacts usually identify a major role for changing land use, particularly the conversion of marginal agricultural areas and pasturage to forest cover, making possible "negative emissions." Tree planting, or simply pledges to leave trees in place, are often the basis for carbon offsets, allowing their purchasers to burn fossil fuels while declaring themselves carbon neutral. The claim at the outset of this chapter that the basis of the climate problem is extraction and combustion of fossil fuels and the solution is to end this practice as soon as possible is apparently contradicted, or at least modified, by all this preoccupation with forests.

It's important to recognize, however, that 1870 is not an often-used baseline year for measurement of human-caused alterations of the greenhouse effect because tree-cutting began in earnest after that date. On the contrary, there had been steady reductions in forest cover throughout the world beginning thousands of years ago with the development and spread of settled agriculture.[28] The best evidence is in Europe, where the development of the saw and rapid population increases after 1000 CE accelerated forest clearing, but similar trends were under way in China and North America. Very rapid acceleration of clearing took place in the nineteenth century and continued into the twentieth (and today). While it is probable that this long history of pushing back the forest has had an impact on the atmosphere, if our carbon problem were due mainly to this factor it would have been apparent long before 1870.

Nevertheless, it is possible that, while land use changes have played a minimal role up to this point, they might help rescue us going forward. The millennia of forest clearing by our ancestors has potentially given us the opportunity to buy time by rebalancing the carbon cycle away from higher atmospheric concentrations. At least it's worth considering.

For many who are closely involved with climate change on a scientific or policy basis, moreover, the benefits of reforestation are obvious and taken for granted. All climate models currently used to predict future greenhouse gas accumulations and assess policy alternatives incorporate a significant role for land use. Public discussions about what needs to be done almost always include it. Large sums of money, as we will see, already stand behind reforestation programs. Even Donald Trump, who called the subject matter of this book a "hoax," advocated planting a trillion trees.[29] Isn't this a settled matter?

There can be no dispute about the need to include changes in terrestrial (and other) carbon sinks in quantitative climate models. These are systems of simultaneous equations, many of which represent fluxes within the carbon cycle. Atmospheric carbon exchange with the oceans has to be in the model, and so do the flows of carbon into and

out of the world's soils. In each time period modelers must account for
the carbon taken up by plants, including trees, as well as the carbon they
release through transpiration or when they decompose or burn. By
tracing all these flows and the ongoing change in the factors that influence them continuously through time, such models allow the future
evolution of the climate system to be estimated with increasing preci-
sion. It would make no sense to leave any of it out, including carbon
fluxes associated with changes in forest cover.

This is the basis for saying that planting a certain number of
trees in a particular location – say, Madagascar – in a given year will
effectively reduce the human contribution to greenhouse gas concentrations in that year and in subsequent years as the trees grow. And so
an airline traveler is offered the option to offset the carbon emissions
resulting from a trip by paying for some of these faraway trees. (They're
far away if you're not in Madagascar.) This offset treats the carbon
introduced into the surface carbon cycle by the extraction of formerly
buried fossil fuels as equal and opposite to the carbon pulled from the
atmosphere by photosynthesis as a new tree begins to make its way
upward. And for the years in which that growth occurs that's correct.

Those offsets are adding up. The global program that consoli-
dates the largest portion of them is called REDD+ for "Reducing
Emissions from Deforestation and Forest Degradation"; the "+" was
added to signify that the program was concerned with positive enhance-
ments to forests and not just reversing their deterioration.[30] REDD+
doesn't sell the offsets itself; rather, it inventories forests, provides
carbon measurements and facilitates certification to support forest offsets sold to buyers eager to acquire carbon credits. Suppose, for
instance, you are an air traveler who decides to offset the emissions
from your trip by donating a few dollars to a special "carbon neutrality" fund. This fund will pool your money with that of other contributors to finance a forestry project somewhere on the planet. The fund's
managers will look for a certified project so they can advertise its
legitimacy; otherwise, you might distrust it and not participate. So what
does everyone get from this?

- You: Your guilt about contributing to greenhouse gas accumulation
  through air travel will be assuaged.
- The airline company: They will not worry that you might choose to
  travel less in order to protect the climate.

- The offset fund: They assess a portion of the proceeds for staff and expenses. These funds are nonprofits, but they provide livelihoods and prestige for their employees.
- The organization implementing the forestry project: Their enterprise, which might be public or private, for-profit or nonprofit, is success-fully financed. Often these projects are in low-income countries where the revenues derived from selling offsets are some of the best eco-nomic opportunities available.

But we have left out certification. This is very expensive, since carbon assessments of forests require hands-on data collection; individual pro-jects have to fit to an overall forest development plan; and plans require forestry expertise and still more data collection. If the offsets had to cover these additional costs they would need to be much more expensive per tonne of carbon, and the entire industry would have difficulty getting off the ground. This is why REDD+ was created: it assumes these costs itself and lets the rest of the industry profit.

So who pays for REDD+? Interesting question. All financing comes from governments; Table 4.1, taken from a recent REDD+ annual report, shows the cumulative funding through the end of 2015.

Nearly the entire funding was from Europe and more specific-ally Norway, which alone accounted for almost 88% of the total. In fact, it wouldn't be too far off the mark to say the worldwide forest offset business supported by REDD+ is a creation of the Norwegian government. Normally, I would be hesitant to speculate about motives,

Table 4.1. Cumulative funding of REDD+ through December 31, 2015, in millions of US dollars

| | |
|---|---|
| Denmark | 8.9 |
| European Union | 11.8 |
| Japan | 3.0 |
| Luxembourg | 2.7 |
| Norway | 234.1 |
| Spain | 5.5 |
| Total | 267.0 |

Source: UN-REDD (2016).

but in this case they are rather clear: Norway is one of the world's wealthiest countries, with large deposits of oil and gas on a per capita basis, and it also prides itself in its progressive values. In other words, it is a major contributor to climate change and profits from it, but also wants to demonstrate it is taking the lead in fighting climate change. Taking a portion of its hydrocarbon proceeds and financing a global program to support reforestation in other countries is just the ticket. Indeed, through its sponsorship of REDD+ Norway might claim that all its production and export of fossil fuels is offset by the forest programs it facilitates.

So, if we consider the internal and external political benefits for Norway, the global forest offset industry looks like a win-win-win-win-win. Buyers are happy. Companies like airlines that promote offsets are happy. Offset fund administrators are happy. Forest investors are happy. Norway is happy. What's not to like?[31]

The one lingering question is whether forestation projects actually withdraw carbon from the atmosphere the same way burning fossil fuels adds to it – whether they constitute measurable negative emissions. After all, placebos make us happy too.

## Forests: A Stopover, Not a Final Destination, for Carbon

To sort out the legitimate from the fictitious effects of forestation, we have to go back to the basics, the surface carbon cycle described in Chapter 1. In a nutshell, if we suppose for the moment that introductions of new carbon from long-term storage – under the earth, in undersea methane deposits and in stable peat and permafrost – equal the transport of carbon back to long-term storage, the surface cycle is in equilibrium, with a constant amount of carbon that circulates through it. This is roughly the situation we would be in if human beings had never discovered fossil fuels.

In that case, the various sinks and fluxes depicted in the carbon cycle graphic would remain unchanged year after year. Their sizes, incorporating only "natural" flows and not anthropogenic ones post-1870, are given in that diagram and summarized in Table 4.2. Of the four major temporary storage locations for carbon, the atmosphere might actually be the smallest, while the ocean is by far the largest – logical in view of the size of the ocean relative to land, horizontally but also vertically. In the absence of human intervention, approximately the same amount of carbon would reside in terrestrial vegetation at any point in time as in the atmosphere. Soils play a larger role but exchange only very slowly with the rest of the system.

A useful way to summarize the relationship between stock (the size of the sink) and flow is average turnover time, defined as the sink divided by the flux. This can be interpreted as the average time a carbon-bearing molecule, like carbon dioxide, spends in a given location before moving somewhere else. Performing this calculation produces the turnover times in the table. Here the atmosphere is clearly the winner, with carbon entering and leaving rapidly compared with the size of the sink, while soils and the ocean see little annual turnover. Carbon in vegetation turns over almost as fast as that in the atmosphere.

Table 4.2 is reasonably accurate for the preindustrial carbon cycle, but human beings have altered it in various ways, especially by extracting and burning fossil fuels. The surface carbon cycle is no longer in equilibrium, and fluxes in and out of the various sinks are no longer equal; this has to be taken into consideration when we think about how this cycle operates today.

Since our topic of the moment is forestation, let's take a closer look at "vegetation." This category is an average of vastly different biomes, including not only forests but also grasslands and even desert. What about forests in particular? A recent study estimated average turnover time in tropical forests at 4.2 years and temperate forests at 23.5 years – interesting in that most forestation projects qualifying for offsets are in tropical regions.[32] Short turnover times do not in

Table 4.2. Natural carbon sinks and fluxes and average turnover times, in gigatonnes carbon per year or average number of years

| Location | Sink | Flux | Turnover |
|---|---|---|---|
| Atmosphere | 589 | 170 | 3.5 |
| Ocean | 38,000 | 61 | 623.0 |
| Vegetation | 450–650 | 107 | 4.2–6.1 |
| Soils | 1,500–2,400 | 2 | 750–1,200 |

Source: IPCC (2014). This table is derived from the sink and flow data provided in the graphic representation of the carbon cycle in Chapter 1.

themselves mean that carbon sinks are any less sink-y, since, in equilibrium, inflows equal outflows. At a superficial level, it's like the difference between a fast food restaurant and a more upscale dining establishment. Both may have fifty patrons at any point in time, but there's more coming and going in fast food. One might ask whether it makes a difference if the goal is simply to keep a certain number of people off the street, and in equilibrium the answer is no.

But we are not in equilibrium, and not even in a steady, predictable disequilibrium. Carbon fluxes are changing for a variety of reasons, some under human control, and others, as the elements of the carbon cycle adjust to new conditions, not. Faster turnover means greater susceptibility to disruption – to relatively abrupt changes in the size of the sink. This in fact is exactly the core problem of carbon accumulation in the atmosphere: we are emitting enough greenhouse gases to fundamentally alter the size of the atmospheric sink in just a few human generations. This would not be possible, at least not without a massive effort, in the ocean, where the sink is immense relative to the size of the flows.[33] And this brings us to forests, especially in the tropics, where a situation similar to the atmosphere obtains. Humans can try to rapidly increase forest sinks through accelerating inflows by planting trees (good), but the sinks are also vulnerable to sudden changes in outflows (bad). Looking only at the first and not at the second is seriously misleading.

With this context in mind, we're ready to face the central problem with forest carbon accounting. Recall that climate models record, as they must, the annual fluxes of carbon to and from forest sinks. It's the job of these models to produce quantitative estimates of annual changes in the amount of carbon in the atmosphere, so the effects of forests are measured in those terms. The reliable prediction horizon of these models is a few decades, and they produce the best forecasts they can under the circumstances.

But the real question we would want to answer in evaluating the climate impact of a forestation project is not just its effect in any given year or even over thirty to forty years, but the net effect over the full life span of the project, or at least over a century or so. We want a life-cycle analysis, even if more distant outcomes are somewhat speculative.

To make things simple, suppose again the carbon cycle is in equilibrium, where inflows to each sink exactly equal outflows from it, and then a new forest project is undertaken. At first inflows of carbon from the atmosphere to the forest will exceed the outflows, which is what conventional measurements capture, but after many years a new equilibrium will be established as biomass growth declines and decomposition increases. In this example we are ignoring all the impacts on the carbon cycle that are unrelated to this particular project. With a little reflection it should be clear that its effect on the equilibrium level of atmospheric carbon is roughly equal to the change in the steady-state size of the forest sink, the amount of carbon residing in the forest prior to the project compared with the amount after the new equilibrium is established. This is the net carbon buildup in forest biomass, and that's what could potentially offset carbon emissions from other sources.[34]

So what can we say about this change in equilibrium carbon sequestration? Alas, not very much. It will most likely be greater than zero: plant a new forest, and you are likely to have more carbon storage in that forest in perpetuity. What the *steady-state* amount will be, however, is much more difficult to predict.

The first point, obvious to anyone who knows about forest ecology, is that "steady state," while it may have a statistical meaning at very large geographic and temporal scales, is a poor descriptor of a mature forest. For any given patch of forest, disturbance is part of the story. Fires, storm damage and the periodic eruption and containment of biological threats are never-ending.[35] The forest project that earned its proud investors many tonnes of carbon offsets may well fall prey to one of these forces, and its carbon value should be discounted by the degree of that risk, but we will see that challenge is largely unmet.

And the situation is worse because we are not in equilibrium, nor will we arrive at equilibrium over calculable time frames. Because of this fact, simple extrapolation from the past is a poor guide to the future of forests planted or protected today.

Thus one important factor is climate change itself. It is virtually certain that temperature and precipitation will change dramatically in many locations, and this will change what types of forests can survive in which regions. Fire risk for forests in the United States has doubled in recent decades, clearly due to climate change. Drought is an increasing hazard worldwide. Warming has exacerbated the toll taken by pests and pathogens. Even more disturbing, these risks to forests are synergistic: each threat increases the impact of the others. Research at the intersection of climate science and forest ecology has begun to shed light on the rising vulnerability of forest sinks, but this awareness has not yet made its way into the realm of offset promotion, like REDD+.[36]

A secondary confounding factor is how future societies will respond to the pressures of a changing world. As we saw in Chapter 2, most analysts now expect climate change to lead to crop losses, with the impacts becoming more severe as global temperatures continue to rise and climate systems are altered. How will people react? It is more than possible they will convert additional land to agricultural uses to make up for losses in productivity, but this would probably entail forest clearing, as it has in the past. It is especially in tropical regions that agricultural impacts will be the biggest, and where most forestation projects are located.

The only reasonable conclusion is that negative emissions through forestation are uncertain in size and all too reversible. We have good estimates of their carbon sequestering effects on a year-to-year basis over the next few decades, but not over the long run. If a tree is planted and absorbs carbon for fifty years, only to release all of it through fire or cutting in the fifty-first year, it has no net effect on atmospheric accumulation over the entire period. In this respect there is no symmetry at all between the negative emissions of planting a forest and the positive emissions of burning fossil fuels. Introducing new carbon into the surface carbon cycle by bringing it up from subterranean deposits is irreversible, given the technologies we possess today and are likely to possess in the future.[37]

Meanwhile, even if we had precise estimates of the long term, steady-state carbon storage potential of forest protection and enhancement, we would still face practical uncertainties about how much of it can be attributed to offsets. Above all, a major reason trees are cut down is that there is demand for them or the land they occupy. Safeguarding a forest stand in one location may lead to increased clearing in another in order to satisfy this demand; indeed, economics predicts exactly this outcome.[38] While it might be possible to estimate this effect over a large scale, like a major region or a country, it is virtually untraceable at the level of single projects – but this is the level at which forest offset programs supported by REDD+ operate. In reality, as Norway's own Auditor General reported in 2017–2018, the large potential for displacement of deforestation, combined with a lack of follow-up on REDD+ projects, and even outright fraud, leave "considerable uncertainty" over the contribution of forest offsets to climate mitigation.[39]

And there is another problem with offsets based on storing forest carbon: it is difficult to know whether the trees planted or preserved under an offset program would have had the same fate if the program hadn't existed. This complication, which we will examine more systematically in Chapter 6, is about the "additionality" of the offset – whether the carbon sequestration it ostensibly finances is truly greater than what would occur otherwise.

Consider, for instance, Pennsylvania Ridges, a 3,800-acre forest in the middle of that state. According to the seller of carbon credits for protecting this property, without a large infusion of extra revenue, almost three-fourths of the trees will be cut down within five years. It sounds like a valid proposition; by purchasing forest credits you can keep this carbon secure far into the future. There is just one problem: the entity selling these credits is the Nature Conservancy, which purchased Pennsylvania Ridges twenty years ago precisely to forestall timber harvests by its previous owner. The offsets provide additional income to the Conservancy but not additional forest protection, unless their earlier campaign to raise money for saving this property was just a ruse. But the Pennsylvania credits are on the market, and the Walt Disney Company has bought 180,000 of them.[40]

Another example was recently provided by the reputable online news organization ProPublica in conjunction with the *MIT Technology Review*. It found rampant abuse of the forest offset component of the California cap-and-trade program, which we will consider in greater detail in Chapter 6. The centerpiece was a case study of a forest owned by the Massachusetts Audubon Society. This nonprofit, which manages its holdings for habitat and conservation, and not timber, nevertheless earned $6 million by selling pledges not to log a parcel of 9,700 acres. This allowed the buyers, mostly oil and gas companies, the right to emit an extra 600,000 tons of carbon dioxide. This further illustrates the perverse incentives that pervade the world of offsets, forest-based and otherwise. Incidentally, it also shows how cheaply emitters can escape California's carbon cap: just $10 buys you a ton.[41]

The verdict on forestry projects is similar to the one we will come to later with other so-called carbon removal technologies: planting new forests and maintaining and enhancing the ones we already have is highly desirable. *Some* increased carbon sequestration is likely to result from all this effort, and it may even turn out to be quantitatively important. *But investments in forests should never be used to avoid reductions in other sources of carbon emissions, particularly the extraction and combustion of fossil fuels.* We simply don't know what the long-term carbon impact of any particular forestry project will be, so we can't legitimately use it to offset a known and irreversible impact from the use of fossil fuels. A better approach is to use policies to curtail the use of fossil fuels to ensure, as far as possible, that we avoid warming in excess of 2°C, and then use forestation and similar interventions into the global network of carbon fluxes and sinks to bring warming down even further.

This is our first intimation that all is not well in the land of offsets. We will see more evidence for this judgment in Chapter 6.

## Conservation and Renewables: The Danger of Positive Thinking

Public opinion specialists tell us the negativity surrounding climate change needs to be expunged.[42] Scaring people doesn't work, and anything that sounds like sacrifice – especially if it can be construed as a tax – is a big turnoff. Instead, we should lead with the positive. Replace the grim talk of climate catastrophe with a glowing picture of our green future, with a solar array on every rooftop and heirloom beans in every pot. Forget about taxes or controls on fossil fuels and point to all the green jobs that will be created in the ecotopia to come.[43] Alas, this exemplifies the wishful thinking the Introduction to this book warned us against.

This thinking is at the heart of the current strategy of centering climate policy on a Green New Deal (GND). The origin of this approach is a 2004 position paper written by Michael Shellenberger and Ted Nordhaus, two marketing consultants whose clients included major environmental organizations.[44] Surveying the failure – already at this time one could use the word "failure" – of environmental activists to get government action to reduce carbon emissions, they argued that the entire mental framework of activism had to change. Rather than defining environmental problems scientifically and proposing actions to achieve technical goals, greens should recast these problems as political in the traditional sense: about values, material benefits and, above all, constituencies. Talk about cutting emissions does none of this; it does not engage established narratives about progress, nor does it promise to put any money in your pocket, and what constituencies have a particular interest in whether invisible plumes of carbon dioxide ascend or don't ascend into the atmosphere?

Their solution was to propose that the climate problem be recast as one of investment in new technology and infrastructure. Invoke the can-do spirit of inventing new and better ways to do things, and emphasize the economic benefits of a green jobs program. Tailor the proposal to appeal to constituencies like labor unions, minority communities and regions impacted by economic decline. The goal, they argue, is to solve not a technical problem about greenhouse gas concentrations in the atmosphere but the political one of assembling a winning coalition.

The timing of the Nordhaus–Shellenberger epistle was somewhat off, and their attempt to get environmentalists to change course fizzled out. In the past few years it has been resurrected by new advocates, however, in the form of a Green New Deal. At this point the GND is still more a slogan than a set of proposals. It takes various forms in activist and political contexts, as well as between the United States and Europe.[45] In some versions it is essentially a wish list, a set of objectives detached from concrete actions to achieve them. When formulations of the GND specify criteria, there is little guidance to balancing the competing goals that might be pursued or how possible costs can be assessed against them.[46] Thus to advocate a GND is to express support for public programs to subsidize the expansion of renewable energy, upgrade the electrical grid, retrofit the housing stock for greater efficiency, improve mass transit and finance new, less-carbon-reliant technology. At the same time, the GND is expected to facilitate full employment, with additional targeted support for workers currently in the fossil fuel sector and racial or ethnic minorities – the "just transition" component.

Before launching a criticism of the GND framing of carbon policy, I want to make it clear that, not only do I not oppose any of these items, I am strongly in favor of all of them. We surely need a rapid increase in green energy production and end-use efficiency, along with new technological options for decarbonization. Promoting a high-employment, high-wage economy is good economics. Opportunities to reverse inequalities inherited from the past should be fully utilized. The GND is excellent economic, environmental and social policy. What it is not, unfortunately, is a sufficient program for avoiding a climate catastrophe. Let's see why.

Imagine a world ruled by a king whose every word is law. For reasons known only to himself, he has decreed that the amount of energy used in his kingdom, measured in units of oomph (the technical term of choice in that land), must remain at a fixed level, not an oomph more or less. At first, all the energy is produced by burning coal, but the king hates coal mines because of how grimy they are, and he doesn't like his subjects going underground where he can't see them. One possibility is that he could command the mines to shut down and force the populace to search for alternative energy sources. Another is that he could order the building of other energy supply systems. For instance, he could direct his royal engineers to build an array of windmills, and, since the total energy consumption must remain constant, every oomph of wind energy means one less oomph of energy from coal.

And there's a third strategy, too. If his wizard can find ways to produce the goods the kingdom needs with less energy, the king can decree a lower level of energy production, which would translate directly into less coal mining. The story is the same in either case: if total energy production can be fixed, then there is an equal and opposite relationship between one energy source and the others, or a direct relationship between the fixed level and the source that produces it.

Of course, we don't live in this kingdom or any place even approximately similar. The total energy used in our society is not decreed by anyone, but arises from choices made by millions of producers and consumers. Over the long sweep of history since the industrial revolution, energy use has gone up and up, and the struggle of poor countries to improve incomes and living standards guarantees that, if possible, this trend will continue well into the future. More energy from one source does not mean that much less from the other, nor does less demand for one type of use mean that overall demand will go down by the same amount. This is a simple and obvious point, but somehow it gets lost whenever discussion turns to the subject of the green economy.

To get a rough quantitative sense of the tug-of-war between renewable and nonrenewable energy sources in a world of expanding consumption, consider Table 4.3. Energy consumption is measured in this table in units of oil equivalents, or how much oil it would take to produce the same amount of energy from other sources. This doesn't correspond to climate impacts, but it does give us a useful sense of the trade-off between fossil and non-fossil energy supplies. While two years also doesn't begin to tell the full story of the ups and downs (or, more

Table 4.3. Global primary energy consumption in million tonnes of oil equivalents, 2017–2018

| Fuel | 2017 | 2018 | Change |
|---|---|---|---|
| Oil | 4,607.0 | 4,662.1 | 55.1 |
| Natural gas | 3,141.9 | 3,309.4 | 167.5 |
| Coal | 3,718.4 | 3,772.1 | 53.7 |
| Fossil fuel total | 11,467.3 | 11,743.6 | 276.3 |
| Renewables | 490.2 | 561.3 | 71.1 |
| Nuclear | 597.1 | 611.3 | 14.2 |
| Hydro | 919.9 | 948.8 | 28.9 |
| Nonfossil total | 2,007.2 | 2,121.4 | 114.2 |
| **Combined total** | 13,474.5 | 13,865 | 390.5 |

Source: British Petroleum (2019).

accurately, the ups and more ups) of energy use over recent decades, it's enough to illustrate the extent to which different sources compete with or simply add on to each other. I have lumped all non-fossil sources together for simplicity, although there are important differences in the environmental and other impacts of renewable fuels, nuclear and hydro-electric power. (Renewables constitute about a quarter of non-fossil energy supplies over this brief period but account for 62% of the growth of this sector.)

Non-fossil energy use increased by 5.7% between 2017 and 2018; how good was that? It's much faster than fossil energy growth, 2.9%, but it's adding to a lower base, since non-fossil sources made up only about 15% of total supply in 2017. The result is that, while oil, natural gas and coal grew at a lower rate, their absolute growth (in oil equivalents) was almost two and a half times that of renewables, nuclear and hydro combined. Now imagine for a moment our hypothetical king who keeps energy use constant: if we had the same growth in non-fossil energy under his regime, fossil sources would have declined by nearly 1% instead of increasing by almost 3%. While that would be far too small in relation to what we need to accomplish, at least it would be in the right direction. I suspect this is the effect many people assume when they hear about expansion in renewable and other forms of non-fossil energy supply: more of the "good" energy means that much less of the "bad" variety. Of course, in the real world there is no royal fixed-energy mandate, and the interesting question is, How large an increase in non-fossil energy would it take to actually get the same 1% reduction in fossil supplies given overall energy growth? The disturbing answer is 25%: at the current size and composition of global energy supply and at the current growth rate of that supply, to cut fossil fuels by 1% would require a 25% growth rate in all the other energy sources.

But as we have already seen, our benchmark rate of carbon emission reduction, which is approximately the same as the rate of fossil fuel reduction, is 3.9% for the world and 6% (or higher) for the United States and other relatively wealthy countries. If the annual rate of increase in green energy production to achieve just a 1% decline in emissions is out of reach, the higher benchmark targets are that much more unachievable if we rely on just this one strategy. In other words, *in a world of expanding energy demand, no feasible amount of investment in renewable or other noncarbon energy sources can sufficiently reduce the use of fossil fuels unless action is also taken to suppress those fuels directly.*

Note, incidentally, that following through on this conclusion would mean ignoring assertions one sometimes hears that current fossil fuel investments such as mines, power plants and pipelines "lock us in" to further years or decades of these energy sources – there is no such "lock." On the contrary, the logic of rapidly decreasing fossil fuel use year after year is also the logic of scrapping such investments, no matter how costly that may be to their owners. (Technically, as we will see in Chapter 6, this need not take the form of mandates to decommission them, but the effect will be the same as a result of making their fuel sources or products so expensive their demand disappears.)

To see the same logic at a national level, consider the energy transition (*Energiewende*) taking place in Germany. Initiated at the federal level in 2011, the goal is to completely transform the country's energy consumption by 2040, with targets for electrical generation, home heating, transportation and general energy usage.[47] Due to Germany's consensus-based system of economic organization, with powerful industry associations, unions, public financial institutions, and integration of education and research with all of the above, it has an exceptional capacity to reengineer itself. And in fact the increase in renewable energy sources as a proportion of total energy use has risen dramatically, as shown in Table 4.4.

Table 4.4. Renewable energy sources and coal as percentage of total consumption, Germany, 2005–2016

|  | 2005 | 2006 | 2005 | 2008 | 2009 | 2010 | 2011 | 2012 | 2013 | 2014 | 2015 | 2016 |
|---|---|---|---|---|---|---|---|---|---|---|---|---|
| % Coal[a] | 24.0 | 24.5 | 25.8 | 23.8 | 22.8 | 23.7 | 24.8 | 25.3 | 25.1 | 25.4 | 25.3 | 24.3 |
| % Renewables | 5.0 | 5.9 | 7.1 | 6.9 | 7.7 | 8.3 | 9.3 | 10.1 | 10.3 | 11.3 | 12.2 | 12.3 |

[a] Includes both hard and brown coal. In general, Germany uses somewhat more hard coal than brown (lignite), which has higher carbon emissions per energy content.
*Source*: European Commission (2020).

Renewables have more than doubled their share of total energy use over this period, and their inroads into electrical generation have been even more impressive, accounting for nearly 30% of the total for 2016.[48] Ambitious plans are in the works to build a virtual forest of offshore wind turbines in the coastal region of the North Sea, with massive transmission lines to convey the energy to population centers in the south. The German housing stock, already well insulated by global standards, is being systematically retrofitted for maximum savings in heating requirements. These and similar measures have justifiably attracted worldwide attention.

But greenhouse gas emissions? This part of the story is not as uplifting. As Table 4.4 also demonstrates, coal has stubbornly retained its importance in Germany's energy portfolio, and cutting back will be difficult since the country has committed itself to shutting down its nuclear industry by 2021. (Nuclear provided 6.9% of all energy consumption in 2016.[49]) The upshot is a decidedly mixed record on the overall carbon front, as we can see in Figure 4.1.

To some extent, the rather stable carbon emissions since 2009 reflect the relative strength of the German economy, which has benefited from robust exports due to the weakness of the euro and continuing demand from China; if Germany had stagnated like most other Eurozone countries its people would be a lot less content, but the climate would be somewhat better off. Indeed, Table 4.5, which uses 2005 as a base year to index carbon emissions, tells us that Germany's progress over the past decade on this front substantially trails the entire twenty-eight-member EU taken as a single entity.

The inescapable conclusion, as strange as it seems, is that the Energiewende has hardly had an impact on overall German emissions; to this point Germany has been outperformed by its neighbors. This

**Table 4.5.** German and EU-28 carbon emission indexes, 2005 = 100

|         | 2005 | 2006  | 2007 | 2008 | 2009 | 2010 | 2011 | 2012 | 2013 | 2014 | 2015 |
|---------|------|-------|------|------|------|------|------|------|------|------|------|
| EU-28   | 100  | 99.9  | 99.0 | 96.9 | 89.9 | 91.8 | 89.0 | 87.8 | 86.0 | 82.8 | 83.3 |
| Germany | 100  | 100.8 | 98.3 | 98.5 | 91.8 | 95.2 | 93.2 | 93.8 | 95.7 | 91.5 | 91.3 |

*Source*: European Commission (2020).

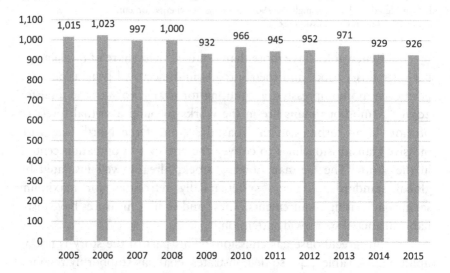

**Figure 4.1** German greenhouse gas emissions, 2005–2014, in millions of $CO_2$ equivalents.
*Source*: European Commission (2020).

observation is so surprising it has acquired its own name: the *Energiewende* Paradox.[50] Increased renewable capacity has *not* been at the expense of fossil fuels – especially coal – and energy conservation in some sectors, like residential heating, has not automatically translated into corresponding reductions in overall demand. The picture is somewhat complicated by energy imports and exports, since surpluses of electricity at times when wind and solar are abundant are shared with other countries on the same grid, but Germany also draws from the grid at other times; a thorough analysis of Energiewende would have to take this factor into account, but we won't.

The German struggle to rein in emissions while sustaining its economy is fascinating and can easily occupy a book of its own. The reason for bringing it up here is much simpler, however: it vividly illustrates the fact that investing in renewable energy is not the same as reducing the use of fossil fuels. There is no monarch decreeing that German energy consumption must remain fixed or that its mix of nonrenewable energy sources is not allowed to change. Germany is entirely capable of making very large investments in wind and solar energy as well as energy efficiency technology *and* maintaining an unacceptably large appetite for fossil fuels, especially coal. Energy is not a zero-sum world.

Nevertheless, it would be unfair to dismiss the value of Energiewende and similar attempts elsewhere to build a decarbonized energy system – a goal of the GND as well. It is indisputable that a climate catastrophe cannot be avoided unless a transformation of this sort takes place. One way to think about it is to redefine what we mean by mitigation and adaptation in climate policy. Normally, mitigation refers to the set of policies that have to do with changing energy use so that atmospheric carbon concentrations can be stabilized, while adaptation has to do with the investments we will need to make to cope with the climate change we can't avoid. From that perspective, installing wind turbines and solar arrays is mitigation, and constructing sea walls or helping farmers switch to new crops is adaptation.

That pair of boxes isn't quite right, however, since it is the amount and type of fossil fuel we use and not how many wind turbines we build that actually determines the extent of mitigation. A better distinction might be one that defines mitigation strictly in terms of carbon emission reduction and recognizes two different kinds of adaptation – adaptation to unavoidable climate change and also to the unavoidable costs of mitigation. Drastic cutbacks in fossil fuel use threaten to reverse decades if not centuries of progress in improving living standards unless we take other steps to soften the blow. That's exactly what investments in renewable energy sources and energy efficiency promise to achieve: they help us adapt to the profound disruption that going on a strict carbon diet would otherwise entail.

In this way, green energy investments, by reducing the human costs of limiting fossil fuel use, also make serious climate measures more politically palatable. It is easier to get the public to support a strenuous tax on gasoline, for instance, if ample mass transit alternatives are in place and if electric vehicles are inexpensive and have access to a thick network of charging stations. (And, as we have seen, also if a large enough portion of the electricity to run these vehicles can be supplied by renewables not subject to a carbon surcharge.) In practical terms, this benefit from green investments may be decisive. On the other hand, it is politically difficult to get support for a truly massive program of green investments without the spur of high fossil fuel prices, an inconvenient chicken-and-egg dilemma.

For the limited purposes of this chapter, however, we don't have to solve this problem. It is enough to recognize that, crucial as they are, programs to expand the supply of renewable sources and reduce the overall amount of energy we need to power our economy have only indirect and unpredictable effects on fossil fuel use. If we take the threat of catastrophic climate change seriously, there is no substitute for actually curtailing the extraction of coal, oil and gas.

# 5 COSTS AND CONSEQUENCES

Some evolutionary biologists say humans developed their keen powers of reasoning as a way to convince members of their group to provide agreement and support.[1] Our ancestors who were good at devising arguments got their way and improved their chances for survival and reproduction. (Pickup conversations must have been fairly sophisticated among the paleolithic crowd.) Even today, in the worlds of politics and academic debate, motivated reasoning appears to be the norm. People often say whatever supports their side and undermines the other.

This is especially true when we look at debates over the cost of acting on climate change. On one side are the climate deniers or those who advocate going slow; they say restrictions on fossil fuels will damage the economy, raise unemployment and divert money that could be spent better elsewhere.[2] Environmentalists tend to take the opposite stand; according to them, kicking the fossil fuel habit will be nearly painless, shaving a negligible fraction of a percent off the rate of economic growth and perhaps even creating more jobs than it eliminates.[3] It's understandable why each side would position itself this way, but the usefulness of an argument for political persuasion is not the same as its actual truth.

In this chapter I will take a renegade stand: even though I am taking a hawkish position on the need for action to forestall catastrophic climate change, I will also make the case that policies at the necessary scale and scope will be difficult to carry out and likely to be economically painful. I didn't use to think this way; a few years ago I was a well-behaved member of Team Green. I too talked about all the low-hanging fruit in improving energy efficiency and how prices for wind and solar energy generation were plummeting to competitive levels. I was converted to pessimism, however, as I delved deeper into the evidence and certainly not because there is any benefit to contrarianism on this front. I truly regret the argument I'm about to make and wish it were false, but ultimately the demands of greenhouse gas mitigation leave no room for dissimulation. One compensation, however, is that facing up to the costs gives us a clearer picture of the political economic dimension of climate change – the barriers to action arising from capitalist power relations and the strategies that might overcome them, a theme we'll return to at the end of the book.

## The Centrality of Fossil Fuels

Let's begin with a reality check. Fossil fuels do not constitute a peripheral, disposable sector of the modern economy; more than anything else, they are the basis for it and the civilization that depends on it. The story of the steady expansion of humanity's deployment of energy, from the force of our own bodies to draft animals, wood, wind and water and eventually mineral fuels, has been told many times and does not need to be repeated here.[4] The record of historical energy use in the United States is depicted in a useful graphic from the Energy Information Agency (Figure 5.1), where BTU refers to British Thermal Unit, a quantity of energy sufficient to heat one pound of water by one degree Fahrenheit.

Until late in the nineteenth century, the primary fuel in the American economy was wood. In fact, because wood was so abundant at this time, its role far exceeded any other source. You can see this in the wonderful Buster Keaton film *The General*, which tells the story of a railroad escapade during the Civil War. Keaton plays a southern railroad engineer whose train is captured by northern troops; he steals it back and finds himself in a high-speed chase against another train. An endless series of gags is built around the need for wood, wood and more wood to throw into the boiler. Aside from the overall skill of Keaton as an actor and film maker, what one notices today is the centrality of wood rather than coal as a fuel in the mid-nineteenth century, and how it is completely taken for granted in popular culture.

Coal begins to emerge at the time of the Civil War but plays a supporting role to wood until the mid-1880s. Petroleum doesn't become

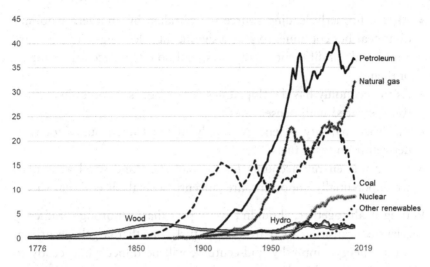

**Figure 5.1** Energy consumption in the United States, 1776–2014, in quadrillion BTUs.
*Source*: US Energy Information Agency (2020).

significant until well into the twentieth century and finally surpasses coal around 1950. The reign of petroleum as the energy leader continues up to the present but is being challenged by natural gas, whose recent upsurge has come at the expense of coal. All other energy sources are far less important. Nuclear energy boomed in the 1970s and 1980s but has stalled since then. Significant hydropower capacity has not been added in nearly fifty years, and wood is a declining factor. That leaves only renewable sources, including not only wind and solar but also biofuels. Indeed, the growth of biomass energy, spurred by ethanol mandates, is the major story among renewables; it accounted for almost half of renewable supply in 2015. Hydropower accounts for another quarter, so wind and solar, while promising, are still clearly in their infancy. When thinking about the future of renewable energy in the United States, it should be noted that hydro capacity is unlikely to expand by much, and biofuels may already be above their sustainable level, given that land is needed to feed people and not only machines.[5]

The purpose of this quick overview is to establish a few broad facts before plunging into the details about cost:

- Large-scale supply of energy is central to the modern economy.
- Transitions from one leading fuel source to another have occurred only at rare intervals, at least half a century apart.

- After a formerly leading source is overtaken by another, it doesn't disappear but continues to play a significant role, suggesting there are a multitude of different energy uses, and no one source is best for all of them.
- As the economy has developed, less energy-dense sources like wood were replaced with denser ones.
- The vast majority of energy supply in the United States today is derived from fossil fuels.
- Renewable energy accounts for a small slice, and wind and solar, while potentially important, are currently a small slice of that slice.

Putting it all together, shouldn't we expect that a thorough, radically accelerated transition away from fossil fuels, one that largely decarbonizes our energy supply by mid-century, will be difficult and costly to achieve? How could it be otherwise?

## A Brief Detour: What about Jobs?

Before taking the plunge into carbon cost accounting, one important point needs to be clarified. Especially in the political arena, many studies trumpet the number of jobs that will be created by switching from fossil fuels to clean energy. In fact, if the most optimistic reports are to be believed, the energy transition could be a net economic benefit, ushering in an era of prosperity and full employment.[6] Can this be true?

The point to bear in mind is one that every economist knows but sounds paradoxical to those who hear it for the first time: employment is a cost, not a benefit. Of course, people don't want to be unemployed, and when job creation numbers go up we all say the economy is improving. All of this is true – but employment is still a cost, not a benefit.

To see why, imagine a hypothetical jobs program: let's eliminate all computers with their word processing applications and reinstate the army of secretaries who used to spend their days typing and filing back in the 1950s (with better gender balance, of course). Overnight, millions of new jobs would be created, tapping out all the memos and reports that are produced electronically today. Even more employment could be generated by bringing back secretarial schools to teach those lost arts.

Why is this a bad idea? It's because, unless you have a special thing for carbon paper and whiteout, no new *value* would be created by going back to the old ways; we would just be doing more work to get the same result. If you wanted to put money in the hands of would-be secretaries, it makes more sense to just give it to them for free, since that way they can put their time to better uses than trying to impersonate computers. For the vast majority of jobs labor is a burden, something we wouldn't do unless someone pays us. That's what it means to say it's a cost.[7]

The reason this sounds paradoxical is that, in most situations, the work people do produces value in excess of the burden. When a new business opens, jobs are created, but with the expectation that the products the business produces will command a price in the market that exceeds the payroll expense. If not, the business will not survive. For public sector jobs, we also expect that the value of the services employees provide justifies their pay stubs. So, when we hear about new jobs being created, it is reasonable to believe that their benefits will be greater than their costs. And, if that's true, the number of jobs and how well they pay is a rough minimum estimate of their social value.

Now switch topics: consider climate change. Simply burning fossil fuels in the future as we have in the past is not a rational option; we have to decarbonize our economy, and this will be expensive. Much of the expense, in fact, lies in the large amounts of labor it will take to rebuild our infrastructure and create products with methods that would not be adopted if we could continue relying on otherwise cheap and abundant carbon energy. In other words, this expense takes the form of jobs. The jobs are a big part of the cost we'll have to absorb: more work to be done just to keep what we have, and more money to pay for it. Of course, these jobs will be entirely worth their cost if they keep the alligators at a safe distance from the Arctic, but they are a cost all the same. The goal of an effective climate policy is to stabilize atmospheric carbon with the minimum necessary cost, and everything else being equal that means the *fewest* number of new jobs it will take to get it done.[8]

## What Do We Talk about When We Talk about Decarbonizing the Economy?

What does it actually mean to decarbonize our way of life? Proponents of a Green New Deal speak the language of investment:

drastically cutting carbon emissions means putting millions of people to work building wind and solar power plants, modernizing the electrical grid and improving the insulation of our buildings. Prophets of a green business boom paint pictures of consumers rushing out to buy electric cars and new energy-efficient appliances. The thou-shalt-not wing of the environmental movement emphasizes what we might have to forgo: a meat-oriented diet, goods produced in distant locations and resource consumption in general. Surely, all of these will have some role to play in a carbon-free future, but how much, and does more of one mean less of the others?

In its last assessment report, published in 2014, the IPCC identified five broad strategies: increasing energy efficiency, replacing fossil fuels with renewable energy sources, electrifying heating and industrial production systems, eliminating the use of fossil fuels in transportation and expanding mass transit, and expanding non-atmospheric forms of carbon storage like forests.[9] This schema helped its authors present a mass of research findings, but I believe it is incomplete, and in any case there is a simpler way to think about the problem.

As we've seen, the core task is to dethrone the position fossil fuels occupy at the center of our economy. There are three layers. The first is to replace them with other, non-carbon sources of energy. This approach takes the demand for energy as given but meets it in a decarbonized manner. If we could expand renewable sources quickly enough and at sufficient scale to supply an ever-growing appetite for energy while keeping our emissions within the remaining carbon budget constraint, that would be a complete answer – but we can't. Investment in clean energy alone is not enough.

This takes us to the second layer, increasing energy efficiency to power our end uses. Each product or service we purchase consumes energy, often extravagantly because of decades of thinking we would have an endless supply of cheap, reliable fossil fuels. If green energy is limited in its abundance, we will have to find ways to get more with less. Fortunately, our very profligacy leaves us with many opportunities to be more frugal. Industrial processes can be retooled for greater efficiency, buildings can be better insulated, and overreliance on cars and trucks can be cut back in favor of less energy-gulping transit and freight alternatives. By making energy go further we can try to reconcile the constrained pace of decarbonizing our energy supply with our continued desire for the services that depend on it. As we will soon see, nearly all models of mitigation pathways are predicated on the assumption that this reconciliation is achievable, or more precisely they specify the requirements that must be met if we are to meet carbon budget targets without sacrificing the end uses we currently consume.

It is possible these two broad strategies, fuel substitution and increased energy efficiency, will do the job. I think that's unlikely, however, for reasons that will soon become clear, and that brings us to the third layer, changing the end uses themselves – altering the composition of the economy to favor goods that require less energy to produce or consume. The following examples will make this clear.

*Transportation.* The first layer is converting our fleet of vehicles to renewable energy. This can be done by using renewably produced fuels, like hydrogen, or shifting from internal combustion engines to electric plug-ins, while also decarbonizing the generation of electricity itself. Since we won't be able to accomplish this quickly enough and at scale to keep carbon emissions under budget, we will also resort to the second layer, meeting our mobility needs with more public transit and fewer cars. We would still be getting around more or less as before, but with less energy, however supplied. If that too proves insufficient, however, we will have to move to the third layer, entailing a change in the consumption patterns that in turn create a need for mobility. This would mean dramatic change in how population and commercial activities are distributed over the coming decades: more densely concentrated cities with intermixed employment, shopping and other services to cut back on motorized travel – what geographers and planners refer to as a change in urban form.

*Tourism.* Layer one begins as it did with transportation except extended to longer distances, especially air travel. As we will see in the final chapter, there is some scope for decarbonization of jet fuels but not much. Travel by train and boat are less fuel-intensive, and trains in particular can be electrified (again) and brought into the renewable realm. Similarly, hotels, restaurants and the rest of the tourism infrastructure can be given a green makeover. With the second layer we search for ways to stretch energy supplies to support continuing growth in tourism capacity. This will likely entail substituting other forms of long-distance transportation for air travel and achieving greater efficiencies in hotels and other structures. But much of the world's tourism investment is closely tied to airline routes and designed for relatively brief, intense bursts of spending; think, for instance, of the vacation packages offered by tour companies.

If non-carbon energy is truly scarce (and expensive), the character of tourism and its place in affluent lifestyles may need to change, a matter for level three. While it is difficult to be specific, it is not hard to imagine a shift away from venues dependent on air links toward others accessible by boat and train and perhaps also from frequent, travel-intensive experiences to longer but less frequent ones that economize on travel costs. Or perhaps tourism itself will diminish, to be replaced by other, more place-bound, restorative activities.

*Tools.* The average household in an upper-income country has an array of tools for all sorts of purposes, from occasional cooking projects to deep cleaning to outdoor maintenance. Gardeners, wood-workers, hobbyists and others have specialized tools for their pursuits. These items require energy, sometimes to operate but always to manufacture, which means they need to be decarbonized along with the rest of our possessions.[10] Layer one points to fuel substitution in production and use: electric rather than gas-powered yard tools, for instance, and greater use of electric power, renewably generated, in their production. In layer two efficiencies are raised at all stages from raw material extraction to final use. In the likely event that these two decarbonization strategies don't take us far enough, we can go the extra distance by shifting away from extensive private tool ownership altogether. There are many possibilities; one just beginning to be explored is the expansion of libraries from books and media to tool-sharing, which could drastically cut down on the amount of production our society devotes to a wide range of items.[11]

Wherever we look we will find some version of this three-layer structure. If we can keep everything else the same and change only where our energy comes from, fine. But that's seldom possible, so the next step is to do more with less energy. If fuel-switching and efficiency together still aren't enough, the additional recourse is to shift from more to less energy-dependent goods and services. This isn't possible for everything we consume (we will still need heat to cook food, for instance), but it is for a large portion of it. This third layer is about structural transformation.[12]

Far-reaching changes in our way of life are unlikely to be undertaken unless some form of pressure is applied; does this mean they will leave us worse off? Most economists, who assume we are, all of us and all the time, rational decision-makers who optimize our "utility," draw this conclusion.[13] But perhaps we are not always such expert judges of our own welfare. For an example that is especially pertinent to the third-layer adjustments we may have to make to avoid a climate catastrophe, consider a study published in 2008 that examined the effect of longer commutes on self-reported happiness. Even though individuals presumably choose where to live and work based on their judgments of what will be best for them, after accounting for other factors it turned out that longer commuting was associated with less happiness; the people being studied (Germans in this case) systematically underestimated how stressful a daily commute can be.[14] The lesson for climate change is that if the pressure for decarbonization forces us to change our travel-demanding choices, we might well end up better off for it. It would be too much to promise that the lifestyle changes needed for climate mitigation will always have such positive outcomes, of course, but it shouldn't be assumed that they will always cause us to suffer either.[15]

Meanwhile, if we compare the simple three-layer model to the IPCC list of strategies we began with, it should be clear that IPCC's numbers 1–4 all pertain to what I have designated as the first two layers. (Number five is not about emissions reductions.) The third layer is not represented; why?[16] There are various possible explanations. Perhaps the simplest is that scientific research, while it can examine and forecast fuel substitution and energy efficiency in great detail, has little to say about the subjective choices people are likely to make if they are pushed to revise their life choices away from energy dependence. This reminds us of the economic calculation problem we looked at in Chapter 3: when open-ended, subjective responses to policy measures have an important role to play, forecasting becomes murky.

Nevertheless, it is virtually inevitable that all three layers will be needed if the pace of carbon emission reduction deduced in Chapter 3 is to be adhered to. The models of decarbonization themselves are prime evidence, since they show that warming targets can be met without structural change only if other, disturbing assumptions are adopted. To see this we now have to turn to one of the central strands of climate research, the modeling of future carbon emissions and climate impacts.

## Getting to Zero Will Not Cost Much: Unless It Does

If you read only the reports put out by governments and think tanks, you might believe that humanity can swap out its fossil fuel economy for a renewable energy supply while hardly breaking a sweat. The cost of wind and solar power is coming down, they say, and the potential of bioenergy is nearly limitless. We have a wide array of energy efficiency-enhancing technologies just waiting to be deployed. If we just stop subsidizing carbon-spewing industries and give the system a modest nudge or two, we can easily dispose of the climate threat. If it were mine to choose, that's the world I'd like to live in.

Unfortunately, these assurances, especially those about how we can shift most of our energy needs to renewable sources quickly and at little cost, need to be approached with skepticism. This is not because there isn't an element of truth; costs of wind and solar have been coming down quickly, and in many situations they are already competitive with fossil fuel alternatives – but this ignores the question of scale.

One problem lies in assuming that the cost of replacing all fossil fuels will be the same as the cost of replacing a small portion of them, as if we could continue using, as we do now, ideal locations for siting renewable energy facilities.[17] Naturally, as the renewable sector develops, the best sites are sought out for new installations, the windiest areas for wind and the sunniest for solar. It's no surprise the cost of electrical generation under these conditions is relatively low. As we saw at the beginning of the chapter, however, the renewable share of energy use in the United States (and similarly around the world), while rising, is still very slim. To replace most existing capacity, not to mention the burgeoning unmet needs of the developing world, will require searching out many less-than-perfect sites for new installations. As we go from windier to calmer and sunnier to cloudier, renewable costs have to rise, and this is a major reason that the lowest current price is not a good guide to the costs of a more thoroughgoing transition.[18]

Another problem is that the economics of renewables depends on storage, which in turn depends on the share of renewable sources in total energy supply. If that share is modest we can get energy from solar when the sun is shining and wind when the wind is blowing, and at other times we can fall back on fossil fuels that burn whenever we want them to. To largely or fully decarbonize, however, we have to take away that fallback option. This means our energy source during renewable downtimes will have to be stored power from hours, days or weeks ago. The problem is that current technologies for storing intermittent renewable energy are expensive. While it is possible that new methods will bring these costs down – and like you I strongly hope they will – we can't count on it, nor can we know today what their costs will be or if they will have supply limitations. On the other hand, storage capacity can definitely be created if carbon prices are high enough, which is the point about the cost of an energy transition.[19]

Moreover, the sheer scale of the renewable energy challenge should give us pause. While annual totals have bounced about, in each of the past fifteen years the United States has generally installed between 20 and 40 gigawatts (GW, billions of watts) of new capacity from all sources, carbon-based and renewable alike. In a prominent recent study of what it would take to substantially decarbonize US electrical supply by 2035, new solar and wind installation exceeds 100 GW each year a decade into the program.[20] Whether that level of resource mobilization is even possible is an open question.

Related to the scale problem is the issue of resource demands. Solar panels and wind turbines, along with the battery storage to offset their intermittency, require specialized inputs, and electric vehicles in particular are dependent on the supply of rare earth metals. One recent study found that this constraint alone would prevent electrification of the transport sector.[21]

So, fortified with our newfound pessimism, let's take a look at an example of a report touting the potential of the green economy, *Pathways to Deep Decarbonization*, issued by a team of nongovernmental organizations connected to the UN Secretariat in New York.[22] Researchers in sixteen countries developed technology-based scenarios, which were combined into a composite study. The news, you will not be surprised to hear, is very good: the world can keep warming below the 2° limit, and the cost we'll bear is minimal and perhaps even negative – it might be cheaper to do this than continue on with business as usual. The only cost to achieving deep decarbonization is the investment in new technology, but we would have to invest in some sort of energy technology anyway. Moreover, clean energy facilities will be much cheaper to operate, so even in standard business metrics we may come out ahead. In their words:

> Energy investment under deep decarbonization requires only a modest increase in the gross energy investment required in the absence of climate policy.... The net cost of deep decarbonization is substantially lower after accounting for reduced operating costs.[23]

Indeed, so compelling is the purely financial case for this energy transformation that government policy, after jump-starting it, can stand
aside and let the market take over:

> As technology costs decline, deep decarbonization starts to
> provide its own momentum: lower costs encourage deployment,
> which can encourage even lower costs. **The "tipping point" in
> this process is when costs decline at a rate and speed sufficient
> to drive their global deployment based solely on their favorable
> economics.**[24]

It's a wonderful vision, but does it get the job done? The answer
depends on what we think the job is, which is where carbon budgets
come in. The critical moment arrives on page 18, where the authors
present the cumulative emissions they anticipate from their program
and compare it with the IPCC's budget constraint. There we find
that their projected emissions over the period 2010–2050 sum to
1,185–1,555 Gt of carbon dioxide depending on extrapolation assumptions.[25] They claim they are within the 2° window, citing an IPCC
budget range over the same period of 586–1,336 Gt. However, their
source, the IPCC Working Group III Summary for Policymakers, in the
same table cited by the Deep Decarbonizers, gives the budget range
(whose provenance we will come to shortly) as 630–1,180 Gt *over the
entire 2011–2100 period.*[26] (Note that the upper end of this range is
roughly consistent with the budget we provisionally adopted in
Chapter 3, which drew on more recent research.) In other words, the
low and perhaps even negative cost program outlined by the Deep
Decarbonization team produces a level of cumulative carbon dioxide
emissions by 2050 that exceeds the top end of the IPCC budget range
over a time period over twice as long.

What's going on? They say they adhere to the IPCC's 2° pathway, but they blow past it by mid-century. How can they have it both
ways? Part of the answer may be simple fudging in the interest of
producing a result the intended audience hopes to hear. Another, more
disturbing explanation is that most of the scenarios considered by the
IPCC in its 2014 report incorporate massive investments in technologies
that create *negative* emissions – that instead of pumping more carbon
dioxide into the atmosphere are intended to withdraw carbon dioxide
from it. This is how a scenario could reach one level of cumulative
emissions by 2050 and then a much lower one fifty years later. That's

not a part of the Deep Decarbonization program at all, nor could it be since there would be no business case for negative emission technologies unless governments were putting a very tight squeeze on fossil fuel use – exactly what the Deep Decarbonizers say we don't need – and businesses could effectively buy carbon permits or avoid carbon taxes by investing in carbon removal. But is that scenario even possible? Can we claim to adhere to a 1,100-plus Gt budget by emitting far more than that and then un-emitting the excess?

We will return to this crucial issue in a moment, but first it should be noted that the Deep Decarbonization report at least measured itself against a carbon budget; most decarbonization-on-the-cheap scenarios don't go this far. As I write this, a popular target is "net zero emissions by 2050," but as we saw in Chapter 3 there is no reason to assume that meeting this goal will also mean keeping our cumulative emissions between now and then under budget. Worse, there is the slippery word "net," which, as we will see, means that emissions will continue but be offset by an equal level of withdrawal of carbon from the atmosphere. Nothing in the world of climate change mitigation is as it initially seems.

In the interest of clarity, the following is a list of questions that should be asked of any policy document that, like the Deep Decarbonization report, claims to vanquish global warming at minimal cost:

- *Do they aim for a target defined by cumulative carbon emissions or only a percentage reduction arrived at in a given target year?* As we saw in Chapter 3, only a carbon budget applied to cumulative emissions allows us to predict climate impacts.
- *Do they adhere to a budget that will give us a better-than-even chance of keeping global warming to 2°C?* If the target is relaxed, of course it will be easier to meet.
- *Do they assume an important role for negative emissions, and do they treat them as symmetrical with positive emissions?* As Chapter 4 demonstrated, withdrawing carbon from the atmosphere with uncertain prospects of permanence does not cancel out injecting carbon from deep Earth storage into the surface carbon cycle.
- *Do they extrapolate from small-scale efficiency and cost estimates to massive transformations of the economy?* It's one thing to build wind or solar installations in the best possible locations to meet a few

percentage points of our energy needs and another to embark on a crash program to obtain most of our energy from them within a few decades. Simply pointing to a few low-cost implementations of a technology does not demonstrate that we have the economic capacity and resource availability to rapidly transfer our entire energy supply to them.

- *Do they provide a model that shows their assumptions and projections are mutually consistent?* A model doesn't have to be complex, but if mutual consistency is possible it should also be possible to demonstrate it.

In my experience, studies that paint a rosy picture of our transition to a post-carbon future inevitably gloss over one or another (or all) of these issues.

## An Introduction to the Art of Modeling Climate Mitigation

If we are looking for the best available prognostications on the cost of forestalling a climate disaster, and not just the most reassuring ones, we should turn to the studies that use modeling techniques – systems of simultaneous equations – based on transparent, reproducible data and methods. A small army of economists and data scientists is employed in this endeavor, publishing what are variously called "emission" or "mitigation" or "energy transition" pathways, scenarios that sketch a future of carbon emissions and climate impacts from some initial year to a predetermined horizon – often 2100. They have important limitations that we'll consider shortly, but taken together they offer the only credible point of departure.[27]

The workhorse of this literature is the integrated assessment model (IAM), which we first encountered in Chapter 2. At that time we surveyed only the IAMs that are outfitted to attach a monetary cost to climate impacts, but there are others that don't and concentrate their resources on better understanding how mitigation might proceed. IAMs have two key components which are augmented in various ways. First, they incorporate equations for the economy, broken out into regions and sectors; these incorporate changes in the size and composition of national and global economies over the model's planning horizon. Second, they include equations that show how the evolution of the economy will generate climate impacts through the emission of greenhouse gases or other mechanisms. They usually provide substantial detail in the energy-producing or energy-consuming aspects of the economy, showing how specific demand and technological conditions will alter our use of different energy sources and how that in turn will affect the climate.

The most important attribute of these models is that they explicitly take into account the consistency of all assumptions and outputs – in other words, they are *models*, unlike simple lists of the potential emissions savings from adopting various technologies. Because they are models, everything affects everything else: energy supplies affect economic growth and economic growth affects energy use, while the human economy affects the carbon cycle and, to a limited extent, climate impacts react back on economic life. Investment in new sources of energy are components of GDP, and resources used for renewable power or carbon-storing land use are withdrawn from other purposes.[28]

There are many IAMs and many runs of them because there are a lot of choices to be made. With limits to the complexity they can encompass and still be solvable, modelers have to decide which components to break out in greater detail. For instance, how many different energy-using sectors of the economy should be given their own growth equations? How detailed should the national or regional breakouts be? At what level of detail should land use changes be represented? There is no single correct answer to these questions, only a range of options that show how different sets of refinements result in different study results. A particular choice of interest is how the economy is depicted. All IAMs have a demand-and-supply framework, where the demand side for energy of various types comes from economic and population growth and their past relationship to a range of end uses, and supply comes from the available technologies and their respective costs. Prices influence both demand and supply and settle at an equilibrium where the amounts people want to buy and sell are equal in all markets.[29]

Incidentally, these models depict time in two strikingly different ways. Some are based on sequential decision-making, with production and consumption outcomes in each time period the result of circumstances in that period only. Effectively, a model that functions this way from 2020 to 2100 has each participant in the economy making one choice per year about everything (a total of eighty choices), each a year apart. Others, however, posit what economists call a "representative agent," a single individual who buys or produces on behalf of everyone in their industry or region. This person has foreknowledge of all economic factors over the model's planning horizon and is anointed with the capacity to make a single all-encompassing decision at the outset that includes all future annual choices in order to maximize economic gains. If that person is you, you will adopt a program in 2020 that specifies decisions for 2020, 2021, 2022 and every year until 2100, and you'll have no need to make any changes to it since every piece of it will be optimal for you. Such depictions of "rationality" are far-fetched, but economists prefer them because they simplify the problem of how to include future expectations into current plans.[30]

Technology assumptions are obviously critical in work of this sort. What technologies will become available? How much will they cost? How quickly can they be scaled up, and how does the speed of deployment affect cost? Are there technical, environmental or social constraints on their use? And how will these answers evolve over the coming eighty years? Every IAM necessarily has to prognosticate on all of this; these are inputs to their analyses, not outputs from them. As we will see, many of the assumptions they make are controversial, so the best work reports the extent to which results are sensitive to them.

It should be clear at this point that IAMs are not crystal balls. They should not be viewed as forecasts, predictions of the course events will take over the years to come – not even conditional forecasts derived from particular sets of assumptions. We can be sure that the decisive events of the future, whether they turn out to be wars, political upheavals, environmental shocks or extraordinary technological breakthroughs, are not remotely envisioned by these models. Not surprisingly, none of them anticipated the coronavirus pandemic of the past year, which has had large, if temporary, effects on carbon emissions. Consider them instead as thought experiments, asking, "Suppose we constructed a hypothetical world out of a number of plausible assumptions – how would a given set of policies play out?" What matters for such an exercise is not the precise outcomes it predicts, but how, in a given model, changes in the underlying assumptions affect the model's results. This can be a rough guide to the logic of the interplay between economics and planet Earth, as well as the general magnitude of the influences back and forth. We will see, in fact, we can learn quite a bit from this enterprise.

Once the assumptions are in place that make it possible to write the equations for an IAM, the critical input becomes the policies countries do or don't adopt to reduce carbon emissions. This is where the "shared socioeconomic pathway" (SSP) framework developed by the modelers comes in. There are currently five SSPs, each summarized by a short narrative that, in modeling terms, can be fleshed out in assumptions about economic growth within and between countries, research leading to the introduction of new technologies, and projections of end use demand. The following is a brief summary.[31]

- *Sustainability – Taking the Green Road* (SSP 1): The world shifts gradually, but pervasively, toward a more sustainable path, emphasizing more inclusive development that respects perceived environmental boundaries.
- *Middle of the Road* (SSP 2): The world follows a path in which social, economic, and technological trends do not shift markedly from historical patterns. Global and national institutions work toward but make slow progress in achieving sustainable development goals.
- *Regional Rivalry – A Rocky Road* (SSP 3): A resurgent nationalism, concerns about competitiveness and security, and regional conflicts push countries to increasingly focus on domestic or, at most, regional issues. Countries focus on achieving energy and food security goals within their own regions at the expense of broader-based development. Investments in education and technological development decline.
- *Inequality – A Road Divided* (SSP 4): Highly unequal investments in human capital, combined with increasing disparities in economic opportunity and political power, lead to increasing inequalities and stratification both across and within countries. Technology development is high in the high-tech economy and sectors. Environmental policies focus on local issues around middle- and high-income areas.
- *Fossil-Fueled Development – Taking the Highway* (SSP 5): Global markets are increasingly integrated. There are also strong investments in health, education, and institutions to enhance human and social capital. At the same time, the push for economic and social development is coupled with the exploitation of abundant fossil fuel resources and the adoption of resource and energy intensive lifestyles around the world.

A model run combines all these elements: a system of equations for the global economy that takes into account climate feedbacks, a set of specific technological assumptions (parameters for the supply-side equations), a given SSP and a designated temperature target typically for the year 2100. The model solves for activity levels – amounts of specific investments, production of energy and end use goods, and the resulting emissions trajectory and other indicators – that meet these constraints. For its 2014 Assessment Report the IPCC commissioned a standardized set of runs across participating models, its "coupled model intercomparison project" (CMIP). It is overseeing an update for its scheduled 2022 Report, and results are beginning to appear.

Climate insiders study these model results carefully, seeing them as the best guide we have to our true, and not just our hoped-for, climate options. Let's see what they're seeing.

## A First Pass at the Model Results

We can begin by surveying the IPCC's 2014 Assessment Report, since we won't have as comprehensive a set of results until their next iteration. While they examined many scenarios, we will zero in on just those programmed to give us a two-thirds chance of keeping warming under 2° by the end of the century.

The good news is that all models were able to generate such scenarios under a wide range of assumptions. There is considerable uncertainty, however, stemming not only from the different assumptions about technology and future economic development that drive the scenarios, but also the error bands around key parameters like the climate's short- and longer-run sensitivity to the accumulation of greenhouse gases and the discrepancies between different model results. We should think of the scenarios not as precise outcomes of a given set of assumptions but as probabilistic, susceptible to both under- and overestimation.

That said, what patterns did the IPCC find?

- Fourteen 2° scenarios provided cost estimates for stabilizing $CO_2$ (equivalent) at 450 ppm in 2100.
- Looking only at mitigation costs, reduced consumption relative to business as usual (no climate policy adoption) in future years ranged from 1 to 4% in 2030, 2 to 6% in 2050 and 3 to 11% in 2100. Note these were snapshots, not accumulated totals, and that business as usual assumes substantial growth in consumption throughout the rest of the century – which means reductions still take the form of growth, but less of it.

- The median reduction in annual economic growth rates yielding these consumption losses are 0.09% over the first twenty years of carbon policy, 0.09% over the first fifty years and 0.06% over ninety years.
- Mean prices per ton of carbon are $60 in 2020, $90 in 2030 and $200 in 2050. This represents an increase of slightly more than 4% per year between 2020 and 2050.[32]

When you consider the benefit from all of this is greatly reducing the risk of a climate catastrophe, the costs are eminently affordable. Since economic growth rates for most countries in non-pandemic, non-financial crisis years are in the 1–4% range (net of inflation), the impact of climate policy would be imperceptible, closer to a rounding error or the sort of statistical discrepancy that shows up in data tables due to measurement gaps. We could go all in on emissions reduction and no one would notice the difference. This story is consistent with the carbon price estimations as well, since a steady, predictable increase in fossil fuel prices of 4% per year is certainly manageable – consider the much bigger year-to-year or even week-to-week swings in oil prices.

It gets even better. In recent years it has become popular for modelers to include "co-benefits," other desirable effects from reducing fossil fuel use in addition to mitigating climate change. The most important of these are the health benefits from reduced air pollution, particularly due to coal. One high-profile estimate of these beneficial side effects appeared in an International Monetary Fund (IMF) working paper in 2014; it found that, across the top twenty $CO_2$-emitting countries, the average co-benefit for 2010 was $57.50 per tonne.[33] Note this is nearly equal to the average carbon price in the IPCC mitigation models for 2030, which means that during at least the first few years of carbon policy there will be net economic benefits, not costs. (The IMF benefit estimate will go down over time because, as fossil fuel use declines, so will the remaining benefits from reducing them further.)

Meanwhile, the models have continued to be updated, and new estimates of climate sensitivity to greenhouse gases have appeared. We don't have a full comparison to draw from, but the International Institute for Applied Systems Analysis in Vienna has made partial results from recent model runs available on its website. To take one example, in Figure 5.2 we see total carbon dioxide emissions between 2010 and 2100 for five models adopting SSP 2 (an intermediate possibility) and

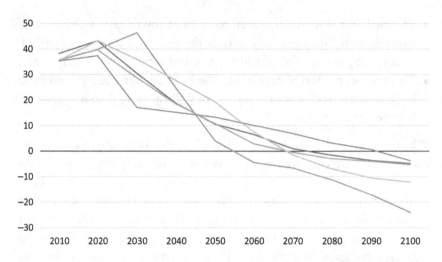

**Figure 5.2** Emissions in gigatonnes per year for five model scenarios targeting 2°C warming.
*Source*: International Institute for Applied Systems Analysis (2021).

targeting 2°C. Again, there is good news: all five models are able to solve for a 2° emissions trajectory. (The number drops to two for the least favorable scenario, SSP 5.) Four begin significant cuts in 2020; the fifth continues to rise until 2030 and then plunges precipitously.

But something else is apparent in this diagram: all five pathways dip into negative territory, with the model exhibiting delayed cutting going extremely negative: −25 Gt per year by the end of the century. What is this telling us? The answer should take us well out of our comfort zone.

## The Costs of Climate Mitigation When You Read the Fine Print

Most scenarios that stabilize at 2° rely heavily on two future technological advances, carbon capture and storage (CCS) and the much expanded use of bioenergy (BE), the combustion of biomass to generate electricity or a natural gas substitute. This shows up in the following four ways:

- CCS allows continued use of fossil fuels – even coal in some scenarios – by extracting carbon from the combustion process and storing it in condensed form in underground chambers.

- BE provides a low to zero net emission source that "buys" a bit of carbon space for continued emissions from other fuels. (BE's net emissions approach zero because carbon released in the combustion of wood, grasses or other biomass is offset by carbon drawn from the atmosphere to grow the crops that replace those that were burned.)
- Above all, the *combination* of CCS and BE allows for the possibility of negative emissions. How? Carbon is pulled from the atmosphere to grow crops, which then produce energy, but, thanks to CCS, there is no return of carbon back to the atmosphere. Every time we do this we get more energy while reducing the amount of greenhouse gases. For every tonne of such negative emissions we can produce a tonne of positive emissions (by burning fossil fuels) and still remain carbon neutral.
- Finally, the possibility of negative emissions on a large scale allows for much greater flexibility in the timing of emission reduction. Costly shifts away from fossil fuels can be delayed, and atmospheric carbon concentrations can be allowed to zoom past 450 ppm during the coming century, since negative emissions can hypothetically bring this number down to 450 again by 2100. Thus we don't need to have the BE/CCS methods in hand in order to delay other forms of mitigation; believing they will come online allows us to run up a massive carbon debt in advance. This pattern of excess emissions in near-term decades followed by years of negative emissions to pay them back is called overshooting.

And the BE/CCS combination is not the only source of negative emissions, or "carbon dioxide removal" (CDR) in modeling lingo. Industrial-scale expansion of forests, an amped-up version of the ostensible silviculture safety valve we considered in the previous chapter, is another option. A more exotic technology, one that would use chemical processes to precipitate carbon out of thin air – literally – with no combustion at all, dubbed "direct air capture" (DAC), is typically part of the mix. With all these supposed opportunities to put carbon emissions in reverse, it is not surprising that overshooting is the norm, not the exception, in 2°-compliant scenarios. And we haven't yet touched the delicate subject of nuclear power and its projected vast expansion.

To get a sense of the overall importance of this constellation of assumptions, consider CDR in total, combining all its technology components. Two analysts, Tavoni and Socolow, dug inside five models,

Table 5.1. Carbon dioxide removal (CDR) in five 2°C modeling scenarios

| Study | Cumulative CDR (Gt $CO_2$) |
| --- | --- |
| Edmonds et al. (2013) | 660–1,380 |
| Van Vuuren et al. (2013) | 800 |
| Kriegler et al. (2013) | 470–910 |
| Chen and Tavoni (2013) | 777 |
| Fuss et al. (2013) | 1, 600 |

*Source*: Tavoni and Socolow (2013).

four of which were contributors to the database used by the IPCC in 2014, and examined how much mitigation was assigned to CDR rather than true emissions reduction.[34] Their findings are presented in Table 5.1.

To make sense of these numbers, recall that the working budget we adopted in Chapter 3 for total cumulative emissions from 2019 to the end of the century is just over 1,000 Gt. Suppose every tonne of CDR corresponds to an extra tonne of carbon emissions from fossil fuels we are allowed to emit and still come in – sort of – under budget. Then, in the least CDR-ish scenario, the first of two in Kriegler et al., almost 50% more fossil fuels can be used compared with an emissions-only budget constraint, and at the upper end, in Fuss et al., the fossil fuel cap can be expanded to two and a half times its emissions-only size.

A similar pattern appears in the more recent modeling exercises. Look again at the five models (Figure 5.3) that kept warming at 2° in SSP 2, and this time consider the role of carbon capture and storage. As in the 2014 runs, this more recent sample from 2018 features extensive use of CCS. In four of the five models negative emissions in this form begin in earnest by 2030; in all of them they play a central role by mid-century, ultimately replacing from half to all of today's fossil fuel emissions by 2100. It is important to add that this reliance on CCS exists in large part because the models allow it; not all models can produce this result based on emissions reductions alone.

For another revealing look at the role of CDR in mitigation models, consider a recent study that compares global CDR-included

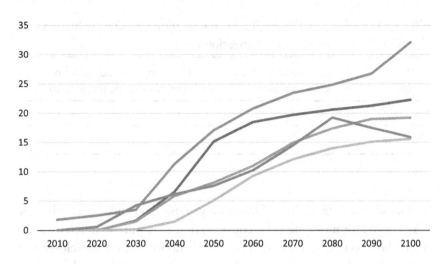

**Figure 5.3** Carbon capture and storage in gigatonnes per year, SSP 2 and 2°C warming target.
*Source*: International Institute for Applied Systems Analysis (2021).

and CDR-not-included scenarios in one such model, TIAM-Grantham. The authors ran it under a range of assumptions: the likelihood CDR (in toto) would eventually prove feasible, the likelihood policy makers at the beginning of the emissions reduction program gave to its future feasibility, whether the target was limiting warming to 1.75° and 2° (with two-thirds probability), and various discount rates that translate future costs into their magnitude at the outset. The program was assumed to begin in 2020 and continue to the end of the century.[35]

Let's look at just a single comparison in which the target is 1.75°, the discount rate is 5%, policy makers know in advance whether CDR will work, and either it will or it won't – no intermediate probabilities. Table 5.2 shows the implications for near-term emissions reduction and the necessary restriction of demand for electrical power. It is difficult to view these results as anything less than shocking. If ample CDR is sure to become feasible, and policy makers can count on it from day 1 of a climate program, for the first ten years emissions can be reduced at the challenging but doable rate of about 3% per year, and the amount of electricity supplied will fall only very slightly. Eliminate the CDR option, and the annual rate of emissions reduction in the first decade leaps to the almost unimaginable level of nearly 11%, while global demand for electricity must somehow fall by a seventh. Of course, these chilling numbers apply to a target, 1.75° warming, that

**Table 5.2.** The effect of CDR feasibility on near-term emissions reduction and electrical demand in a climate mitigation model

| CDR feasibility | Annual rate of emissions reduction, 2020–2030(%) | Electricity demand reduction relative to no-policy in 2030(%) |
|---|---|---|
| Yes | 2.9 | 1.5 |
| No | 10.9 | 14 |

*Source*: Grant et al. (2021).

is more stringent than the 2° I take as a provisional benchmark, which is why I opted for it despite valid concerns that 2° is still too much. Bear in mind, however, that each year we delay taking action the closer the remaining carbon budget for a 2° target begins to resemble the budget for 1.75° – and also that for any target we might select whether or not we forecast the availability of CDR makes an immense difference.

It's crucial to recognize that this starring role for carbon removal is the basis for the "net" in the so-called net zero carbon target that now dominates public policy debate. It seems that everyone measures climate commitment by whether and how soon net zero will take hold, from US President Joe Biden (by 2050)[36] to Chinese President Xi Jinping (by 2060)[37] to the activists of the Extinction Rebellion (by 2025!)[38] On this magic date carbon emissions from burning fossils fuels will be far from zero themselves, but they will supposedly be fully offset by increases in forestation, carbon capture and storage and other sources of negative emissions. This vision of future carbon removal, usually decades into the future and largely predicated on technologies that do not currently exist, makes it possible to make sweeping promises without difficult reductions in emissions for years to come.[39]

So how dependable are the negative emission technologies that underpin these results and allow policy advocates to advertise their net-zero-by-some-distant-future-date credentials?

*Carbon capture and storage*. This is not a new idea; there have been abortive attempts to set up pilot projects for decades. It remains a futuristic technology, a hope, but it looks like a sure thing in the modeling literature, as Figure 5.3 demonstrates: putting Figures 5.2 and 5.3 together, it is clear that all five model runs depend on CCS-fueled negative emissions in the later decades of the century to offset what would otherwise be excess emissions during the early decades. This is a big bet.

Some studies have constrained model runs to not use CCS to see what difference it makes. The general result is that the cost of adhering to the 2° limit at least doubles, assuming no limitations on other uncertain technologies.[40] That likely understates the true effect, however. Many models are simply unable to produce a 2° scenario without CCS; for instance, one study of nine different IAMs found that more than a third of model runs were unable to produce a feasible solution under this constraint if action were begun in 2020. If stringent climate policies are delayed for another ten years, more than three-fourths fail.[41]

So a lot depends on CCS, according to the modeling studies now on the table. And this technology might indeed play a big future role in keeping the alligators safely out of the Arctic – or it might not. Two rather sober analysts, Kevin Anderson and Glen Peters, remind us that "Two decades of research and pilot plants have struggled to demonstrate the technical and economic viability of power generation with CCS, even when combusting relatively homogeneous fossil fuels."[42] The last bit refers to the extra challenge of scrubbing carbon from biofuels that will differ from one batch to the next in their chemical composition. A major review of exotic technologies, including CCS, to permit climate mitigation while still burning fossil fuels was published by the National Academy of Sciences (NAS) in 2015. Their judgment, which strikes me as balanced and reasonable, is the following:

> it is important to keep in mind that today with the existing five CCS projects in place ... sequestration is only taking place on the order of $MtCO_2/yr$ ... Hence, it is uncertain whether the injection and sequestration of 18 $GtCO_2/yr$ is a reasonable estimate. Furthermore, these studies are misleading since none of the cost estimates include compression or sequestration, but only capture. In addition, it is important to keep in mind that there are many challenges associated with accurately determining sequestration potential and that geological sequestration technologies are still in their infancy.[43]

A sum of 18 Gt (total, not per year) is the level of CCS required to offset 1 ppm (out of a target of 450) of atmospheric carbon (a gigatonne is 1,000 times a megaton [Mt]). CCS is an infant technology, still unproven at small scale, much less the massive deployment assumed by most pathway scenarios. The NAS rightly calls for ramped up research on this option, but to not depend on it.[44]

*Bioenergy and BE/CCS.* The human use of biomass as a fuel goes back to the earliest stage in human evolution and perhaps even earlier. As we saw at the beginning of this chapter, wood remained the primary fuel source in the United States until late in the nineteenth century, and it was superseded primarily because fossil energy sources are more dense: more energy output per unit of mass and therefore more versatile and transportable. But as we have come to learn about the risk of disrupting the carbon cycle, renewable, plant-based energy is starting to win reacceptance. The mitigation scenarios we are considering all make use of this energy source, as they should, drawing on crops like specialized grasses (suitable for growing on marginal lands), timber and marine algae. Above all, they combine biofuels with CCS in order to continue substantial use of coal, oil and natural gas, thereby keeping costs down.

The dependence of aggressive mitigation on biological carbon withdrawal strategies shows up in the Representative Concentration Pathway (RPC) framework adopted by the IPCC. In the runup to the 2014 Assessment Report, modelers were asked to devise scenarios that targeted a few selected (representative) greenhouse warming impacts. The scenarios were named for the greenhouse intensity they embody, measured in units of energy per surface area. RPC 2.6 corresponds to the 2° pathway we have taken as a benchmark; model runs qualifying for membership in the 2.6 club have a two-thirds chance of keeping temperature increases under this ceiling over the duration of the century. Of the entire family of RCP 2.6 scenarios collected by the IPCC for its fifth assessment report, almost 90% relied heavily on BE/CCS, 12 Gt per year in the median case.[45] We will see what this reliance will look like in the Working Group III Assessment Report scheduled to be released in 2022.

But such an extensive reliance on biofuels would require us to devote an immense portion of the Earth's land area to achieve the intended scale. It's difficult to say just how much, since nothing like this has ever been done, and much would depend on what crops can be grown where and with what efficiency – not to mention the infrastructure and logistical demands of bringing all that far-flung biomass to

CCS facilities. One recent assessment, published in *Science*, noted that estimates of how much land would be needed to produce 12 Gt of negative emissions ranged from 0.4 to 1.2 billion hectares, which corresponds to a staggering 25–80% of all land currently devoted to raising crops and which itself accounts for about a tenth of all land on the planet.[46] To sharpen your sense of scale, consider that India has about one-third of a billion hectares of land, so we are envisioning somewhere between roughly one and four Indias devoted solely to growing biofuels – so that carbon goals can be met without giving up fossil fuels.[47] Of course, not only is this image of Biofuel Earth dubious from a purely engineering point of view, it also depends on the assumption that we can radically improve agricultural productivity so we don't starve in the process.[48]

*Other exotic carbon-removing technologies.* As futuristic as it sounds, direct air capture (DAC) plays a role in many mitigation scenarios. It makes its appearance as the 450 ppm barrier is about to be breached or even later, to bring atmospheric concentration back down to 450. Models regard it as a backstop technology, since it is likely to be expensive (no surprise) but is otherwise handy in a tight spot.[49] The view of the National Academy of Science panel that studied carbon removal in 2015 is even less optimistic, however, noting DAC facilities will be highly energy-intensive, raising the demand for even *more* low- or non-carbon energy sources. In addition, even compared with other aspirational technologies (like BE/CSS), DAC is at a very early stage of development, with no practical experience to draw on.[50]

And there are even more exotic options on the drawing board. One which caught the eye of the NAS is enhanced weathering of atmospheric or industrial $CO_2$. This is an attempt to augment the natural fixing of carbon in mineral formations, which plays an important role in the carbon cycle (Chapter 1); the extra carbonates can then be buried underground or in the deep ocean. The general idea is to increase the amount of carbon-incorporating minerals that come into contact with airborne $CO_2$, a marriage that can be consummated either terrestrially or in the ocean. This is an intriguing idea, but one obvious problem is that the natural process it mimics is extremely diffuse, spread out over the entire Earth, and difficult to engineer at human scale. Another is the potential for dangerous side effects, especially if we try to alter the chemistry of the ocean. Still another is that, at the scale required to make a dent in humanity's carbon footprint, the technology would require digging up and transporting a lot of rock, perhaps 100 billion tons per year if enhanced weathering is called on to play the main role in mitigation, compared with about 1 billion tons of crushed stone now mined in the United States annually.[51] If a massive carbon weathering operation of this sort lies in our future, we are headed for a new stone age.

*Nuclear power.* Another entire book, at least, would be needed to properly address the controversies surrounding nuclear power. I have my opinions, but I won't try to support them here. Suffice it to say that (1) most mitigation scenarios that adhere to RCP 2.6 entail massive investments in new nuclear facilities, and (2) there are serious doubts regarding the feasibility of this undertaking.

To get a sense of the scale of nuclear expansion envisioned by the modelers, consider just one scenario, admittedly on the upper end, a 2°-compliant pathway generated by the WITCH integrated assessment model.[52] It starts the policy clock in the year 2020, and in just a decade *triples* global installed capacity by over 800 gigawatts.[53] How likely is this in a world in which some countries, like Germany, are already phasing out their nuclear plants?

*Overshooting.* This is truly the dark secret of carbon mitigation modeling. We like to look at mitigation scenarios as a deck of cards splayed out with the invitation to pick one, any one of our choice. It is reassuring to think that the 450 ppm option is available even if the political will to pull it from the pile is lacking. But there is a surprise in store: most of the scenarios promising to place us at 450 ppm in 2100 take us well beyond this ostensible limit over large portions of the coming century. First they overshoot the target, then they use carbon removal technologies (negative emissions) to pull us back to it. To be clear, this pattern is not a secret to the climate modelers themselves, and there is a spirited literature in which they discuss their disquiet with it, albeit in the uninflected style of academic science. Word has not yet spread to the general public, however. For them this is likely to come as an uncomfortable surprise – it did for me.

How dependent are 2° pathways on overshooting? Nearly all of them, as the 2014 IPCC summary makes clear.[54] One comparison study, examining scenarios produced by four different IAMs, found *no* scenario adhering to a 1,000-Gt carbon budget (the "bright line" promulgated by the IPCC) was able to do so without shooting past this limit and then backtracking to it.[55] It is not an exaggeration to say that, without the possibility of overshooting, there would be almost no scenario modeling for a 2° future.

As you can imagine, the modeling community is not entirely happy about this state of affairs. An entire special issue of the journal *Climatic Change* was devoted to this topic in 2013, and several articles have appeared since then which explore the possibility of escaping the overshoot gamble while adhering to modeling protocols and climate constraints – and found it unlikely.[56] With a few exceptions they are cautious in how they describe the problem, but the attention they give it leaves no doubt it is a central issue in their professional circles.

Overshooting is a big bet in three ways. First, it assumes the technologies we'll need to achieve net negative emissions – carbon withdrawals in excess of unavoidable emissions from the continued presence of carbon in our economies – will be available when we need them. Second, it assumes that governments will be prepared to implement these technologies, no matter how economically costly, environmentally damaging or otherwise forbidding they may prove to be. And third, it assumes that temporarily higher global temperatures, triggered by above-450 ppm carbon concentrations, won't set in motion natural feedback processes that increase warming even more, thereby shutting the door behind us.

Consider the third of these. There are several feedback mechanisms that could play this frightening role, such as the loss of forest habitat or increased wildfires, but a primary suspect is the release of stored methane, from either marine (clathrates) or terrestrial permafrost deposits. Only one study has thus far examined this risk, and only for permafrost, but what it found is sobering. Andrew MacDougall wrote his doctoral dissertation on this topic and published a shortened version of it with three coauthors in 2015.[57] To understand his analysis, consider what a carbon budget means in a world with overshooting.

There are two phases to a mitigation pathway: the first, which takes us to the peak of the overshoot, and the second, which brings us back down to the finish line in 2100. Suppose that a budget of a bit over 1,000 Gt, if adhered to between now and the end of the century, would give us the hoped-for two-thirds chance of staying with 2° of warming. One way to stick to it would be to stick to it. Another way, the overshooting way, would be to exceed it and then pull excess carbon out of the atmosphere. If we chose this route, we might emit, say, 1,300 Gt between now and 2070 and depend on carbon removal technologies to bring it back down to 1,000 over the course of the following thirty years. Except 1,000 wouldn't do it any more, because the extra warming we had instigated by 2070 would have altered the global carbon cycle in such a way as to require even more emission cuts. How much more? The permafrost methane release effect that MacDougall studied would, according to his simulations, require a 40% average reduction in the carbon budget to reach the same goal of 450 ppm in 2100. In other words, in our simple example, having allowed ourselves to exceed an original 1,000 Gt budget in 2070 by 300 Gt, we would now need to withdraw 700 Gt – the 300 overshoot plus the 400 budget tightening – in the three decades from 2070 to 2100. As MacDougall and his coauthors put it, overshooting our carbon budget constraint is like borrowing and having to pay it all back with interest – but, to extend the metaphor, accepting the risk of methane releases is like borrowing from a loan shark.[58]

## The Problem of Capital

All the problems I have outlined – the dangerously optimistic assumptions about nuclear power, carbon removal technologies and the reliance on overshooting – are well understood and regularly debated in the mitigation modeling community. My only role up to now has been to call your attention to them. Nevertheless, I think the underlying methodology of the models themselves disguises a further cause for concern, their treatment of the capital stock. Except for the energy sector, capital is represented as a purely financial substance, a sum of money that can be shifted instantly and costlessly from one use to another.[59] This is convenient from a modeling standpoint, but it conceals enormous potential for economic disruption.

To begin, consider that everything our economy produces requires some sort of specific capital. To build an airplane requires an airplane factory; to build a car requires a car factory. Retail sales require stores and warehouses in particular locations accessible to the markets they serve. Everything everywhere requires an infrastructure for transportation and communication, not just in the abstract but in particular places using particular technologies to accomplish what we ask of them. The capital stock we have today is the product of hundreds of years of economic evolution. While technologies have come and gone and populations have moved across the globe, we can read this history in the specific equipment, structures and locations that make up our stock of capital if we know how to look for them. Yet throughout this long period of change and accumulation, there has been one constant, an unending availability of ever more productive and inexpensive sources of carbon energy. A visitor from some other planet would immediately notice how finely tuned our capital stock is to a world of abundant coal, oil and gas.

Going on a crash diet to largely phase out fossil energy over the course of two generations will profoundly impact the value of this capital. We will almost certainly find that we have inherited a configuration of invested wherewithal from past generations that will no longer serve our purposes in a decarbonizing world. Many goods whose value to consumers depended on fossil fuel supplies, such as all those cars and planes, will be worth less, perhaps a lot less, and it may be costly to switch the capital stock over to the production of their replacements.[60] Other productive systems will be disrupted by changing energy costs; this may prove to be the case for industrial agriculture, for instance, which depends on large energy inputs. Above all, the location patterns of the economy – where we have built our homes, stores, businesses and the roads that connect them – may be out of sync with the new energy realities. We may have the same amount of "capital" available to us in financial terms, but not in the physical form we need to meet our needs. Rebuilding the global capital stock does not appear in the IAMs, except for energy supply.

Actually, the problem is even greater than this, precisely because capital *is* financial as well as physical. It is likely that the upheaval stemming from drastically altered energy prices will trigger large capital gains and losses in specific investments.[61] This in turn raises the specter of potential defaults. With so much income shifting between different sectors of the economy and the investments they draw on, it is inevitable that many of today's financial commitments will not be met in a carbon-squeezed future. Alas, no model currently in use allows for even the possibility of default.[62]

Humanity has never experienced anything before like a radical, planned change in its energy system, so it's difficult to imagine what it might be like to live through one. Consider, however, a radical but unplanned shock to the value of productive assets that can serve as a sort of parable: the post-1989 opening of Eastern Europe to the world economy.

We remember the year 1989 mostly in political terms, as communist dictatorships crumbled and the walls that prevented the free movement of people fell. But 1989 also inaugurated a cataclysmic economic change, not all of it benign. The walls that separated people also prevented most trade in goods, shielding the Eastern Bloc from competition from the West. Prior to 1989, virtually anything that was produced in these countries could be sold, since there were widespread shortages, and consumers didn't have alternatives. Looking back on this era, we tend to make fun of the clunky goods on offer, as reflected, for instance, in a movie that was a big hit in Germany, *Goodbye Lenin*. It's about an elderly woman who remains a true-believing Communist, holed up post-1989 in her East Berlin apartment. She doesn't know her beloved regime has collapsed, and because she's also in frail health, it falls to her sons to try to shield her from the truth. There is one joke after another making fun of the shabbiness of the East, and how the dutiful children have to pretend it's really the apex of civilization. It doesn't play nearly as well in the United States, where few people know how dismal the goods of everyday life were in the Communist world.

But without warning the walls came down, and western goods flooded into the East. Instantly, the gaps in quality were apparent to everyone, and the market for domestically made products collapsed. Entire industries were revealed as having the wrong machinery and methods, the wrong designs and the wrong skills. It was as if the people of the Soviet Union and Eastern Europe woke up one morning and discovered their countries had the wrong capital stock. The result was that large parts of these economies simply shut down, leaving their former workforce unemployed. Figure 5.4 lays out the extent of the catastrophe. These were serious depressions by any measure. They resulted not from a shortage of inputs or an upsurge in costs, much less a lack of demand, but instead from the necessity to write off a large portion of the capital stock. Economic recovery set in only as new investments were made, often with foreign capital, to replace what had been lost. The two countries that suffered the least damage in this group, Hungary and Poland, had experimented with markets and competition prior to 1989, so many of their industries were somewhat competitive at the point the walls came down. They also benefited from a faster infusion of western capital, in part precisely because their economies were already partially adapted. Meanwhile, economically weak Romania had less prosperity to lose.

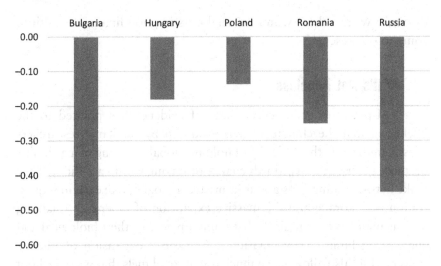

**Figure 5.4** Cumulative reduction in GDP during the 1990s. This figure displays the percentage reduction in inflation-adjusted GDP measured in local currencies from its 1989 level to the nadir of its post-1989 decline. The trough occurred in 1999 for Bulgaria, 1993 for Hungary, 1991 for Poland, 1992 for Romania and 1998 for Russia. The IMF does not report data for Russia from 1989 to 1991, so its time series is filled out with data from the World Bank's World Development Indicators. The Bank and Fund data for 1992 differ by less than 1%.
*Source*: IMF (2020).

How is this episode relevant to climate policy? The shock the no-longer-Communist countries underwent was the result of having a large portion of capital – both physical and human – that had suddenly and unexpectedly become uneconomic to operate. This is likely the situation all of us will face if there is a rapid global turn toward decarbonization at the pace required to keep warming under 2°. The assets likely to lose value are not just those directly tied to the production of fossil fuels; the third layer, structural transformation, of our three-layer model of climate mitigation points to a wide array of potential at-risk investments.

And just as there are tipping points in nature, there are tipping points in an economy. Production can continue under increasing costs and reduced profits, but only up to the point at which production itself is a losing proposition.[63] If substantial portions of existing investments, made on the basis of forecasts that do not include stringent limitations on carbon emissions, become uneconomic, we will experience something similar to what the countries of Eastern Europe went through. Worse, there won't be neighbors in good financial health to come to our rescue.

## It's Not Hopeless

Up to this point every piece of evidence has pointed to the likelihood that the climate models produced by academic researchers grossly understate the difficulty of holding global warming to a 2° limit – or, more precisely, a two-thirds chance of staying within a 2° limit. They make heroic assumptions about future technologies, like carbon sequestration and storage and the massive expansion of bioenergy (planting over as many as four Indias), that bump up against their biological and engineering limits. They envision a breakneck expansion of nuclear power, while also allowing so much use of fossil fuels that we overshoot the 450 ppm atmospheric carbon barrier and rely on negative emissions to work our way back – all the while hoping that no Earth processes like permafrost methane release are triggered that would render 450 ppm unattainable forever. Finally, the models are based on an incomplete rendering of economics, overlooking the role of dedicated capital and the financial repercussions of having to rapidly and unexpectedly replace one capital stock with another. If you were to end your climate explorations with this paragraph, you might be ready for a steady diet of antidepressants.

But here begins a new paragraph and new hope. The economic assumptions on which IAMs are based are also unduly pessimistic and rule out the potential our economies have to dramatically alter their structure: what they produce, how they produce, and how we meet our needs – the third layer of mitigation. Unfortunately, the argument for this proposition is necessarily technical, but its practical implications are enormous, so it's worth spending some time on it.

The core output of an economic model like the ones we are considering is a series of year-by-year changes in the actions of businesses, households and governments. It is expected that consumers will alter the mix of goods they buy, while firms alter the mix of inputs they use, and governments as well make changes in their role as both producers and consumers. The key instigator of all this change is movement in relative prices: as some goods become more expensive relative to others, people buy less of them and more of the now-cheaper things. The responsiveness of a change in demand to changes in relative prices is called its *price elasticity*. We expect that the amount of something people will buy is negatively related to its price, but elasticity tells us by how much.

There is no single elasticity for everything in a modern, complex economy, nor should it be assumed that elasticities will remain constant over time and changes in context. Economic models, however, cannot be so detailed. The IAMs we have surveyed all aggregate the economy into just a few sectors and apply a single elasticity to changes in composition between each of them. The only exception is energy, where different energy sources are broken out, their prices noted, and a range of elasticities used to predict how price changes will alter the energy mix. Since the whole point of such models is to trace out paths of substitution in energy supply and end use, the key step is to specify the elasticities. When possible these are taken from empirical evidence; when not they are just postulated.

I don't want to second-guess the elasticity choices built into these models. What should be questioned, however, is the deeper assumption that economic change occurs item by item, each according to a fixed responsiveness to price shifts.[64] This is easier to tell in the form of a story than in the abstract, so imagine we are in a simple world that allows only substitution between travel and music lessons: people can spend their money either on going from one place to another or on learning how to play instruments and forming music groups. Of course, life can't be all one or the other, so people spend some money on each, and they begin with a particular mix. Since travel is more carbon-intensive than music, this is also a story about mitigating climate change.

Now consider how an IAM mitigation scenario might generate changes in spending patterns. As carbon prices go up, the ratio of transportation to music costs goes up as well. The elasticity parameter plugged into the model determines how the change in the price ratio will translate into a corresponding, opposite-direction change in the consumption mix: less travel, more music. The process is tracked over the first year, the second, and every succeeding year until the finish line is reached in 2100. In each time period it is essentially the same: a percent change in prices gives us a percent change in spending choices. It is this structure that makes mitigating climate change intrinsically so difficult, for only ever-increasing prices (and shifts to ever-more-expensive energy sources) can produce ever-decreasing fossil fuel use and carbon emissions.

Behind the mathematical structure of this hypothetical IAM lies an implicit view of how economies function, based on isolated individuals making isolated choices. With a given shift in the price ratio the elasticity parameter tells us what proportion of these individuals will trade in their car for a piano or a synthesizer system, and if the model's target requires more people to make the switch year after year, the price must go up again and again and again. It's as if all the people in this economy were lined up according to their preferences for driving versus jamming, and as the price ratio marches steadily toward more expensive transportation, one after another they leave the first camp for the second.

There is a different view of economic life, however, in which what people want is not just an unchanging reflection of their unique, fixed preferences but also changes depending on what other people want and are doing to get it. A society in which travel by car has become very expensive will see dramatic changes in land use patterns: new, denser cities with closer links between work, home, shopping and recreation, and also more mass transit options – more Tokyo and less Denver.[65] Similarly, a society can make a collective decision to promote musicianship, as Finland has, and the greater prominence of music in everyday life can alter individual preferences in that domain as well.[66]

The general argument is that much as a river can jump channel when a critical mass of groundwater flows have shifted, an economy can make a relatively abrupt shift to a different pattern of production and consumption as the choices made by separate individuals and organizations react on one another. If there are indeed tipping points in social change, as there almost certainly are, we don't have to depend on an eternity of ever-rising prices and more costly substitutions to arrive at a sustainable way of life. Of course, pointing to the general possibility of such a transformation is not the same as demonstrating when and how it might take place, but it should give us at least some cause to believe that our prospects are not as dim as we might otherwise conclude from our study of mitigation modeling.[67]

While it would be a mistake to specify an alternative, decarbonized economy in detail, the type of shift it would embody can be described in a general way. In affluent countries it would incorporate, in addition to the altered location patterns sketched above, more leisure and less work, more personal services, and above all a greater role (and share of income) for craft and design embedded in the products people buy. All of this will tend to lower carbon emissions, and if goods last longer and are valued for their quality there would also be less need to discard them and the materials used in their production. A transition to this sort of redefinition of affluence would require a change in expectations and social norms as well as worker skills, and in that sense is subject to the clustering dynamics sketched above. We often bemoan our conformist tendencies, but sometimes an element of herd response is a good thing.

In poorer countries the conflict between improving the quality of life and suppressing carbon emissions will be more difficult to manage, but there is also a benefit from delayed commitment to fossil-fueled affluence: the possibility to leapfrog this technological byway and move directly into a cleaner future.[68] This too implies a clustered response to technological and social change.

In the face of a century-long agony of taxing ourselves, bit by bit, into a fully decarbonized economy, the notion of a systemic shift in this direction is our main source of hope. We need to keep it clearly in mind even though it is ruled out by the assumptions of the mitigation modelers. Of course, it is exactly the potential for rapid structural transformation that also makes the potential for capital losses so large.

## Why Honesty about Cost Matters

We sometimes lie in a good cause. "You look fabulous!" "That's a wonderful idea; we'll consider it closely." "Hold still, this will hardly hurt at all." Why not shade the truth a bit in the name of climate sanity? Perhaps staying under 2° will be expensive – a lot more expensive than the headline predictions let on. But we don't know for sure, do we? Maybe new technology will make it easy, maybe not. Since it's all a big unknown, why not just tell people it's not a serious problem so we can get policy out of the starting blocks? Later on, if it looks like the costs will be big, we can adjust our story.

I think minimizing the question of costs – the problem of wishful thinking flagged in the Introduction – is a big mistake for three reasons. First, it's not convincing. Second, by anticipating the costs we can make them somewhat smaller and more manageable. Third, it obscures the political economy dimension of the policy conundrum. I'll take them one at a time.

*Not convincing.* For most people, the notion that we can largely eliminate fossil fuels from our lives within a few decades, beginning immediately, and that this will have minimal economic impact, is implausible. They are aware of the general context presented at the beginning of this chapter and may also remember how much disruption the oil price spikes of the 1970s delivered, even though our consumption of that fuel hardly disappeared as a result. If the costs of decarbonization are being soft-pedaled for political expediency, it's not a good strategy. It will likely have the opposite effect, reducing the trust many of our potential allies have in climate advocacy.

*Not precautionary.* The biggest single difference between the economic collapse experienced in 1989 by countries transitioning out of communism and the difficulties all of us face in transitioning from fossil fuels is that our problems are largely predictable. Imagine the public in Eastern Europe knew in advance 1989 was on the way, rendering much of their capital stock obsolete. Seeing it coming, they could have prepared. Public enterprises might have brought in western partners prior to 1989 to begin making changes to design and product quality, and efforts could have been accelerated to incubate new industries. At a minimum, safety net programs could have been beefed up so families thrown into unemployment would be able to tide themselves over until new jobs could be created. Much of the post-1989 cost could have been avoidable or at least managed a lot better. Of course, the fall of communism was not foreseen, and no preparations were made.

We're in a much better position today. Stringent climate policy is very likely to be imposed; in fact, one of the purposes of books like this is to convince you that it's urgent to decarbonize as quickly as possible. We know such a policy, if it's going to be effective, will have the primary objective of keeping most fossil fuel reserves in the ground. This will mean much less availability and far higher prices for the energy we do continue to use. The vulnerability of each participant in our economy – each individual, organization or business – can be studied and assessed. Action can be taken ahead of time to reduce the impact. We can strengthen the firewalls that protect the overall economy from the coming carbon crunch and plan the investments that will allow the economy to flourish even as fossil fuels are phased out. The costs of decarbonization are not written in stone, but to shrink them we have to face them honestly.

In the next chapter, I will discuss at somewhat greater length the forms that adaptation to climate policy can take. Here I want to put in a plea for economists to shift their focus from the futile and unproductive task of calculating the social cost of carbon to the crucial one of anticipating and minimizing the costs of transition. What we need are studies of capital stock vulnerability, as well as potential bottlenecks where the timetable for phasing out fossil fuels moves faster than the introduction of substitutes and alternatives. We can see immense challenges on the horizon; why aren't we getting ready?

*Political economy.* The single most important fact about the world's response to the climate crisis is that it has barely begun. There has been immense resistance to taking decisive action, and that can only be due to perceptions of the cost. This in turn means that understanding these costs – measuring them as precisely as possible and, above all, examining who will be paying them – is the key to unlocking the frozen political process. This will be taken up in the final chapter of this book, but the analysis begins with an honest, unblinking look at how large these costs are likely to be.

# 6  THE CARBON POLICY TOOLKIT

If climate change had a single moment when it burst into public consciousness and political controversy, it was probably the appearance of James Hansen, then director of NASA's Institute for Space Studies, and two other scientists before a US Senate committee on June 23, 1988. Washington, DC, was in the grips of a heat wave, and Hansen told the senators, "Global warming has reached a level such that we can ascribe with a high degree of confidence a cause and effect relationship between the greenhouse effect and observed warming. It is already happening now." Hansen's testimony received front-page treatment in the *New York Times*, whose headline announced, "Global Warming Has Begun, Expert Tells Senate."[1]

But the following day the paper's top stories were about exchange rates, the crack cocaine epidemic and presidential candidate George Bush's pledge to not raise taxes. Climate change had been portrayed as an urgent crisis one day and practically disappeared the next, setting a pattern that would continue for decades.

It is now more than thirty years later, and we are still waiting for policy to rise to the challenge. During this time many people have become frustrated, turning their attention away from politics to what they can do on their own without waiting for the government to step up. I share their frustration and believe the many independent initiatives taken by activists, companies, organizations and individuals are not only well intentioned but may even have made a small contribution to reducing emissions. It's crucial to recognize, however, that these dispersed efforts cannot possibly be sufficient to achieve the scale and scope of decarbonization we need to accomplish within a time frame sufficient to meet the 2° maximum. To limit recommendations to measures that can be taken one person at a time is to succumb to the individualist illusion described in the Introduction to this book. As difficult as it is to unfreeze the political process, there is no substitute for it.

One sure nonsubstitute is voluntary renunciation of fossil fuels at either the individual or community level. I wouldn't mention this except that it is often presented as the most "militant" solution to climate change by some activists.[2] According to this view, agitating for laws to phase out coal, gas and oil is a distraction from the real job, shutting them down altogether in whatever location we find ourselves. While the sentiment of taking direct personal responsibility is admirable, the strategy is hopeless. As a matter of simple fact, an immediate cessation of all fossil energy production, the cold turkey approach, is impossible, and if some locales ban the production of these fuels while others don't, the carbon-producers can supply most or all of the fuels the carbon-banners have disowned. There will even be a strong incentive for them to do this: because the action of some activists will make fossil fuels more scarce (the whole point, right?), remaining supplies will become more valuable, increasing the financial return to those who continue to produce them.

The logic of keeping an increasing portion of carbon energy supplies underground, unexploited, implies exactly the opposite approach: not voluntary renunciation but laws against their development, rigorously enforced on everyone. Penalties need to have real bite. Society tolerates a certain amount of illegal alcohol and cigarette smuggling, for instance, which have emerged in response to relatively moderate taxes; it can't afford to allow a contraband trade in fossil fuels to defeat the much heavier taxes or other controls we need to keep them out of the carbon cycle. The road to a stable climate leads, like it or not, through the enforcement power of the state.[3]

But what kind of government action are we considering? That's the topic of this chapter, and its premise is that there is no substitute for establishing a price – a stiff price – on carbon. This too brings us into dispute with some activists, who think that "markets" are the cause of the climate problem and therefore can't be used to solve it.[4] Why not just control fossil fuel use directly, for example, using rationing coupons as the main combatants did in World War II? Wouldn't that be fairer and more certain?

But wartime economic controls are not a good model for the kind of program we want to live with for the next century. As we saw in Chapter 3, the direct and indirect carbon content of the millions of goods we consume is beyond calculation – for one thing, it changes from time to time and place to place – and the consequences of personal and business decisions for their ultimate carbon impacts are impossible to trace. And even if it were possible, would we want the degree of government control over our day-to-day life rationing entails? Fossil fuel use is the result of a myriad of choices we make each day in everything we do, and government regulation of the entire spectrum of them would be totalitarian and stultifying. The advantage of using some form of carbon pricing is that it steers decisions toward reduced fossil fuel use while allowing each of us, at each moment, to determine for ourselves where to make the deepest cuts. It encourages decarbonization at each level of use and each moment in time, rather than setting a floor below which further cuts are unrewarded. It also rewards those who find new ways to meet the needs of society that use even less of the now more expensive energy sources.

The day we know we have a serious climate policy is the day we have a serious carbon price, but this doesn't tell us whether the price is the policy or only its result. The confusion over this issue is immense, and before we can do anything else we have to confront it.

## A Fork in the Road: Taxes and Permits

To stay within a carbon budget, we need to make fossil fuels ever more scarce, year after year. Items that become more scarce become more expensive, but cause and effect can work in either direction. We can put a tax on these fuels to discourage their production and use, or we can curtail their supply directly, and the resulting scarcity will drive up their price. The first approach, carbon taxes, is somewhat more market-based; the second, which operates through a system of carbon permits, has a stronger element of direct control.[5] In some ways they are similar, in others quite different.

A carbon tax is a per unit tax on carbon energy levied by the government. Such a tax is typically proposed according to a tonne of carbon dioxide, with the amount per unit of fuel determined by each fuel's carbon intensity. It can be applied at any stage, from the original extraction or importation of the fuel to its end use. A familiar example is the tax levied on gasoline in all developed countries. Although many justifications have been provided for it, it is also a carbon tax, although it is applied to only one fuel source, petroleum. It generates income for the government and financially penalizes us for each gallon of gas we burn. In principle, the tax could be imposed higher up the supply chain, for instance, at oil refineries. If it were applied only to fuels eventually destined for gas stations, the result would be approximately the same: its cost would be passed along, more or less, to drivers, who would continue to see a higher price at the pump.[6]

A gas tax is not a very effective carbon tax, however, because it doesn't cover the majority of fossil fuel uses in the economy. This can lead to significant misincentives. For instance, a higher gas tax encourages more drivers to switch to electric vehicles, but the fossil fuels, especially coal, used to generate the electricity that powers them are not taxed. This makes electric vehicles seem much less environmentally demanding to operate compared to cars with internal combustion engines than they actually are. An effective carbon tax would cover all carbon fuel sources in all uses, and of course also carbon emissions from nonenergy sources.

The alternative is to require a permit for any introduction of new carbon into the economy, with the proviso that the total number of permits issued is capped. The core idea is the one we see in hunting or fishing permits. If the public were free to fish as much as they want, the result would be overfishing and the depletion of the fish population. (This, of course, is the reality for many commercial species in international waters.) To prevent this, the government can require anyone catching fish to have a permit, with its biologists determining the number of permits consistent with sustainability. Carbon permits work the same way. Applied at the top of the supply chain, for instance, it would mean that companies would need permits for all the fossil fuels they intend to extract or import, and by limiting the number of the permits we would be limiting the resulting carbon emissions. Permits essentially make the extraction of fossil fuels illegal, but not all at once.

Such systems are often, misleadingly, referred to as cap-and-trade. The trading of permits can be an important part of the design, but it doesn't have to be. For fishing permits, to continue the example, whether trading is allowed is secondary. Should people who have fishing permits but don't need them be allowed to sell them to people who want them but don't have them? In general, I'd say the answer should be yes in the interest of flexibility, but it is not a make-or-break question. Similarly with carbon permits, if an energy company acquires permits to supply a certain amount of coal, oil or gas but changes its plans, should it be allowed to sell them to another company that wants to increase its supply? Again I would say yes and for the same reason, but it is the permit requirement and the cap on how many are issued and not the trading arrangement that primarily determines how much carbon is emitted. Later we will see that the importance of trading in real-world permit systems arises because of damaging loopholes inserted into them, not because of any inherent logic in the approach.

So where does the carbon price come from in a permit system? Since fewer permits are issued than people want – that's why it's effective – permits are valuable. Let's be specific: suppose we establish a carbon permit system that restricts the availability of fossil fuels. Since supply has been constrained, the price will go up; we will all have to pay more, just as consumers did when the supply of petroleum was restricted in the 1970s by the Organization of Petroleum Exporting Countries (OPEC). Companies that have permits to put these fuels on the market will take in more revenue per unit of energy. The permits that allow them to collect this money are valuable to the extent of the price increase they make possible. That raises the question of how much the permits will cost, and this is an absolutely crucial design choice. Carbon will have a price, but who pays and who benefits?

If the government gives away the permits for free, companies that acquire them are being handed a license to rake in super-high profits (referred to by economists as rents). Do I have to add that, whenever the topic of carbon permits comes up, business interests argue that it is absolutely essential for many reasons, which they creatively devise, for all or most permits to be free? They swear on a stack of economics textbooks, which contradict them at every turn, that they will never, ever raise prices for consumers, and then of course they do. Any permit that gives its holders the opportunity to benefit from a regulated shortage, whether it's a taxi medallion, a liquor license, or a carbon certificate, will be valuable in exactly the same way. The logical implication is that the government should *auction* the permits to the highest bidder; that way the permit buyers transfer to the government the super-profits they would otherwise capture from consumers. The price that emerges from such an auction will reflect this extra scarcity value that consumers can be charged – and that's the carbon price.

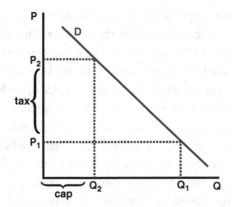

Figure 6.1 Carbon taxes and permits under demand certainty.

In a nutshell, from this very abstract vantage point, taxes and permits are like mirror reflections of each other. A tax sets a price for carbon and allows the market to determine the amount of carbon emissions that ensue, while a permit system fixes the amount of carbon emissions and allows the market to set the price on the basis of this policy-imposed scarcity. Figure 6.1 can be found in almost any introductory economics textbook; it presents this fundamental logic in the form of geometry.[7]

On the horizontal axis is the amount Q of some sort of pollution that could be emitted; here it's measured in tonnes of the carbon dioxide emitted when a corresponding quantity of fossil fuels is burned. On the vertical axis is the price P of this pollution. The straight line labeled D is a demand curve, which represents the relationship between the price and quantity. It's downward-sloping under the assumption that, the less expensive something is, the more of it people will want to buy; or, conversely, the more scarce something is, the higher the willingness to pay of those who outbid others for the privilege of acquiring it.

The diagram requires a bit of interpretation, since it's reflecting the price and quantity of two different things – the carbon emissions and the fuels that incorporate these emissions. It may help to think of more Q meaning more carbon emissions *and* more fossil fuel use, while higher P means a higher price placed on carbon emissions *and* on fossil fuels. Strictly speaking, we might demand multiple diagrams, one for the emissions and the others for each of the various fuels, but, since the logic is the same in each case, we can leave out the detailed labels and use one bit of geometry to represent everything.

So back to Figure 6.1. Suppose we start out at an initial situation in which emissions are very high at $Q_1$, while the price paid for them is very low at $P_1$. In fact, in most of the world the price of carbon emissions is at or near zero. If we want to reduce emissions to the level of $Q_2$ we have two options. One is to impose a tax that raises the price of carbon to $P_2$. According to the demand curve D, raising the cost of fossil fuels would reduce the amount of fuel use such that emissions would fall to $Q_2$. The tax that accomplishes this is measured vertically as the difference between the initial price $P_1$ and the new, post-tax price $P_2$. Mission accomplished!

The other way to do the job is to institute a permit system for emissions and limit their number to $Q_2$. By making carbon, and therefore carbon fuels, scarce, this makes permits valuable. Based on the same demand curve D we can determine that the value per permit is $P_2 - P_1$, the amount the price is raised due to the restriction imposed by the permit cap. This value could show up in one of two ways. If the permits are given out for free, this is the extra amount those who have them can charge for the fossil fuels that generate these emissions: since oil, gas and coal have become scarce, permit holders can raise prices, just as oil companies do today when petroleum becomes scarce for one reason or another. If the permits are auctioned, however, the difference between $P_2$ and $P_1$ is the maximum amount that energy companies would bid for them, the amount returned to them in the form of higher prices for the energy they sell. The full scarcity value of permits equals the auction price if the auction market is competitive, which would have to be monitored, of course. Another mission accomplished!

The point is that, according to this model, it really doesn't matter which approach we use. Either a carbon tax or a corresponding system of carbon permits – if they are auctioned – will give us exactly the same result. If we prefer taxes, we can raise the price to $P_2$. If we prefer permits, we can set the cap at $Q_2$, but either way we will end up with $P_2$ *and* $Q_2$. In this hypothetical world any debate between tax and permit adherents is essentially a waste of time. In fact, economists are often bemused by the intensity of this debate in policy circles, since they tend to see Figure 6.1 as an approximately accurate portrayal of the real-world situation.

## But Taxes and Permits *Are* Different, and It Matters

As soon as we begin to drop the extreme assumptions on which our first diagram is based, there is a parting of the ways between taxes and permits. Perhaps the most important element of realism is to pivot from a fixed, known demand curve to an economic environment of uncertainty. The treatment of uncertainty in this context was pioneered by Martin Weitzman, who also appears in the Appendix as the author of the "dismal theorem" that the costs of climate change can be unbounded. Here he speaks to us about the difference between price instruments like taxes and quantity instruments like permits when the relationship between price and quantity is not altogether known.[8]

Let's rerun the analysis above, but now with the proviso that, while we know the price ($P_I$) and quantity ($Q_I$) of carbon in the initial situation, the further from it we go, the wider our margin of uncertainty about where the demand curve should be drawn. To avoid clutter, we will consider the matter twice, first from the vantage point of a carbon tax, and then from that of a permit system (see Figure 6.2). Demand, instead of being a simple line, is now a cone, widening as it goes outward from the known starting point of $Q_I$ and $P_I$.

By the time we get to the post-tax price $P_2$, the uncertainty about quantity ranges from the low to the high level indicated by the bracket. Maybe at that price, demand for burning carbon will be choked off, and the quantity used in the economy will be at the leftward end, or maybe the higher price will have less effect, and the economy will situate itself at the rightward end, or perhaps somewhere in between. The logic is simple when you think about it: by fixing the price at a given level with a tax, we are allowing the quantity used to fluctuate based on the (partially) unpredictable effect of that price hike.

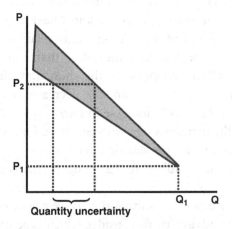

Figure 6.2 Carbon taxes under demand uncertainty.

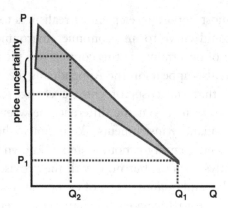

Figure 6.3 A cap on permits under demand uncertainty.

The comparison to a quantity approach like permits is revealing, as shown in Figure 6.3. Now the shoe is on the other foot. The demand relationship is the same as before, with a known starting point and greater uncertainty radiating outward, but now the policy is to set carbon emissions at $Q_2$ and let the price find its own level. This creates a zone of uncertainty about price effects; the cost of carbon could be at the bottom end of the bracket, the top end, or somewhere in between. The underlying logic is that, by fixing the quantity with a permit cap, it is now the price that is free to fluctuate with (partially) unpredictable economic forces.

How large are these potential brackets on the quantity or price sides? In other words, how much or little do we know about the way the economy will process very large reductions in allowable emissions or increases in carbon prices? The answer is that we know next to nothing at all. We have a fairly good idea of the price–quantity relationship in recent historical experience, for instance, the effect that rising and falling oil prices have on oil consumption in the short and medium run. A decent rule of thumb is that for an x% decrease in energy consumption there needs to be a 2x% increase in energy prices.[9] This applies to supply or price fluctuations we have experienced for a variety of reasons, but none approximates the drastic interventions in carbon energy we would have to make to adhere to a 2° budget. That is simply an unknown territory.[10]

When economic uncertainty is substantial, as we can be certain it is, Weitzman's approach advises us to consider which type of variability we would rather accept. If we go with taxes, we know the price of carbon, but we don't know if we'll come over or under budget. If we go with permits, we know how much carbon we'll emit – it's right there in the cap – but we won't know how much individuals and businesses will have to pay to use fossil fuels. There are also hybrid systems, such as permit arrangements that adjust the cap to stay within a given carbon price range, so it's not all or nothing, but there remains a fundamental decision to be made about what worries us most. If you are like me, what scares you more than anything else is the prospect of alligators in the Arctic. You will be willing to put up with a lot of price uncertainty if the result is that we can be sure we are adhering to a carbon budget. Businesses, in general, are more terrified of the unpredictability of carbon prices under a pure permit system. They want to be able to plan ahead, especially since their investments are often irreversible over multiyear time frames.

This is a trade-off we will return to in the final chapter. For now, be aware that opting for a hybrid does not resolve the question, because, whatever the combination of price and quantity instruments, the trade-off remains. We can always shift to more quantity certainty at the cost of more price uncertainty and vice versa. I believe, however, that the supreme urgency of forestalling catastrophic climate change indicates that the primary tool of policy should be quantitative, requiring permits for fossil fuel extraction or importation, limiting the number of permits, and auctioning them off. This commitment can perhaps be modified a bit, while keeping an eye on the atmospheric carbon meter. The political economy of modification and adjustment is an important topic in Chapter 8.

It's worth pausing for a moment to consider the political ramifications of the case for carbon permits in an uncertain world. It has become common for the most militant and leftward wing of the environmental movement to denounce permit systems and demand taxes. In her first book on the climate movement, *This Changes Everything: Capitalism versus the Climate*, for instance, Naomi Klein denounces reliance on markets, commodification of nature and giving in to the demands of business – and then endorses a carbon tax as a centerpiece of climate policy.[11] This is surprising, since a tax works its effects through markets by commodifying carbon emissions; it is a "capitalist" approach par excellence. Moreover, as we have seen, it prioritizes business's need to stabilize prices over the competing ecological need to stabilize emissions.

Perhaps the explanation for the bias of Klein and others lies in the compromised design of existing permit arrangements, which compare poorly to an idealized tax. Tax proponents, however, should pay attention to the reality of other types of taxes in modern economies: tax codes normally make for grim reading by anyone but tax avoidance professionals. Another possible reason for the view that taxes are more "radical" is that the very word "tax" has an antagonistic connotation: if something is bad, we should tax it. Meanwhile, words like "permit" and "allowance" seem to connote approval, suggesting carbon emissions are okay. But this is all just semantics. As we have seen, from the standpoint of what they actually do, permits apply stricter control over emissions than taxes do.

But there is another, even more fundamental critique to be made of the tax-and-cap-equivalence story portrayed in Figure 6.1: a stable demand curve for something as fundamental and interconnected with the rest of the economy as fossil fuels doesn't exist. The line labeled "D" in Figure 6.1 is illegitimate. The reason for this is that any such line, even one we don't have enough information about and therefore lies in a zone of uncertainty (Figures 6.2 and 6.3), depends on a set of background assumptions that often go unmentioned. When we imagine a demand curve, we are supposing there exists a stable, predictable relationship between the price of some good (like fossil carbon) and the amount of it that will be demanded. Any such relationship requires that we assume that other factors in the economy – the prices and availability of all the other goods and services – be held constant; this is referred to as the "ceteris paribus" (things being equal) assumption and marks the demand curve as a figment of what economists call partial equilibrium analysis.

Consider what this means in our case. We are supposing that if the price of fossil carbon rises by a given amount, the demand for it will fall correspondingly. That's the interpretation of saying we go from a situation like $P_1$ and $Q_1$ to another like $P_2$ and $Q_2$. Such predictions can be made only by isolating just this one piece of the economy and making the assumption, at least temporarily, that nothing else is changing in a way that would interfere with the relationship summarized by "D." For relatively small price or quantity shifts in relatively peripheral markets, that's a reasonable assumption to make. If there were a revolution in the production or availability of toothbrushes, it's likely that the rest of the economic universe would proceed on its way with little alteration, so it makes sense to study the toothbrush market in isolation.

This is not true with fossil fuels! When the political will materializes to put our societies on a strict carbon diet, and when the price of fossil energy rises to unprecedented levels, it will affect everything else we do. It will change the design of and demand for a large portion of the goods we consume, alter decisions about where to live and work, and many other aspects about our lives it is difficult to predict in advance. Here you may notice I am making the same argument about "clustered," or interdependent, dynamics I made in the previous chapter – our glimmer of hope in an otherwise discouraging world of mitigation modeling.

The channels through which this will happen are both human and technical. On the technical side are all the relationships between energy and other goods – how energy costs affect choices in building design, agricultural practices and anything else you might think of, and how those choices in turn affect demand-driven energy costs. On the social side, what we want and how we pursue these wants are a function of what others want and how they pursue it. Consider again a fairly obvious example, personal transportation, mentioned briefly in the previous chapter. As the price of energy rises, people will drive less. Rather than make a car trip for food shopping twice a week, some people will consolidate to get by on one trip, as many have during the pandemic. More commuters might carpool rather than go to work as solo drivers. This is a well-known response, one we've seen in past episodes of oil price rises, and we have a statistical basis for making rough estimates of it.

But suppose prices rise well beyond the level they have in the past, and there is confidence that climate policy will see to it that fossil fuels become ever scarcer. It is likely that the entire configuration of land use and the geography of where people live, work and obtain services would change. There would likely be a new desire for mass transit systems and for infrastructure that supports bicyclists and pedestrians. Since what one person wants – the costs and benefits of various location and transportation options – depends on what others do as well, the entire system could "jump" to a new pattern. These considerations, which are speculative but not unreasonable, profoundly violate the notion of ceteris paribus (holding the rest of the world constant) that gives us permission to draw a line like "D" in Figure 6.1.

You might think this is simply a matter of the passage of time; after a few years the economic ramifications of a strong climate policy would cause markets to shift around. In a sense, this is true, since all events take place over time, and the world will be a different place after a few years of policy, as it would also be without policy. But the point of the previous paragraph would hold even if time were held still. The way to see that is to do a thought experiment about planning. Suppose you could ask each person what changes they would make in their lifestyle, and each business in their operations, if the price of oil, for instance, were $40 per gallon ($10 per liter). Each would tell you, and then you would tell everyone what everyone else had said and ask them to revise their plan. You would then share these revisions, get new plans and so on until the revisions became too small to matter. This is what is referred to in economics by the term "general equilibrium." If the number of revisions is not infinite, which is the same as saying that the revisions get smaller with each round, the equilibrium is stable.

But an important question is whether there is just one such equilibrium – one pattern of living and working, production and consumption – associated with each hypothetical oil price. In short, the answer is no, and figuring this out is one of the major achievements in economics over the past several decades. There are many reasons for this conclusion, but one is that the interactions between all the individual decisions people are called on to make allow multiple patterns to emerge. Where there are multiple equilibria, there is the potential for tipping points that send the economy on one path rather than another, and as we raise energy prices it is plausible – predictable, even – that such tipping points will arise.[12]

This view of deep economic, social and technical interconnection, multiple potential outcomes and discontinuous tipping points suggests that the simple, stable pattern represented by the demand curve in Figure 6.1 is misleading. Yes, the pattern likely holds for small changes in energy prices, but as we move further away from the current situation in the direction of prices higher than anything we've ever seen, there is no basis for expecting any regular pattern within energy markets in isolation. This has important implications for the merits of taxes versus permits. Suppose, to take a simple but entirely likely example, that much higher energy prices instigate a widespread shift away from cars and toward public transit, accompanied by a resurgence of urban density.[13] By changing from one pattern to another, consumers would reduce their demand for gasoline not just for the price at the tipping point but for a range of prices below and above it. In effect, their

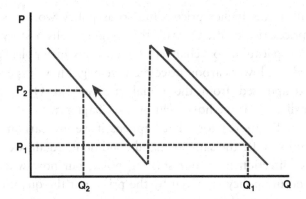

**Figure 6.4** Carbon permits with a discontinuous jump in the demand for fossil fuels.

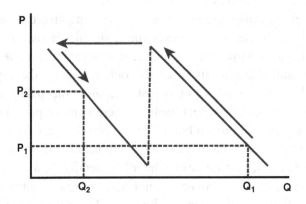

**Figure 6.5** Carbon taxes with a discontinuous jump in the demand for fossil fuels.

demand curve would have jumped – the river metaphor again! – as depicted in Figures 6.4 and 6.5, first for permits and then for taxes.

Here we imagine that, beginning with a high initial energy use at $Q_1$ policy systematically restricts supply. The arrow pointing up and to the left indicates the direction the economy will move as policy takes hold: progressively less fossil fuel availability and higher carbon prices. At some price tipping point, myriad interconnected decisions in the economy are triggered, and there is now less demand for fossil energy at any price. A new demand relationship is established on the left side of the diagram, causing a substantial price drop, even at the much lower level of energy availability. But along this new relationship less availability still means higher prices, and so as policy works its way down to $Q_2$ prices rise to $P_2$. Overall, this diagram tells a story of a reduced permit cap leading to a changed economy in which policy goals can be achieved at a lower carbon price than we might have expected if we simply extrapolated from the initial situation at $Q_1$ and $P_1$. Diagrammatically, this is the hope held out in Chapter 5.

Now see Figure 6.5 for what happens if we use carbon taxes instead of permits under the same demand conditions. Again we move in a northwest direction from our starting point, but now when the tipping point occurs policy is driven by the price, not the quantity. At that price the economy shifts to an extremely low demand for fossil fuels, well below the target of $Q_2$. To undo this excessive, and perhaps very painful, tightening, carbon taxes will need to be reduced, leading ultimately to the destination of $Q_2$ and $P_2$.

To sum up, both approaches get to the same target price and quantity but by different routes. Taxes run a significant risk of over-shooting, applying the same price medicine, at least initially, to the new, post-jump demand relationship as to the old. Adjusting the cap on permits, on the other hand, can't overshoot, since the policy being adjusted is the number of permits itself.[14] There is more price fluctuation under the permit approach but a better controlled path for energy supply. This illustrates a more general phenomenon about multiple equilibrium situations, that quantity controls generally do a better job of managing the transition between equilibria than price controls, but that takes us well beyond the scope of this book. In the context of fossil fuels the story is easy to understand. Pushing the public to a new configuration of energy use by relying on prices runs the risk that once the configuration has changed the price will be much too high, exacerbating the impacts of policy. If quantitative controls, using a permit approach, are employed instead, the quantity of fossil fuels used in the economy will be whatever we determine it to be.

There is one more difference between taxes and permits that has little to do with economics but a lot to do with politics and culture. Up to this point I have simplified the problem of carbon policy. In the above diagrams the goal is to get to a particular, known-in-advance level of carbon emissions, $Q_2$. In Chapter 3 I simplified by signing on to a plausible carbon dioxide budget, which I then translated into an equal annual percentage cut in emissions. By waving away complications it's easier to focus on the central issues. In real life, however, the objectives are not nearly so clear. There are multiple views on what the appropriate carbon budget should be, and new information will continue to change how we think about this. It might be desirable to start a bit slower on decarbonization and then pick up speed, or perhaps we should try to front-load as many of the reductions as we can and then slow down when we get to the really difficult choices. Whatever else we may think about carbon policy, we can be sure it will be an arena of ongoing debate. Where taxes and permits differ is on the *terms* of this debate.

Opting for a tax approach to decarbonization invokes the discourse of taxation. Future policy alternatives will be couched in the language of how much to tax and what the appropriate carbon price should be. Some will argue that prices are already too high and taxes should be cut, others that prices need to be still higher. Adopting a tax as your primary instrument puts you in this world. If we choose to rely on permits, on the other hand, we will have a discourse centered on amounts of carbon released into the atmosphere. On one side will be those who think we can get away with burning more, on the other those who say we need to burn less. For many economists, I suspect this is a reason to go for taxes; they believe policy should be calibrated according to the social cost of carbon, which translates into thinking in terms of prices. For those who see the policy imperative in ecological terms, however, a debate that centers on gigatonnes of carbon is the better choice. In addition, we might want to consider the resonance that "taxation" has, at least in the English-speaking world, compared with something like "allowable permits." The decision of whether to adopt a tax- or permit-based approach is politically fateful, and serious thought should be given to its consequences.

## Exemptions, Handouts and Offsets: The Art of Policy Failure

It would be much too simple and effective to have a general price on carbon, from either a carbon tax or a permit system, to dial up the price over time to adhere to the necessary budget constraint, and to let individuals and businesses figure out solutions for a less carbonized life. No, that would be too easy. Instead, programs to reduce carbon emissions have been fantastically complicated, a tangle of loopholes and special procedures that supposedly fine-tune policy before it ever reaches the public. Very generally, there are three kinds of outs that can be written into law by lobbyists with special interests to defend. The first is exemptions, carving out a portion of the economy so it won't be covered under climate rules. The second is handouts, allowing favored businesses to dodge the carbon price. The third is offsets, releasing businesses from their obligations under carbon policy in return for their cooperation with some favored activity.

*Exemptions.* In essence, this is "carbon permits or taxes for thee but not for me." Businesses claim they are too important or vulnerable or intrinsically virtuous to be held accountable under carbon policy. Maybe they are defense-related. Or critical to international competitiveness. Or operating with low profit margins on the verge of being tipped into insolvency. Or maybe they have a sterling track record on climate issues going back many years, and this absolves them from the need to pay taxes or hold permits in the present. When legislation is being debated, business associations inundate lawmakers with arguments of this sort, backed up by the clout of their owners, workers or customers. There's always a reason, and almost any reason can be reason enough. In practice, no system of emissions reduction has universal coverage, and some cover only a small portion of the emissions they are ostensibly placing under control.

The most egregious form of exemptions occurs when carbon policy is applied downstream. In this metaphor, the movement of carbon through the economy is pictured as a river flowing from its source in the wells and mines where carbon energy is extracted, through industries that process it and use it as inputs into production, and ultimately arriving at the end consumer. The further upstream the regulation occurs, the more comprehensive it is and the more leeway is given to the economy to adapt to it. The ideal point of implementation is where carbon enters the economy, from either its extraction from the earth or its importation. This is going to be the simplest level for monitoring and enforcing the policy, since there are relatively few entry points to keep track of.[15] It is comprehensive, since it includes all fossil energy used downstream, for whatever purpose. It removes the temptation for legislators to pick among more or less favored sectors of the economy because decarbonization has already taken place before energy products are delivered to their various users. Upstream is best.

But business lobbyists hate upstream control for all these reasons. They *want* legislators to be able to grant or withhold favors so they can have targets for their ample powers of persuasion. And legislators want the freedom to pick and choose for the same reasons. As a result, everywhere there is a carbon tax or permit system in effect it is at least somewhat downstream in its implementation.

Unfortunately, there is a current within the environmental movement that also favors downstream controls, even more downstream than what business has in mind. In their view justice demands that each person's individual carbon footprint be determined by their proper ethical claim, either set equal to everyone else's or subject to adjustment based on historical use, current relative privilege and the validity of the purposes their carbon emissions will serve. This requires rationing at the individual level, and, according to this view, businesses that produce "bad" or unnecessary products should face more severe carbon constraints than those that pass the virtue test, which consists of some combination of local, small and green.[16]

Rather than debate the advantages claimed for policies that use aesthetic and political judgments to parcel out carbon allotments, I want to emphasize the costs. First, downstream caps, however noble their motives, result in coverage gaps when there isn't the will or administrative capacity to include all sectors and ensure their combined emissions will adhere to an appropriate carbon budget. Upstream caps, on the other hand, are inherently comprehensive, and their impact on cumulative emissions is transparent. If we allow fuels generating no more than 1 Gt of carbon dioxide emissions into the economy, the claim on the remaining budget is capped at 1 Gt. To put it differently, under a downstream permit system it takes extra effort to keep the total below a specified economy-wide maximum. Under an upstream system it takes extra effort to create exemptions that will exceed it.

The second problem with downstream caps is a bit more complicated to explain but just as important: the further downstream permits are assigned, the less flexibility we allow for the economy, meaning all the individuals, businesses and organizations that comprise it, to adjust and adapt. As an example, consider the movement of freight. Suppose there are only two ways to ship goods, by truck or train. If we restrict our view to just this one economic function, a more upstream approach would require permits for freight movement without specifying which mode, while a more downstream one would allocate a given quantity of permits to trucking and another quantity to railroads. If we choose the downstream option, we allow truckers to figure out ways to reduce their emissions and rail operators theirs, but we limit freedom to substitute one mode for the other. If we pull back further and consider the choices that underlie the need to ship goods in the first place, an even more upstream approach, one that applies an economy-wide cap, allows for even greater substitution: individuals and companies can relocate, change where they get their goods from or even change the goods they want to acquire. If a given number of permits are assigned to freight, or even specific freight modes, however, shrinking the amount of shipping we need is ruled out as an adjustment. The general point is that the more upstream the permit system, the more scope we allow for the sort of structural transformation that Chapter 5 held out as our chief hope for a not-too-costly path to decarbonization.

If there is still a political insistence on favoring one sort of activity or portion of the economy, rather than gutting the permit system, the way to implement it is through subsidies, targeted investments and regulations. Later in this chapter, I will argue that at least some such policies are in fact essential.

*Handouts*. Putting a price on carbon means someone will have to pay it. Of course, no one particularly wants to, and some interests, usually businesses, are influential enough to get a free pass. If the policy relies on permits, this takes the form of permit giveaways to some or all of the firms that are required to hold them. With taxes, this can arise if firms are rebated their tax payment or given credits for other taxes on one pretext or another.

Free distribution of permits, rather than selling them at auction, has plagued most permit systems since the beginning of carbon policy early in this century. As discussed above, this is really a license to print money, since, if the permit allowances have actual bite, fossil fuel scarcity causes higher prices. It would not be an exaggeration to say this practice constitutes a bribe to the business community to buy their support for emissions reduction. In public the key players all solemnly swear that the purpose of the free handout is to protect consumers and that no one – perish the thought – would ever consider charging what the market will bear for scarce energy products. In practice the only circumstance that protects consumers from paying higher prices is that usually so many permits are issued there is hardly any scarcity at all.

Incidentally, there *should* be higher prices for fossil fuels and the goods that require plenty of fossil fuel input; there is no other way to alter the choices of the billions of us who will need to do things differently if we are to decarbonize. If this isn't immediately obvious, consider the case of air travel. Under a system of upstream carbon permits, a company that wishes to bring petroleum into the economy must acquire one. The cost of the permit is passed along to the refinery, which passes it along to the company that sells jet fuel to the airlines, which passes it along to passengers in higher ticket prices. Of course, air travelers don't like this, but part of the process of reducing carbon emissions is reducing the amount of air travel, and that's what higher ticket prices accomplish. If decarbonization weren't inconvenient for us it wouldn't be so difficult to achieve.

Now suppose the permit for supplying petroleum to refineries is given away to oil companies. If the number of permits is restricted as before and leads to a reduced availability of fuel, the price refineries have to pay to will go up. In turn, airlines will pay more for each gallon of jet fuel, and to recoup their costs they will pass them on to their customers. Once again we will see higher prices for air travel, leading to fewer seats being booked.

The difference between these two scenarios is that in the first prices go up at each stage in the process, but the public recaptures this extra cost via an auction; in the second the prices go up for everyone except the oil companies, who pocket the extra cash.

Turning carbon taxes into handouts is typically more devious. Assuming no exemptions, firms pay for the carbon energy they use. But tax systems typically have reams of fine print, and if you look closely enough you will find that firms can sometimes get some or all of a tax assessment back. They can write it off as a deduction against other taxes, for instance, or use it to speed up complex depreciation formulas, or off-load it to ostensibly independent entities that just happen to be registered under other, more compliant tax regimes. Very clever people are paid large sums of money to take advantage of these possibilities, which were planted in the first place by other (or perhaps the same) clever people via their influence over those writing the tax laws. If carbon taxes are not awash in such ploys, they will be the first such taxes in a long time.

*Offsets.* The concept of an offset sounds plausible on the surface. Suppose there are two operations that currently generate carbon emissions, and it is much cheaper to reduce most of the emissions from the second than even some from the first. Why not allow the people affiliated with the first operation the opportunity to waive their carbon obligations if they agree to finance greater reductions in the second? Example: suppose the first operation is an oil refinery, and the second is a proposed wind park. To reduce emissions, the refinery would have to completely rebuild itself, and even then its potential is limited because it is, well, a refinery. However, instead of paying, say, a million dollars in a carbon tax or the equivalent to buy a carbon permit, why not let them take that money (or a bit less) and invest it in the wind park, where lots of renewable energy can be produced quickly and cheaply? Then perhaps a different refinery or other fossil fuel installation can be shut down thanks to the infusion of new wind power. It's win-win-win, we're told: a win for the refinery, a win for the wind park, and a win for the planet.

With offsets the devil is typically in the details. From a climate protection point of view the essential question is whether a given amount of emission nonreduction due to the offset is fully matched by the extra reduction promised by the program the offset supports. This is difficult to ascertain for three reasons.

The first can only be described as metaphysical. It goes like this: to justify the offset, a venture that promises to reduce emissions must demonstrate that, had it not been for the support of the company claiming the offset, its project would not have gone forward. Technically, this is called "additionality." If the wind park would be set up with or without the financial support of the refinery, its energy can't be attributable to that support, and the refinery should not be granted the offset. The refinery should be required to demonstrate that its investment truly results in energy that's additional.

But how do we know what's additional? This is where metaphysics comes in. The refinery's case is that we can imagine two parallel universes, the same in every respect except that in one they provide money to the wind park and in the other they don't; then the difference in the wind energy output between Universe 1 and Universe 2 can be deemed additional. The problem is that, in the universe we actually happen to live in, only one of these possibilities can be actualized. If the offset is certified and the investment goes forward, we have only this particular sequence of events to observe and record. The claim that it would have been different in Universe 2 is, in the end, metaphysical – and being metaphysical it's very difficult to disprove. How do you *know* that the wind energy would have been generated anyway? How can you prove the refinery is wrong and their offset shouldn't be honored?

The second problem is that offsets are frequently for the support of projects that increase energy efficiency or the supply of renewable energy sources or temporarily transfer a bit of atmospheric carbon to forest biomass, but as we saw in Chapters 3 and 4, these are not actually (negative) measures of carbon emissions. Here the point made earlier needs to be emphasized: there is nothing wrong with increasing energy efficiency or renewable energy supply or forest cover. All of these have important contributions to make. The problem is that their relationship to actual carbon emissions, and therefore adherence to a budget, is uncertain. A wind park is likely to have *some* effect on reducing the demand for coal- or gas-fired power plants, but how much is hard to say, since there is no law of constant energy at work in the economy, and the same applies to efficiency gains. Forecasting the future of forests over the next century, meanwhile, is practically an exercise in metaphysics itself, an interesting recursive problem since the answer depends on our own future choices, which depend on the consequences of our current choices and so on. The only conclusion we are justified in drawing is that, whatever their other virtues, investments in renewables, efficiency and forests should not be used as a pretext to do *less* actual emission reduction. Since offsets are the mechanism by which this pretext is applied to tax or permit mandates, it's an argument against them.

This brings us to the third problem, which arises from basic economic reasoning. Consider an average event in the daily life of an economy, such as when someone purchases a pair of pants at a clothing store. What guarantee is there for the quality of the merchandise? The government has quality standards for some goods but not most, and generally not for clothing. There might be a manufacturer's or retailer's guarantee, but it's not required, and even when there is one it's not self-enforcing. The result is that everyone who is party to this transaction has a reason to pay at least some attention to quality. Naturally, buyers have the main motivation, since they want their clothes to be well made. But this also rubs off on both the store and the manufacturer; if the products are too obviously shoddy, it will leave a bad impression and detract from future sales. This doesn't mean that every pair of pants sold in the economy belongs in the Fiber Hall of Fame, but the worst quality tends to get weeded out, and there may even be an upward drift of quality over time. As the example of 1989 demonstrated in the previous chapter, while markets may not always produce the level of quality we are looking for, they aim higher than production systems where consumers have little or no choice. This situation is so obvious we often take it for granted, but we shouldn't.[17]

Now let's take a look at *offsets*: Who has the incentive to demand quality in this market? Not the buyer, the company that is relieved of its burden under a tax or permit system because it has made an investment that qualifies as an offset. The company's motive is to avoid obligations it would otherwise have; whether the offset actually reduces carbon emissions is, as we have seen, difficult to determine and in any case secondary. If it's expensive to inquire into, why would the company bother? If it found that there weren't true emissions reductions on the other end of the transaction it would only get in the way of a possibly lucrative option.

And what about the enterprise on the receiving end of an offset investment? Its objective is to acquire funding. To that end it will say whatever it needs, extolling the environmental wonders its work accomplishes and swearing earnestly that its offset revenue is indispensable; everything good would come to an end without it. They can hardly be expected to argue against their own interests.

And then there are the parties whose independent judgment is relied on to certify that the offset is worthy of its claim. The country in which the project receiving the investment is located? They want the business. Third-party certification agencies? Maybe, but whom do they fear if they stretch the truth a bit? Both the company that gains the offset by subsidizing an investment (that wind park) and the company obtaining the subsidy really, really want the deal to get a seal of approval.

In other words, an offset is not subject to the same market forces that promote quality in other contexts. To the extent any incentives are at play, they militate against quality. Moreover, since even in the best case the additionality of offsets is difficult to discern, the lack of incentives is deadly. We should expect – and we will in fact see – that real-world offset markets are beset by questionable judgment and even outright fraud. It should be stressed one more time that these failures are costly because an offset is a loophole in a climate program: every offset granted to businesses *reduces* the amount of decarbonization the main instrument of the program, its tax or permit regime, otherwise mandates.

At the beginning of this chapter, when introducing the concept of permits, I argued that in a well-constructed permit system there need be little or no trading. By now it should be clear that most of what is called "carbon trading" in policy debates is about offsets. Get rid of them, and most of the trading will disappear as well. Any trading that's left, between parties that are all adhering to their requirements to pay for or hold valid permits for carbon emissions, is neutral with respect to the goal of forestalling catastrophic climate change.

## Carbon Pricing: A Reality Check

So much for theory, but what do tax and permit systems look like in the real world? Here the news is not so good.

The world's premier carbon emissions reduction program is the European Trading System (ETS). It was instituted in 2003 and began operations in 2005 with its first allocation of carbon permits. In its first phase it covered only the electrical power sector and some of the emissions of the largest industrial firms and has gradually, as Phase II has given way to Phase III, been expanded to encompass about half of all European greenhouse gas emissions. In other words, it was assertively downstream rather than directed against carbon at its upstream source. Moreover, at the outset all permits were handed out for free, and only over time has the portion subject to auction risen. The EU's definition of "auction" is rather expansive, but under a normal understanding of the term, the proportion of the total actually sold has not yet reached 50% and is not expected to do so for several more years.[18] Offsets have played a key role in the system, totaling about 10% of covered emissions since the introduction of Phase III in 2013.

The detail is important and instructive.

*The cap.* The ETS initially covered only carbon dioxide emissions, not other greenhouse gases, and only in electricity generation and manufacturing. It has expanded to other gases and sectors, but there are no plans to include transportation and freight (other than by air) or home or commercial heating, to mention only the most important. Originally, each country was charged with developing its own national action plan, assigning permits by sector, but the process of monitoring and merging them proved overwhelmingly bureaucratic.[19] With Phase III the EU has switched to a centralized system of permits, determined in

Brussels. The overall cap was originally designed to shrink by about 1.75% per year, which if reciprocated in the uncovered portion of the economy was intended to bring total emissions down to 67% of their 1990 levels by 2030; this rate of tightening has been increased to 2.2% in the most recent round of reforms. However, it turns out the cap has barely been binding; a combination of very slow economic growth (largely attributable to the Eurozone crisis that prolonged the 2008 recession) and the profusion of offsets created a large surplus of unwanted permits. In order to prevent the permit price from collapsing altogether, the EU has purchased allowances in excess of two billion tonnes, placing them into an account from which they can be released in the future if the cap becomes more constraining. Currently, the accumulated surplus exceeds the total number of permits allocated within a single year.[20]

*The price.* Because the allocation of permits, even after withholding the surplus, nearly satisfies the full demand, prices were very low, 5 euros or less, until 2017. At the time of this writing, however, a permit to emit 1 tonne of carbon dioxide fluctuates in the low to mid-20 euros, still far lower than the price most analysts regard as necessary to achieve a 2° climate stabilization, even as a starting point.

*The handouts.* When the ETS was introduced, it mandated that at least 95% of the permits had to be distributed freely in the first phase (2005–2007) and 90% in the second (2007–2012). It was written this way to actually *prevent* countries from auctioning a larger share if they democratically chose to do so. The main effect was on electrical utilities, which – of course! – raised their rates and received windfall profits. In response the European Commission decided to require utilities to reinvest a portion of the value of their (free) permits to modernize their operations, and they called this earmarking an "auction," or more precisely they added the earmarked funds to the revenues earned from actual auctions and called the sum "auction revenues." This earmarking is expected to amounted to 4% of the entire value of the cap over the duration of Phase III. But this still left the "auction" total below the level they wanted, so they also categorized a portion of the surplus permits put into reserve (see above) as also "auctioned," under the presumption that they would eventually be sold rather than given away at some future point. In this creative manner, about 10% of the permit total designated as "auctioned" has not in fact been put up for auction.[21]

There's another twist to the free distribution process: the formula for determining how many permits each company receives. This formula is somewhat complicated, but it partly depends on how fully the company's capital stock was utilized in the previous year, with more prior activity resulting in more permit handouts. Activity levels are in brackets of 25%, 50%, 75% and 100%, so companies producing near the top of one bracket have an incentive to increase output and make it into the one above. In other words, in order to obtain more free permits (and their associated windfall profits), firms increase their production and their resulting carbon emissions; rather than permits reducing emissions, emissions increase permits.[22] While EU policy is easy to criticize in this case as in so many others, it should be recognized that it is difficult to avoid perverse impacts in any formula for allocating permit giveaways.

*The offsets.* The ETS allows companies to emit carbon without a permit if they instead hold an offset certificate, up to a maximum of 10% of all covered emissions. These offsets can be dedicated either to the Clean Development Mechanism (CDM), about which more shortly, or to the Joint Implementation (JI) program, which oversees projects to modernize the power sector in countries transitioning from Communism. After repeated publicity disasters for the CDM, the European Commission has restricted one after another of their project types and is looking to eliminate them altogether in the future.[23]

*The auction revenues.* As an increasing share (although less than half) of the permits is sold at auction, the question of what to do with the proceeds arises. Given the EU's federal fiscal structure, the money reverts to the national treasuries of the member countries. They are subject to the guideline that somewhat under half should be devoted to "energy and climate related" expenditures, but it is nearly impossible to determine additionality (whether programs that would have been funded anyway are simply shunted over to the auction revenue budget), and the language of the directive in fact acknowledges this.[24]

*The rebates.* Manufacturing businesses with carbon-intensive production processes lobbied successfully for the ETS to compensate them for most of the extra costs of doing business attributable to the permit system. There's a formula for this, but the core idea is that a firm reports how much carbon energy it uses directly and indirectly, the impact of requiring carbon permits is calculated, and payments are made to minimize the firm's financial consequences. The argument is that compensation is needed so European producers are not placed at a disadvantage in competition with companies in countries that don't put a similar price on carbon. Of course, this compensation also reduces their costs in their European home markets, allowing them some combination of more sales and higher profits. One result, however, is that the incentive effect behind pricing carbon in the first place, pushing individuals and businesses to alter their choices in line with decarbonization, is blunted. Over a fifth of auction revenues are recycled back to businesses in this way.[25]

*The bottom line.* So how effective has the ETS actually been in reducing European carbon emissions? During the period of 2004–2014, measured emissions in countries that were part of the system from the beginning fell by 20%. This is partly attributable to poor economic performance, especially resulting from the eurozone crisis. Over these years total industrial production (value added) in these same countries increased only 5%. In addition, there were other factors that might have played a role in causing emissions to fall, such as fuel substitution and improvements in energy efficiency.[26] The large research literature on the role the ETS itself played was summarized by Ralf Martin and two coauthors, and their conclusion was cautious: it's hard to say.[27]

Overall, the ETS could serve as a poster child for how not to design an emissions reduction system. Each aspect of its operations has been eviscerated by critics, many with language much harsher than mine. You might wonder why supposedly knowledgeable and intelligent officials would concoct such a misbegotten enterprise. Didn't they know going in how poorly and inequitably it would function? And the answer is yes, they knew going in. All the ex post criticisms were made – elegantly and in multiple languages with simultaneous translation – ex ante. It wasn't a problem of ignorance or carelessness. In general, observers have chalked it up to "politics," but that doesn't quite go far enough. Many of the defects of the ETS are costly to large majorities of the European public. In particular, the free handout of permits, with the further insult of compensation payments, has literally dipped into the pockets of consumers and taxpayers and transferred billions of euros to corporations. In what system of politics is this a reason *for* such policies?

That's not a rhetorical question, and if we reflect further there is an answer: a politics of business dominance. Business interests in

Europe, as elsewhere, weigh more heavily in the political process than those of the rest of the population. The situation is even more severe in the EU, where opportunities for ordinary people to influence decisions at the European level are few and feeble, while the voice of business practically resounds in Brussels. I admit this is only a hypothesis, and perhaps there is evidence waiting to be gathered that will contradict it. It seems to me to be the only plausible story, however.

Second to the EU ETS, the most widely studied system is California's Cap-and-Trade Program, administered by the California Air Resources Board (CARB). Inaugurated in 2013, Cap-and-Trade is part of a larger package of regulations intended to return California's carbon emissions to their 1990 level by 2020, an unambitious goal surpassed in the first three years.[28] A new goal envisions a further 40% reduction by 2030. Arguably, the most important policy tools are the state's renewable portfolio standards for utilities (mandating a minimum level of renewable power), fuel efficiency standards, standards to reduce the carbon content of fuels used for transportation, and energy efficiency standards for home heating and appliances. The Cap-and-Trade mechanism sits on top of all of these – but how easily?

Like the ETS, California's system is downstream, requiring users of fossil fuels to acquire emission permits, although this may be unavoidable given the close integration of California's economy with that of the surrounding states. For instance, about 30% of the electrical power used in California was originally generated out of state and imported via the grid.[29] The only way to incorporate this indirect use of fossil fuels is to require permits for the utilities on the importing end. To its credit, California has rapidly extended the system to cover about 75% of all emissions, making it far more comprehensive than the EU's.

All the other indicators are worse. Carbon permits were initially handed out for free, and while an auction system has been introduced, only about half currently fall under it. Price floors and ceilings, to be enforced by either withholding or releasing permits, were established from the beginning, but only the floor has mattered, and it has been difficult to sustain. As with the EU, the Cap-and-Trade administrators found themselves accumulating large numbers of surplus permits, and even so, prices have risen only sluggishly, plateauing at about $17 per tonne at the time of this writing.

Why did this happen? To some extent it was a function of the limited role assigned to the Cap-and-Trade system from the beginning.

CARB, in designing the policy, expected 80% of the emissions reductions to result from other regulatory measures, so the role of emissions permitting was residual, to pick up opportunities for decarbonization not addressed elsewhere. If you are an optimist, you would say that the weakness of Cap-and-Trade is the result of California's smashing success in energy efficiency, renewable portfolio standards and so on.

Unfortunately, there's much more to the story. First, the scheduled emissions reductions were so modest to begin with it would take only small improvements in efficiency or fuel substitution to create a situation in which the number of permits exceeded the emissions they were supposed to limit. Second, firms were allowed to substitute offsets for nearly half the permits they would otherwise have to hold.[30] Finally, and this is important, electrical utilities were practically invited to game the system through a technique known as "shuffling" their energy sources. As mentioned above, almost a third of the state's electricity is imported from the interstate grid, and it's produced by a mix of energy sources including coal, natural gas and renewables. Through the use of shuffling, California utilities are able to claim that *their* electricity imports are derived from renewables, while utilities from other states, not subject to California's Cap-and-Trade, could be left with the ostensibly dirtier electricity. This is essentially the Renewable Energy Certificate dodge we encountered in Chapter 3.

When a problem like this arises, we like to think it's a mistake of some sort, and that careful administrators will fix it in due course. That's difficult to argue in this case. CARB, when it was establishing the rules of the road, commissioned a report from a well-regarded group of academic energy experts. They modeled the system and predicted that, if it were not prohibited, shuffling would lead to as much as 360 million tonnes of bogus emissions reduction claims per year, slightly more than the entire annual permit issuance.[31] CARB accepted the report – and ignored it. One can only conclude that the enormous free pass given to the state's energy sector was a feature, not a bug.

Finally, the system was struggling for several years because its legal status was clouded, due to a provision in the state constitution that requires a two-thirds' vote of the legislature to approve any tax increase – and the permit system could be interpreted as a tax. (It did not pass with a super-majority vote.) Recent developments on that front have been favorable, however, and Cap-and-Trade has now been successfully reauthorized.

Meanwhile, carbon taxes and permits have been introduced or are planned for many other jurisdictions – several provinces in Canada, the northeastern United States, the Nordic region, a number of developing countries, and also, interestingly, China. Those that have a track record mostly have, like the ETS and California's Cap-and-Trade, a light touch, with ample fine print detailing exemptions, rebates and offsets.

A summing-up of the current situation is provided by the World Bank in its annual report on carbon pricing.[32] The sixty-one jurisdictions that have or are planning such systems are almost evenly divided between tax and permit approaches. In all, about 22% of global emissions are covered, but programs are not nearly strong enough to have much impact. Only about $45 billion in carbon revenues were collected in 2019; this may sound superficially like a large number, but it represents just 0.05% of the global economy.[33] The average price per tonne of carbon dioxide was an uninspiring $2.[34] From the perspective of what we need in the face of a climate emergency, this is indistinguishable from zero.

## Real-World Offsets: The Case of the Clean Development Mechanism

Our brief survey of real-world policy wouldn't be complete without a look at the offset industry. We've already considered forest offsets in Chapter 4, but what about programs that allow businesses to avoid the need to hold a permit or pay a tax if they help finance some other ostensibly emissions-reducing program? Here we will focus on the Clean Development Mechanism (CDM), the largest and most important offset certification outfit.[35]

It will warm the heart of a theorist but dismay those who care about climate change that the CDM in practice confirms the suspicions registered earlier in this chapter. Recall, for instance, that the criterion of additionality was viewed as essentially metaphysical, embodying the notion that in a hypothetical world the same as our own except for the absence of CDM funding, particular projects would not materialize. In practical terms, this means that entrepreneurs seeking funding need to file papers showing that (1) there is a baseline business-as-usual scenario (the alternative universe) in which a certain amount of carbon emission will take place, and (2) there is a CDM-funding scenario in which it won't. Such claims would be difficult to justify in any case, but the evidence is there is little to no scrutiny. Jinshan Zhu and Yingkai Tang cite seven previous studies, based on reviews of samples of approved projects, that show a high level of certification of applications that ought to have failed the additionality test.[36] The smoking gun, however, appeared in a diplomatic cable released by Wikileaks in 2011. It describes a meeting held in Mumbai in 2008, in which employees of the US Consulate, accompanied by fact-finders from the US Government Accountability Office (GAO), interviewed key officials responsible for vetting CDM applications from India; India accounts for about an eighth of all carbon offsets issued by the CDM. The US representatives wanted to know how much scrutiny was applied in India, since criticisms of the process had already become widespread. The cable quotes the highest-ranking CDM official in India as saying that his office "takes the project developer at his word for clearing the additionality barrier." In other words, no scrutiny at all, although it took an unauthorized disclosure to communicate this to the rest of us. At least the metaphysical complications are avoided.[37]

In Chapter 4 much was made of the difference between expanding the supply of renewable energy and actually keeping fossil fuels in the ground. If we could be sure the total demand for energy always remains constant, more of one energy source would mean less of another, but that is not generally the case. This assumption is especially inappropriate in developing countries where energy is seriously under-supplied to a population eager to have access to the appliances and services taken for granted in rich countries. We will return to this issue in the next chapter, but its relevance to the CDM should be obvious. In fact, the CDM guidelines for approving projects that provide low- or no-carbon electricity generation simply assume that they will replace higher-carbon alternatives, existing or anticipated, on a one-for-one basis, even though nearly all such projects are situated in energy-starved economies. In a careful study of the problem, Jinshan Zhu and Yingkai Tang found that more than half of all carbon credits are for cleaner electrical power and that 90% of this portion is in just three countries: China, India and Vietnam. All are undergoing massive electricity expansion to meet burgeoning economic and social needs. As they argue, the most likely prospect is that the offset-finance projects will simply add to supply, not supplant other sources.[38]

Incidentally, permits are granted not only for carbon-neutral power generation through renewable sources, but also for natural gas-fired plants, based on the hypothesis that this has less greenhouse impact than coal. Of course, if the coal plants remain open, which has been the case up to now and will remain likely for years to come, the offsets are simply financing *additional* fossil fuel emissions. This version of additionality is a lot more plausible than the other kind.

But that is not the worst of it. Of all 1.7 billion offsets issued to date under the CDM, about 32% are for HFC-23. This is down from more than half a few years ago, for reasons that will be explained in a moment.[39] What, you say? All those offsets in California, or at Microsoft, or for my airplane ticket are for what? HFC stands for hydrofluorocarbon, and HFC-23 is better known as freon-23, but first we need to back up.

The starting point is actually HCFC-22, a widely used refrigerant best known under its commercial name freon-22. Because it has powerful ozone-depleting effects when released into the atmosphere, it is gradually being phased out in accordance with the Montreal Protocol.[40] Countries have different timelines, with the United States slated to achieve complete phaseout by 2030, while developing countries are on a somewhat slower track. In addition to its ozone impacts, HCFC-22 is also a powerful greenhouse gas, 1,800 times the effect of carbon dioxide. Unfortunately, in the course of production, HCFC-22 generates another gas as a side product, HFC-23, which we encountered in the previous paragraph. HFC-23 is an *extremely* potent greenhouse gas, with a carbon dioxide equivalence of 12,400. Obviously, we should try to keep this out of the atmosphere.

That is where the CDM came in. Producers of refrigerants, companies manufacturing HCFC-22, proposed projects in which they would not allow their HFC-23 byproduct to escape, but capture it instead. These were readily approved, since the parallel universe was one in which there was no CDM funding and producers simply vented their HFC-23.

But, like the broomstick water-carriers in the Sorcerer's Apprentice, the offsets were way too productive. To earn an offset certificate for the equivalent of a tonne of carbon dioxide, it was necessary to finance the capture of only 80 grams of HFC-23. Even with offset prices at their bargain basement rate, the revenues refrigerant producers could get for capturing HFC-23 vastly exceeded the cost. Indeed, it became so profitable to bring in this CDM funding that companies *increased* their output of freon, even though this product was supposed to be tapering off under the Montreal Protocol. Companies were earning more profits from the intake of offset money than from selling their products. There was no practical limit to this strategy, because the offset market moved en masse to refrigerant projects. Recall that at their peak, HFC-23 projects accounted for half of all CDM offsets, and even now, after they have been phased out, they still account for over 30% of the accumulation up to this point.[41] Moreover, producers didn't have to capture all the HFC-23 to be rewarded with CDM-approved funding; it was enough just to capture more than zero. The upshot is that the global CDM mechanism, the centerpiece of the world's system of carbon offsets, became a giant machine for increasing the production of refrigerants that were supposed to be in the process of being phased out, and even increasing, in all likelihood, the very byproduct, HFC-23, they were supposedly trying to control.[42] The reason no further credits are being awarded for this travesty is that the scandal became too egregious to contain. The EU announced it would no longer allow offsets for industrial gases (including HFC-23) and the CDM itself had to commit to exiting the business.

The lesson of the HFC-23 saga is that the logical conundrums of the offset market show up in real life. There was no incentive on the part of any market participants – not the companies purchasing offsets, not the refrigerant producers raking in the subsidies and not the certifying agency itself, the CDM – to police the quality of the program. Only an aroused public, and even then only after years of angry protest by environmental organizations, could have an effect. And the untethered nature of the hypotheticals that supposedly justify certification – the hypothetical world of no CDM and some projected future HFC-23 emissions versus the proposed world of a certified project – created the sort of murkiness in which cynical motives could flourish.

This is not to say all CDM projects have been valueless. Building a small wind farm in a developing country may be a wonderful idea and have some ultimate impact on carbon emissions. The problem is that the benefits are speculative and might not outweigh the costs. In a careful overview of the factors that affect how the CDM both increases and decreases carbon emissions, Erickson and coauthors concluded, "On balance, the overall net mitigation impact of the CDM remains difficult to assess with certainty, and it would be a mistake to assume the net decreases cancel out the net increases."[43] Even if the CDM can be reformed so a net benefit is more likely, it should not be used as a basis for reducing the decarbonization commitments that businesses in upper-income countries would otherwise be held to.

This suggests a more general point. Climate change is a global problem, driven by the sum of carbon emissions across the entire world. But countries do not confront it on an equal footing. There is vast poverty in what is referred to as the Global South, and a compelling need for more access to energy for electrification, infrastructure and improvements in agriculture and industry. Under these circumstances, the logical conclusion is that the wealthier economies of the North need to decarbonize even more than their proportional share in order to offset the effects of this essential development in the South. It is bizarre that the global offset regime is set up to reverse this logic and use the need for development as an excuse to allow the North to decarbonize *less*.

## The Rest of the Toolkit

This chapter began with the claim that the centerpiece of any effective climate mitigation policy is putting a stiff price on carbon, because only in that way can we bring about a revolution in personal and business choices widespread and deep enough to make a $2°$ budget attainable. After all the ups and downs of the analysis of taxes and permits, that's still true. Nevertheless, an effective carbon policy has to do a lot more than establish a price or even limit fossil fuel use directly. While I won't delve into the specifics of the other measures we need to adopt, I will sketch them here for balance and completeness. I hope the amount of ink spilled in analyzing carbon permits and taxes in this chapter does not leave you with the impression that the rest of the climate agenda is optional. On the contrary, the following proposals are essential if we have any hope of achieving a viable transition to a decarbonized world. The reason they get less attention here is that they get much more elsewhere, and I have tried to make it clear that they should supplement direct controls on fossil fuel use, not substitute for them.

*End fossil fuel subsidies.* This should be the very first thing we do, and there's no reason, other than political will, why we can't accomplish it immediately. Every country subsidizes carbon energy to one extent or another, but the scale is sometimes surprising. According to a recent comprehensive survey, direct subsidies by the G20 countries, the world's largest and/or richest, in the form of tax breaks or spending to boost private production and consumption amounted to an average of $78 billion per year. The US share of this total was $20 billion. Other potential forms of subsidy are more difficult to cost out. Many countries have state-owned energy companies, and it is likely that a portion of their costs is borne by taxpayers and not consumers. Similarly, many countries have public banks or sovereign investment funds that they dip into to finance fossil energy projects, and here too there may be a hidden subsidy, but we can't say for sure how much. Taken together, these second two categories come to an additional $374 billion – again, an undetermined portion of which is truly a subsidy.[44] The point is that all too often carbon has a *negative* price: businesses and consumers are being paid to use it. While it would certainly arouse opposition from energy and other influential interests, most of these subsidies could simply be terminated.

There is another point to be made about subsidies. One of the reasons environmentalists tend to be enthusiastic about using carbon revenues for green projects – a subject we'll explore in the final chapter – is that governments often claim they can't afford them due to a lack of funds. The existence of widespread fossil fuel subsidies gives us a different perspective on that problem: the barrier is not necessarily revenue, but priorities. Money withdrawn for the support of fossil energy production can be repurposed for environmental uses. Of course, there are also plenty of other large public expenditure items that add little to social well-being – or even detract from it – and which could be swapped for investments in decarbonizing the economy.

*Regulation.* Having a stringent carbon permit or tax system removes much of the need for public regulation; if we adopt a permit approach, for instance, the permit cap itself limits the total emission of greenhouse gases, doing the job we would otherwise need regulations to accomplish. Consider renewable portfolio standards, which specify the minimum share of electricity to be derived from renewable energy sources; they become superfluous if limits are placed directly on non-renewable fuels. But regulation can serve many positive purposes besides simply limiting emissions. Perhaps the most important is establishing standards for energy efficiency across a wide variety of goods, ranging from appliances to vehicles to buildings. The energy demands for operating them are difficult for consumers to research or make sense of; in some cases there may be legitimate doubt about whom to trust. The government has a crucial role to play in setting performance standards and issuing labels and ratings that help consumers navigate their way through a challenging energy landscape.

In addition, there are smaller but still important sources of carbon emissions that do not take the form of fossil fuel extraction and will not be sufficiently touched by policies that consider only energy. For instance, cement production accounts for about 4% of global greenhouse gas emissions, according to the IPCC.[45] Much of this is due to chemical reactions that take place during the production process rather than the fuels that drive it, so energy policy alone is not enough. Similarly, there is concern that the heat-trapping effect of the contrails produced by airplanes may contribute as much or more to climate change than the fuels the planes burn as they fly.[46] For these and similar sources of climate risk it will be necessary to develop detailed specifications for how certain goods and services are produced and used.

*Infrastructure and public goods.* A decarbonized economy will look very different from the one we have today. It will have a radically different spatial organization and rely far more on public transportation and human-powered mobility. It will be built on the foundations of a much more robust infrastructure, including not only traditional cement and steel fixtures like roads, bridges and sewers, but also smart electrical grids and robust, universal broadband. (Many of the things we do in person today will need to be done virtually in the future.) This much is apparent from current technology, and we can be sure that new technology will emerge that makes its own infrastructure demands. Every economy in human history, whatever its principles of organization, has relied on public works to provide these shared goods and services, and ours will be no exception. Our infrastructure needs would be daunting enough if they were based only on the extent to which we have allowed the current stock to age and deteriorate, but they now require not only renovation but reinvention. As an aside, it is extraordinary – and I mean extraordinarily obtuse – that, at a time when our public investment needs are so immense and interest rates so low, even negative in real terms, that many political leaders are still fixated on a fictitious need to avoid public debt. Borrowing at the right time and for the right reasons is how we build wealth.

*Research and development.* We might possibly be able to transition to a decarbonized economy based on the technologies we now possess, but it would be extremely difficult. At the least, it probably entails a period of falling living standards for much of the world's population. To keep alligators out of the Arctic *and* humans at a reasonable level of comfort will require advances in knowledge that governments are best placed to finance and, in some instances, organize. For several decades the mantra has been repeated that the public sector is stagnant and oppressive, and only private entrepreneurs can take on the daring task of "disrupting" our current systems of production and consumption. Not so, as Mariana Mazzucato has pointed out in *The Entrepreneurial State*, a deservedly popular analysis of modern techno-logical dynamism.[47] Public research and development has been crucial to nearly every advance we associate with the private sector, and we need to expand this pipeline now that new discoveries in energy supply and use are no longer luxuries but necessities.

*Interventions to protect basic needs.* A high and ever-rising price on carbon is essential if we are to wean ourselves from fossil fuels, but it will also have side effects that, if not countermanded, will imperil the survival of much of the world's population. The most powerful example is the conflict between biofuels and food for human consumption. High fossil fuel prices mean high prices for substitute fuels made from biomass – crops grown for fuel and not for food. Consumers in the higher income parts of the world will bid up the price of biofuels and the land that produces them, and this will in turn lead to much higher prices for food as well. Even aside from technical questions about the net carbon benefits of biofuels, the effect on the food supply of the widespread conversion of agricultural land is unacceptable. Left to their own devices, markets will do what they do best: allocate resources to the production of goods that earn the highest return. There is no decent choice except to override market forces and insulate a sufficient portion of global agriculture to enable all the world's people to be well fed.

Similarly, climate policy will elevate carbon emissions to the very top of environmental concerns, potentially eclipsing other side effects of production that are damaging but carbon-neutral. This may become especially important as new technologies are developed that rely on exotic materials and production processes; the emergence of nanotechnology may be a harbinger of this new set of concerns. Pricing carbon does not diminish the need to regulate other threats; on the contrary, the pressure to do almost anything to reduce carbon emis-sions, if left unchecked, may lead to greater noncarbon risks. An economic upheaval as immense as decarbonization will almost certainly present us with a new environmental agenda.

*Carbon removal.* Despite the uncertainties I've drawn attention to, programs to expand forest cover, enrich organic soil matter and sequester carbon scrubbed from combustion processes have an important place in climate policy. If we are lucky, they may at some point become inexpensive enough at a large enough scale to make a difference in how much warming we will have to endure. These approaches should be used not in place of restrictions on fossil fuels but in addition to them. Specifically, taken together, they offer whatever hope we have of limiting warming to 1.5° C rather than the 2°C I've used as a benchmark. There is a big difference between a 1.5°C and 2°C world: less sea level rise, fewer deadly heat waves, less extreme weather, smaller impacts on agriculture and greater preservation of biodiversity. There is also less risk of triggering feedback mechanisms that might send the alligators on their way.[48] Unfortunately, the window of opportunity to achieve this outcome through reductions in fossil fuel use alone is essentially closed.[49] What *is* possible, and what this book strongly advocates, is that we put policies in place to restrict fossil fuels that can assure us of atmospheric carbon dioxide concentrations not exceeding 450 ppm, and then supplement them with other, less certain measures that, it is hoped, can withdraw further carbon from the atmosphere and reduce ultimate warming below 2°C. To put it another way, we should consider having two targets. One is the absolute maximum level of atmospheric carbon we will allow, to be attained in as certain a manner as possible. The other is a desired level beneath it which can be approached by supplementing our mandatory carbon budget with less certain but potentially effective interventions to remove carbon from the atmosphere even after we've burned it.

*Employment and social protection.* As we saw in the previous chapter, a fossil fuel–restricting program adequate to the challenge will predictably lead to large capital write-offs across the economy. Whole sectors will shrink or disappear altogether, and millions of workers will lose their jobs. This is likely to happen quickly, as it did when Eastern Europe was opened to international competition in 1989. What we are picturing is a macroeconomic meltdown far beyond what the world experienced in the wake of either the 2008 financial crisis or the 2020 and continuing pandemic. The good news is we can see it coming. That being the case, it is essential that any stringent climate program be

188 / The Policy Toolkit

accompanied by measures to minimize the impact of unemployment and falling incomes.

Large-scale investment programs targeting housing, infrastructure and renewable energy supply address this need, but there are limits to the rate at which the economy can absorb new inputs. Mass transit systems can't be built all at once, nor can wind turbines, improved power grids or denser, energy-efficient dwellings. To cope with the wave of shutdowns and layoffs we will need additional public spending on projects that may not be climate-related but are beneficial in other ways and sustain high levels of employment. In this context it should be noted that employment or other guarantees earmarked for workers in the fossil fuel sector, while politically attractive, do not address the seriousness of the economic problem and in some ways exacerbate it by identifying a particular segment of the work force for favored treatment. What are needed instead are comprehensive employment policies that can benefit *all* workers impacted by climate policy. In addition, and to be safe, we should plan to shore up the social protection safety nets in health, nutrition, housing and child care for those who might, for any reason, fall through the cracks – but we should be doing this now as well.

Taken together, these items closely parallel what has come to be known as the Green New Deal in the United States.[50] I hope it is clear that nothing in this book should be taken as a criticism of that approach; on the contrary, while there can be debate about the particulars, its broad direction and sweep get my full endorsement. The only caveat that emerges from this analysis is that a Green New Deal should be understood as a guide to what needs to be done *in addition* to keeping fossil fuels in the ground, not a substitute that somehow accomplishes this goal on its own.

*The last resort.* This book may appear to take a pessimistic stance, but it is actually rather optimistic in face of the challenge in front of us. It assumes that most of life will go on in a normal way, that large-scale political and social structures will not erupt in conflict and that a complex, globalized economy interwoven with markets will continue to function. There is another scenario to consider, however. Events could take a serious turn for the worse. This could happen because terrifying feedback mechanisms in the global carbon cycle begin to take effect sooner and more visibly that we now expect, or the consequences of "moderate" climate change prove far more severe than we can cope with. It could happen because our institutions are more fragile than we realize, and environmental pressures may cause them to shatter. Or perhaps another threat, unrelated to the ones we're considering here, may prove devastating. Whatever the reason, it is possible that routine mechanisms will break down, and we will find ourselves in a single-minded mobilization for survival, much as occurred during the world wars of the last century. Under those conditions we are likely to adopt a rigid system of administrative controls; carbon pricing and related refinements would appear as quaint notions from an innocent past. If that is where we are heading, I believe it can only be viewed as a colossal defeat for values of liberty, democracy and humane progress. I certainly hope it never comes to this, but it would be naive to assume that it couldn't.

Lock this last paragraph in a drawer you rarely open. With luck we won't need it.

# 7 THE GLOBAL DIMENSION

A number of years ago I was doing research in Ghana, interviewing people in a fishing community just outside Accra, the capital city. Local fishermen would take their boats, which resembled large, motorized canoes, out onto the Atlantic, dipping their nets to catch whatever could be sold on the local market. They did this most days; I met them on an off day when the boats were drying out on the beach with the nets spread out between them as the crews worked on repairs. After I had the information I needed, out of curiosity I asked, "If you could have one thing that would make your work easier, what would it be?" The answer: a refrigerator. These fisherman had to land their catch and sell at whatever price they were offered or the fish would spoil. With a refrigerator they could bargain.

In much of the world refrigerators and the electricity that powers them are privileges of the few, and this applies to many of the other features of modern life that people in wealthier countries take for granted. It forms the backdrop to debates over how the planet's shrinking carbon budget should be allocated, a dispute that has made it difficult to achieve meaningful international cooperation on climate mitigation. Wealthy countries warn the biggest increase in carbon emissions is expected to be in the Global South, so that is where programs to reduce them are most needed. Poorer countries reply that the developed world, in acquiring its wealth, has already used up more than its share of the available carbon space, so it should now go on an even more stringent diet.

There is truth to both sides, although, from an ethical point of view, it is difficult to argue with the demand that climate policies need to allow everyone, and not just a fortunate few, to enjoy the benefits that increases in energy make possible. How can we both stick to a global carbon budget that forestalls catastrophic climate change and also accelerate improvements in the standard of living for the billions who today lack the basics? To set the stage, let's begin with a look at refrigerators and the other accoutrements of a more comfortable way of life in order to better understand the tension between eradicating poverty and decarbonizing the economy.

## Cold Comfort: Refrigerators, Air Conditioners and Their Consequences for Carbon Emissions

Few inventions have had as dramatic impact on living standards as the refrigerator. Without one, fresh foods have to be produced or purchased the day they're consumed. It's not possible to take advantage of cost savings from buying in bulk. The risk of food-borne illness rises. Everyone who doesn't have a refrigerator wants one. I've lived without a refrigerator at times and know what a difference it makes.

We don't have data on refrigerator ownership for all parts of the world, but household surveys asking about assets give us a picture for all the large countries and many smaller ones. In China, for instance, 69% of households have refrigerators, but the proportion is only 13% for India. Sub-Saharan Africa, with a population of almost 900 million people, trails with just over 10% of households. Overall, in the poorest half of the planet well under half the population lives in a household with a refrigerator.[1]

But to have a refrigerator you need to have access to electricity, not just from time to time but regularly. Here the numbers are more encouraging, although reliability of supply can vary considerably. China has universal access to electricity, and 75% of Indians have access as well. On the other hand, only a third of those living in sub-Saharan Africa have access to electricity. In many parts of the world, supply is intermittent, and to run an appliance like a refrigerator requires a backup generator.

As the world gets hotter, which it unquestionably will, air conditioning (AC) in tropical regions will become less a luxury than a necessity. In May 2015 a devastating heat wave struck India. Temperatures were in the low to mid-40s Celsius, or roughly 110–115°F for weeks. At their peak they approached 120°F. Over

2,300 deaths have been attributed to it, as well as extensive economic disruption.[2] Blast furnace temperatures struck again in 2016, setting a new record of 51°C, although causing fewer deaths.[3]

Of course, excess heat is not only a problem in developing countries. The heat wave that hit Europe in the summer of 2003 was one of the deadliest on record, with one study using an excess mortality methodology – looking at the deviation of deaths during this period from their previous trend rather than case by case – and finding it cost 70,000 lives.[4] Unlike India, the problem was less the inability to afford air conditioning as the unprecedented ferocity of a heat wave that struck a region where people could typically get by without it.

We are only at the early stages of serious warming, and, as we saw in Chapter 2, the prognosis is for increasingly severe heat events that will dwarf what we've seen so far. By mid-century some heat-prone regions will be experiencing wet bulb temperatures beyond the point at which human beings can survive without AC. For instance, a recent study that looks at the implications of two different carbon emissions scenarios for Africa finds that extreme heat waves will become the norm, not the exception. In measured terms, the authors conclude that some regions will become "uninhabitable" and warn that "the projected increase in extreme heat waves in the coming decades can result in humanitarian crises of unknown dimensions."[5] Under these conditions, providing near-universal, reliable electricity and AC devices becomes an essential piece of the climate adaptation agenda – although, even if we manage to achieve this, the effects on agriculture are likely to be horrific.[6]

So where do we stand today with respect to air conditioning? The numbers are difficult to find. Household surveys conducted by the World Bank (the Living Standards Measurement Surveys) have sometimes asked respondents about household appliances, including AC. There is a compilation of population averages computed from these data in an EPA study from 2011, but many countries of interest are missing, and the survey dates range from 1992 to 2003.[7] Instead, I've taken estimates of the number of AC units owned by households assembled by a team from Lawrence Berkeley National Laboratory and divided them by the number of households per country.[8] The report used confidential sales information from AC producers and, incorporating information on expected replacement rates, estimated the total number of units as of the time of writing.[9] Household data for some

Table 7.1. Number of households and air conditioning units (in millions) and AC per household (percent), 2015, selected countries

| Country | Households | AC units | AC per household |
| --- | --- | --- | --- |
| Brazil | 57.3 | 17.5 | 30.5 |
| India | 248.4 | 23.0 | 9.3 |
| Indonesia | 61.2 | 10.5 | 17.2 |
| Pakistan | 28.0 | 1.7 | 6.1 |
| Thailand | 30.3 | 8.4 | 41.4 |

*Sources*: Government of India, Ministry of Home Affairs (2016), Government of Pakistan, Statistics Division (2013), Shah et al. (2015), Thailand, National Statistical Office (n.d.) and UN Department of Economic and Social Affairs (2016).

countries is available from the UN's Demographic Yearbook, but others had to be obtained from the statistical offices of the countries in question. The results can be seen in Table 7.1.

These numbers should be approached with care, as always when combining data from different sources. The AC figures are proprietary and can't be validated independently. Above all, it is quite possible for a single household to have more than one AC unit, so the final column should be taken as an upper bound for the true percentage of households, and people, who have air conditioning. (Households without AC may well have higher average size than those with, although we lack recent evidence.) These estimates for Brazil, India, Indonesia and Thailand are much higher than what we find in the older World Bank surveys, but we would expect rapid growth in AC purchases in all these countries.

And what about Africa? A recent report offers snippets of proprietary information from an industry market analysis firm, which is summarized in Table 7.2. Except in South Africa, the proportion of households that currently have AC units is 20% or less, with each country expected to increase its level by 5% in the coming years. Clearly, very few people with low income in this region have AC access or will soon acquire it.

The implications of this brief overview for the future of climate policy are immense. In fact, there have been a number of high-profile studies recently that attempt to forecast future energy demand as low-income countries in tropical regions move up the income ladder

Table 7.2. Percentage of households in selected African countries with at least one AC device

| Country | Current | 2023 (projected) |
| --- | --- | --- |
| Ethiopia | 10 | 15 |
| Ghana | 17 | 22 |
| Kenya | 15 | 20 |
| Nigeria | 20 | 25 |
| South Africa | 55 | 60 |

Source: Collaborative Labelling and Appliance Standards Programme (CLASP) (2020). Data on residential AC are attributed to BSRIA, a "global strategic market intelligence company" according to their website at www.bsria.com/us/?geoh=www.bsria.com&geoc=us. The exact year for "current" AC penetration is not given, except for Ethiopia, where it was 2018.

in a warming world.[10] My view is that forecasts of this sort are more useful as general pointers to the issues at stake than actual prognostications. There are too many uncertainties, such as:

- Demand for air conditioning depends on income, and we have little basis for predicting how income will evolve anywhere, including the developing world.
- Air conditioning units vary widely in efficiency, and if there's a trade-off between efficiency and affordability, the units most demanded in lower-income countries may draw more electricity.[11]
- The implication of increased energy use for carbon emissions depends greatly on the relative role of various fossil fuels in generating electricity to power the ACs.
- Finally, and this may be the most important point of all, future AC adoption in tropical countries is a *political* question, one we ourselves will answer, for better or worse, by the policies we adopt. As the world gets hotter, air conditioning becomes a matter of survival, and whether the billions of people at risk can pay out of their own pockets is not the end of the story. Support from those who are better off for increasing access to electricity and AC is central to climate adaptation, and at the political level mitigation and adaptation are intertwined. In the end, how widely and rapidly AC is disseminated depends on what path we – all of us – choose to take.

As a footnote to this discussion, it should be recognized that the needs of the world's majority go beyond cooling food and bodies, important as this is. Large numbers of people still use wood, dung or similar fuel sources for cooking – 80% in sub-Saharan Africa, for instance.[12] Switching to electricity or fossil fuels is important for public health, as well as to curtail deforestation. Of course, as those without safer, more efficient cooking fuels acquire more income, they will act on their own to make this shift.

The increase in the portion of the world's population who own automobiles will also have a profound effect on our carbon future. Currently, the United States can serve as a benchmark; there are about 800 cars for every 1,000 people (of all ages), which is probably about as much car ownership as a society can sustain. The corresponding number for China is 58, for sub-Saharan Africa 28 and for India 18. The issue is not whether people in these countries "should" have cars or not; the evidence is overwhelming that, as they can afford them, they buy in ever greater numbers. It makes no more sense to deny someone in India or Kenya the right to buy a car than it does to forcibly take a car away from someone who already has one in the United States. It shouldn't happen and it won't.

The conclusions that should be drawn from this overview of energy needs in the Global South are that (1) the growth in future per capita fossil fuel consumption will be much higher in the developing world than in the upper-income countries that already benefit from ample energy use, and (2) if the North doesn't reduce its emissions further in order to offset justifiable and unavoidable emissions from the South, there can be little hope of forestalling catastrophic climate change. Recall from Chapter 3 that a benchmark budget to hold warming to 2° is a constant 3.9% carbon dioxide emissions reduction per year, with none of the escape valves (or fudges) like carbon removal we looked at in Chapter 5. That is the global rate. But we also saw in the same chapter that energy demand is expanding by nearly as much per year, most of it in lower-income countries. If the South is cutting its carbon emissions less, or even temporarily increasing them to meet urgent needs, the North has to reduce that much more.

This is well known in climate policy circles, and there have been various efforts to develop a conceptual framework for reconciling the demands of climate stabilization and international development.[13] In its overview of this topic, IPCC Working Group III puts forward four general principles that ought to inform global coordination: responsibility, capacity, equality and the right to sustainable development.[14] A brief translation: responsibility highlights the much greater role of the developed countries in bringing about currently high atmospheric carbon concentrations; capacity refers to the resources countries can bring to climate mitigation based on their wealth and technological capabilities; equality points to the equal right of each individual to enjoy the possibility of a fulfilling life; and the final principle upholds the necessity for allowing all countries the opportunity to achieve a satisfactory level of development, given the environmental constraints that apply to all of us. As it so often happens, the value of these broad ideas is best seen through the prism of actual, real-world problems, like refrigeration and air conditioning. It is clearly unacceptable that wealthier countries in temperate climates have near-universal access to these technologies, while poorer countries most exposed to the risk of extreme heat must suffer without – and especially that the past carbon impacts of the Global North would be used as an excuse to obstruct the future spread of these life-saving benefits to the Global South.

But when it comes to writing diplomatic language that codifies such differentiated responsibilities, the process virtually freezes. The most minimal agreements, such as Paris, are hailed as breakthroughs simply because they happen, despite the fact that they (1) do not incorporate collective adherence to a meaningful climate budget, (2) lack accountability mechanisms and (3) take us no further toward resolving the distributional disputes between richer and poorer countries. Like Burning Man, these agreements celebrate their own existence. But what is the solution? Will better-defined or better-articulated principles of equity convince governments to arrive at a common understanding? Is there an architecture, a particular set of political procedures, that can help governments iron out their differences and guide them toward greater cooperation?

## Why Cooperate?

But first we need to understand why international cooperation is necessary at all, since the answer isn't immediately obvious. Why can't countries tackle climate change individually, each in its own way? If the United States or the EU or China wants to take action along the lines of the previous chapter, using taxes or permits to put a high and rising price on carbon, what's to prevent them? Perhaps the morass of international negotiations is just an excuse for inaction at the national level.

The starting point is to recognize that climate mitigation is a collective action problem. There is an immense academic literature on collective action that builds on game theory, laboratory experiments and real-world case studies, and we can hardly do justice to it here, but a few general principles will serve us well.

Perhaps the most famous version of a collective action problem is the Prisoner's Dilemma (PD), named for the hypothetical story that was used to illustrate it in 1950 by its authors, Merrill Flood and Melvin Drescher, who were working at the time for the US Air Force's RAND project. There were said to be two prisoners suspected of committing a crime together, grilled separately by the police – but this is not a good example for our purposes because cooperation between the prisoners (each remaining silent) is detrimental for society, while cooperation on mitigating climate change promotes the public good.[15]

First, let's establish the logic of the PD and then see how it can be applied.[16] We can bypass the model's underlying algebra to describe its conceptual structure verbally. In a PD, there are two or more players who each has two options, one which sacrifices some individual benefit for the common good, and another that puts individual advantage over cooperation. In this constructed model, several things are assumed to be true. First, if any individual player cooperates unilaterally, they will be worse off than if they had acted uncooperatively like everyone else, because the disadvantage of self-sacrifice will be felt but not the advantage of cooperation (which isn't reciprocated). Second, if any individual eschews cooperation while others act cooperatively, they will be better off than by sharing cooperation, because the benefits of cooperation are enjoyed without the costs. These two characteristics make it unlikely that a self-interested player would choose to cooperate if the game is played just once: no matter what the others do, cooperate or not, each individual is personally better off by not cooperating. And that leads to the prediction that in such a game general cooperation is improbable. Yet the third feature of a PD, also by assumption, is that all the players are better off under shared cooperation than if they all forgo it. What is individually rational for each of them is collectively irrational for all of them.

It needs to be emphasized that the PD is simply a logical model formulated out of pure algebra, an elaborate if–then construction: *if* a

social situation has all these characteristics, *then* we predict this outcome. It hardly fits all real-world contexts, but it does come close
enough to a number of them that researchers in many fields have found
it a useful tool. Arguably, it applies rather well to the problem of climate
mitigation at the global level. Cooperation in this context means curtailing carbon emissions; it comes at a cost (see Chapter 5), but its
benefits, *if there is general reciprocation around the world*, are even
greater (see Chapter 2). The kicker is the condition that, in order to see
the benefits of cutting our carbon emissions, enough others have to be
doing the same thing. If a single country goes on a strict carbon diet and
absorbs all the resulting costs while the rest of the world continues
business as usual, the lone cooperator faces the first condition of a
PD: all pain and little or no gain. If the rest of the world pulls together
and radically cuts emissions, it will make little difference for climate
outcomes what a single country does (if it isn't a carbon behemoth like
the United States or China), so a free rider option is possible – the
second PD condition. Thus, it's difficult to achieve high levels of buy-
in, just as the theory predicts.

Fortunately, a dog-eat-dog, go it alone world is not our destiny,
even if climate action is a PD. One reason is that players in a PD can
coordinate: they can establish a structure that effectively compels them
to cooperate. An example of this in the sports world is drug testing. The
possibility of taking performance-enhancing drugs that carry a certain
amount of health risk sets up a potential PD if the benefits of winning a
competition are large compared with the health costs. This has been the
case, for instance, in professional cycling. If all the cyclists but one are
doping, the abstainer is at a big competitive disadvantage and will
probably give that more weight than the benefit of avoiding the possible
health effects that may not materialize for years or decades – the first
condition.[17] If all cyclists but one are not doping, the one who dopes
now enjoys a big competitive edge and may well regard this as more
compelling than the risks – the second condition. And so, if cycling isn't
regulated it may devolve into a chemical arms race with ever-mounting
risks to the longevity of each rider. Instead, however, cycling *is* regulated. Riders are tested and severe penalties are imposed. If media
reports are to be believed, this is popular not only among sponsors
and fans but the cyclists themselves. They know how the sport would
devolve if testing were ended, and it's in their collective interest for the
regulation to be effective enough to prevent it.[18]

By analogy, our climate players, the countries reaping individual benefits from the use of fossil fuels but fated to suffer far more if climate change tips into catastrophe, might choose a strong system of regulation. If it were like cycling, it would involve regular monitoring to see that carbon commitments were maintained, with violators facing severe repercussions. That would be what a really serious international treaty would look like.

We don't have one, however. In general, there are three reasons for this. (1) Different countries, unlike cyclists, have rather different interests. If carbon is a drug, it is also true as we have just seen that many countries see a need to increase, not decrease, their dose, at least for many years to come. Of course, those who don't have this need don't want others to emit more than they do. And so we get difficult, almost intractable conflict. (2) The players aren't actually countries, but governments. The policies of governments are determined by the strength of domestic political forces, and in most countries business interests play a preponderate role. As we will see in the next chapter, this is a likely explanation for widespread lack of will. (3) Sanctions, which play the key role in a regulatory solution to the PD, violate the principle of national sovereignty. The weak justifiably fear the power of the strong if the principle of sovereignty is set aside, and the strong, of course, have no intention of discarding their own freedom from external constraint. Every attempt to create a system of punishments within a global climate treaty framework has failed utterly.

So the test 'em and disqualify 'em approach that works for professional cycling is not (yet) an option for the world of global climate policy. That's not the end of the story, however. There are two aspects of carbon mitigation that offer hope for an alternative solution. The first is that, while a bike race is an all-or-nothing competition with a few winners and lots of losers, our fortunes on planet Earth are subtly shaded. Climate risk can be dialed up or down slightly by emitting somewhat more or less carbon, and the costs of taking action are also on a continuous scale. The cyclist's doping decision approximates yes-or-no; the country's decision is more along the lines of "how much?"

The second feature of the climate policy PD that favors international cooperation is that it is ongoing. It is not as though countries make a decision at a single moment on what carbon measures to adopt and then stick with them forever. These questions are always up for renegotiation, and every time the players weigh the costs and benefits it's a new game. The reason this matters is that, in the international context, a choice of what steps to take has two sets of consequences. One is direct, the immediate costs and benefits of that choice. The other is indirect, the effect your choice has on the choices that other players will make in the future, when the game is played again and again. Every country should rationally want all the others to be climate hawks. The United States (minus some miscreants in one of its two dominant parties) wants China to get off coal as soon as possible and cheers every new wind-powered generator in Germany, because the more *other* countries reduce carbon emissions the less climate change there will be for *us*. And of course the same is true in the opposite direction(s). Each country acts in part on the basis of its own internal balance of economic and political interests, but each is also more likely to go further in reducing emissions if it thinks that, by doing so, others will be more likely to follow suit. This was a clear theme, for example, in Obama's promotion of a Clean Power Plan, which was intended to encourage China and other developing countries to go further with their own climate policies.[19] Countries may do more than they would otherwise to build trust and nudge the others to do more too.

Yet despite the somewhat encouraging messages coming to us from the abstruse world of game theory, an immense gap exists between the current state of climate policy around the world and what's needed to keep the alligators at bay. How can we use our understanding of climate mitigation as a collective action problem to find a way forward?

## From Top-Down to Bottom-Up Coordination

What should be the first step any country's government should take, for either launching its own policies or setting in motion the process of international coordination? The Extinction Rebellion, whose direct action strategy will be considered later, demands that governments begin by "tell[ing] the truth by declaring a climate and ecological emergency."[20] As I hope should be clear by now, this call is fully justified, but it leaves the policy content still to be addressed.

On the issue of international coordination, leaders typically begin by announcing they will engage in diplomacy – again a reasonable if unrevealing initiative. Soon after his election as president, for example, Joe Biden appointed John Kerry as a special envoy for climate. Since Kerry had previously served as Secretary of State under Barack

Obama, this was seen as a signal that Biden was serious about the issue.[21] Still, as of this writing it remains to be seen what actual measures the US government will take or propose.

The logic of this book, on the other hand, points to a concrete first step that establishes a framework for all subsequent policies, as well as criteria by which they can be judged. It applies equally to domestic and international policy, although it is the international dimension I will emphasize here. It is simply that the government publicly announces the remaining carbon budget for its own country it pledges to adhere to. This announcement is a unilateral action. It doesn't need to be negotiated with anyone or even, initially, justified. It simply recognizes that acting against catastrophic climate change requires a carbon budget and that, in the absence of any international authority, these budgets will have to be applied at the national level. At the outset such a budget could be purely aspirational, not backed by any policies that force compliance with it, meaning it wouldn't even require legislation; a political leader or high-level administrator could simply proclaim it.

What makes this a first step is that it naturally leads to more steps. First, by setting a standard by which it invites others to judge it, a government with a carbon budget puts policy on the agenda. Observers will logically ask whether existing measures do enough to make the budget limit stick, and if there is a glaring gap between aspiration and action there will be demands to close it. Now demands are not the same as results, and there is no guarantee that governments will back up their fine proclamations with programs that can get the job done, such as the toolkit discussed in the previous chapter. But there are no guarantees in any event; what we can say is that there will be more pressure for meaningful action with an announced carbon budget than without one, and that the standard for "meaningful" will become much more precise and transparent.

The second step is giving consistency to the budget commitment. It is always possible for officials to say one thing and then, after the next reshuffling of government, for their replacements to say something else. Again, at this stage there are no guarantees. However, the advantage of having a declared carbon budget is that it puts the question to each successive administration: Will you continue to be guided by this budget or do you intend to change it in some way? This makes it at least possible to *talk* about policy consistency in a way we can't if we're not specific about carbon budgets. When new administrations come in they will always make policy changes, and in the area of climate change they will explain their actions as being more efficient, or smarter, or more practical, or more visionary or something else. Without a fixed standard for measurement, which is what a carbon budget provides, there is no obvious way to escape the rhetorical miasma. But a budget is a number, and changing a number means moving to either a higher number or a lower one. Any retreat from consistency becomes explicit.

The international aspect emerges as multiple countries make such an announcement. If enough countries take this step, the total for the world and its relationship to a recognized standard like a 2° budget is a matter of simple arithmetic, since budgets, unlike emissions targets for varying years, are additive. It is virtually certain that the sum of these nationally self-chosen carbon allotments will exceed what nearly all informed observers recognize as a viable global total. This will clarify the challenge we all face, one that has been largely obscured during the long decades of smoke and mirrors policy. On this basis there can begin to be honest discussions about how the available carbon space should be apportioned.

What might these discussions look like? At first officials and experts from various countries might simply present to each other the reasons for their national emissions objectives and, assuming the sum of the national budgets is manifestly too high, their preferences for who should cut back the most. We shouldn't expect this process to be amicable or to immediately converge. Actually, it is unlikely there will be any settled agreement over the decades to come, since not only attitudes but also facts will continue to change. No global carbon budget is set in stone, and new findings in climate science and related fields will cause it to go up or down. The impacts of climate change may be less or more severe than we expect, and the relative vulnerability of different parts of the planet may also evolve. Some countries will undergo spurts of economic growth while others fall behind. The objective is not to find a single set of carbon allotments to adhere to, come what may, but set in motion a process that can translate the challenge of reconciling climate, development and adaptation goals at the international level into rational political debate within countries.

But what about the goal of cooperation? If no general agreement comes out of this process, aren't we still in a world of unilateral decision-making and the frustrations of a Prisoner's Dilemma? Not necessarily, since "national versus global" is a false dichotomy; in between lies a vast arena of potential coordination that is international but not universal. Seeing this is critical to making progress.

The core problem with the global agreement template is that it requires unanimity among all participants; that's how all treaty-based institutions operate. Of course, treaties are not strictly universal; they have to be ratified, and countries that refuse to sign are not party to them. Famously, the United States never ratified the Kyoto Protocol and was therefore never included in it. But the goal of negotiators is always to get maximum participation, and buy-in especially from the countries that may be least open to an agreement but are – as measured by their size, wealth or level of carbon emissions – key players. That obviously means the United States, but also India and other nations reluctant to make significant commitments. It would be wonderful if these holdouts changed their policies and became enthusiastic about mitigating climate change, but in the meantime there are many options open to groups of countries that want to accelerate progress.

A small group of countries (or other actors) willing to band together to achieve a common purpose is called a "club" by political scientists; the concept of a carbon club is especially associated with David Victor, who has written effectively on its behalf.[22] The way it works is like this: governments believing climate action to be especially urgent would meet and draw up an agreement just for themselves; there would be no effort to widen the group at the cost of watering down its commitment. The institutions they establish would possess real, if less than universal, force. In addition, the club would create incentives for new members to join in the form of both positive benefits for insiders and costs to those who stay outside. In effect, this is a bottom-up rather than a top-down approach to gaining global cooperation, where national governments are the individual actors that constitute the "bottom."

Do such club-ready countries exist today? There are certainly many governments that are intensely concerned about climate change and want to act in a bold way, but they largely represent small populations, such as the Association of Small Island States (AOSIS). AOSIS represents thirty-nine countries or protectorates that, because of their geography, are especially vulnerable to the sea level rise resulting from a warming planet.[23] They are a vocal presence at international climate conferences, but their clout is practically nil; the fact that some of them will simply disappear under the waves does not give them bargaining power. They would be enthusiastic supporters of a carbon club, but are not large or powerful enough to get it off the ground. Many large and influential countries, as well as the European Union, have made public statements of support for aggressive climate mitigation, but so far their performance does not match their rhetoric. In the case of the EU, for instance, we saw in the previous chapter that their trading system (the ETS) appears to be deliberately designed to be ineffective.

The honest conclusion would be that a carbon club of the type I've sketched is purely hypothetical at this point, but even if there isn't yet a constituency for it, that isn't reason to dismiss it. For one thing, it's the only plausible path to international cooperation, since it has a lower bar to surmount than a global agreement. For another, raising the issue of a carbon club potentially puts the matter on the agenda. It can be a way to sharpen the politics of climate mitigation at the national level, so more momentum for membership can be created. In that sense, it sits alongside the other policies considered in this book, like carbon permits and taxes, the setting of carbon budgets, and the elimination of loopholes like carbon offsets and exemptions for favored businesses. These ideas are not politically viable today, but by clarifying them, communicating them to others, and especially by using them as a basis for organizing, we can try to bring them about – and so also with a climate club.

## The Climate Club: Privileges of Membership

The primary purpose of a climate club is to have an impact on climate change that exceeds what any one country could do on its own, or even what all the member countries could do separately. There are two particularly important functions.

*Reducing the collective action problem.* In the simplest version of a Prisoner's Dilemma the logic of noncooperation is overwhelming, but the problem of international climate coordination offers opportunities for evolving step-by-step initiatives. One difference is that the options open to the players in a classical PD are binary: whether to cooperate or not. The same bifurcation appears in the cycling example, as riders decide whether or not to dope. But climate action can be measured on a continuum from doing nothing (or making the problem worse, for instance, by subsidizing fossil fuels) to extreme, emergency measures to reduce emissions. This means *some* international cooperation can be better than none, and it can make enough of a difference that countries might individually choose it. The reason is that gradations of costs and benefits of cooperation moderate the force of the two incentives that characterize a PD, the disincentive to being a lone cooperator and the attraction of being a lone noncooperator.

To be precise, a climate club, even if it doesn't muster enough cooperation on its own to achieve adherence to a 2° carbon budget, can reduce the odds of catastrophe enough to matter. The bigger the club, the more the risk dial is turned, even well short of universal cooperation. In cycling, on the other hand, if 80% of the riders stop taking drugs but the other 20% continue, the costs for the cooperators in their own decreased competitiveness are almost the same as if the proportions were 20–80.

Another consideration is that a climate club can reduce some of the costs of emissions reduction stemming from international trade. As with the ecological benefits, the reduction in economic costs is not an all-or-nothing proposition. If a group of countries forms a club, and if they all go on a similar carbon diet, trade between them is, in this respect at least, on an equal footing. The more countries that join, the wider this "carbon fair trade" zone will extend. It is important to recognize that international trade is not evenly distributed across the globe; every country has a few others with which it has especially close trading relations. The United States, for instance, trades intensively with Canada – far more than, say, with Russia. In this way, countries can significantly reduce the costs of taking serious climate action if some of their key trading partners join them in a carbon club.

Even if carbon budgets vary within a climate club, the potential economic costs they impose on the most ambitious carbon cutters are less than disparity between those with meaningful climate policies and those with none. In addition, a climate club can negotiate internal trading rules with a variety of mechanisms to mute distortions. It is the commitment to acting forcefully on reducing warming and aligning other policies to minimize the costs that makes the club a club.[24]

The other wrinkle we considered earlier, the difference between a one-time-and-out PD and an interaction that is frequently repeated, also points to the value of setting up a club. For one thing, a club provides structure that can promote trust, the key factor in a process that moves toward greater cooperation over time. It could standardize the measures that qualify as "committed" climate action, and its common policies would be more transparent and, hopefully, permanent than the occasional, disconnected proclamations by political leaders we see today. Above all, the importance of institutionalizing trust should not be overlooked. A country, by joining the club, would assume obligations that would be formalized, and they could count on their fellow members to carry out the same obligations on their end. The more a country can rely on a reciprocating effect of its own commitments, the more likely it is to make them.

Perhaps the best feature of a club in this context, however, is that it can expand. It can begin with a few founding countries, and, as others see it is working, they can consider whether to join. Rather than having to overcome the collective action barrier all at once, a club can chip away at it, bit by bit. If, as is almost certain, the advantages of cooperation grow in tandem with the size of the club, it will acquire momentum. It might take only a modest amount of benefit to convince some country on the cusp of joining to take the plunge; then, with the club having grown and now offering that much more for its members, another country now occupies the cusp, and so on. If it's likely that there will be a tendency for a viable climate club to grow over time, the most important thing is to get it started.[25]

*Sharing common costs, especially research and development.* An ambitious climate policy encompasses a number of activities whose costs can be shared. The most important is investment in research to find new technologies that reduce society's dependence on fossil fuels. Much effort already goes into this, of course, but the landscape will be redefined if meaningful prices are placed on carbon. Technologies that might have seemed uneconomic in a world of unregulated fossil fuel use may be more attractive as policy tightens. The struggle of modelers to find a nondisruptive path to stabilization at 450 ppm carbon dioxide, which we saw in Chapter 5, indicates that a still higher research and development effort is called for, and this need is only intensified when we contemplate a $1.5°$ warming target instead. But research in this field (and others) has an aspect of what economists call a public good: if a breakthrough is achieved, knowledge of it will be disseminated all around the world – as it needs to be – whether or not those who benefit contributed to the costs of discovery. That creates an opportunity for countries to become free-riders, not putting up their share of the costs yet taking advantage of the investments of others. A carbon club can at least share these costs equitably among its own members. This is not a complete solution, since nonmembers can still free-ride, but it is better than no cost-pooling at all. In this situation we should take what we can get.

## Carbon Revenues and Climate Finance

The benefits of membership described above are intrinsic to the nature of a carbon club: what it is and what functions it performs. But a club can adopt additional policies that, while not centered on reducing carbon emissions directly, provide further inducements for new countries to join – a strategy game theorists refer to as "side payments." One intriguing possibility is using the rebate concept, which we will discuss in the final chapter at the international level.

Consider the following scenario. Suppose, to make things simple, all countries (or at least all countries for which the World Bank has data) are members of this club. (In that case it wouldn't be a club, but this is just a scenario.) Let's suppose this club has a shared carbon pricing mechanism, either a permit system or a tax. Every tonne of carbon dioxide emitted results in a payment, and the payments are collected in a common pool. Now imagine the pool has an administrator who once a year divides up all the revenues and returns the money to the countries in the club on the basis of population *only*. In other words, if the countries were to turn around and divide this rebate equally among their own citizens, each person in the whole club, no matter where they lived, would get the same sum of money: an individual in Burkina Faso would get the same as someone in Switzerland.[26]

Of course, the governments of these countries would not be obligated to disburse their refunds they receive from the pool, but the principle is that the carbon fund belongs to all of us equally, where "us" is people, with the expectation that governments will use the money on our behalf. Our question here is, What would be the distributional effect of such a system? Which countries would put in more than they get back and vice versa? We can answer this question with data assembled by the World Bank and included in the World Development Indicators database. Table 7.3 provides the results of this simulation for a carbon price of $1 per tonne, using the income categories into which the World Bank has sorted all the individual nations. They use four broad groups: high, upper middle, lower middle and low income, based on national income per capita, and data are for 2016, the most recent year for which the Bank reports carbon emissions.

**Table 7.3.** Net flows resulting from a $1 per tonne carbon price and equal per capita rebate, in dollars (per capita) and billions of dollars

| Income group | Population (billions) | Payments (billions of $) | Receipts (billions of $) | Net transfer (billions of $) | Net transfer ($ per capita) |
|---|---|---|---|---|---|
| High | 1.2 | 12.7 | 5.5 | −7.1 | −5.4 |
| Upper middle | 2.8 | 16.7 | 12.7 | −4.0 | −1.4 |
| Lower middle | 2.8 | 4.2 | 12.7 | 8.5 | 4.0 |
| Low | 0.6 | 0.2 | 2.8 | 2.6 | 4.3 |

*Source*: World Bank (2021).

To make sense of this exercise, it first helps to know a bit about how the countries are sorted. The cutoffs in per capita annual income (measured using market exchange rates) are $1,035 (US) between low and lower middle, $4,045 between lower and upper middle, and $12,535 between upper middle and high. Examples include Haiti and Ethiopia (low), Egypt and Honduras (lower middle), Brazil and China (upper middle), and the United States and South Korea (high); for the full list, consult the World Bank's Country and Lending Groups web page.[27]

The first step in constructing the table was to calculate carbon payments by country income group; this was simply their collective carbon emissions in tonnes times the $1 price per tonne. The second was to calculate rebates; this was the sum of all carbon payments divided by the share of the total population accounted for by each group. The final step is the net transfer, deducting the payments leaving each group from the rebates returning to it.

Several caveats are in order. The carbon emissions data are based on production, not consumption, as many analysts would like; we'll take a look at that issue shortly. Second, it assumes there are no changes in carbon emissions resulting from instituting the carbon price – an absurdity, since that's the whole point. In other words, this means the calculation applies at best only to the first year in which the program is in operation. Third, it assumes there is a reliable, costless mechanism for collecting all this money and rebating it back to the countries who should receive it. Finally, since it is likely governments will keep some or all the money they receive and not distribute it to their populations, we face thorny questions about accountability and sovereignty. (Rebates to governments based on their populations rest on the assumption the money will benefit the people.)

Nevertheless, despite its obvious simplification this exercise provides a useful glimpse at what an internationally administered carbon price could accomplish. On the basis of two widely accepted principles – payment based on the amount of emissions and rebate based on an equal claim to the global commons – we would arrive at a progressive global redistribution system that could accomplish a lot of good. Keep in mind that this table gives the results of a $1 per tonne carbon price, but obviously an actual price would be much higher. Suppose, for instance, that the main portion of the carbon pricing system is administered at the national level and only a fraction is international. If this international piece is $10 per tonne, multiple all the numbers in Table 7.3 by ten. In that case the very poorest countries would receive $26 billion in net income, while the far more numerous group just above them, the lower middle income category, would net about $85 billion. And every year the carbon price would continue to rise and the transfers would rise with it.[28]

In this simple example the combined transfers associated with a $10 per tonne carbon price exceed the $100 billion climate finance pledge made by developed countries first in Copenhagen in 2009 and then repeated in Cancun in 2010 and Paris in 2015. The dismal story of this pledge deserves a closer look, which will help contextualize the hypothetical transfers stemming from a shared carbon pricing system. To strike a deal with developing countries, which were balking at any global agreement, even a purely symbolic one, in Copenhagen, the upper income countries promised to create a fund that would provide $100 billion per year in financing for climate adaptation and mitigation by 2020. This fund, they assured us, would be additional, on top of already existing money for development projects and other purposes.

To keep the Global South on board, the pledge was renewed at high-level meetings in 2010 (Cancun) and 2015 (Paris). Unfortunately, no precise definition of what constituted "funding" or climate "adaptation" or "mitigation" was offered, nor was any mechanism set up to monitor performance of this pledge. Instead, we heard vague, reassuring statements by European and American leaders claiming that the fund is on track and will arrive at its promised magnitude by the 2020 deadline and hailing a misleading OECD report supposedly documenting progress.[29] As the deadline approached, however, it became impossible to cover up the gap between rhetoric and reality. The most recent study of the adaptation side of the pledge – $50 billion – found that, once the misrepresentations of wealthy country governments were corrected, actual finance was likely less than $10 billion. This figure is for 2020, the year the pledge was supposed to be fulfilled.[30]

In this light, an *automatic* system that funnels more than $100 billion per year to the world's poorer countries has quite a bit to recommend it. It is explicitly additional. Its operation is transparent and can be monitored by all parties. Since the payments wouldn't be parceled out by government agencies in the Global North but flow routinely according to explicit rules, there wouldn't be pressure on lower-income countries to purchase the exports of donor countries or borrow money from their lending facilities, both of which have been documented in previous reports by Adaptation Watch, an NGO that scrutinizes climate finance.[31] Of course, there would need to be a structure to ensure that funds are actually used for some form of climate adaptation, and this is not a trivial matter, but by bringing the process out into the open there is hope for an acceptable solution.

The benefits of the transfer mechanism we've been considering are clear, but note that it is predicated on a shared, international system of carbon pricing and rebates – and that's the sort of thing a carbon club is especially designed to do. There wouldn't need to be an agreement on the precise policies club members would implement. For instance, a higher-income country might establish a ceiling on carbon emissions that resulted in a price of $200 per tonne, while a low-income member's price might be only $50. Even so, $10 or some other common portion could be dedicated to the shared fund; in fact, a division along these lines that strikes a balance between equity within countries and between them would be expected.

So imagine that such a system has been set up, but only for countries that agreed to join it. The prospect of being net recipients of carbon funds would serve as a powerful inducement for lower-income countries, those roughly on the bottom half of the global income ladder, to participate. True, the prospect of being net payers might provoke some hesitation on the part of those in the upper-income countries, but (1) under such a system they could reach a critical mass of global support for a stringent carbon budget, (2) they can afford it, (3) they may value fighting poverty and improving global equity for its own sake, and (4) the portion of the total carbon price that is shared internationally can be adjusted up or down to maintain politically sustainability. How far the Global North is prepared to go in sharing carbon revenues with the Global South remains to be seen, but it is not wildly optimistic to think that the portion could be large enough to bring most of the developing world into the carbon club.

## Climate and Development: A Shared Agenda

A system of sharing carbon revenues through equal per-capita rebates would work wonders for global cooperation and meeting the adaptation finance goals already on the table, but why stop there? The biggest mental step we can take is to pull back from tunnel vision about climate change, as urgent as it is, and see the larger situation of global development and inequality as a whole. Cooperation on carbon is just one aspect of larger set of interconnected problems, and what we do on each affects the others. To put it very directly, if we want development goals to bend toward climate imperatives in some ways, we need to provide extra support for these goals in other ways. Policy makers in poorer countries are justifiably reluctant to relax the struggle against poverty (to the extent they are actually waging it), but they may be more open to policies that reduce fossil fuel use if they are embedded in a broader antipoverty agenda.

The logical place to start when thinking about this is with the global goals initiated at the end of the twentieth century. The process began with the Millennium Development Goals (MDGs), formally launched at a UN-sponsored summit in 2000.[32] The MDGs established numerical targets in eight broad areas: extreme hunger and poverty, primary education, gender equality, child mortality, maternal health, infectious disease, environmental sustainability, and global cooperation (including aid). The approach embodied a form of management by objectives, reflecting impatience with vague promises and insufficient performance. The intention was to reach as many of the targets as possible by 2015; in the end the MDGs met with mixed success but did achieve important results in education and health. In 2016 the baton was passed to the Sustainable Development Goals (SDGs), which at this writing have not acquired the prominence of the MDGs but nevertheless remain a reference point for global discussion.[33]

From the outset it was apparent the global goals framework was limited by a lack of funding. Education and public health, for example, are not cheap, and cutting corners defeats the purpose. To mobilize financial support, a long list of donors, development agencies and other interested parties created the Leading Group on Innovative Financing for Development in 2006.[34] Its membership today includes sixty-six countries, including China, Japan and the EU; international agencies like the IMF and the World Bank; major foundations (Gates, Rockefeller); and a wide range of NGOs like Oxfam and the Climate Action Network. The only significant holdout is the United States.

The Leading Group has explored a number of initiatives to transform financial support for development from a sporadic, strings-attached instrument of big power foreign policy to a routine, rule-based system. The name that has arisen to describe this perspective is "global public finance."[35] Just as governments at a local or national level do not pass the hat when they need revenue, and voters in one neighborhood don't deliberate each time a need for spending arises across town, so international needs should be met not by ad hoc measures but a similarly institutionalized system of taxation and budgeting. Building up such a system, piece by piece, is the program of the Leading Group.

Thus far only one step in this direction has been (partially) implemented, but it is instructive. Ten countries, most prominently France, have banded together to implement an "airline solidarity tax." The levy varies from country to country, but most of the money has been collected by France, which charges flyers traveling coach to pay an extra euro for a domestic ticket or 4 euros for an international ticket, and ten times this amount for those traveling business or first class. The money goes to UNITAID, an international fund devoted to combating AIDS, malaria and tuberculosis.[36] Up to this point, almost $1.7 billion has been raised from this tax, a revenue source that's predictable and exerts no leverage over the politics of countries on the receiving end.[37]

Among the other revenue-generating proposals under consideration by the Leading Group is a tax on international financial transactions. From the standpoint of financial stability, the goal would be to lessen the volatility of foreign exchange markets, but its potential to support development programs is significant as well. A very modest version of this tax was examined by a team assembled by the Leading Group, which reported that it was feasible and could be expected to raise about $15 billion per year.[38] There are also ongoing explorations of measures to reduce tax avoidance on the part of corporations and the ultrarich, which takes a very high toll on developing country finances.[39]

I hope by now the general picture is clear. There is an emerging international consensus that the needs of development, especially involving education and health, are compelling and that, to get the job done, a regular, institutionalized flow of finance is required. What holds back progress at this point, above all, is the opposition of the United States, which has been absolute from the beginning and not discernibly different from one administration – red or blue – to the next. Meanwhile, even relatively orthodox institutions like the IMF are supportive, although, of course, there is a range of opinion when the details of these proposals are discussed. What would take this agenda to the next level would be its fusion with climate policy, both adaptation and mitigation. One could imagine a global package combining serious emissions reductions framed by a global carbon budget, and accompanied by a global public finance initiative that would fund both development and adaptation needs.[40] Initially, it would need to be on a club basis, since at least one key player, the United States, refuses to play, but it might well attract participation from virtually the entire rest of the world. As one thinks about it, it seems artificial to *not* link the large financial flows of carbon policy with the financial imperatives of providing a decent standard of living to the billions who now lack it.

## What about Trade?

The issue of international trade looms large in discussions about climate policy, not always constructively. For some reason, many climate activists have come to believe the use of fossil fuels to move goods around the world is a major contributor to carbon emissions. On an intuitive level the idea seems to make sense, since at every major port one can see a vast expanse of shipping containers that shuttle back and forth around the world – surely a major draw on our carbon budget. And yet, not so much. A modern ship can carry 15,000 containers, so the fuel use per item shipped is extremely small; a much greater concern should be short-distance trucking. The International Council on Clean Transportation estimates 1,061 megatonnes of carbon dioxide equivalent was emitted in 2015 in the course of international marine shipping;

this is about 2.2% of global greenhouse gas emissions for that year from all sources.[41] This is not nothing, but it is small relative to the other uses, and interesting concepts involving hydrodynamic ship design and a partial return to wind power are being explored that could reduce emissions for the same amount of cargo.[42]

A different and more interesting question is how international trade affects calculations of carbon emissions. The standard measurements, such as the one used a few pages ago to calculate the effects of a carbon pricing and rebate mechanism at the global level, are based on estimates of emissions within each country's territory. This is a production-based footprint, since it is where goods are produced that determines who is given responsibility for their emissions. There is a good case to be made, however, for a consumption-based footprint, assigning responsibility to those using these goods, no matter where their production occurs. Consider a refrigerator, for instance. Suppose it is produced in Korea but sold to a consumer in the United States. Producing the refrigerator generates carbon emissions, especially if some of the refrigerant gases, with their intense greenhouse impacts, escape into the atmosphere. Under a production footprint these emissions would be assigned to Korea, under a consumption footprint to the United States. Insofar as demand ultimately elicits supply, it is the US consumer whose choices play the decisive role.

All the officially published data, such as the World Bank indicators, use production footprints since they are much easier to calculate, but there have been several studies over the years that have tried to estimate consumption-based alternatives. This is complicated, because carbon emitted from the production of a finished good loaded for export can't simply be deducted from that country's production footprint; in the contemporary integrated world economy intermediate goods used along the way may themselves have been imported from elsewhere. There is no way to make the statistical adjustment without taking into account all the flows of parts and materials at every stage of the process. Since there are several competing models of these linkages in the world economy, studies produce somewhat different numbers.[43]

While no single set of estimates can be regarded as definitive, Table 7.4 presents results from one recent study that suggest the magnitude of the production/consumption difference. For many countries these are quite large adjustments. In general, developed countries have

**Table 7.4.** Consumption minus production $CO_2$ emissions as percentage of production, selected countries, 2008

| | |
|---|---|
| Brazil | −0.4 |
| China | −18.9 |
| France | 40.7 |
| Germany | 28.8 |
| India | −10.5 |
| Japan | 15.6 |
| Nigeria | −27.6 |
| South Africa | −33.4 |
| UK | 29.1 |
| US | 8.4 |

*Source:* Peters et al. (2011).

higher consumption footprints, because they are net consumers of goods produced in the developing world. By this measure, for instance, France's emissions would be undercounted by almost 30% if a production footprint were used, while China's would be overcounted by about 23%.[44] The United States, incidentally, is less affected by this recomputation, despite its very sizable trade deficit. The reason is the United States specializes in exporting resource- (and therefore carbon-) intensive goods, as it has since its first settlement by Europeans.[45] There is one very large and one smaller caveat to be aware of regarding this table, however. First, note the year, 2008. This was when international trade reached its peak as a proportion of the world economy, just before crashing precipitously in 2009. It hasn't fully recovered since, and this suggests more recent adjustments would be smaller. Second, regarding France and Germany, the euro was also at a peak in 2008, and this made eurozone goods less competitive on world markets. The result was that people in Germany, France and the rest of the zone were consuming more and producing less than they were a few years later, when the euro had lost 30–40% of its value.

Looking at the world as a whole, as international trade became a larger component of global output, so did the carbon emissions embodied in traded goods. One study found that the share of all emissions that went into the production of traded goods increased during the early years of this century, peaking at 38% in 2008.[46] This is a gross rather than net measurement, since it records embodied emissions in each country's exports and imports and not just the differences between them.

What do these numbers mean in practical terms? The answer depends on the policies we adopt. Production-based carbon pricing schemes in the richer countries will miss the carbon that enters through imports destined for their consumption; this missing carbon is called "leakage." On the other side of the trade connection, a developing country like China that imposes a carbon price on itself can expect to pass a portion of the cost on to wealthier consumers in the Global North. The difference between consumption and production footprints is also invoked in discussions of ethical responsibility; it's given as a reason why wealthier countries should do more than their pro rata share, if that share is based on standard production-based accounting.

Perhaps the most controversial aspect of the intersection between trade and climate policy has to do with the effects on global competition when some countries adopt carbon pricing while others don't. The fear among many in developed countries is that a tough system of emissions controls will drive up costs, while low-income competitors, using low-cost or even free carbon, will take their markets away. In fact, every time a carbon policy initiative is introduced in a developed country this fear is voiced, and it often carries considerable political weight.[47]

A potential antidote is a carbon tariff. If enacted by a country that has chosen to price carbon, it would add a tax to every item imported from countries without such a policy based on the amount of carbon emissions used in its production. In conjunction, a country could also offer export subsidies for domestic firms competing for markets in countries with lower carbon costs, although this is technically more challenging. Together these are called "border adjustments" by economists, and they have several objectives:

- They cut down on leakage, making the policy's actual contribution to emissions reduction greater than it would otherwise be.
- They may preserve employment in the country adopting the policy.

- They "level the playing field," at least in this respect, between producers in different countries. In theory this should promote more efficient outcomes, since less efficient firms wouldn't be able to conquer markets just because they happened to be located in countries that hadn't yet begun to price carbon.
- They generate better incentives for producers and consumers alike. Consumers would have a financial stake in reducing the carbon content of the goods they buy no matter where they were produced. Producers would have a stake in less carbon-intensive methods no matter where they were located.
- They reduce the incentive for firms to relocate to countries with low or nonexistent carbon pricing – the "pollution haven" effect.
- By doing all of the above, they might make it easier to gain political acceptance for tough carbon policies in countries that compete in international markets.

Analysis of the pros and cons of such measures has occupied a small army of researchers.[48] There are many issues to consider that would affect how well border adjustments would work in practice, or even whether their benefits outweigh their costs.

To start with, there is the legal dimension: Would they violate the rules of the World Trade Organization (WTO), and if so, what then? We won't know for sure until the WTO actually rules on a carbon tariff or subsidy, and none has yet been implemented. That hasn't stopped legal experts from sifting through relevant treaty language, precedents from previous rulings, and the various fine points of policy design. Since the WTO has endorsed the "polluter pays" principle, most observers believe *some* types of tariff could gain approval, at least more readily than subsidies, but the question is which kinds.[49]

But the practicality of border carbon adjustments doesn't hinge only on their legal status. As we have seen, any estimate of the direct and indirect carbon content of an individual traded good can be only approximate, and there will need to be credible rules for producing such numbers if they become the basis for tariffs and subsidies. Above all, from both an ethical and a political perspective, the rules need to be seen as fair by both exporting and importing countries as well as higher- and lower-income ones. The closer such a system comes to being consensual rather than unilateral, the better it will be. An international body, perhaps drawing on both trade and climate science expertise, could perform a large service by facilitating agreement on border adjustment schedules.

Meanwhile, the political economy of trade regulation has been upended in recent years by the profusion of complex value chains. Much of what we assume about the interests of importers and exporters is based on the simple notion that goods competing in international markets are the products of individual countries and the corporations based there. This was implicit, for instance, in the example of the Korean refrigerator exported to the United States. But such goods are now assembled from parts made from all over the world, including the country to which the finished product is ultimately exported. And parts are themselves made from distantly sourced parts, making it difficult to calculate national value shares in many cases. This has important implications for climate policy: if producers in a country with high carbon prices import intermediate goods from countries with low ones and then turn around and export back to them, a carbon tariff will actually *reduce* their ability to compete.[50]

To sum up, border carbon adjustments? Probably, but they can't make the collective action problem of global policy we considered earlier in this chapter go away. The most important steps that can be taken on that front are to get a carbon club constituted as soon as possible and to institute measures, especially those that incorporate support for global development – that would still be worth doing even if climate change were not a problem at all – to bring as many countries on board as possible.

# 8  POLITICAL ECONOMY FOR ALLIGATORS

On November 27, 2012, President Obama pulled out a pen and signed into law the only act relating to climate change ever passed at the federal level. Despite the bitter controversies surrounding all things climate, this bill sailed through without a peep of opposition: it had been approved in the Senate by unanimous consent and then the House by a voice vote.[1] Despite its singular status in the history of US climate policy, its passage was unremarked by any major news service. Readers of the *New York Times*, the *Washington Post* and Reuters, not to mention the popular online news and commentary blogs, would have heard nothing about it. What was this law, and why was it invisible?

Its name says a lot: the European Union Emissions Trading Scheme Prohibition Act of 2011. (A year passed between its introduction and passage.) Recall the ETS was designed as a downstream, industry-by-industry carbon cap – at first fragmentary but covering more sectors over time. In 2011 the EU extended the trading system to airlines, and the United States, along with several other countries, was outraged. How could the EU unilaterally require carbon permits for planes landing at or taking off from European airports? Wouldn't that cut into the revenues of US-based carriers? Doesn't an action of that type undermine the right of each country to ignore its carbon emissions if it chooses? How dare they? For the record, the Obama administration and airline lobbyists argued the ETS initiative would interfere with the development of more effective global controls on air travel – controls that have not come any nearer to realization (no surprise) during the past nine years.[2] So the purpose of the Act was to prohibit any US-based airline company from participating in the ETS by acquiring carbon permits.

The only federal law on climate change is one that made it illegal to cooperate with a (weak) system for controlling carbon emissions.

And what about the invisibility? The salient fact about this law was that its passage was not an issue. There was no opposition in either house of congress or the executive branch. This is not to say there were no voices that questioned such a blunt attack on climate policy: a coalition of environmental groups protested it, and the Brookings Institution, a respected centrist policy analysis organization, calmly argued it was the wrong approach.[3] But they could have held their breath, since no one in a position of political influence was listening. And because there wasn't any dissent within the two major political parties or between them, it wasn't a topic the news media felt there was any need to cover.

What happened in 2012 was just a somewhat more extreme version of the events and nonevents that occur each day in the politics of climate change. The main themes of this book have been the extraordinary, unprecedented urgency to respond to the climate challenge, the necessity of phasing out fossil fuels as rapidly as possible, and the evasions, distractions and denials that, in their different ways, justify inaction. But there is one final question, perhaps the most important of all, that remains unaddressed: *Why* the triumph of confusion and delay? Is it a failure of messaging? Some inherent shortcoming of politics or even human nature? What can explain the lack of progress in countries and regions as different as the United States, the European Union, and China? And what do we have to do differently in the future to get serious policies to control carbon off the starting blocks?

The premise of this final chapter is that the *political economy* of climate change is as challenging as the economics, and only when we face this honestly will we be able to make real progress. The term "political economy" has been used in different ways; here I mean simply the intersection of economic and political power – especially the role of concentrated wealth in guiding and constraining the political system. I will not argue for one theory of this tangle of interconnections over another but use a general approach to explain why climate action is so difficult to bring about. The primary problem is that pursuing the agenda described in Chapter 6 would cause a sudden, massive loss of wealth, and those who stand to lose it have a virtual veto power over ostensibly democratic systems of government. Under these conditions the only way to get a climate initiative approved is to compromise it to the point of ineffectiveness. Worse, putting a price on carbon would transfer vast sums of money – literally trillions of dollars – from the general public to whoever collects the carbon revenue, and using these funds to compensate the wealthy leaves the majority, the voters, holding the bag. These observations aren't particularly obscure, but it has been considered impolite to bring them up.

Alligators hoping to extend their range may cast a crooked smile on these simple political economic considerations, but humans should view them as the agenda behind the agenda – what needs to be overcome so we can take decisive action to keep carbon in the ground.

## Carbon and Capital

When I started as a neophyte local news reporter many decades ago, I was pulled aside by a veteran and told that 90% of municipal politics is about land values. What's the issue? Is it a zoning change, extending a sewer line or widening a road? Do a little research, find out who owns the land whose price could go up or down, and that will tell you most of what you need to know about why the item is up for consideration and who will line up on which side. It was good advice, and not just at a local level. Look beyond land to other assets, change the topic to climate protection, and it works nationally and even globally.

What does it mean to say the cost of adhering to a 2° carbon budget could be expensive? Who pays these costs, and in what form? In Chapter 5 we surveyed the existing knowledge, but we didn't consider the crucial question, *Who pays?* Now we will.

An obvious place to start is fossil fuel companies. Over the past ten years multiple studies have been conducted that show the amount of coal, oil and gas on the books of corporations (and in many cases governments) – resources that make up much or most of the value of their enterprises – greatly exceeds the amount that can be extracted and burned if we are to adhere to a proper carbon budget. Of course, potential fuel that remains in the ground has no economic value. A company that thought it owned $100 million of oil reserves, for instance, might find it owned only, say, $20 million post-policy.

This in turn means the value of the company itself, which is approximately the value of what it owns, would also be that much less.[4]

The term of art for fossil fuel reserves companies have paid money to locate and develop, which constitute a substantial portion of their net worth but will have to be left in the ground under a vigorous carbon policy, is "stranded assets." All assets have a lifespan, of course, and depreciation envisions the gradual, planned loss of value as they age and either deteriorate or are superseded by new investments. Assets are stranded, however, if this process exceeds its planned rate due to unanticipated changes in regulations, technology or other factors. In everyday terms, it means a portion of the asset's value has to be written off; this is simply a reduction in the wealth of the owner.[5]

So how much wealth loss is on the table with carbon policy? Most research has been limited to fossil fuel assets alone. Perhaps the most influential voice belongs to Carbon Tracker, which put 80% of carbon energy reserves in the stranded category, conditional on stringent climate action. They don't estimate this portion in monetary terms but note that large, privately owned companies in this sector have a combined market valuation of $4 trillion. Clearly, a considerable sum is at risk.[6]

The potential for fossil fuel reserves to become stranded assets if the world gets serious about carbon is no secret. Bill McKibben, perhaps the most prominent climate activist in the United States, made a profound impact with his article on the topic, "Global Warming's Terrifying New Math," published in Rolling Stone in 2012; it is a virtuoso piece of writing.[7] In the world of finance, a comparable splash was made by Mark Carney, the governor of the Bank of England, who warned of the banking system's exposure at a talk given in 2015 at Lloyds of London; for Carney the potential loss of value of fossil energy corporations constitutes a risk to financial stability.[8] In subsequent years the term "carbon bubble" has become part of the standard financial lexicon, embodying the fear that energy sector valuations could collapse just like the dot-com implosion at the end of the 1990s or the mortgage meltdown of 2007–2008. A spate of studies has appeared, investigating whether the financial system is as exposed today to this bubble as it was to its predecessors.[9]

Fossil fuel reserves are the most obvious candidate for assets at risk from rapid decarbonization, but they are not alone in that respect. As concern for climate policy risk exposure has percolated through the financial world, attention has spread to other sectors. A few research-ers have tried to develop criteria that could be applied to any invest-ment to determine its vulnerability to changes in carbon pricing.[10] A common choice is the extent of greenhouse gas emissions in relation to value added; another is the direct connection to the fossil fuel industry, particularly as consumer or supplier. It seems to me these indicators, while relatively easy to research, are not very informative. Ultimately, only two criteria really matter for the risk of asset write-offs: how vulnerable to policy change is the *demand* for the goods or services an investment supplies, and how flexible is that investment – what portion of its value needs to be written off as a result of the demand shift?[11] For instance, a rapid rise in energy prices will lead consumers to prefer appliances like washing machines and refriger-ators that are more energy efficient. If the capital stock currently used to produce these goods can be readily retrofitted to meet the shift in market demand, it will suffer little or no loss of valuation. On the other hand, a freight company that owns a large fleet of semi-trailers may find they are worth little more than scrap value if the cost of fossil fuel becomes prohibitive.

Thinking about the cost to capital assets rather than just oper-ating costs due to higher energy prices constitutes a profound paradigm shift. The two key differences are timing and who bears the burden.

*Timing.* Asset depreciation is instantaneous as soon as new information arrives that alters forecasts of future profitability. Consider the trucking company scenario, for instance. Let's suppose a climate law is passed putting a steadily increasing price on fossil fuels, so that, five years from now, it will simply be uneconomic to ship many goods by long-haul trucking. A freight company doesn't have to wait; its fleet will lose value immediately. If its stock is publicly traded, share prices will fall as soon as the law is passed. And companies that build these trucks will be in the same boat (or trailer): their manufacturing assets will be subject to an instant write-off.[12]

The front-loaded nature of capital losses contrasts to the slow unwinding of operating costs. Companies that purchase trucking ser-vices will experience a slight cost increase the first year the climate law goes into effect, a larger increase the following year and so on. There is time to adjust and look for substitutes. Of course, as substitutes, such as new technologies employing renewable energy, become available, there will be profit opportunities for investments in them, but these potential assets are glimmers from the future compared with the losses that materialize up-front.

*Economic burden.* As we will discuss in more detail shortly, the operating costs incurred by businesses resulting from increased energy prices will be almost entirely passed along to consumers. All of us will share in footing the bill. But capital losses are borne primarily by those who own the assets; they assumed the risk and now they reap the (negative) reward. To the extent any burden-sharing exists, it operates through the financial system. If asset owners default, for example, their creditors suffer. Or risk-hedging strategies, such as those employing derivatives, may be applied to spread the losses. Even so, from a social standpoint, it is a narrow stratum of the population that bears most of the burden from stranded assets. Both sides of this distinction – the downward transfer of operating costs and the upward concentration of capital costs – will play key roles in the political economy of climate policy.

## Tallying the Threat to Wealth

We are at a double disadvantage at trying to put numbers on capital at risk from carbon policy: there has been little investigation of this question, and what literature exists is based on a methodology unlikely to reveal the full extent of the problem. Simply identifying industries with above-average carbon emissions is unhelpful.[13] Unfortunately, incorporating demand, while the right approach, requires case-by-case research. We know (or think we know) that demand for air travel would shrink dramatically under stringent carbon pricing, with predictable consequences for both airline companies and producers like Boeing and Airbus whose capital stock is not easily switched to other products – but what about trucking? How much demand for their services will migrate to other freight options, how will this affect manufacturers of trucks and related products, and how will changing distribution channels affect investments in commercial real estate? Questions like these can't be answered by consulting existing statistics on carbon emissions; there is no substitute for the painstaking study of specific markets and the investments geared to them. We have barely scratched the surface.

In a recent paper, I performed a preliminary analysis of four sectors related to air travel: airline companies, aerospace manufacturing, airport ownership and operation and international tourism, and for the purposes of this chapter I am adding a fifth, air freight and logistics.[14] This was inadvertently prescient, since the pandemic gave us a preview of the air travel apocalypse that might be on the horizon. But the pandemic, devastating as it has been, is expected to be an episode, not an endless future, avoiding the need for widespread capital write-offs. A stringent carbon policy, by contrast, will raise jet fuel prices permanently, and at least for the foreseeable future it is unlikely they can be significantly offset by efficiency improvements or replacement by alternative fuels derived from bioenergy feedstocks.

How vulnerable these sectors are will depend on how far and fast carbon prices rise. While there is no way to know for sure, I will use a scenario in which the starting price is $100 per tonne and then rises at 8% per year; after thirty years this would result in a price of about $1,000 per tonne. These end-point prices are roughly consistent with the estimates the IPCC produced in its 2018 report that compared 1.5° and 2° warming targets.[15] To be sure, this would constitute a very large price jolt but not out of proportion to the immense effect it aims to produce.

Based on this price trajectory, the historical relationship between fuel and ticket prices, and the price elasticity of demand for air travel, it is possible to approximately identify the extent of capital at risk in these sectors. Incidentally, I have used valuations prior to the onset of the pandemic to avoid blurring the projected impact from one cause with the actual one from another.

1. *Air travel.* As of January 17, 2020, the combined market capitalization of the twenty largest air carriers was $259.1 billion.[16] If past demand relationships continue to hold, a carbon price of $100 per tonne, which is a plausible early outcome of a 2° policy, would reduce air travel by 22% from its pre-pandemic level, rather than allowing it to increase as currently anticipated (and reflected in current investments). Within a couple of decades or so the carbon price would reach or exceed $1,000 per tonne, and air travel would decline to less than a quarter of its former level. It is speculative to apply these projections to the market value of these carriers, but a conservative estimate would be in the range of $100 billion.[17]

2. *Air freight and logistics.* Applying the same stranding fraction to this sector – clearly fraught with uncertainty – we can provisionally estimate 39% of $172 billion, or $66 billion of capital write-offs.[18]

3. *Aircraft manufacture.* Market capitalization in this sector was estimated in 2018 at $838 billion.[19] If we assume the commercial share of revenues is reflected in the allocation of capital, 47% of the total, or about $400 billion, should be assigned to investments in designing, producing and assembling commercial aircraft parts.[20] Rather than taking a percentage of this total, as with air travel, however, I believe it is appropriate to consider the entire amount as potentially stranded. This is because manufacturers produce for replacement and expansion of the existing fleet, and under likely future conditions, demand for new planes will fall to near zero. In fact, putting only $400 billion in the "stranded" box may be conservative, since governments too may reconsider their military priorities in aerospace if fossil fuels become prohibitively expensive.

4. *Airport ownership and operation.* Travelers may not be aware of this, but quite a few of the world's major airports are either owned or operated by private firms. The top fifteen airport enterprises have a combined capitalization of $137 billion.[21] Here it is difficult to prognosticate, since airports can make up for reduced traffic by investing further in shopping and other amenities, possibly appealing to new clientele in addition to air travelers. Suppose capital in this sector might be marked down around 10 to 50%, or $14 billion to $69 billion.

5. *International tourism.* Our problem here is that capitalization is not broken out between intra- and international tourism, but suppose it is apportioned according to revenues; in that case, 29% of the sector's total market value, or $273 billion, is devoted to servicing the international market.[22] A further uncertainty is how much of this market depends on air travel; suppose it is half, and apply this same fraction to market capitalization. With air travel declining by an initial 22% and dwindling to all but about 22% of its current level, and bearing in mind that a portion of existing investment targets an anticipated *increase* in demand, writing off half the air travel–dependent capitalization seems reasonable. This amounts to $68 billion in stranded assets. Of course, a very large margin of error surrounds this guesstimate.

Summing up these five sectors gives us roughly $650 billion to $700 billion; is that a lot or a little? For one thing, it amounts to 28–30% of the total market value of these sectors, based on the data sources used for estimating potential stranding. That includes the entire global tourism sector, which probably inflates the calculation for "air-related" investment. If we use the lower estimate for the portion of capital invested in global tourism, the stranded component jumps to 39–42%. This would represent nothing less than a catastrophe for those who had invested in these enterprises, and it helps to explain the singleness of purpose that swept aside all opposition to the European Union Emissions Trading Scheme Prohibition Act. True, the impact of the EU's trading scheme was minuscule, but it should not surprise us if interests connected to air travel would strongly resist taking even the first step down this (for them) cataclysmic path.

A different perspective emerges if we compare our estimate of capital losses in air travel–dependent sectors with those in the energy sector itself. As we saw earlier, most of the discussion to date has identified asset stranding as a problem for investments in fossil fuels and the energy infrastructure reliant upon them, so it makes sense to ask how adding this new source of capital risk adds to the old. Perhaps the most widely noted study of stranded assets from climate policy is the 2017 report of the International Renewable Energy Association (IRENA) referenced earlier in this chapter.[23] It considered two carbon policy scenarios, with the high-cost option being one of delayed implementation (myopically allowing for more fossil fuel–oriented investment) followed by drastic carbon emission reductions and correspondingly high carbon energy prices. In that simulation, it estimated $7.1 trillion in stranded assets in the fossil fuel sector and an additional $1.9 trillion in electric power generation, a total of $9 trillion in what are regarded as the core sectors vulnerable to a drastic shift in carbon pricing. Our rough estimate of capital loss in five air travel–related industries ranges from roughly 7–8% of this amount. In itself this is not so dramatic, but the air-dependent portion of the economy is just one of many that will feel the impact of decarbonization.

Where else might we look for investments at risk? Consider Table 8.1, which tallies the market capitalization of a number of other potentially vulnerable sectors. The universe of firms is drawn from the S&P 500, so it encompasses only the United States and only large, publicly traded market participants. Share prices are as of March 2, 2020, down 8.7% from their high six weeks earlier but well above their trough during the subsequent pandemic spring.

Each of the listed sectors could be the subject of a potential story of how its market capitalization might suffer in the event of an unanticipated switch to aggressive carbon policy. With drastically

**Table 8.1.** Market capitalization of selected sectors in billions of current US dollars

| Industry | Market capitalization |
|---|---|
| *Consumer discretionary* | |
| Auto components | 116.9 |
| Autos | 668.4 |
| Distributors | 33.7 |
| Hotels, restaurants and leisure | 750.9 |
| Household durables | 390.4 |
| Multiline retail | 147.8 |
| Specialty retail | 683.2 |
| *Financials and real estate* | |
| Real estate investment trusts | 1,230 |
| Real estate management and development | 83.2 |
| Mortgage real estate investment trusts | 75.7 |
| Thrifts and mortgage finance | 96.3 |
| *Industrials* | |
| Industrial conglomerates | 503.4 |
| Machinery | 685.9 |
| Road and rail | 489.9 |
| Trading companies and distributors | 173.2 |
| *Materials* | |
| Chemicals | 731.4 |
| Metals and mining | 680.4 |
| Paper and forest products | 53.9 |
| **Total** | 7,594.6 |

*Source*: Fidelity Sectors & Industries Overview (2020).

reduced availability of fuels and much higher prices at the pump, demand for automobiles might shrivel, and housing stock along with retail and service infrastructure tied to automobility would experience losses in asset values as well. Freight and logistics would be disrupted, including both rail and over-the-road. Manufacturing processes dependent on cheap energy would need to be retooled, with some requiring reengineering from the ground up. Increased cost and decreased availability of hydrocarbon feedstocks could call into question some investments in chemicals. To some extent, the production and distribution of bulky intermediate and final goods would need to be relocated to minimize expensive trucking.

What proportion of the total investment might need to be written off? This, of course, is purely a matter for speculation at this point, since the problem is entirely unstudied. If only 10% is truly at risk, we would add it to our air-related estimate and anticipate nearly $1.5 trillion in stranding – this in addition to the trillions of write-offs in the energy sector itself – but there are two caveats. First, 10% is actually a small proportion, since market up- and downswings often exceed this in the course of normal turbulence. If sectors are truly exposed, we should expect to see larger valuation impacts. Second, the capitalization data are taken from the restricted world of large, publicly traded corporations. A significant portion of corporate ownership is now delisted, either because it never went public in the first place (e.g., Cargill) or because it was bought out by private equity (e.g., Hilton hotels). Moreover, much of the capital at risk – in real estate, retail, services and agriculture – is in small- and medium-sized enterprises and escapes the statistical scrutiny of market analysts. Finally, recall that the IRENA estimate for stranded assets in energy was global; to truly compare energy and nonenergy stranding we need to scale up US numbers to account for the rest of the world.

There is no point to spurious exercises in number-spinning. With virtually no prior research in the location and degree of capital at risk from climate policy, all we can justify at this point are general impressions. On the basis of a cursory look at one set of sectors related to air travel and an even more cursory survey of the scale of investment in vulnerable aspects of the economy, it seems clear that potential nonenergy stranding is almost certain to exceed by a large margin the energy write-offs that have thus far attracted the most attention. Moreover, these investments at risk are widely distributed geographically and by type of activity, to the extent that it is difficult to differentiate between the class of investments vulnerable to decarbonization and wealth in general.

Why should we care?

## Capital and the Politics of Climate Change

Given the apparent trillions of dollars of capital at risk from action on climate change, why have there been so few ripples in the financial world? Banks, pension funds, equity funds, endowments and other big players continue to hold vulnerable assets as if oblivious to the risk of suffering serious losses. Economists and financial analysts have proposed various hypotheses, such as psychological blinders and weak incentives, and have expressed alarm that the global economy is unprepared for the collapse of the carbon bubble.[24]

There is a different way to look at market nonresponse to what appears to be substantial asset risk: investors, unlike outside observers, aren't writing off their own opposition to policies that would erase a large portion of their wealth. And why should they? How often do countries take actions, with the possible exception of going to war, that confiscate a large portion of the wealth of their richest and most powerful citizens? Who is the victim of over-optimism, investors who expect their carbon-based assets to retain value or advocates of climate policy who expect governments to finally take this challenge seriously – after decades of obfuscation and delay?[25]

We have already seen one episode in this ongoing battle between capital and the climate, the showdown over carbon emissions in aviation. The immediate stakes were small, a weak carbon permit system that barely limited the contribution of air travel to atmospheric carbon and relied largely on toothless offsets to maintain the appearance of responsible action. Yet even this was too much, and when industry played its tune the political system practically danced in its sleep. If this continues to be the future of carbon policy, the airplane manufacturers and other companies that depend on an uninterrupted flow of dollars from air travelers can safely ignore academic studies of stranded assets and carbon bubbles. How representative was this skirmish, however?

Let's begin with outright denial. There is evidence that the decades-long movement to discredit climate science that culminated in the 2016 election of Donald Trump was substantially bankrolled by corporate sectors other than fossil fuels. In a forthcoming study, sociologist Robert Brulle identified twelve key coalitions behind the denialist movement in the United States and over 2,000 organizations that were members of them. He classified each organization according to the interest it represented, dividing economic interests into eleven sectors. If we were to believe the usual political rhetoric on this issue, nearly all the economic impetus behind the denialist coalitions should have been coming from oil, coal, gas and cement – but this is not the case. On the contrary, non–fossil fuel interests accounted for the bulk of participation. Brulle looked at industry associations that were members of one denialist coalition and then more narrowly at those that belonged to at least two. Of the first group, fossil fuel and related interests comprised just 28% of the membership, of the second, which represents a greater commitment, still only 46%.[26]

More recently, an important battle was fought in Oregon, where Democrats in control of the legislature and the governorship attempted to pass a somewhat comprehensive, if weak, carbon tax.[27] The bill passed the lower house, but Republicans in the state senate went into hiding, denying supporters of the tax the quorum they needed to bring it to a vote. The holdouts returned only after they were assured renegade Democrats would join them to defeat the bill if a vote were taken. *The Oregonian*, the state's largest newspaper, published an analysis of the main corporate contributors to the campaigns of the anti–carbon tax senators. As one might expect, fossil fuel interests, primarily in the form of the Koch brothers, were a significant factor, but at 16% of the total they placed only third, behind timber (56%) and trucking (18%): trucking because higher fossil fuel prices would cut into the return on their investments, and timber because it is a key industry in Oregon and depends heavily on trucking.[28] Rhetorically, these politicians also invoked agricultural and related concerns, which are entirely plausible.

There is little doubt that corporate interests have been supportive of only the weakest climate measures at best, with many firms hostile to any action at all, but how effective have they been? Are they the main barrier to progress or just one of many? It is almost impossible to answer this question with confidence, since the various strands of political causation all act on one another, and there are many confounding factors that affect any given issue, including climate change. That said, we do know a bit about the interplay between wealth and power in modern democracies.

One approach is to look at the concrete mechanisms by which money influences politics. The work of Thomas Ferguson, for instance, has repeatedly buttressed his "investment" theory, that wealthy donors regard political donations as investments that are expected to, and do, earn a rate of return in the form of favorable legislative and regulatory actions. In two recent papers, he and his coauthors have demonstrated that big money donations significantly affect congressional races and that contributions to legislators pay off in the form of changed votes on matters of direct economic interest.[29] While it is useful to document these channels, money almost certainly has deeper, more systemic effects.

To see this, consider a study by Martin Gilens and Benjamin Page that sent a shock wave through the world of political science research. Gilens and his team of students and assistants had assembled a data set of 1,779 policy proposals that had both a polling and a legislative history, and he and Page examined it to see what impact measures of public support had for whether the policies were enacted within four years of the opinion survey. Logically, if the "majority rules" view of democracy is correct, the more support for a policy in the polls, the more likely its enactment. And that proved to be true for survey respondents whose income placed them at the 90th percentile – that is, those who earn more than 90% of the population but less than the top 10%: if more of these well-off citizens liked an idea, the idea was also more likely to pass. But it turned out not to be true for the median respondent, the one right in the middle with 50% earning more and 50% earning less. In their case what they thought made no difference at all; the likelihood of policy adoption was unrelated to their polling preferences.

To put this as simply as possible: the US political system was portrayed as operating democratically for those near the top of the income ladder but not for those down below, meaning political strategies based primarily on mass persuasion and bolstering polling numbers would be unlikely to be effective. However – and this is extremely important – Gilens and Page also found that mobilization, the formation of interest groups with resources and significant membership, also made a difference. Voters whose economic position is about average have no clout as individuals (their opinions as stated to pollsters don't affect outcomes), but they do if they engage in collective action.[30]

These provocative findings were controversial. Other prominent political scientists challenged them, and a period of dueling studies ensued.[31] The core problem is that differences between the median and 90th percentile voters exist against the backdrop of substantial agreement; the correlation across the entire sample of policy questions is 0.78, where 1 would represent identical political preferences between the two groups and 0 complete disagreement. If you are looking for a wide gap between elite and common opinion, you won't find it in the United States, at least not among the issues they analyzed. This leads to two further problems. First, the true sample isn't the full 1,779 issues but the much smaller portion that is truly disputed. Different definitions of the boundaries of "truly" in this context yield different samples and therefore different results. Second, when the explanatory forces are disentangled, the opinions of average and elite voters are so congruent that small changes in the way the model is set up – such as the cutoffs for disagreement that narrow the sample and definitions of what winning on a given issue entails – can have substantial effects on the findings.[32]

A recent contribution to this debate by Jarron Bowman has shed new light on these complications in two ways.[33] Bowman constructed a relative measure of political influence – how much your group's opinion counts when it agrees with the other group compared with when it doesn't – that reduces the murk of correlated opinions, and he tried out a wide range of sample selection choices and definitions of the outcome (the meaning of "winning"), reporting the results of all of them. When he averaged across all his models, he found that policies supported by the middle-income group but opposed by the rich had no greater likelihood of enactment than those opposed by both, while policies supported by the rich but opposed by the middle had the same likelihood as those supported by both. He concludes, "These findings offer strong evidence for Gilens's claim that while high-income preferences have a sizable independent impact on policy, the preferences of the middle have little to no impact" (1031).

Meanwhile, supporting evidence has arrived from Germany, where a similar methodology was applied to German policy debates.[34] The German study had the advantage of distinguishing policy views not only between the median and the 90th income percentile, but also the 99th slice at the top as well as by occupational category. The results parallel what we've seen for the United States: substantial influence exerted by the rich and higher-ranked occupations, and little – or even *negative* – influence by those in the middle or at the bottom. This is notable because the German political system is tightly regulated to reduce the impact of money on politics. If you visit the country just before an election, or live there, you will see equally sized posters for each political party, large or small, displayed at the approved advertising locations. Compared with the United States, the money spigot plays a minor role, but political outcomes are skewed toward the rich all the same.

It has been worth spending a bit of time on this academic dispute because the stakes are immense for how we should think about politics in general and those of climate change in particular. We often talk as if it were obvious that the reason carbon regulation has been so slow in coming is lack of public support, with the corollary that the main political challenge is cultivating public opinion, but what if this isn't true? The evidence is still being sifted, but if the skeptics are right, and they currently have the stronger case, public support as measured by opinion polls is nearly irrelevant; as things now stand it is only the support or opposition of those at the top that matters. If we can't count on bringing this exalted group firmly on the side of aggressive action against climate change, the only other option is to challenge their outsized influence over this issue. More on this shortly.

But let's return to the strong correlation between the views of average citizens and those well above them. One interpretation is that economic status doesn't have much to do with political outlook one way or the other, which could be true for many social issues but is unlikely to hold for economic matters.[35] Another is that elites are successful in molding the position of the majority, as in the Gramscian view of hegemony.[36] A third view, which I suspect provides at least part of the explanation, is that there is already a selection process that determines which proposals will be placed on the public agenda, and only policies with substantial support of elites will make the cut. To phrase it differently, elite views largely define the Overton window, the range of "acceptable" policy ideas we are asked by pollsters to opine on.[37] Which hypothesis best explains the convergence between average and elite opinion is uncertain at this point, but the latter two both characterize a political environment that, in general, is favorable to higher-income groups. This too is a concern when thinking about climate policy.

The influence of wealth on politics is a function not only of the greater power the wealthiest members of society possess in general, but also of the degree to which they agree with one another. If the rich are split 50-50 on an issue, we can't even define what "the power of wealth" means in operational terms. Even if the split is, say, 80-20, one might expect the wealthy minority to wield enough clout that the issue will enter democratic debate, and the general public may have a chance to weigh in. But if there is virtual unanimity among the upper stratum around a particular position, and if it is a matter of great concern to them, they are far more likely to get their way, and the issue may be resolved quietly behind closed doors – as happened with the airlines and the "threat" of carbon permits. If this hypothesis seems implausible, consider: What could be of greater importance to wealth-holders than preserving their wealth, not having it diminished by "reckless" government policy? Can we imagine a viable political campaign, whether in the United States, Europe or another relatively prosperous country or region, whose platform was the deliberate destruction of a substantial share of the stock of wealth? But – and here we again look ahead to the implications for climate activism at the conclusion of this chapter – isn't this *exactly* what we need to envision and even bring about?

To tie together this portion of the argument, recall the litany of ineffective, compromised policies surveyed in Chapter 6. In theory carbon controls should be upstream; in practice they are downstream so favored firms and industries can be exempted. In theory there should be few if any offsets, since additionality is difficult to enforce and no project has the same carbon-cutting effect as not burning fossil fuels in the first place – but offsetting is rampant. In theory permits should be auctioned so policy-created scarcity doesn't lead to excess profits; in practice permits are often given away. Above all, emission targets are so unambitious that existing climate programs serve primarily to give only the appearance of activism, with scarcely any impact on the trillions of dollars of assets whose value depends on maintaining a carbon-intensive economy. We see this pattern in countries where conservatives claim that climate change is a hoax, and we see it where they claim to be just as concerned about the problem as everyone else. Articulate, carefully reasoned studies by policy analysts have no effect; their writings are simply ignored. Policy is crippled everywhere and in approximately the same way: exemptions, handouts and timid targets are put forward to win the support of business, beyond the point where the consequences are self-defeating. Political brokers certainly act as if the investor class has a veto on policy – are they wrong?

## Follow the Carbon Money

Let's put aside the question of wealth for the time being and turn our attention to the added costs of producing goods and services that would result from rapidly phasing out fossil fuels. Who will pay them, and where will the money go?

Recall the diagrams from Chapter 6 featuring a demand curve for fossil energy. We have a vague sense of the shape of this curve in the vicinity of the status quo, where energy prices have fluctuated primarily due to market forces, without much regulatory interference. (This is what the elasticity discussion was about.) We don't know much about where the curve will lie once policy begins to dictate prices, raising them well beyond past experience, but we can be fairly certain it will slope upward to the left – meaning a price increase for energy will cause less to be produced and consumed, or that a cap on production will cause prices to rise.[38] This fundamental relationship between the price of fossil fuels and the amount extracted and burned is the basis for all that follows. There is no escaping it; it can't be legislated away or transcended through some transformation of consciousness, and even if we could we wouldn't want to, since the energy-related choices of billions of the Earth's people need to change, and there is no reasonable alternative to the use of higher prices to accomplish this.

So we will pay more for energy – all of us – and the goods and services that draw on it. That will feel like a sales tax, a surcharge on everything we buy based on its direct and indirect carbon intensity. The money will go to whomever is selling us these things, and the sellers will pay more to their suppliers, and so on up the chain until it ends up in the hands of the ultimate suppliers, the companies that sell fossil energy.[39] This is why, if we adopt a permit system, the permits need to be auctioned; that will ensure those who are in a position to charge higher prices have to pay for that right, and if the auction is fair the amount they pay will approximately equal the extra revenue from owning a permit.

If carbon policy is serious about adhering to a 2° budget, we will find ourselves rapidly climbing the demand curve as it ascends to the left, into the region of lower carbon quantities and higher carbon prices. The amount of money changing hands will be immense. As a first pass, note that US emissions of carbon dioxide for 2019 were approximately 4.8 billion tonnes.[40] Suppose the starting price placed on a tonne, either by a tax or permit cap, is $50. This will lead to different percentage changes for different energy products, since they have different carbon contents, but let's use the case of petroleum as a starting point. Each dollar of the carbon price translates into approximately one cent more per gallon at the pump. At the time I am writing this a gallon sells for about $3.50, so a $50 $CO_2$/tonne surcharge would increase this price by about 14%. Using an elasticity of –0.5 (see the elasticity discussion in Chapter 6), we would expect to see a 7% reduction in emissions – again using petroleum as a stand-in for the entire energy sector. With this reduction our emissions would fall to about 4.5 billion tonnes. Multiply 4.5 billion times $50, and we find about $225 billion in extra energy revenues will flow from consumers up the energy supply chain to fossil fuel producers. That's approximately 1% of US GDP for the year, but remember this is just a beginning.[41]

Our emissions need to fall far more than this over the coming decades, of course, which as we have seen could eventually require carbon prices at or above $1,000 dollars per tonne. Of course, as emissions fall there are fewer tonnes to pay on, but until the demand curve shifts as a whole its inelasticity guarantees that prices will rise faster than emissions fall – perhaps twice as fast. Before long the 1% of GDP would become 3%, 4% or more. To put it in different terms, every 1% of our economy in 2019 was about $650 per person, so we are anticipating that each of us (children and the elderly too) will pay this amount to start, with costs rising to several thousand dollars as the pace of decarbonization intensifies. (Again, this is per person, not per household.)

Any analysis of carbon policy that doesn't face up to this reality is seriously deficient.

Of course, per person costs are just averages, and actual carbon payments will be more or less than this depending on a variety of factors. The first consideration is how much of the increased cost of fossil fuels will be passed along to the buyers of products that use them as inputs, directly and indirectly, versus other suppliers to those product (who may be paid less) or the companies producing them in the form of lower profits. For instance, consider the effect of a large tax on the carbon content of natural gas, much of which is used to generate electricity. Companies, public or private, that produce electricity can pass on their higher fuel cost to consumers, offset it by striking a harder bargain with their workers or other firms they contract with, or they can eat a portion of it in lower net revenues, that is, profits.[42] When it comes to empirical evidence in the energy sphere, the extent of pass-through to consumers is uncertain, but a reasonable approximation is all of it.[43] That is roughly how it works for the effect of gas taxes on prices at the pump, for instance.

A second consideration is how and to what extent household incomes will be affected by carbon prices; after all, if a household's costs go up but its income goes up even more it has little to complain about. Economists have spun elaborate models to produce forecasts of how carbon pricing will affect income distribution, but their results, highly sensitive to the assumptions they're based on, can be viewed as little more than speculative at this point. Once again, we can make the simplifying assumption that, while incomes will be buffeted by the economy-wide impacts of scrapping a portion of the capital stock, a problem explored in Chapter 5, we can set aside the question of how these effects will be distributed – excepting the obvious point that capital write-offs will be felt primarily by those who own the most wealth.[44]

This leaves us with a third and crucial point: in general, higher-income consumers will pay more because they also spend more, but it is also typical that spending does not rise as rapidly as income, so carbon payments as a percentage of income are likely to be lower for those on the upper rungs of the income ladder. In the language of public finance, sales taxes, of which a carbon price is one example, tend to be regressive. Most empirical estimates of carbon pricing in developed countries come to this conclusion, although a minority position is that costs could be proportional to income.[45]

Figure 8.1 presents one such calculation, performed by two economists affiliated with the Political Economy Research Institute (PERI) at the University of Massachusetts, Amherst. I prefer their approach to others, such as a comparable study from Resources for the Future, because the PERI analysis is conducted entirely in terms of money incomes and expenditures and not "utility," which is an arbitrary and perhaps fictitious metric.[46] What we see is increased household costs as a percentage of household income when a $49 per tonne

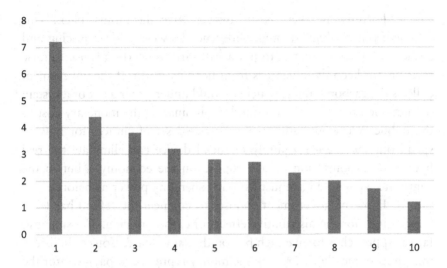

**Figure 8.1** Carbon expenditures as a percentage of household income, assuming a carbon price of $49 per tonne. The percentage of household income spent absorbed by the carbon price is highest for the lowest-income households.
*Source*: Fremstad and Paul (2017).

carbon price is in effect. The population is divided into deciles, with the lowest income tenth on the left and the top on the right; calculations are based on consumer expenditure patterns by income group, combined with the estimated direct and indirect greenhouse gas emissions of those expenditure items. The carbon tax is a great burden on the poorest tenth of households, increasing their costs by more than 7% of their income. This burden falls as income rises, amounting to little more than 1% for the best-off tenth.

This impact of carbon costs is painful for two reasons. First and quite obviously, it exacerbates economic inequality, which has risen to levels even moderate observers regard as excessive. It would be disastrous social policy to enact a program that drove even more families, including their children, into poverty. Second, the substantial burden borne by most households constitutes a political impediment to getting serious policy off the ground. Politicians will be reluctant to vote for proposals that impoverish a substantial portion of their constituents. Opponents of climate action, including the holders of vulnerable assets discussed earlier, can be expected to seize on this issue; in fact, this is exactly what they have done. If we don't have an answer for this strategy, we are in deep trouble.

Fortunately, there is an answer: give the money back. This follows from the biggest single difference between carbon pricing and a sales tax, that the reason to put a stiff tariff on carbon is not to raise revenue but keep the alligators from heading north. If the government collects the carbon money, which it would under either a tax or a system of auctioned permits, it can refund it, eliminating the monetary cost to the public. We would still face a restricted set of choices for how to spend our income – no purely financial device can eliminate the real burden decarbonization would impose on the economy – but in the aggregate we would have just as much spending power as before.

How the government chooses to engineer the refund has large implications for the distributive effects of carbon pricing. The simplest, fairest approach is to give each person the same share. You could justify this philosophically by arguing the money represents a payment for the use of environmental space – the cost of putting additional carbon in the atmosphere – and all of us are equal owners of that space. That is the approach taken by Peter Barnes, who has perhaps done more than anyone else to popularize the idea of equal per-capita refunds of carbon revenues.[47] It also makes sense pragmatically, since it addresses the twin problems of economic inequality and the potential for carbon costs to derail the politics of climate action. It is also the easiest to implement, as demonstrated by the efficiency with which the state of Alaska has administered its Permanent Fund, which distributes oil revenues to its citizens on an equal per-capita basis.[48]

Logically, these refunds will be relatively more advantageous to those on the bottom of the income distribution than the top, since they represent a greater share of overall personal income, but what happens when the disequalizing burden of putting a price on carbon is combined with the equalizing effect of equal rebates? The answer can be seen in Figure 8.2, again adapted from the simulation conducted by Fremstad and Paul. The bottom tenth of households would average a net gain of over 12% of their income, as their refund earnings would swamp extra carbon costs. (Note that multiple individuals live in households, pooling their refunds.) In fact, only the top 30% of households would end up in the red, reflecting the fact that higher expenditures on carbon-intensive goods are concentrated among those with the highest incomes.

A different way to picture this same result is to consider the portion of each decile whose extra costs are fully covered by carbon

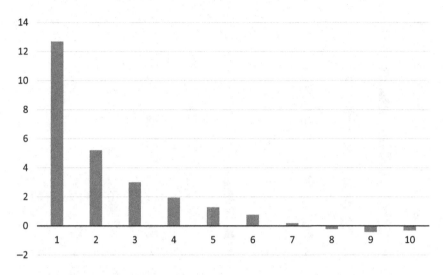

**Figure 8.2** Net receipts from carbon costs and rebates by income decile as percentage of household income. The net return from deducting carbon costs from carbon refunds is a higher percentage of household income the lower the income decile.
*Source*: Fremstad and Paul (2017).

refunds; this addresses the political concern that people might vote their pocketbook and, without a mechanism for recycling carbon revenues, turn against climate policy. Figure 8.3 shows this percentage, which, incidentally, is independent of the extent of the carbon price (in this analysis). It is important to note that, even in the lowest income groups where refunds loom largest relative to carbon costs on average, not everyone comes out ahead – but most do. This suggests that refunds alone may not be enough to address the burden some households may face as a result of carbon policy, a topic we'll get back to shortly. Overall, Fremstad and Paul find that 61% of all households, a solid majority, have their carbon costs fully offset.[49]

To sum up the argument at this point, while the impacts of carbon policy on asset values affect primarily the wealthiest segment of the population, impacts on the costs of the things we buy are passed down to all of us. This fact is exploited by opponents of climate action, but a well-designed system of carbon pricing can largely neutralize it and even use carbon revenues as a tool to reduce extreme income inequality. It is difficult to overstate how important this is to the political economy of climate change.

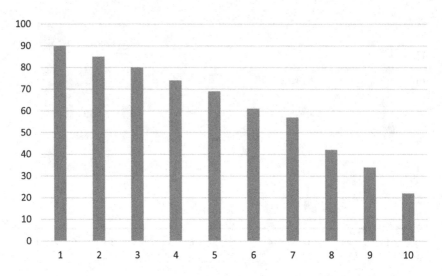

**Figure 8.3** Percentage of households whose refunds equal or exceed their carbon expenses, by decile. The proportion of households whose carbon expenses are fully returned by a per-capita rebate falls from about 90% to 22%, from the lowest to the highest income decile.
*Source*: Fremstad and Paul (2017).

## The Competition for Carbon Revenues

The logic of per-capita refunds of carbon revenues is pure and compelling, but nowhere do we see such a system in action. Where does the money go?

By far the greatest leakage is the giveaways to business we saw in Chapter 6. If carbon permits are just handed out, for instance, the higher costs paid by the public do not end up as government revenues, so they can't be given back; instead, they remain in corporate coffers as extra profit. Permit systems are also usually watered down with offsets, which, although they impose a cost to firms that purchase them, are also revenue sources for those on the receiving end.

Why is the first claim on carbon revenues always by business, and especially businesses with carbon-intensive operations? My hypothesis has been that, to neutralize business opposition to policies that would endanger asset values, politicians see no alternative but to try to buy them off. Yet this effort is not only bad policy but also bad politics, since it leaves climate advocates exposed to a backlash from the majority of voters who are left to foot the bill. Until we escape this damned-if-you-do, damned-if-you-don't dilemma, there is little hope for significant progress.

A second leakage, rather less prevalent than the first, takes place at the urging of many economists who play a role as policy designers and analysts. It is an article of faith for much of the economics profession that markets generally "get the prices right," only to have government, through its tax system, get them wrong again. For instance, if one believes markets produce the "correct" level of wages for all workers, taxing labor income or business payrolls distorts it. In the standard diagrams used in economics textbooks to depict the efficiency loss of taxation, the prices of things being taxed are typically assumed to reflect their "true" costs and benefits to society. Taxes can only make matters worse – except of course for a carbon tax, which corrects a price that would otherwise be inefficiently low, since it wouldn't include the social cost of carbon (Chapter 2). Thus, on theoretical grounds alone, economists who believe markets operate efficiently except for carbon want to substitute carbon revenues for practically any other type of tax.[50] There is also a large "empirical" literature on this topic, in which hypothetical utility functions (which purport to represent each individual's well-being) are calibrated with survey data to estimate the precise efficiency cost of a given tax rate.[51] Such models can be used to estimate the increased utility that can be expected if carbon taxes substitute for income or business taxes.

As soon as we move from calibrating hypothetical models to examining the data without preconceptions, however, the relationship between the level of taxation and reasonable measures of economic performance becomes murky. This was the judgment of the Congressional Research Service after examining US data, and the same conclusion holds if we look at the international record.[52] Figures 8.4 and 8.5, for instance, show the relationship between taxes, growth and the level of income for thirty-four countries whose economies were designated as "advanced" by the International Monetary Fund.[53]

What can we see in these two pictures? Figure 4 looks like it might be capturing the sort of negative relationship between taxes and growth economists typically presume. There are two caveats, however. First, only about 20% of the variation in growth rates is "explained" by the relationship embodied in the trend line, which is what its $R^2$ measures. Second, this is almost entirely due to a group of low-tax outliers in Eastern Europe and high-growth outliers in East Asia;

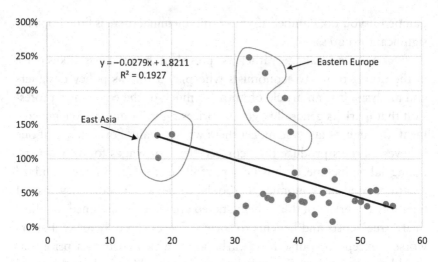

**Figure 8.4** Taxes as a percentage of national income and growth in national income per capita, 1995–2019. Notes: Tax rates are averaged for the period 1995–2019, with the exceptions of Israel, Latvia and the United States, whose tax revenue data only become available in 2000, 1998 and 2001 respectively. National income per capita is in constant PPP dollars. Economic growth is the cumulative percent increase in national income per capita between 1995 and 2019. The formula for the linear trend is given in the upper left, along with adjusted $R^2$, a measure of how well the line fits the scattered points.
*Source*: IMF (2021).

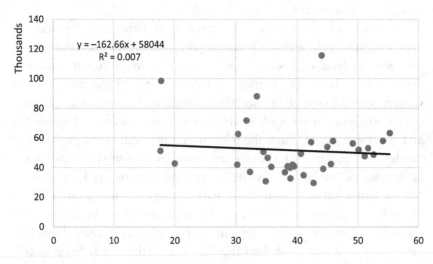

**Figure 8.5** Taxes as a percentage of national income, 1995–2019, and national income per capita, 2019. National income per capita is in constant PPP dollars.
*Source*: IMF (2021).

remove them from the mix and the relationship disappears.[54] Worse, Figure 5 shows essentially no correspondence between tax rates and the level of a country's income per capita, whatever its particular history or geography; not surprisingly, its $R^2$ borders on zero.

Obviously, many factors affect the level and growth rates of national income besides the tax share of national income. A first look at the evidence provides little basis for believing that markets are paragons of efficiency and that by taxing them we impose suffering on the economy. Whatever the other justifications (largely those of political philosophy) for wanting to cut taxes, there is little empirical reason to suppose our economies will function much better one way or the other due to that policy choice alone.[55]

Nevertheless, under the sway of economists, governments have sometimes turned to the tax system to implement revenue recycling. Because direct and indirect tax payments are at least somewhat correlated with income, returning the money to the public in this manner is less progressive, often much less progressive, than doing it via per-capita refunds.[56]

If these first two revenue leakages appeal to business and policy professionals, a third usually arises at the urging of environmentalists themselves: to have the government keep the carbon revenues and spend it on currently underfunded programs. These can be measures for climate adaptation, investments in green infrastructure or renewable energy, subsidies for research and development or, increasingly, social programs earmarked for workers or racial or ethnic minorities.

It is understandable there would be considerable support for treating carbon money as one more addition to the government's revenue stream. Public budgets in the United States and many other countries have been squeezed in recent decades as hostility to the public sector (neoliberalism) has flourished. Social needs, and not only those related to climate change, have continued to mount as the resources of government have shrunk. Carbon money appears to be the first good news on this front in a long time. Moreover, carbon pricing will create its own new set of needs. For instance, as it becomes more expensive to get around in private automobiles, we will depend more than ever on government to help us substitute other modes of transportation and make the investments needed to facilitate rapidly changing land use patterns.

A particular focus of activism in recent years has been the call for a "just transition" to a decarbonized economy. This seems to have two components. One involves workers who risk losing their jobs due to carbon pricing; to protect them activists call for using carbon revenues for expanded employment and training programs. Presumably, workers laid off in carbon-impacted industries would be given priority over those unemployed in an "ordinary" (noncarbon-related) manner. The other is for increased funding for organizations supporting poor and minority communities. This reflects a desire to prioritize resource allocation according to a calculus of compensation for past oppression, where the most oppressed groups have the greatest claim on any new source of funds. Since most of the public paying higher carbon costs is in the "relatively less oppressed" category, social justice is held to require that they not receive rebates so as much money as possible can be redirected to the truly oppressed.[57]

Yet even when spending priorities are well thought through, there are serious disadvantages to having the government retain carbon money. First, as with offsets, there is no guarantee spending from carbon revenues will be additional. Suppose, for instance, there is a stipulation that half the revenues be devoted to energy efficiency and renewables. Many such programs already exist, and they could be off-loaded from the general budget to the newly created carbon fund, freeing up more of the government's budget for other, nongreen purposes. An even greater problem, however, is the regressivity of carbon pricing, as illustrated in Figure 8.1. It is extraordinary that the current wave of social justice advocates is so determined to finance new public spending with money disproportionately drawn from lower-income groups; apparently, they are not bothered by who foots the bill. I would encourage anyone concerned about a "just transition" to a sustainable future to make a copy of Figure 8.1 and display it somewhere they will see each day. This is not a trivial matter.

Nevertheless – on the third hand – there is still a case to be made for earmarking a portion of carbon revenues for public spending. As we saw in Figure 8.3, even though lower-income groups come out ahead from per-capita rebates on average, there will still be many households left behind. This might be due to geography or special needs that require more spending on carbon-intensive goods and services.[58] In addition, while refunds enable people to restore their consumption as individuals, sometimes they will be better off through collective consumption organized by government. A refund check will allow me to spend more money on other transportation options to make up for higher gasoline prices but in itself may not expand the options I can choose from.[59] Finally, as a simple matter of democracy, voters have a right to decide whether some other uses for money have a priority over having it returned to them.

Elsewhere I have made a case for a periodic process through which voters can divide carbon revenues between rebates and spending earmarks, which I see as preferable to setting a once-and-forever rule at the time a climate policy is implemented.[60] The merits of particular spending and recycling philosophies aside, there is little purpose to be served by internecine warfare between groups that all ostensibly favor stringent action to reign in carbon emissions. We can figure out how to split the difference, and to split it again if circumstances or political priorities change.

## From Political Economy to Political Action

Now is the time to take stock: in view of the enormous, utterly unprecedented stakes presented by the climate challenge, humanity is failing miserably. Everywhere there are promises, plans and regimes, but nowhere are they remotely adequate to what needs to be done. To put it bluntly, *the alligators are winning*. The purpose of this final chapter is to present the political economy perspective on that failure, that it is due above all to the threat serious climate action poses to capital and the predominant power wealth exerts over the political process, whatever our ostensible commitment to democracy. Secondarily, we face popular resistance to the everyday costs of decarbonization, stoked by those whose real concern is more often the threat to their own portfolios.

The fear that climate policy will gouge the finances of the citizenry can be countered through intelligent policy – per-capita rebates – but the wall of opposition erected by business interests presents a more difficult challenge. Up to now, backroom policy negotiation has been about finding an arrangement acceptable to capital, but if the analysis in this chapter is correct, there is simply no possibility of a deal that safeguards wealth *and* brings us under a 2° carbon budget: any scheme that maintains the value of existing investment fails as climate stabilization. This means the very framework of climate policy needs to change: instead of cutting a better deal, we need to be strong enough to not cut a deal at all. Business as usual, whether in the form of carbon spewing from a smokestack or politicians trying to balance business interests against the imperative of survival, can't continue.

Fortunately, we know from experience that democracy *can* overpower wealth. Perhaps the most familiar example from recent American history is the Civil Rights movement that erupted in the 1950s, spreading through mass demonstrations and direct action. While media attention has centered on a few leaders like Martin Luther King Jr. and a set of iconic confrontations – Rosa Parks refusing to give up her bus seat, the attack on the Selma-to-Montgomery march in 1965 – in fact, every town in the South had committed activists, and the overall movement was a mosaic of local, regional and national organizations representing a variety of political strategies and goals. During the long decades of official segregation, companies based in the North and South alike were perfectly willing to do business on racist terms, and the tactical alliance of pro-business conservatives and southern segregationists erected a wall against reform once the impetus of the New Deal was exhausted. Their resistance went far beyond normal politics and extended to the terror of lynchings, Ku Klux Klan attacks and routine police violence. A mass movement was necessary to break the power of the old order, and while the South today remains a bastion of conservativism, a large enough counterforce was created to win important victories in the struggle against racism.

Broadly speaking, the Civil Rights movement had two prongs. One was electoral, legal and legislative, including running candidates for local office, pursuing court challenges to segregation and lobbying for federal laws to outlaw discrimination and protect voting rights. These actions were essential; there was simply no substitute for the force of law in ending paramilitary violence and forcing businesses, public services and government agencies to respect the rights of each citizen equally. A century of gentle attempts at persuasion had hardly made a dent.

If activists had had a magic wand to implement this program on just the basis of needing and deserving it, the "movement" part of the Civil Rights movement would have been unnecessary, but the whole point of the hegemonic power of segregationists was to forestall it. How do people without the right to vote get a voting rights law? How do people threatened with violence for speaking out bring that violence under control? How do parents whose children are restricted to schools with inadequate funding gain access to the schools and resources controlled by other parents in the school district? Only a mass upheaval that made the status quo unsustainable could break through the barriers to change.

What makes this phase of the Civil Rights movement exemplary is its ideal coordination of the two prongs of institutional reform and direct action. The movement had a program that, if implemented, could abolish some of the structures of oppression that had existed for generations, and it also had a strategy for bottom-up, disruptive action to carry its program to victory.

Every movement for reform needs both elements, and this applies with special force to the movement to end humanity's reckless gamble with its planetary home. What we know from the researches of political scientists and the recent, discouraging history of climate policy is that sedate methods will continue to fall short. Candidates committed to dramatic action to curtail carbon emissions will not be elected in sufficient numbers, or if they are, their commitment will erode as they are forced to seek compromises with unelected but even more powerful business leaders. Environmental lobbyists can court legislators with their arguments for why stringent policies need to be adopted, but they will be outlobbied by a united bloc of financial interests.

This is why there is no substitute for a movement of massive public action – demonstrations, civil disobedience and even strikes if the possibility exists. It is important not to fetishize actions of this sort; their effect is not an automatic product of the numbers activists can mobilize or the passion they express. But they do have a reinforcing effect on participants, because self-confidence and resolve take hold when we move from an "I" to a "we" mode. Collective action, especially when it is disruptive, challenges the expectation of those in power that they can get their way without complication or conflict. Perhaps most important, people have many interests, public and private. There might be a potential majority for a proposed policy, but few are paying attention. Waging a highly visible campaign of mass action brings a specific issue into focus, at least temporarily, allowing the weight of public opinion to coalesce behind it.[61]

For these reasons, and because of the large political economic obstacles to serious climate policy we have considered in this chapter, a direct action component of the movement to restrict carbon emissions is indispensable. This has been realized by activists in groups like Extinction Rebellion and Fridays for the Future, made famous by Greta Thunberg. As of this writing, protest activity is in abeyance due to the pandemic, but it is likely to return as health threats diminish – and it needs to.

On the other hand, these and other groups are missing the programmatic prong a movement needs to accomplish lasting change. Street activism and school strikes, however impassioned, can't put a stop to the burning of fossil fuels; only the power of government can do this. Mass participation can't remain at a high pitch indefinitely, and proposals have to be in place, ready to be enacted, so when public opinion reaches a crescendo its force can be transferred to the political sphere. Finally, and crucially, climate activists should expect governments to try to co-opt them or pretend to respond while barely changing their actual policies. Movement demands should center on proposals that not only would be effective if adopted but are also transparent, limiting the ability of politicians to say one thing and do another.

This is why I have emphasized the importance of demanding, as an initial step, that governments announce a carbon budget against which every other policy can be measured. The moment such a budget is established the clock begins to count down, and actual emissions can be compared with those needed if the budget is going to stick. And being a number, the carbon budget can't be finessed by fine rhetoric or fine print.

But policy sophistication will be needed for the steps that follow as well. As we've seen, whenever climate policies are unveiled the same dodges appear: spotty downstream coverage, giveaways to business and offsets that undermine goals that were weak to begin with. In the face of this history the only proper attitude is skepticism, and activists will need the tools to recognize and expose the deeper layers of official resistance and not just the surface ones.

Looking down the road, we should expect that a single political breakthrough will not be enough. It is crucial to muster support for legislation along the lines sketched in Chapters 6 and 7, and this will require far more political muscle than climate advocates have yet mustered. But that is just the beginning. Circumstances will change, and climate policy cannot be put on autopilot. New estimates of climate sensitivity and feedback risks will emerge, and new technologies will become available. I have adopted a precautionary stance toward carbon removal, for instance, but perhaps this will turn out to be a feasible option. Or maybe there will be a public relations campaign to persuade us it has become feasible even though it hasn't. We don't know what battles lie ahead. What we do know is that the dominance of concentrated wealth over climate policy has to be broken not once, but in perpetuity, so future decisions can truly be made on their merits.

This two-pronged strategy of sophisticated electoral pragmatism and urgent grassroots boldness demands a sort of double vision. It's as if we need to know how to live both on land and at sea, one moment staying close to the ground, carefully measuring each step, and the next taking a deep dive to stir up the waters.

It's a thing we could learn from alligators.

# APPENDIX: DEMYSTIFYING THE ECONOMICS OF CLIMATE CHANGE

This appendix extends Chapter 2's critique of "optimal climate mitigation" as promulgated by many economists.

## The Quest for the Social Cost of Carbon

During the Obama administration the US Environmental Protection Agency, working with the Office of Management and Budget and the President's Council of Economic Advisors, had a working group whose job was to estimate the "social cost of carbon" (SCC).[1] The SCC is the cost of one tonne of carbon emissions over its lifetime of impacts, measured in dollars; because these impacts will occur over time, their calculation depends on the choice of discount rates. In addition, the estimation methodology generates probability distributions of costs: very low costs if we turn out to be lucky, higher if our luck is poor, and an average somewhere in between. Table A.1 gives a range of SCC estimates based on discount rates and the projected year of emissions. As we can see, at a 3% discount rate the central cost estimate started at $36 in 2015 and was projected to slowly rise over time, nearly doubling by 2050.[2] EPA economists expected the SCC to drift upward as climate-related problems become more intense and society moves closer in time to more damaging impacts.

What was EPA up to here? In administrative terms, they wanted to have a number to put on the benefits they expected to get from programs that reduce carbon emissions. If a regulation was intended to reduce emissions by 1,000 tonnes of $CO_2$ in 2020, for instance, and if

Table A.1. The social cost of a tonne of $CO_2$ in 2007 US dollars

| Year | 5% average | 3% average | 2.5% average | 3% 95th percentile |
|------|-----------|-----------|-------------|-------------------|
| 2015 | $11 | $36 | $56 | $105 |
| 2020 | $12 | $42 | $62 | $123 |
| 2025 | $14 | $46 | $68 | $138 |
| 2030 | $16 | $50 | $73 | $152 |
| 2035 | $18 | $55 | $78 | $168 |
| 2040 | $21 | $60 | $84 | $183 |
| 2045 | $23 | $64 | $89 | $197 |
| 2050 | $26 | $69 | $95 | $212 |

Source: EPA (2016).

they had chosen to use a 3% discount rate for estimation purposes, their midpoint value for benefits would have been $42,000 (in 2007 dollars). They could then compare this with the cost of the regulation to do a cost–benefit analysis – a requirement for all large government regulations since the Reagan administration.[3]

But there is a deeper purpose behind the SCC enterprise. Conventional economics is centered on the concept of optimization, both descriptively and prescriptively. On the one hand, economists usually assume that all participants in the economy make optimal choices given their goals and preferences: consumers maximize "utility" (the well-being they get from the goods they buy), and businesses maximize profits. When pressed, economists will admit this assumption is a bit extreme but has the virtue of making the economy much easier to model. Unless they can attribute clear rules to decision-makers, economic model-builders will have a hard time predicting how policies will alter the future course of events.

But economists are also wedded to the notion that it's their job to advise the public on what policies to adopt in order to maximize the benefits to society as a whole. In the case of pollution, for instance, they want to identify the *optimal* level of pollution that society should aim for – not too much, not too little, but just right. The SCC is the crucial piece of information that makes this possible for climate change. Any regulation that reduces a tonne of $CO_2$ emissions for less than $42 in

2020 (at a 3% discount rate) is a go; any that costs more should be rejected. This works only if the SCC measures the actual damage caused by a tonne of emissions, so economists want to get it right.

Let's follow their logic in more detail. There are four steps to calculating the SCC:

1. Identify the impacts of a tonne of carbon dioxide emissions on things people value. How much extra sea-level rise will it generate? Storm damage? Crop losses? Of course, this can't be done literally for just a tonne, since that's too little to trace through the system. Instead, analysts will perform this calculation for a much larger amount, say, 100 million tonnes, and then divide by the number of tonnes to get the impact of a single unit. But this step is fraught with uncertainty, since natural systems like the Earth's climate are immensely complex, and the timing of impacts is also difficult to gauge. Rather than set forth a single expected set of impacts, analysts will generate a range of possibilities, with probabilities attached to each.

2. Put monetary values on these impacts. Environmental impacts are measured in "natural" units, like square miles of coastal land flooded or number of tropical disease cases that arise in temperate regions. To figure out the optimal level of pollution, however, economists need to convert these impacts into a measure that reflects the value people place on them. This common measure is money, of course, but the techniques for doing this are not always straightforward. The simplest possibility is that the natural units will have market prices, such as bushels of wheat that might not be grown if there are negative impacts on agriculture. Often, however, there are no markets in the goods or services suffering impacts, and economists must be more devious. What is the value of a case of malaria or the historic district of a coastal city? How can we put prices on the loss of species due to the effect that climate change will have on their habitats? The economics literature offers methods for valuing almost anything; if all else fails, simply conduct a survey and ask respondents how much they would be willing to pay to avoid an undesirable environmental impact. In this way the heterogenous effects from Step 1 are converted into a single metric – a sum of money.

3. Discount the value of impacts to get their present value. There are long lags in climate change. This is because the accumulation of greenhouse gases takes place slowly over time as more fossil fuels

are burned, and consequences of warming, such as the melting of terrestrial ice masses, take still longer to fully materialize. The time element of these impacts plays an important role in economic valuation.

When time is tracked from the present to the future, its effect often takes the form of compound growth: a sum of money worth $100 today, if it grows at a constant rate of 3% per year, will be worth $103 a year from now, $106.09 in two years and so on. Discounting tracks money from the future to the present, so at a 3% discount rate $100 a year from now is worth $97 today. The higher the discount rate, the less any given future amount will be valued in the present.

It should be obvious that, with long lead times before the most severe climate impacts take hold, the selection of the discount rate plays a key role. This can be seen in Table A.1, for instance, where reducing this rate from 3 to 2.5% increases the present value of a tonne of carbon dioxide emitted in 2050 from $69 to $95, a hike of about 38%. But why does the EPA give us a table with three different discount rates? Why not just pick the "right" one and tell us what it thinks the SCC is?

The answer is that economists disagree vehemently about what discount rate should be used to calculate present values. Some argue that, once we've converted climate impacts into monetary equivalents, what we have is simply money, and the discount rate should be a benchmark risk-adjusted real interest rate that we expect savers to be able to earn on their accounts. For them 3% seemed like a reasonable figure in 2011, as 2% does now.[4] Others think that, while the valuation process (Step 2) has converted impacts to money, this is not "real" money, like the kind you'd invest in a bond, but a monetary measure of the well-being people would lose because of sea-level rise, extreme weather and so on. In that case, they say, the discount rate should reflect the present-mindedness of the average person – how much they would pay to postpone a negative effect on their well-being for a year. Most people are very present-oriented in that sense, and the corresponding discount rate should be much higher than 3%; perhaps even 5% is too low. Finally, many economists say that, when we do a present value calculation of some impact 50 or 100 years in the future, we are actually asking how much the well-being of those currently alive compares with the well-being of our descendants. They argue that everyone should count the same, so the discount rate should actually be close to zero.[5]

The problem is that all these arguments have at least some merit; they all capture some aspect of the way the passage of time alters the significance of events, or does not. The EPA can't adjudicate this debate, and neither can I. By showing different estimates for the SCC at different discount rates, they are passing the problem along to the reader.

4. Calculate the expected value. Climate impacts are highly uncertain. To take one example, a certain amount of sea-level rise is rather predictable if we know how much additional heat will be transmitted to the ocean, since it will cause thermal expansion, but beyond this everything depends on the stability of land ice. Will the ice sheets that currently blanket Greenland and Antarctica remain frozen in place, or will they fracture and melt? And how long will it take before this process turns a one-meter, mostly manageable problem into a many-meter onslaught of disasters? The reality is we don't know. We can construct scenarios and more or less arbitrarily assign probabilities to them, but that's the limit of our knowledge at this point.

Each set of potential climate impacts can be valued (Step 2) and discounted to the present (Step 3), but this results in a wide range of possible cost estimates, each tied to a particular scenario. In theory, the ideal way to condense all the scenarios into a single cost number would be to use some sort of probability function that assigns a likelihood to each possible outcome; then we could multiply each cost outcome by its probability and add them all up.

Unfortunately, it's misleading to compare the foggy prognostications of climate change with known uncertainties like rolling a pair of dice or spinning a roulette wheel; when it comes to climate risk, we have to make it up. This step is inherently arbitrary, but it's unavoidable if we want to collapse all the scenario outcomes into a single number like the SCC. And so *every* economic study that puts an estimated price tag on climate impacts does this one way or another. Analysts are usually transparent, putting in print the probabilities they are guessing at, but beyond this there is little more they can do to fulfill their scientific obligation of reproducibility.

To their credit, EPA has taken an extra step. In Table A.1 the final column reports not the expected value calculation but an estimate of the SCC at the upper tail of the distribution of scenarios. Specifically, it tells us the present value cost, using a 3% discount rate, of the scenario for which, according to their estimates, there is only a 5%

chance that the outcome could be worse. Naturally this is a bigger number, roughly three times the expected value, which is identified as "average." Their admirable goal is to give us a sense of how much risk there is that the expected value will prove to be too low.

I have gone into quite a bit of detail on the methodology for producing the SCC (although nowhere near as much as you'd find in whole books on the subject) because I am about to argue that each step is wildly inappropriate to the problem at hand, with the result that the entire enterprise of estimating the monetary value of reducing carbon emissions is essentially pointless.

## The Social Cost of Carbon: A Chimera

Let's return to the four steps involved in estimating a SCC, now with a critical eye.

1. Identifying the impacts of carbon emissions and climate change. A SCC is a bit like a tax return. If I report some of my income to the government but not all of it, I'm going to be in trouble if I get audited. Similarly, the SCC can't include some of the costs of carbon emissions but not others – it has to be complete. Unlike tax reporting, however, the problem is not diligence but information. Analysts are not keeping climate impacts "off the books"; they simply have no way to know whether they've included all of them. The problem is the famous "unknown unknowns" that Donald Rumsfeld, in what may have been his greatest contribution as a public official, referred to in the run-up to the invasion of Iraq.[6] Some of the consequences of climate change are eminently predictable. Some are issues of concern but unpredictable. And finally, there will probably be impacts, perhaps quite severe, that we can't even imagine today.

This is because of three aspects of the situation. First, the sheer magnitude of what human beings are doing to the carbon cycle takes us far out of the realm of the familiar. What is at stake are not only incremental changes in Earth physics, chemistry and biology, but radical shifts with the potential to create new, unanticipated effects. Suppose, for instance, that rapid climate alterations cause a massive depletion in biodiversity. What might that entail for the stability of ecosystems, the resilience of plant and animal communities to random disturbances? What could this mean for marine food chains? The nutrient cycling that sustains forests? Should we be surprised if we encounter surprises?

Second, there is little precedent for the types of changes to natural systems brought on by human actions. We have surveyed the Paleocene–Eocene Thermal Maximum, but that is just a single episode in Earth history and one for which we have just a few shreds of evidence.

Third, the systems we are disturbing are extremely complex; we are only in the early stages of discovering their dynamics. Life on Earth has coevolved: species have the characteristics they have and are distributed in various communities due to their simultaneous, mutually influenced reproductive success. How sudden, sizable changes in biodiversity will play out is largely unfathomable.

To be very specific, suppose, through a combination of direct carbon emissions through fossil fuel combustion and the secondary effects of positive feedback mechanisms, human ingenuity manages to trigger a new thermal maximum. What would this mean for regions of the Earth that are currently tropical or subtropical? Would the threat of unsurvivable heat waves cause mass migration? If so, would that in turn lead to war or social chaos? Would changes in temperature and precipitation cause substantial losses in agricultural productivity? If so, how would human populations react to life-threatening food shortages? It is simply bizarre to think that we can catalog and describe all the potential futures that lie before us to the degree we would need if we were to put economic valuations on them.

2. And that brings us to the matter of converting physical and biological outcomes into sums of money. The reason for computing a SCC in the first place is to identify the "optimal" amount of carbon emissions reduction, exactly balancing the costs of cutting back on fossil fuels or taking other measures to reduce greenhouse gas emissions with the expected benefits in the form of reduced impacts. Optimality requires us to compare apples with apples, which means the costs and benefits of each kind of action have to be measured in the same units. Costs and benefits are viewed as impacts on some overarching notion of well-being, and the units are monetary

There is a powerful bottom-up critique to be made of the methods economists use to convert outcomes like the inundation of coastal cities and the spread of disease into sums of money, but there is a simpler, more direct way to make the argument – that inferring changes in well-being from market data may make sense for small disturbances in economic life but fails altogether in the face of a radical upheaval like catastrophic climate change.[7] This is the problem of scale.

## Time Out for Fish

To see how misguided economic reasoning can be in this context, consider the panel on "Valuing Climate Change Catastrophes" held on January 3, 2016, in San Francisco as part of the Allied Social Sciences Associate Meetings, the annual gathering of the American Economic Association and several smaller affiliated professional groups. I was in the audience along with forty to fifty other economists or economist-watchers, wondering how the speakers were going to address this challenge to the assumptions of standard policy analysis. There were four presentations: "Shutting Down the Thermohaline Circulation" (the oceanic convection system that undergirds the global climate system), "A Potential Disintegration of the West Antarctic Ice Sheet" (which would substantially raise forecasts of sea-level rise), "Ecosystem Impacts" (defined as the collapse of entire ecosystem types – biomes – worldwide) and "Economic Effects of an Ocean Acidification Catastrophe" (resulting in the decimation of marine life). One after another, the speakers pruned and trimmed the dimensions of the crisis under examination, applying current market prices to prospective impacts and coming to the conclusion that the worst-case scenarios for climate change have only modest economic consequences.

How was this possible? Let's take a closer look at the final paper, written by Stephen Colt and Gunnar Knapp of the University of Alaska, although we could just as well pick any of them. Colt and Knapp consider two impacts of ocean acidification: a collapse of the marine food chain that puts an end to all harvesting for human consumption and the complete destruction of the world's coral reefs. They take the worst-case scenarios in biological terms as given and apply themselves to converting these outcomes into monetary losses.[8]

The easiest call, from their point of view, is the loss of the coral reefs. The only value they possess in human terms, at least from the perspective of these authors, is given by the willingness of tourists to pay to travel and look at them. They suggest a range of $54–$1,765 per hectare of reef, which can then be multiplied by the number of hectares, 28 million, to give a total economic value.

Only slightly more complicated is the valuation of an end to all ocean-harvested fish. This is not the same as the size of the industry (which would fall to zero), since the costs of harvesting have to be deducted from its benefits. In conventional economic terms, there are two forms of net benefits from this, as from any other, industry – economic profits (also called rents) and consumer surplus. The first is the same as the normal notion of profit, except that it takes into account the value of the capital invested, which could have been used for some other purpose. In other words, it is net of the opportunity cost of capital. The second is the gap between the most that consumers would have been willing to pay for the fish and seafood and the amount they actually have to pay at market prices. To take a simple example, suppose we are talking about just one fish. Let's say it costs $10 to harvest (including the opportunity cost of capital, like fishing boats); the market price is $15 dollars; and the consumer who buys it would have been willing to pay as much as $20. The net value (sorry) of the fish equals $10, since its ultimate benefit is $20 and its cost is $10. This number is equal to the sum of the profit earned on the fish, $15 – $10 = $5, and the consumer surplus, $20 – $15 = $5. So Colt and Knapp set themselves to estimating these two magnitudes over the entire industry.

The problem with estimating economic profit in fishing is that there is massive overfishing around the world, which not only reduces fish populations but also drives up the cost paid by fishing fleets. Colt and Knapp use a World Bank study, however, that claims that global fishing profits could be in the range of $49–75 billion if the industry were rationalized and stocks given a chance to rebound. Thus the upper bound of the lost profits attributable to the destruction of all marine life is the high end of that range, $75 billion.

Consumer surplus is also difficult, since we don't have surveys asking everyone around the world how much they value fish and seafood. Instead, Colt and Knapp rely on an earlier study that estimated the ratio of consumer surplus to profits in the global mollusk industry. Multiplying this ratio, 1.4, times $75 billion gives $105 billion as the high end of consumer surplus that will be lost.

And there are other users of marine fish stocks, subsistence and recreational fishers. Without going into detail, we shouldn't be surprised if their value is somewhat lower than that of the world's

**Table A.2.** Worst-case losses from ocean acidification in billions of 2014 US dollars

| | |
|---|---|
| Capture fisheries | |
|     Producer rents | 75 |
|     Consumer surplus | 105 |
| Recreational fisheries | 52 |
| Subsistence fisheries | 20 |
| Coral reef recreation | 49 |
| Total | 301 |

*Source*: Colt and Knapp (2016).

commercial fishing industry. Table A.2 sums up the authors' evaluation of the worst-case scenario.

Three hundred billion dollars – is that a lot or a little? One way to put it into perspective is as a proportion of world GDP, which was 0.28% as of 2016, and which could be lower if the world economy continues to grow between now and when the marine food chain collapse occurs. This isn't nothing, but remember this is a worst-case scenario resulting from what most people would regard as an almost unimaginable catastrophe, the rapid end to all marine life. It could be fully offset by an almost imperceptible uptick in the rate of economic growth, and it hardly justifies policies to significantly reduce carbon emissions if they entail more than minor economic costs.

What's the problem here? Let's assume that all their calculations are correct or at least not far off the mark, since the issue is not a few billion dollars, or even a few hundred billion, more or less. What really ought to bother us is something deeper, that these market impacts are being equated with the full human concern for something as drastic as the elimination, within the lifetime of our children or grandchildren, of all oceanic life. It's instructive to push further and try to identify where these two notions, market impact and human significance, diverge. As an aside, I will not question the underlying assumption that only consequences for human beings matter in this calculation – that nonhuman life has no interests that merit (or permit) valuation – since it's important to show that even human-centered values are misrepresented.[9]

We can begin by asking just what it is that money is supposed to measure in studies of this sort. It's not all "real" money, in the sense of actual expenses or revenues that actual people will spend or earn. Yes, lost profits are a deduction from real income in this sense, but not consumer surplus, and this latter category plays a fundamental role in the whole enterprise. In the end, if the value of fish is, above all, the value we humans acquire from eating them – net of the cost of bringing them from the sea to our table – consumer surplus is where this primarily shows up. Its monetary equivalent, like the $105 billion in Table A.2 (augmented by more than another $100 billion in other consumer benefits for tourists, recreational fishers and subsistence harvesters), represents the "value" we lose if the fish all disappear. But consumer surplus is not money that anyone pays; on the contrary, monetary payments are deducted in order to calculate it. It is a sort of psychic money, which economists refer to as *utility*.

Utility is not just a catchall term for psychic value or the well-being that results from access to a good or service; in order to be given consistent monetary measurements, it has to follow a set of rules. First, the market choices people make have to be consistent, since otherwise there would be no way to infer the invisible realm of well-being from the visible indicators of market behavior. If I'm willing to buy a pound of one type of fish for as much as $10, and a pound of another for as much as $15, the five-dollar difference measures the difference in utility I get from the second compared with the first, but only if there is a consistent relationship between my "inner" well-being and the visible purchases I'm willing to make. This relationship is *assumed* by economists to hold for nearly all people and nearly all goods; it is what is meant by terms like "rationality" and "utility maximization." Note also that, to be measured in money equivalents, utility (like money) needs to be fungible. If I get a certain amount of utility from eating fish equivalent to $100, and the fish is no longer available, then given that $100 I can derive the same utility by consuming something else. That is certainly the central message of the Colt and Knapp study: they claim that, in the worst-case scenario, people around the world will lose $300 billion in utility from the elimination of all marine life, and it makes sense to prevent it only if the cost of doing so is less than this amount. Why spend $400 billion to avoid a loss of $300 billion?

Evaluating the theory of utility, and the field of welfare economics constructed from it, is beyond the scope of this book. I believe the difference between what we now know from behavioral economics about how people *really* make economic choices and the effect of those choices on their well-being, and how economists *assume* they behave, is fatal to welfare economics, but that will have to wait for another day. Let's give our economic analysts the benefit of the doubt, and say for now that, even if utility theory isn't precisely correct, it works tolerably well most of the time. The maximum amount of money I'm willing to pay for a toothbrush may not perfectly represent its utility to me (and maybe utility offers a poor account of my inner life), but we muddle through the market-organized world of dental hygiene products well enough. I'm mostly rational in my choices, and the prices I'm willing to pay roughly reflect what I get from these products. If it works for toothbrushes, why not the totality of the world's marine life?

An important part of the answer is that there is a large difference between small, incremental valuations that typically occur in the marketplace and the kinds of large, nonincremental impacts that are associated with a climate catastrophe. This is evident even in the relatively mundane realm of fish consumption. Let's do a little arithmetic exercise to see how this could unfold.

Every two years the UN's Food and Agricultural Organization (FAO) issues a report entitled *The State of the World Fisheries and Aquaculture* that provides a wealth of statistics regarding fish production and consumption.[10] In its most recent release, the FAO gives the numbers shown in Table A.3 for global fish production. Total production of fish includes both marine and inland harvest of wild fish, in addition to aquaculture. The marine share of total output is roughly 47%, just under half.

The FAO also reports that, between 2015 and 2017, fish from all sources provided 7% of all protein in the global human diet and

Table A.3. Global fish production in millions of tonnes, 2018

| | |
|---|---|
| Marine capture | 84.4 |
| Total production | 178.5 |
| Marine share of total | 0.47 |

*Source*: FAO (2020).

17% of all animal protein. So suppose marine fishery output plunges to zero: if we use relative tonnage as an indicator for relative protein supply, this would mean that the world would have to get by on 8% less animal protein and 3.3% less protein overall. With careful planning, including a reallocation of nonfish protein sources to vulnerable populations, and with no other threats to our food supply, we could survive this loss, but how does it compare with the Colt and Knapp forecast of a 0.28% reduction in world GDP?

If I go to the store to buy fish, and there's no fish in the cooler today, I can substitute something else. If fish and the substitute food are the same price, but I would have been willing to pay more for the fish, the difference in my monetary valuation (reflecting my personal demand curves) is a plausible indicator of my disappointment in finding myself fishless. Is this the same, however, as a situation in which *everyone* simultaneously loses access to about half the fish they normally consume, and not just for a single day but the rest of their lives? The problem of substitution would be substantially larger, since small shifts from one consumer to another and temporary vacations from fish consumption would no longer be enough.

To put it more precisely, there is room for substitution – of course – within the category of "protein," but no possibility of substitution away from protein for some other economic good or even some other nutrient, at least for people who are at the low end of their protein budget, which constitutes a large fraction of the human race. If the world's supply of protein takes a 3% hit, this by itself implies a reduction in global living standards of something more than 0.3%, the Colt and Knapp figure – and the loss in food supplies is just one of the potential impacts of ocean acidification.

And we can take this one step further. Climate change will not be influencing fish stocks in isolation; there will also be massive effects on agriculture, with the potential for losses in livestock and legume production. Much of the world's soy crop, for instance, is grown in regions that could be susceptible to drought due to changed precipitation patterns.[11] If marine fisheries are decimated due to acidification at the same time other protein sources are undermined, the potential for a larger crisis becomes apparent. It doesn't take much investigation to see how the multiple food production effects of a climate catastrophe could interact and generate threats to living standards that are effectively outside the bounds of measurement, but economists won't even have the opportunity to consider the matter if their only measuring rod is the market signals arising from localized, incremental trade-offs.

## The Dilemma of Scale

At a very general level, the story economists tell about utility and prices makes sense, if at all, only if the rest of the world is held relatively constant. How much people value the loss of fish or some other food source in the world of today, the submersion of a particular historic landmark along the coast, or the increased risk of extreme weather events or any of the other impacts of climate change *measured separately and in small doses* is no guide at all to how our lives will be altered by the systemic effects we will encounter in a world whose climate is far different from the one we have known. And this is true not only for climate change, but any multidimensional, large-scale disruptive event. How much people are willing to pay for an extra square meter of housing during normal times tells us nothing about the horrendous effects of mass homelessness in wartime, when essential services have ceased, bombs are falling everywhere, and whole populations have nowhere to go. On a personal level, the same is true for life-threatening illnesses that make normal activities impossible, cause intense pain and upend the frameworks of purpose and meaning that usually structure our lives. Extrapolating from individuals' willingness to pay to avoid small amounts of pain or make marginal adjustments to their exposure to certain types of risk in order to put a dollar value on what it means to have leukemia, for instance, is simply beside the point. Market-based utility analysis has at best a limited sphere of relevance, and climate change is outside it.

A simple diagram can show us how scale can play havoc with valuation methods using market prices. To begin, recall the distinction between the total benefit of some type of good and its marginal benefit. The first is the sum of all the benefits we get from this good, just as its name implies. The second is the additional benefit we acquire from an additional bit of this good, which in theory (if consumers are rational and there are no monopoly, externalities or public goods problems) is the effect generally captured by market prices.[12] Of course, the benefit we acquire from something, marginal or total, is also the cost we bear if they are taken from us. So consider Figure A.1, which shows two hypothetical total benefit curves, $B_1$ and $B_2$, for some item x. Note that

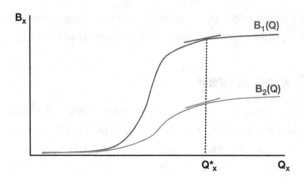

**Figure A.1** Two hypothetical total benefit curves.

there are no units of measurement; this is a thought experiment, not a depiction of empirical reality. Two depictions of a total benefit curve for some good x are shown. The quantity of x available to society, $Q_x$, is displayed on the horizontal axis; the benefit derived from it, $B_x$, is on the vertical axis. More of x means more benefit from it, although we are unsure whether the right depiction is that of $B_1$ (higher) or $B_2$ (lower).

Figure A.1 embodies the assumption that the total benefit curve is sigmoid; it vaguely resembles the letter "S." The reason is that we have in mind a natural resource like fish in situ, going about their business in their watery home. If there are very few fish, it is expensive to locate and catch them, so their value is low – essentially zero until they achieve sufficient numbers. At very high populations their total benefit levels off because human demand is largely satiated at a price sufficient to cover the cost of landing them. This explains the general shape of the total benefit curve, but it doesn't tell us whether that benefit will be relatively low ($B_2$) or high ($B_1$).

Consider a particular quantity of the resource like $Q_x^*$. At that level a little more or less of x will take us slightly up or down the B curve according to the slope indicated in the diagram. (A slope is the change in the vertical attribute divided by the change in the horizontal attribute.) This slope indicates the marginal benefit of an additional input of x. The height of the total benefit curve at $Q^*$, on the other hand, is the total benefit of all of x up to that quantity. They are very different.

Benefit curves such as B(x) are seldom measurable directly. It would be a large research project to determine, fish by fish, the benefit the world acquires from the global stock of tuna or salmon or some other species. What we do have in abundance are market prices, which under the best circumstances are a guide only to marginal, not total, benefits. But what is the relationship between the marginal benefit, the slope of B at Q\*, and the total benefit, its height at Q\*? In a word, none. As drawn above, the upper slope might be steeper or shallower than the lower one, or two equal slopes, upper and lower, might correspond to entirely different total benefits. It is not just that marginal cost is an imperfect guide to total cost; it is no guide at all.[13]

This is a product of scale. At small adjustments, up and down, in Q in the vicinity of Q\*, the marginal benefit is a useful piece of information. That would be the case if environmental impacts that reduce the stock of fish are relatively minor. If we are trying to assess massive impacts, however, such as those that might wipe out a fish stock altogether, the marginal benefit captured in market prices does us no good at all. This problem is devastating for the analytical tools on which the SCC rests.[14]

## More Economics, Less Information

We have said enough now about the economic compulsion to place market values on all the biological and physical consequences of climate change, and the bizarre conclusions to which this obsession can lead. But let us suppose that, despite all that has been said, it turns out to be possible to identify the full set of relevant outcomes and place a monetary value on them. Even in that case, the final two steps in the recipe for a social cost of carbon (SCC) are vulnerable to criticism. Here we will argue that, rather than creating new insight or information, the methods used to discount future impacts to a present value and to condense a range of possibilities into an expected value both end up *eliminating* useful information.

3. Discounting future impacts to get their present value. Recall that, to adjust bottom-line economic values for the fact that costs and benefits occur at different points in time, economists use a discount rate to convert future to present values. Future events have less weight in the present the further out they occur and the higher the discount rate. At even modest discount rates, like 3% per year, very substantial costs that will be incurred 100 years from now have rather modest footprints in the present. For instance, the present value of a cost of $1 million 100 years from now, discounted at 3%, is just over

$52,000, only about 1/20 as much. Since the biggest impacts of climate change are likely to take place many decades or even centuries from now, discounting is crucial and highly controversial. Economists have been splintered into different camps, some favoring higher discount rates on the basis of time preferences revealed in markets, while others call for rates as low as possible to reflect the equal consideration we should give to each generation. All make valid arguments.

But why discount at all? The reason is that the ultimate purpose is to produce a single number, the SCC, so time has to play a role in the calculation. If the cost is deemed to be $1 million this year plus $1 million 100 years from now, is the bottom line $2 million (a zero discount rate), $1,052,000 (a 3% discount rate) or some other total? The commitment to adding the costs together leads inescapably to a demand for discounting.

So the question is really, why add up? This is actually about the SCC itself. If we can liberate ourselves from the need to produce a single, overriding number, the discounting problem vanishes. Instead, the time profile of costs and benefits becomes a visible part of the story.

Let's be slightly more realistic. Suppose the cost of a particular climate impact will be $100 billion dollars 100 years from now, while the cost of preventing it is $10 billion today. If we think in terms of a SCC, and if we accept a discount rate of 3%, we are better off letting the impact occur, since in today's (present value) terms, it would be irrational to spend $10 billion to avoid a cost of $5.2 billion. On the other hand, if we believe the correct discount rate is only 1%, the present value of the future cost is $37 billion, so avoidance pays for itself. The debate over whether or not to act is buried in a potentially arcane debate over the "right" discount rate, one which does not have a clearly correct answer.

But disputes over discounting don't change the projected costs themselves: it is still $10 billion today versus $100 billion in 100 years. This is a rather straightforward choice, even if it may tax our powers of judgment, and there's no reason to shield ourselves from it. On the contrary, any discount rate, however chosen, obscures the nature of the choice being made.

Suppose a 3% discount rate is chosen – although this argument would work at *any* discount rate. At this rate a $5.2 billion cost today is exactly the same as a $100 billion cost a century from now. Both are given the identical present value, $5.2 billion. Unless you delve into the calculation, you have no way to know which kind of cost – near term and smaller or long term and bigger – is under consideration; the information you are given, the bottom line, is exactly the same in either case.

But does it really make no difference at all which type of cost you face? If you thought it was an immediate expense of $5.2 billion, but it turns out to be a distant expense of $100 billion, would you feel that no new information had been acquired? If you accept the logic of discounting the answer is yes; these two costs are identical in all meaningful respects. Yet this is prima facie absurd. The balancing of costs of very different magnitude over long periods of time raises ethical and speculative issues that don't arise when all the costs occur at the same moment. We might want to explore how we think we *should* undertake such balancing, for instance, but "shoulds" of this sort don't play a role when all costs are expressed in present values and their occurrence in time is hidden. Without predetermining how such discussions might be resolved, we should agree that the mere possibility of having such a discussion demonstrates that the difference between knowing and not knowing the time distribution of costs is meaningful.

In practical terms, the public should be informed in a concise, easily understood way what time trade-offs are involved in climate policy. If it is being proposed that certain costs be assumed today in order to avoid risks of much greater costs several generations from now, that should be the message. It is not difficult to create visualizations that capture the gist of the problem. Economists should be in the business of conveying information, not obscuring it.

4. Calculating the expected value. The future holds a universe of possibilities, but the SCC has to be condensed into a single number. It won't do, according to this perspective, to say that a certain level of carbon emissions is optimal if the future takes one direction but not another. The expected value formulation is used to squeeze a single measure out of the different cost scenarios that might or might not occur.

Can we be sure it is possible to do this? Let's take a look at the most widely used probability function, the normal, or Gaussian, distribution depicted in Figure A.2, familiar from its use in a wide variety of situations. The value of some fluctuating variable (like the cost of

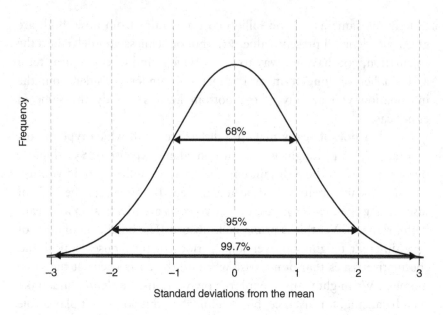

Figure A.2 A normal distribution.

climate impacts) is on the horizontal axis, while the likelihood of each of them occurring is on the vertical axis. Normal distributions are popular for several reasons, one of which is that they are very convenient to work with mathematically. Each such distribution is fully defined by only two parameters, its mean and standard deviation, where the first indicates the average value of the variable (as well as the value of its peak likelihood, the mode) and the second how bunched up or spread out the distribution is. The average value of a normal distribution is simply its mean, while the standard deviation tells us how much uncertainty surrounds this average.

This figure tells us something else as well: the horizontal axis is calibrated by how many standard deviations from the mean any given point is, and additional information is given on what proportion of potential values fall within one, two or three standard deviations. The middle of the distribution is zero, since there is no distance from the mean. The point indicated by "1" is one standard deviation above the mean. For instance, if the mean were 86 and the standard deviation were 10, that point would be 96. The point labeled "−1" is one standard deviation below the mean, 76 in our example. To continue the example, "2" is 106, "−2" is 66, and so on. Just over two-thirds of all observations are within one standard deviation from the mean, such as between

76 and 96, while about 95% are within two standard deviations and 99.7% are within three. These proportions hold for all normal distributions no matter how large or small the standard deviation is, either absolutely or relative to the mean.

It turns out that this property has important implications for the use of a normal distribution in calculating the SCC. Suppose we are measuring the cost of climate impacts, and we believe them to be normally distributed. The first thing we notice is that the distribution is symmetrical, so that there is a 50% chance that actual costs will prove to be greater than the mean – whatever the mean might be. Now, how likely is it that the costs will turn out to be greater than one standard deviation above the mean? Answer: the probability is about 16%, because there is a 32% chance that the value will be further than one standard deviation from the mean in either direction, and the distribution is symmetrical. Next, what is the probability that the cost will be greater than two standard deviations above the mean? By the same logic the answer is about 2.5%. And there is just a 0.15% chance that the cost will exceed three standard deviations above the mean.

This property of normal distributions (referred to as the "empirical rule" in statistics) is crucial for our ability to calculate the mean in the first place. The formula for doing this multiplies each value, like "cost of climate change," by its corresponding probability. As we move rightward along the distribution, further from its center, the costs get larger but the probabilities get smaller. For the total to converge on a single number, the mean, the probabilities need to diminish faster than the costs increase.

Very conveniently, the normal distribution guarantees this is exactly what will happen. Each step of one standard deviation from the mean is equal in size, but the probability this step will occur falls by much larger percentage reductions (32% to 2.5% to 0.15%); this is why the distribution even has a mean. To put it into context, if future risks are normally distributed, very extreme possibilities (like alligators in the Arctic) will have such low probabilities that they will not materially influence our central estimate of the cost of climate change.

Unfortunately, many things in this world are not normally distributed. The most important alternative framework is given by power laws; the right half of a typical power law distribution is depicted in Figure A.3, superimposed on the right half of a normal distribution. Once again, the value of potential outcomes, like the cost of climate change, is

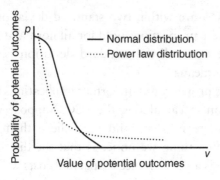

**Figure A.3** A power law distribution versus a normal distribution.

measured on the horizontal axis, while their probabilities are given by the height of the curve on the vertical axis. The right-hand side of two distributions, normal and power law, are compared, where $v$ is the value (like cost) of a potential outcome and $p$ is the probability it will occur.

The difference is striking. As values become more extreme in the normal distribution – as we move further to the right – the probabilities fall precipitously. The power law distribution, on the other hand, exhibits a "fat tail," such that ever more extreme values are associated with only slightly lower probabilities. Returning to our context, this means that, as we contemplate the increasingly cataclysmic possibilities of climate change, their probabilities fall only slightly, and extreme costs dominate our average forecast. It becomes impossible to calculate a SCC, because costs that are essentially beyond measure weigh too heavily. The only way we could pin a number on the mean is to arbitrarily truncate the calculation, by either refusing to consider the most extreme possibilities or placing a cap on how costly we allow them to be. This result was labeled the "dismal theorem" by its late creator, Martin Weitzman.[15]

So, how common are power law distributions, and when do we expect to see them? They turn out to be extremely common, especially in situations where above- or below-average outcomes at one moment change the odds for the next. A classic example is income distribution. The distribution of incomes in a given society is not at all "normal": it is not remotely symmetrical, and there is a fat tail extending into the very highest incomes. The reason is the Matthew Principle, named for a passage in the New Testament, Matthew 13:12: "For to him who has shall be given and he shall have abundance; but from him who does not have, even that which he has shall be taken away." Money begets money.

If you are lucky one year and enjoy an income bounce, you are that much more likely to increase your income in the years ahead. In the end most individuals are bunched up near the mean, while a long tail extends to the Bill Gates of this world. A similar distribution can be found in the size of cities, since, as cities grow, they attract still more growth.

There is every reason to suppose that climate impacts will also be distributed according to a power law. For example, if climate alterations prove to be more severe than we expect (or hope), this may reduce the amount of forest cover, which in turn could release more stored carbon into the atmosphere, worsening climate impacts and so on. In fact, it is positive feedback loops of this type that are the focal concern for extreme climate risk, such as the thermal maximum sketched in the Introduction. The mathematics of power law distributions is telling us that middle-of-the-road estimates of the SCC are naive in the face of extreme possibilities whose likelihood is *not* extremely low.

## What's the Alternative?

Economists devote themselves to estimating a social cost of carbon because they believe their function in society is to tell us the optimal level of emissions control. Without this magic number, they believe, there will be no way to set social objectives, to decide how much policy effort is sufficient or even excessive. It takes a leap of the imagination for them to visualize a world without such guidance.

Ironically, however, we are already in that world, and the economists engrossed in SCC-tweaking don't realize it. The IPCC, which is as close to an agenda-setting organization on climate change as the world possesses, has chosen to reject the SCC framework and instead proposes hard limits on carbon emissions derived solely from scientific considerations. Regarding the SCC, its view was summed up in the fifth (and most recent) synthesis report:

> Estimates of the incremental aggregate economic impact of emitting one more tonne of carbon dioxide (the social cost of carbon) ... are incomplete and depend on a large number of assumptions, many of which are disputable. Many estimates do not account for the possibility of large-scale singular events and irreversibility, tipping points and other important factors, especially those that are difficult to monetize, such as loss of biodiversity.[16]

So instead of searching for an economically optimal level of emissions, the IPCC deduced it from a target of 2°C warming it selected on purely prudential grounds, to which it subsequently added a second potential target, 1.5°C.

A nice summary of the division of labor implied by this approach is supplied by Brock and Xepapadea. William A. "Buz" Brock is one of the world's foremost economists and a pathbreaking modeler of ecological-economic interactions:

> In some sense we are taking the position that the climate science community has the expertise to set the limiting global average temperature increase that the climate system can tolerate and the economic science community's job is to design the best set of policies to maximize the welfare of the world economy, subject to this cumulated carbon emissions budget constraint.[17]

Exactly. The search for a social cost of carbon has been a wild goose chase. It has kept hundreds, maybe thousands, of economists employed for years but has contributed nothing of substance to what we need to know to avert catastrophic climate change. And what is the alternative program?

- Our main job is to avoid a climate catastrophe (and thereby also minimize the severe, if less-than-catastrophic, impacts that climate change also impends).
- This requires adhering to a stringent carbon budget for long-lived greenhouse gases like carbon dioxide, one that sets limits to cumulative global emissions.
- The budget should be based solely on our best understanding of the biological, chemical and physical processes that govern the Earth's climate system.
- And the contribution of economics is to devise policies that can adhere to this budget with the least disruption to other human goals, particularly those that address the needs of the planet's poorest and most vulnerable populations.

# NOTES

## Introduction

1 The source for this and the following description of Mary Dawson's Ellesmere research is Eberle and McKenna (2007). Important early publications by Dawson and other members of her team include Dawson et al. (1975, 1976) and Estes and Hutchison (1980).

2 Gehlera et al. (2016) and Beerling and Royer (2011).

3 For an interesting summary of the findings of the Eberle team, see Eberle and Greenwood (2012). Alligators are just the beginning.

4 Precise dating and duration continue to be debated; see Röhl et al. (2007), also Westerhold et al. (2009) and Beerling and Royer (2011).

5 This is documented in Beerling and Royer (2011) and confirmed in Suc et al. (2020). For a general discussion of the use of proxy measures in paleoclimatology, see Pagani et al. (2014).

6 Gehlera et al. (2016) and Beerling and Royer (2011). For a more recent analysis that raises the temperature estimates for both the pre-PETM and the PETM itself, see Inglis et al. (2020).

7 See the references cited in Pagani et al. (2014).

8 See Aze et al. (2014). Little is known about terrestrial temperatures at subarctic latitudes during the PETM, and for a time the fragmentary evidence seemed to be at variance with marine estimates. Recent research may have reconciled land and sea, as reported by Naafs et al. (2018).

9 For an overview of earlier work that gives prominence to orbital factors, see Sluijs et al. (2007). An excellent recent overview, based on improved methods for estimating global carbon sources and balances, can be found in Gehlera et al. (2016). It should be emphasized that one reason most research attention has been given to events that may have generated greenhouse gas emissions compared with changes in insolation (solar radiation) is that there are no proxy measurements for the latter. But this means, just as insolation can't be "ruled in" as a factor, it can't be ruled out either.

10 For a dramatic account – if you read between the technically abstruse lines – see Storey et al. (2007). Much of the debate has to do specifically with the role of methane, controversial because estimates of the amount of it available to be released

as a global warming feedback mechanism vary immensely. The role of marine methane releases is downplayed by Ruppel and Kessler (2018), who note that current natural (not human-caused) methane releases to the atmosphere exceed some estimates of similar releases during the PETM. A similar skepticism was expressed by Archer (2007); his estimate of the methane hydrate inventory at that time is insufficient to generate the requisite warming, nor, in his view, does the evidence regarding its release correspond to the timing of the warming event. Varying types and degrees of corroboration for the role of methane, however, can be found in Carozza et al. (2011), Dickens (2011), Rudmin et al. (2018) and Yao et al. (2018). Note that methane quickly (in geological terms) converts to carbon dioxide, and it is in this form that its PETM-inducing potential has to be evaluated. We will discuss methane feedback possibilities in greater detail in the following chapter. Finally, attention has recently been drawn to the possibility that changes in cloud cover might have been triggered by a buildup of greenhouse gases that would have caused a further burst of global warming, but this remains speculative; see Schneider et al. (2019).

11 See Rae et al. (2021).

12 See Brinkhuis et al. (2006).

13 "Normal," for millions of years after the PETM, was still pretty warm. For a recent overview of the PETM's place in longer-run temperature trends, see Pagani et al. (2014).

14 Fuller discussion and documentation of this process will appear in Chapter 1.

15 The 25% reduction reflects the decline in $CO_2$ emissions documented by Forster et al. (2020). They found an immediate reduction by 30% globally, stabilizing two months later at 25%. My extension of this reduction over five years is much longer than their projections; it is a very worst case scenario solely for the purpose of showing how the pandemic in itself will likely have little effect on the accumulation of atmospheric $CO_2$.

16 Schneider (1996).

17 Strictly speaking, economics does not have its own Nobel Prize; the categories were laid out at the end of the nineteenth century by Alfred Nobel himself in his will. Economics was added in 1968 by the Swedish Central Bank and given a nameplate that suggests equal Nobelishness.

18 See Nordhaus (2013) and Boyce and Bradley (2018).

19 The group that originally spearheaded the move toward feel-good environmental policy is the Breakthrough Institute, whose website can be found at https://thebreakthrough.org. A helpful summary of their approach can be found in Atkinson et al. (2011). I critique their position in Dorman (2020a). The notion that only polluters will (and should) pay higher prices for carbon energy in response to climate policy is widespread among activists. The demand that this "free" source of revenue should be used for environmental and social programs prioritizing minority communities was the basis for the opposition to a 2016 carbon tax referendum in Washington State by most of the political left, assembled in the Alliance for Jobs and Clean Energy. After the 2016 measure failed, they brought their own initiative before the voters in 2018, and it failed likewise. The Alliance's website can be accessed at https://jobscleanenergywa.com/.

20 A plethora of organizations promote the view that their signature grievance is the "true" cause of the climate crisis. A useful compendium of these claims can be found in Klein (2014). Klein blames the accumulation of greenhouse gases on something she calls "extractivism," a term that amalgamates the sins of neoliberalism, the pursuit of economic growth, scientific rationalism, alienation from nature, disrespect for indigenous people and their spiritual traditions, globalization, mass incarceration, colonialism, militarism, racism and sexism. Fortunately,

all we need is for everyone to embrace a new consciousness free of these evils to put the climate conundrum behind us once and for all. I scrutinize her position in Dorman (2016a). Of course, critiquing this position does not mean ignoring the many other injustices we face apart from extreme climate risk, and we can certainly tackle more than one issue at a time. The problem stems from the false belief that carbon emissions will automatically cease when some other social objective is reached, and that we therefore don't need to take the difficult actions discussed in this book.

# Chapter 1

1 Unless otherwise indicated, the source for the explication of the science in this chapter is IPCC, Working Group I (2013). I relied especially on Chapter 6, "Carbon and Other Biogeochemical Cycles."

2 Valley et al. (2014).

3 Knoll (2015).

4 To put that in perspective, the air that supplies us with oxygen is 40% thinner at 7,100 meters, or about 23,300 feet. Most mountaineers use oxygen tanks at these very high altitudes.

5 Berner (2003).

6 Only a portion of the carbon stored in permafrost takes the form of methane. The majority is organic matter housed in frozen soils.

7 The question of how much methane lurks in marine environments, available to be released if conditions permit, is one of the most controversial in all of climate science. Those who think the amount is relatively small, perhaps under 1,000 Gt, point to theoretical models that substantiate this prediction. These models have not (yet) been validated by the quantities and locations of methane deposits uncovered or not found, however. The empirical problem is essentially one of sampling. It is expensive and difficult to search for methane hydrates, and only a few such probes have been made. If we knew the underlying distribution of sites, so we could infer whether or not our scatter of data points is representative, we could produce estimates with greater confidence. Unfortunately, we don't. If we don't trust the models, the data by themselves point to a much higher inventory, 10,000–20,000 Gt. For various perspectives, see Boswell and Collett (2011), Dean et al. (2018), Dickens (2011) and Sparrow et al. (2018).

8 The Bureau of Economic Analysis has unveiled a new data framework for the US economy that similarly integrates stock and flow accounting; see US Bureau of Economic Analysis (2020).

9 Metric weights are based on volumes of water; thus Crater Lake in Oregon, formed by an ancient volcanic eruption, contains somewhat less than 20 cubic kilometers of water and weighs in a bit under 20 Gt. For a land-based comparison, consider that an average rail car hauling coal carries a load of about 90 metric tonnes; so a 100-car train is moving about 9,000 tonnes. A gigatonne of coal would therefore require more than 110,000 of these trains. Each tonne of coal produces at least two tonnes of carbon dioxide since, while only a portion of coal is carbon, when it is burned each carbon atom is augmented with two heavier oxygen atoms. This means half as many coal trains, 55,000 or less, are needed to move the coal that can generate a gigatonne of carbon dioxide. For conversion factors that translate coal BTUs, a heat metric, into quantities of carbon dioxide, see Hong and Slatick (1994).

10 Allen et al. (2010). For the potential of tipping point shifts between forest and savanna land cover, see Davis et al. (2019) and Staver et al. (2011), also Hirota

et al. (2011). A biome is a characteristic assemblage of plant and animal species over a relatively large geographical space, such as a forest.

11 For a worst-case scenario, see Pistone et al. (2019). Arctic warming and sea ice loss is monitored in National Oceanographic and Atmospheric Administration (2019).

12 Schneider et al. (2019). For an overview of recent research, see Pearce (2020).

13 New research suggests methane release from permafrost melting may arrive sooner than previously thought; see, for instance, Farquharson et al. (2019).

14 As with marine methane inventories, there is also a vigorous debate about the susceptibility of hydrates to dissociation and the fate of any methane released in that manner as it makes its way through the water table. On one side are those who think the gas will not only be oxidized but reabsorbed, and that it will encounter physical barriers that prevent its escape to the atmosphere. On the other are those who think most of it will ultimately enter the atmosphere as $CO_2$, and that this has in fact happened at various points in Earth history. It's important to bear in mind that there is plenty of intermediate ground between these two positions, and that it's not necessary for any single feedback mechanism to pose a catastrophic risk in order for us to be at risk of a catastrophic outcome. For a sample of the debate, see Dean et al. (2018), Petrenko et al. (2018), Ruppel and Kessler (2018) and Sparrow et al. (2018). Interestingly, the recent Assessment Report of the IPCC's Working Group I presents skepticism toward marine methane releases as a matter of scientific consensus, but does so by citing only studies taking a skeptical stance. See IPCC, Working Group I (2021), chapter 5, 8–81.

15 Di et al. (2020).

16 Liger-Belair (2003).

17 An important compendium of research summaries in the field of abrupt climate change, primarily centered on recent ice ages and the interglacial periods between them, that discusses the role of feedback mechanisms in great detail is Rashid et al. (2011).

18 Steffen et al. (2018). There was a follow-up warning by an overlapping group of authors in Lenton et al. (2019).

19 Clearly, I am not giving much credence to schemes for geoengineering, such as massive interventions to increase atmospheric reflectivity or to fertilize the oceans to serve as biomass farms. It is outside the scope of this book to assess specific proposals, which seek to mitigate one set of risks by creating new ones just as alarming. For a recent assessment of some of these options which steers a middle course by pointing out the risks while calling for more research, see National Academies of Sciences (2021).

20 Ricke and Caldeira (2014).

21 Zickfeld and Herrington (2015).

22 For a useful summary of existing knowledge and future research objectives, see Jones et al. (2019).

23 Huybrechts et al. (2011).

24 Of course, the revolution in life expectancy has essential cultural, social and political dimensions as well as technological ones. See Riley (2001). While mortality is a specialized topic in itself, it is usually discussed in conjunction with fertility in the context of the "demographic transition." For a succinct summary, see Lee (2003).

25 Carbon capture and storage (CCS) is an immense topic, far beyond the scope of this book to explore in detail. Much of the specialized literature is by researchers dedicated to finding technological solutions; as in nuclear power, they tend to be optimists. See, for example, Rackley (2017). Independent assessments tend to emphasize the large uncertainties regarding developments affecting future costs and

reliability, for example, Budinis et al. (2017) and Metz et al. (2005). Reliability in this context pertains to both the potential for modest carbon releases and general sequestration failure, and in addition to technical influences, it also depends on the confidence we have that private operators of these facilities will refuse to cut corners in design, construction and maintenance, despite the asymmetric incentives stemming from limited liability. (This parallels a similar problem with nuclear power.) The view of CCS taken in this book is similar to that of mitigation strategies other than the phase-out of fossil fuels: it is worth investing in and might turn out to play a positive role, but is too uncertain to serve as our primary defense against the risk of catastrophic climate change. To put it differently, it can enhance a program to rapidly decarbonize our energy supply, but it shouldn't be seen as a substitute for such a program. This argument will be developed in greater detail in Chapter 5.

# Chapter 2

1  US Environmental Protection Administration (n.d.), US Department of Justice, Office of Legal Policy (2012). The $9.5 million value of statistical life represents an adjustment to 2020 prices.
2  Economists themselves are well aware of this problem, and cost–benefit analyses are generally accompanied by acknowledgments that important aspects of the question under examination can't be given monetary equivalents. In practice this doesn't lessen the tendency for cost–benefit bottom lines (net cost or net benefit) to be interpreted as dispositive.
3  Unless otherwise indicated, the material in this chapter is drawn from IPCC, Working Group II (2014).
4  Diffenbaugh et al. (2017), Emanuel (2017), Kossin et al. (2016), and Wing et al. (2015).
5  Seo (2015).
6  Mendelsohn et al. (1994).
7  Burke and Emerick (2016), and Nelson et al. (2014a).
8  Trenberth et al. (2014).
9  Rahmstorf et al. (2015).
10  Myers et al. (2014).
11  For more detail on forecasts of agricultural impacts stemming from climate change, see in particular chapter 7 of Part A, "Food Security and Food Production Systems," of IPCC, Working Group II (2014). For a useful reflection on the variability of these forecasts, see Nelson et al. (2014b). The most recent IPCC assessment of climate change and agriculture is IPCC (2019).
12  Barnosky et al. (2011), Kolbert (2014), and Stork (2010).
13  Anadón et al. (2014).
14  Raymond et al. (2014), and Snover et al. (2013).
15  See the references cited in the previous paragraph.
16  Palmer (2016).
17  Hönisch et al. (2012). See also the discussion of ocean acidification in IPCC, Working Group I (2013), Chapter 3.8, and IPCC, Working Group II (2014), Chapter 6.
18  Hauri et al. (2016).
19  Pal and Eltahir (2016). Their work was updated, with similar conclusions, in Im et al. (2017).
20  This is the maximum sustainable temperature for our skin, which needs to be slightly cooler than our heat-generating core.
21  Im et al. (2017), and Pal and Eltahir (2016).

22 Raymond et al. (2020).

23 For a recent review of research on the heat/humidity risks of continued climate change, see Matthews (2018).

24 Disease impacts stemming from climate change are the topic of IPCC, Working Group II, (2014), Chapter 11.5. The paucity of material – the section pertaining to infectious diseases is only four pages long – primarily reflects limited research and the large uncertainties of disease evolution rather than relative unimportance.

25 See the discussion of potential interactions between the tipping points of four outcomes – the collapse of the Greenland and West Antarctic ice sheets, disruption of the Atlantic Meridional Overturning Circulation and dieback of the Amazon rainforest – in Wunderling et al. (2021).

26 IPCC Working Group 1, (2013).

27 Farquharson et al. (2019), and Turetsky et al. (2019).

28 For wildfires, see Struzik (2020). Meanwhile, we are already beginning to see a disturbing rise in methane emissions, much of it unattributable to the direct combustion of fossil fuels. There is uncertainty about the exact causes – releases from wetlands, livestock or other sources – and of course no assurance the trend will continue at its present pace. See Fletcher and Schaefer (2019) and Hubau et al. (2020).

29 IMF (2020).

30 This applies to the cost–benefit methodology officially employed in the United States and many other countries, which is also the view of most economists. Some countries, such as the United Kingdom, use the cost-effectiveness approach in which the value of reducing a tonne of carbon emissions is set by its least-cost method. Cost-effectiveness is closer to the position I'm advocating, but many of the arguments I make on the benefit side can also apply to costs.

31 The most prominent IAM of this sort is the Dynamic Integrated Model of Climate and the Economy (DICE), painstakingly developed and maintained by William D. Nordhaus. For recent documentation of his work, see Nordhaus (2017a, 2017b). Readers should be advised that a competing model, the Climate Framework for Uncertainty, Negotiation and Distribution (FUND), developed by Richard Tol, is less credible. Tol has been an influential voice for the view that climate change will likely have positive economic effects, at least for the next several decades. Issues with his work undermine his credibility, however. For detailed discussion of two of his recent articles, see Ackerman (2014), Retraction Watch (2015) and Gelman (2014). The last of these has a substantial exchange between Tol and statistician Andrew Gelman in the comment thread. A fuller discussion of IAMs in general, especially those that consider only the carbon cycle, climate responses and the interaction of both of these with the economy, and which do not try to monetize climate impacts, will appear in Chapter 5.

32 This appears as Equation 3 in Nordhaus (2017a).

33 We may even drill down to smaller marginal costs: the marginal cost of not releasing an acre-foot of water from a dam's reservoir to offset low stream flows or of not constructing a fish bypass channel.

34 There is a more detailed explanation for why methods such as Nordhaus' do not address the scale problem in the Appendix.

35 Two behavioral classics are Ariely (2008) and Kahneman (2011). But for a different view, see Gigerenzer (2010).

36 A similar critique of market-oriented decision-making in environmental contexts was eloquently expressed by philosopher Mark Sagoff in the first edition of his influential book, *The Economy of the Earth: Philosophy, Law, and the Environment* (1988). In

the second edition, published in 2008, he adopted a more Hayekian conception of the problem, espousing libertarian economics. This drift was characteristic of a number of antitechnocratic thinkers in the final decades of the twentieth century – even the iconic Michel Foucault; see Zamora and Behrent (2015).

A common retort to the call for public deliberation in place of market calculation is that political mechanisms are hopelessly corrupt or ineffectual. How to reconcile the demand for public reason with the shortcomings of actually existing democracy is largely beyond the scope of this book, although its method of argument and intended audience reflect the conviction that the task is not hopeless. Later chapters will consider some of the nuts and bolts of public decision-making, including overcoming the suborning of political institutions by concentrated wealth, in the particular context of climate policy. For a more general grounding of the case for public deliberation, see the work of John Dewey, in particular Dewey (1954, 1999). Dewey was notoriously foggy in much of his writing, and a massive secondary literature has arisen to interpret him. An excellent starting point for a journey into Dewey is Westbrook (1993).

# Chapter 3

1 Sobel (1995).
2 Penney (2020).
3 The US Environmental Protection Agency, for example, offers an online footprint calculator at www3.epa.gov/carbon-footprint-calculator/.
4 See, for instance, the final pages of Haupt (2011).
5 Joppa (2020).
6 Adler (2016). A similar, more recent analysis can be found in Cho (2020).
7 The company's announcement of the electricity deal with its supplier, Chelan Public Utility District, makes oblique reference to this fact: "No additional infrastructure is required in Chelan's service area to be able to send power from Chelan PUD to Microsoft." See Microsoft News Center (2019).
8 More precisely, carbon footprint methodology distinguishes between three "scopes." Scope 1 includes emissions from direct operations, like the carbon dioxide and other gases that come out the tailpipes of a company truck fleet. Scope 2 covers the emissions from energy the company purchases, including electricity. Scope 3 scoops up emissions from employee activity, capital, intermediate and raw material goods purchased from external suppliers, and the processing and disposal of goods the company produces after they are sold. See World Resources Institute and World Business Council for Sustainable Development (2020).
9 I am giving an extremely brief summary of the socialist calculation debate that was conducted via dueling academic papers during the 1920s, 1930s and 1940s. Supporters of socialist planning (in this debate) argued for a decentralized system of allocation that mimicked existing markets; their opponents said this mimicry wouldn't work because real markets perform functions that accounting calculations can't. Some of the specific reasons given by those on the "antisocialist" side are relevant to the shortcomings of carbon auditing: much of the important knowledge about how goods are used and respond to social and economic demands is local and tacit (unavailable to those not directly involved), transitory and in constant flux, subjective (dependent on choices governed by perception and attitude) and acquired only through discovery (revealed through trial and error). We will see practical examples shortly. As for the debate itself, I find I largely agree with the "Austrian," antisocialist position, although I also regard the scope of the debate as

too limited to assess the merits of socialism due to the socialists' embrace of an unrealistic conception of general equilibrium and allocative optimality. I also think the shortcomings of the Austrian position, which are severe, were unexploited by their opponents. A full discussion would obviously take us far from the concerns of this book. My thinking has been influenced by Lavoie (1985), which puts the Austrian arguments in their best light. In my view, a proper rebuttal has yet to be written.

10 Delucchi et al. (2013) and Nordelöf et al. (2014). For a recent, optimistic study, see Märtz et al. (2021). They assume nearly complete decarbonization of electrical generation over the coming decades and conclude that a near-term switch from internal combustion to batteries will take best advantage of it. Of course, by making this assumption about electricity a starting point of their analysis, they are not in a position to incorporate the effect of greater demand for electricity stemming from vehicle electrification itself on the speed and extent of the makeover of electrical generation.

11 Graff Zivin et al. (2014).

12 Schipper (2000). A recent meta-analysis of the effect of increasing fuel efficiency on vehicle miles traveled was undertaken by Dimitropoulos et al. (2018). The effect was found to be stronger in the long run, which makes sense since a lot of driving is tied to slowly evolving decisions over where to live, work and shop; they report estimates in which an initial cost saving is reduced by more than a quarter due to greater consumption.

13 Hawkins et al. (2013).

14 Evergreen State College (2015).

15 University of New Hampshire (2016).

16 Gillenwater et al. (2014).

17 Alas, while Evergreen had experienced a dramatic loss in enrollments and associated revenues even before the pandemic struck, and while this may result in future changes to its governance and operations, it is unlikely to result in its disappearance.

18 Schendler and Toffel (2011).

19 Data on Microsoft's publicly reported political donations are reported by Open Secrets (2020). It should be acknowledged that Microsoft is a corporate member of the Climate Leadership Council, a modest counterstep in the right direction. CLC advocates, as this book does, national-level pricing of carbon emissions, with the revenue rebated to the public. On the other hand, they support an initial price of slightly more than $40 per tonne of carbon dioxide, far too low to meet the goals we will discuss shortly. See Climate Leadership Council (2019). For Microsoft's participation, see Smith (2020).

20 The particular model implicit in this discussion is the prisoner's dilemma, a staple of introductory courses in economics, political science and game theory. A useful survey can be found in the *Stanford Encyclopedia of Philosophy*, s.v. Prisoner's dilemma, https://plato.stanford.edu/entries/prisoner-dilemma/. There are other types of collective action problems as well.

21 On the uncertain translation of the Paris commitments to impacts on carbon emissions, see Benveniste et al. (2017) and Rogelj et al. (2017).

22 The following paragraphs are taken from Dorman (2015).

23 Geometrically, atmospheric carbon accumulation is represented by the area under the curve that plots emissions over time.

24 This is true for carbon dioxide but not for short-lived greenhouse gases like methane, a complication we will take up later in the chapter.

25 The baseline for warming is the "preindustrial" level of the mid-nineteenth century. Approximately one of these two degrees has already come to pass.

26 The concept of probability in this context is rather fraught: in IPCC and related budget calculations, it refers to the percentage of mitigation scenarios (which we will discuss in Chapter 5) that establish this outcome. But the scenarios themselves are dependent on current understanding, data and modeling choices; they are not the random generators that conventional probability concepts apply to. The truth is, we cannot pin true probability estimates to budget choices; if we select a quantity of cumulative carbon emissions for which a higher proportion of modeling scenarios produce a temperature increase beneath the targeted level, we are taking a more conservative stance, but the use of this metric as a proxy for true probability has only the justification that it's the best we can do.

27 Masson-Delmotte et al. (2018).

28 To be precise, we know that warming is proportional to accumulated $CO_2$, but with a limited range of past $CO_2$ concentrations to extrapolate from, small uncertainties in the exact historic relationship yield larger uncertainties in future climate response. See Rogelj et al. (2019).

29 Of course, half a centigrade degree is hardly trivial when climate scientists agonize over the choice between $1.5°$ and $2°$ warming targets. For a partial survey, see Goodwin (2019), Jones et al. (2019), Ricke and Caldeira (2014) and Williams et al. (2017).

30 Rogelj et al. (2019).

31 This point also applies to the zero emissions commitment forecasts just cited.

32 Other short-lived greenhouse gases include fluorinated gases and black carbon. An important intermediate case is nitrous oxide ($N_2O$), which remains in the atmosphere for somewhat more than a century. For the prospects of including this gas in broader greenhouse gas budgets, see Kanter et al. (2020).

33 Of course, this will be a geometric rather than arithmetic mean.

34 For some of the thrust and parry on these questions, see Allen et al. (2016, 2018), Rogelj et al. (2019) and Schleussner et al. (2019).

35 Lindsey (2020).

36 Mikaloff Fletcher and Schaefer (2019).

37 Rogelj et al. (2019). Note they had a large error bar around it, from 500 Gt less to 250 Gt more. This exemplifies the uncertainty we face.

38 See Matthews et al. (2021) and Natali et al. (2021). The first appeared in the context of estimating the remaining carbon budget that would give us a two-thirds probability of limiting warming to $1.5°$, but the same logic applies to a $2°$ target. The second notes that recent advances in permafrost research reveal the potential for more rapid carbon releases due to wildfires and landscape disruption, but this hasn't yet been incorporated into mitigation modeling or estimates of the remaining carbon budget.

39 This is consistent with the observation that, when these models are fed lower discount rates, which increase the present value of costs incurred decades in the future, they frontload a higher proportion of the total emission reduction. See, for example, Grant et al. (2021).

## Chapter 4

1 There have also been many climate disruptions caused by volcanic emissions of gases and particulates over a period of one to a few years. These have had major impacts on plant and animal life, but the mechanism was one that primarily blocked

incoming, not outgoing, radiation. The role of carbon in generating greenhouse effects was not involved.

2 Daly (1973), and Georgescu-Roegen (1971).

3 An important statement of the degrowth position can be found in Jackson (2009). Degrowth went mainstream with the success of Klein (2014), earning her an audience with Pope Francis; see Scammell (2015). There is also a "Marxist" version of degrowth, or at least nongrowth, advocacy as exemplified by John Bellamy Foster and Richard York. Rather than espousing socialism because it will outperform a sputtering capitalism in sustaining economic growth, the traditional claim of the Marxist left, they endorse it because it will make possible an end to growth. See Foster and York (2011).

4 For a more polemical version of some of the following arguments directed against a prominent degrowther cited in the previous note, see Dorman (2016a).

5 It is beyond the scope of this discussion to examine exactly what is included in GDP measurement according to the standards of national income accounting, and what is left out. Very generally, GDP measures the fungible portion of the economy, goods and services that are traded for money and can therefore be converted into one another – acquiring less of one such item allows you to acquire more of another. You can spend less on transportation and more on yoga classes, or the other way around. You could spend less on both and fund, with increased taxes, more advanced satellites for weather forecasting. Fungibility is an important quality, since it allows you to choose what you want over a large set of alternatives, but many of the essentials of life are not fungible, which is why increasing GDP should not be regarded as an end in itself.

6 There is an immense literature on economic growth–$CO_2$ decoupling and the lack thereof. Two recent panel data analyses of note are Cohen et al. (2018) and Schröder and Storm (2018).

7 Klemettinen (2007).

8 US Bureau of Labor Statistics (2016).

9 Emissions data were downloaded from World Bank (2021). Incidentally, I have chosen the Great Recession as an example of the effect of reductions in GDP on carbon emissions rather than the coronavirus recession since the pandemic is ongoing as this is written, and because the virus-induced downturn was concentrated in only a few economic sectors.

10 Real global output is also available from World Bank (2021).

11 Steele and Koprowski (2003).

12 OECD (2021). Note that these averages don't reflect wide disparities in work hours within countries, where some work far less than they wish and others far more; see Messenger (2018).

13 OECD (2016).

14 Eurofound (2016).

15 Pencavel (2018).

16 Blyth (2013).

17 This should obviously not be taken as an endorsement of Chinese economic policy. China itself has been shifting attention to the environmental costs of always putting growth ahead of other goals.

18 Stern (2006).

19 Of particular note is World Bank (2012).

20 For a recent assertion of this sort, see Ripple et al. (2017).

21 Except to say that anyone who thinks human populations obey the same laws as the populations of other organisms studied by biologists should look up the term "fertility transition."

22 These and other population numbers in this paragraph were taken from WorldoMeter (2021).

23 In fact, the closer a pair of countries are to each other the more they trade, as reflected in gravity models of international trade. For a recent discussion, see Chaney (2018).

24 International Maritime Organization (2014).

25 The localization and degrowth movements have crossed paths in a way that demonstrates that two wrongs can just be doubly wrong. The starting point appears to be a textbook on ecological economics by Herman Daley and Josh Farley published in 2003. In it they claim that, since exports are a component of GDP and also a form taken by international trade, buying local tames the evils of economic growth. This argument was picked up by Naomi Klein in the work cited previously. The only problem is that it is not exports but *net* exports (exports minus imports) that enters into calculations of GDP: exports raise GDP and imports lower it. The volume of net exports for a given country is not related in any way to the volume of trade, since you could have perfectly balanced trade (zero net exports) and yet trade could absorb a large share of national income. Meanwhile, net exports summed over planet Earth *must* equal zero, however large or small the portion of output traded across borders. See Daley and Joshua (2003), also Klein (2014).

26 Like other "true" causes of climate change considered in this chapter, the separation from nature thesis can be found in Klein (2014).

27 Wallace and Karra (2020).

28 A readable introduction to the history of deforestation is Williams (2000) or, in longer form, Williams (2003), which, despite their age, capture the revolution in modern understanding of prehistoric land use.

29 Friedman (2020).

30 A detailed description of REDD+ can be found on its website, UN-REDD Programme (2021).

31 There has been persistent criticism of the offset business for putting carbon sequestration ahead of other values. In some instances, monoculture plantations, particularly of fast-growing eucalyptus trees native only to Australia, have been financed despite their paucity of ecological services. In addition, forests are home to millions of people, many with ancient, forest-centric cultures. Managing a forest strictly for carbon can constitute a threat to them. The administrators of REDD+ are aware of these charges and claim to have mended their ways. Whether they can now be trusted is a crucial issue but beyond the scope of this book.

32 Carvalhais et al. (2014).

33 Although small percentage increases in the overall oceanic carbon sink can lead to devastating changes in pH, as we saw in Chapter 2.

34 This conclusion depends on the additional assumption that little of the forest carbon is transported to the ocean, altering the equilibrium size of the ocean sink. This is approximately true, and most ocean carbon flux occurs through direct exchange with the atmosphere.

35 Barnes et al. (1998).

36 This paragraph summarizes the findings from a survey of recent work on the projected impact of a changing climate on forests; see Anderegg et al. (2020).

37 I am not alone in harboring these doubts. The National Academy of Sciences report on carbon removal technologies states, "It is unclear, however, how a changing climate will affect sequestration. If climate change results in widespread forest disease

or accelerates the decomposition of carbon stored in soils, terrestrial ecosystems could become a net source rather than a sink of GHGs, further contributing to climate change." National Academy of Sciences (2015), 41.

38 Displacing rather than reducing deforestation is called "leakage" in policy circles.

39 Norway, Office of the Auditor General (2017–2018). The report is also critical of follow-up on social and environmental impacts of climate-motivated forestry projects. For a disturbing journalistic report on forest projects in Brazil, see Song and Moura (2019).

40 Elgin (2020).

41 Song and Temple (2021).

42 Portions of this section were previously published in Dorman (2020a).

43 This is not the only view, of course, but it is a constant theme in popular discussions of how to go about climate messaging. For representative examples, see Campbell (2016), Townsend (2017) and Nisbet (n.d.).

44 The original proposal can be found in Shellenberger and Nordhaus (2004). For a history of the circumstances surrounding the release and reception of this report, see Kallis and Bliss (2019).

45 US Congress (2019), Data for Progress (n.d.), and GNDE (n.d.).

46 There is a tendency in the GND world to adhere to the "good begets good" heuristic, according to which good actions generate only good results, and the attainment of more of some types of good does not require any sacrifice of other types. GND policies are expected to reduce poverty and racism, promote health and a higher quality of life for nearly everyone, and promote political and economic equality. They have no identifiable costs except to very wealthy people in the fossil fuel sector. For a discussion of the "good begets good" heuristic, see Leiser and Aroch (2009).

47 There are many informative overviews of the Energiewende. See, for instance, Beveridge and Kern (2013), Hake et al. (2015), Jacobs (2012) and von Hirschhausen (2014).

48 European Commission (2020).

49 European Commission (2020).

50 For example, Nimgaonkar (2015). A Google search on "Energiewende Paradox" (with the quotes) turns up over 17,000 hits.

## Chapter 5

1 Mercier and Sperber (2017).

2 A prominent source of criticism of aggressive climate action is the so-called Copenhagen Consensus, the creation of Bjorn Lomborg, a statistician who has made a career of disputing environmental science. It opposes "Global annual carbon emission reduction targets for example, 2°C reduction below pre-industrial level [because they are] extremely costly due to a lack of low-carbon energy sources." Of course, the goal of strict climate policy is to hold the *increase* in temperature to 2° *above* the preindustrial level, but why nitpick? See Galiana (2014).

3 We will look at a few examples shortly.

4 For a popular introduction to changing energy sources in global history, see Smil (1994).

5 Searchinger and Heimlich (2015). We will return to the potential role of biofuels in future carbon scenarios later in this chapter.

6 To pick one example of many, a US consulting firm, ICF International, released a report in 2015 promising an economic boom if the transition to noncarbon energy were to continue. It was touted on many widely read environmental websites: "Our

Clean Energy Economy" (NextGen Policy), "Clean Energy Economy Drives Job Creation" (Climate Solutions), "Economy Would Gain Two Million New Jobs in Low-Carbon Transition, Study Says" (Inside Climate News), among others. The study they refer to has been pulled from the ICF website, however. See ICF Resources (2021), Lashof (2015), McGarry (2016) and Sadasivam (2015).

7  Long ago, in the pre-desktop computer era, I worked for a spell as a secretary. It certainly felt like a burden to me.

8  One complication is the presence of excess unemployment in most of the world: people are looking for jobs and not finding them. With unemployment, the cost of providing a job is less than it would be otherwise. True, work is still work, and a lot of it is something most of us would rather not do for free – a personal burden – but the *opportunity cost* of employment, the social cost that arises when we are tied up in one particular job and unavailable to do other, socially beneficial work, is reduced. Moreover, if a green jobs program is financed in part or wholly by public borrowing, it does not result in an equal reduction in spending elsewhere, at least under conditions of excess unemployment. Thus the cost side of employment can be less than it appears, even while the climate benefit remains the same. But the same logic applies to *any* debt-financed program under depressed economic conditions. We could pay currently unemployed people to build or refurbish schools or spruce up our parks. We could expand child or elder care and employ people that way. There are lots of unmet needs in society. So, while the opportunity cost of the extra work it will take to minimize climate change is less than it would be in an economy that's already fully employed, it is well above zero.

9  IPCC Working Group III (2014).

10  Manufacturing is responsible for a third of global carbon emissions: Bataille et al. (2018).

11  Agnew (2014), and Brown (2015).

12  I have presented the layers as a sequence, but in real life they will be determined simultaneously. As a generalization, however, it is fair to say that the first level tends to be more convenient than the second and the second more than the third.

13  For a typical example, see Williams et al. (2015). They compare a series of options for spending or rebating carbon revenues – a topic we will take up in Chapter 8 – according to how the economic burden is distributed. Their measure of burden is the reduction in consumer surplus, estimated on a set of demand functions that presume utility maximization. If you substitute away from your initial consumption choices due to a price increase for one of the items, it means you have lost utility by switching from a higher- to a lower-valued set of goods.

14  Stutzer and Frey (2008).

15  In Chapter 6 we will see that interaction effects between many simultaneous choices can produce a situation in which a structural change overriding our separate preferences could nonetheless improve our quality of life.

16  The absence of end use demand in mitigation pathway analysis is widely recognized; see, for instance, the discussion in Sharmina et al. (2021).

17  For examples, see the widely cited Phadke et al. (2020), similarly Heal (2020).

18  Covert et al. (2016).

19  Covert et al. (2016).

20  Phadke et al. (2020).

21  Ballinger et al. (2020).

22  Deep Decarbonization Pathways Project (2015). This is actually a more careful and better-documented study than most.

23  Deep Decarbonization Pathways Project (2015), 32.

24 Deep Decarbonization Pathways Project (2015), 30. Emphasis in the original.

25 The Deep Decarbonization team examined only some sources of carbon emissions and some countries, so they had to extrapolate in both dimensions to arrive at a global total.

26 See Edenhofer et al. (2014), 12, Table SPM.1. For all parameters, the 10th to 90th percentile of the scenarios is shown.

27 For a relatively accessible discussion of how well these models are meeting their purposes, see O'Neill et al. (2020).

28 For a general introduction to IAM methodology, see Clarke et al. (2014).

29 The word "equilibrium" is tricky in economics. It means only that a market doesn't have a level of either excess supply or demand that would cause prices to change. It doesn't mean "beneficial," much less "optimal," unless many further (and implausible) assumptions are made. For our purposes equilibrium should be understood descriptively without any additional baggage; markets could be deemed to be in equilibrium even as a new thermal maximum sets in and alligators embark on their northward crawl. Also, since the IAMs employ a simple supply-and-demand framework, they assume that all markets continuously clear. This includes the labor market, which is represented as always in a state of full employment – no excess of labor supply over labor demand at the going wage rate.

30 This distinction between IAMs is similar to one in macroeconomics forecasting. The dominant approach from the 1950s to 1970s relied on economic trends disaggregated by sector. These had an inertial aspect (in the absence of changed circumstances people will continue doing this period what they did last) with passive reaction to external change. If taxes go down, people will find themselves with more money, so they'll spend a portion of it based on the portion they spent in the past when their income went up. Starting in the 1980s, a new approach emerged, said to embody "microfoundations." The "micro" in this case was a hypothetical individual or household representing the whole society who was given a simple utility function to maximize, such that choices were now proactive rather than reactive. This entity was assumed to have knowledge of future states of the economy and could therefore maximize intertemporally; if an economic event is anticipated ten or twenty years into the future, it can alter choices made today. The models adhering to this second approach are said to display "dynamic stochastic general equilibrium" (DSGE). Debate over these competing modeling strategies has been heated. Economist-turned-blogger-turned-columnist-turned-Substacker Noah Smith has played an important role in conveying the issues to a broader public; see Smith (2014, 2016).

31 The narratives are excerpted from Riahi et al. (2017).

32 Clarke et al. (2014).

33 Parry et al. (2014).

34 Tavoni and Socolow (2013).

35 Grant et al. (2021).

36 US White House (2021).

37 Farand and Darby (2020).

38 Extinction Rebellion (n.d.).

39 For a scathing critique of net zero rhetoric that exposes the political motives behind the ever more speculative carbon removal technologies incorporated in policy pronouncements and the climate mitigation models underpinning them, see Dyke et al. (2021). Of course, the Extinction Rebellion target date of 2025 is immune from their criticism that it allows too little effort in the near future, but without a nuclear conflagration, wayward asteroid or much deadlier pandemic to spur it along, it is not remotely possible either.

40 See, in addition to Gambhir et al. (2017), Dessens et al. (2016) and Riahi et al. (2015).

41 Riahi et al. (2015). See also Rogelj et al. (2015), where a feasible solution was achievable only under optimistic assumptions about future energy demand. Incidentally, the fact that many model runs fail to limit likely warming to less than 2° affects estimates of the cost of the technology. These estimates are based on the successful scenarios only, a form of sample bias. Correcting for this might lead to doubling or tripling cost estimates, according to Tavoni and Tol (2010).

42 Anderson and Peters (2016), 14.

43 National Academy of Sciences (2015).

44 This verdict was largely reiterated in an updated NAS assessment from 2018 (National Academy of Sciences [2018]). Among the recent academic studies is a particularly comprehensive review by Fuss et al. (2018), which concludes, "Based on our assessment, large-scale deployment of NETs, as implied by some of the current literature on 1.5 °C scenarios, appears unrealistic given the biophysical and economic limits that are suggested by the available, yet still patchy, science today. The same concerns of realism apply equally to 2 °C scenarios that delay action until 2030. The direct policy implications of this NETs review are thus that, given the assessed uncertainties, strategies should aim at limiting warming to below 2 °C with the least possible assumed dependence on NETs. Simultaneously, NETs should be further researched, but until they are demonstrably available at the global scale there should be no delay in a global peak and decline of $CO_2$ emissions" (p. 35).

45 Field and Mach (2017). Current $CO_2$ emissions are about 33 Gt in total.

46 Field and Mach (2017).

47 Anderson and Peters (2016).

48 This was underlined by the National Academy of Sciences reports discussed earlier and also Boysen et al. (2017).

49 One survey pegged the cost of DAC at \$1,600–\$2,000 per tonne of carbon removed, a pricy option when carbon costs under stringent mitigation policy are likely to be in the low to middle three digits per tonne. See Smith et al. (2016).

50 National Academy of Sciences (2015).

51 National Academy of Sciences (2015).

52 WITCH stands for the World Induced Technical Change Hybrid. See European Institute on Economics and the Environment (n.d.).

53 Gambhir et al. (2017). Current global capacity is taken from International Atomic Energy Association (2017).

54 IPCC Working Group III (2014), 478.

55 Van Vuuren et al. (2016). See also Van Vuuren et al. (2011) and Van der Zwaan et al. (2013).

56 Tavoni and Socolow (2013). See also Anderson and Peters (2016), Boysen et al. (2017), Dessens et al. (2016), Fuss et al. (2014), Gambhir et al. (2017), Krey et al. (2014), Luderer et al. (2016), Riahi et al. (2015), Smith et al. (2016) and van Vuuren et al. (2016).

57 MacDougall et al. (2015).

58 MacDougall et al. (2015), 8.

59 In the language of economic modeling, this is called a "putty" representation of capital, as opposed to "clay."

60 One recent study examined the loss of asset value of firms in liquidation. It found that, on average, only just over a third of the replacement value of physical assets

could be recovered, implying that the greater part of the value of tangible capital is tied to its use at the firm level. See Kermani and Ma (2020).

61 Economists lack a modeling framework for incorporating changes in capital valuation, as pointed out by Roth (n.d.).

62 Such models employ a methodology known as computable general equilibrium, and of course there are no defaults in equilibrium.

63 This is presented as the case where average variable costs fall below unit revenues in economics textbooks, but this fails to take into account the possibility of defaulting on debt. To the extent that investment is financed through credit, the shutdown decision approaches the more commonplace "no profit" criterion.

64 This is formally incorporated into these models through the assumption of constant elasticity of substitution production and utility functions. Apparently an innocent mathematical simplification, this actually entails the extrapolation of entire demand and supply curves from estimated price–quantity relationships at a single point (or over a small range), much like the Leader was cloned from his nose in Woody Allen's film *Sleeper*. In fact, there is no other way, since the only empirical evidence we have for these foundational economic relationships comes from past experience, and that experience is clustered around a narrow set of prices and quantities demanded or supplied. To put it simply, elasticities are seen in nature (to a statistical approximation), but supply and demand curves aren't. The latter can only be extrapolated from the former.

65 The World Bank attributes 21.5 per capita $tCO_2eq$ to residents of Denver and only 4.89 to Tokyo, but bear in mind the caveats concerning carbon accounting considered in Chapter 3. See World Bank (2010), Part III, Table 4.

66 Finland's program to promote widespread musical education was discussed in the previous chapter.

67 I have made the case for modeling economies under the assumption they possess multiple equilibria (separated by tipping points or transitions between basins of attraction) in a number of papers. For a very simple statement of the general principle with application to the theory of the firm, see Dorman (2016b).

68 This argument has been made many times, provocatively if not yet convincingly. See, for example, Boyce (2004).

## Chapter 6

1 Shabecoff (1988).

2 This is the implicit model underlying Naomi Klein's encomium to "Blockadia" in Klein (2014). Local communities will do what government won't, shutting down the fossil fuel industry one rail route or pipeline at a time. There is no discussion of government policies or a political strategy to bring them about anywhere in her book.

3 The effect of higher contraband prices on the need for more stringent enforcement is clear in the case of cigarettes. In the EU it has been found that, because enforcement is lax, a 1 euro increase in the tax on a pack of cigarettes can be expected to result in a 5–12% increase in the share of the market captured by illegal trade; see Prieger and Kulick (2018).

4 As Chapter 4 argued, the cause of our predicament is not "markets" but the extraordinary usefulness of fossil fuels, which for understandable reasons people around the world embraced enthusiastically, not realizing their hidden poison. Even if the cause were markets, however, it would not follow logically that markets could not also be used for the opposite ends. Activists are fond of quoting the late poet

Audre Lorde: "The Master's Tools Will Never Dismantle the Master's House," but I have never understood this. Wouldn't these be exactly the tools you would want – especially if the toolbox included hammers? See Lorde (2018). Moreover, the argument that markets can't be part of the solution if they're part of the problem is visibly untenable in other contexts. For instance, labor markets are part of the reason why many workers are paid poverty-level wages or worse, but what sense would it make to oppose an increase in the minimum wage on the grounds that, by altering the price of labor and operating through markets, it utilized "the master's tools"? For additional arguments against anti-market fundamentalism, see Dorman (2018).

5 A small point of terminology: I will use "permit" instead of "allowance" because it is more familiar in other contexts, nonetheless recognizing that real-world systems usually refer to allowances. Of course, changing the name in either direction doesn't change the policy tool.

6 Exactly what portion of a carbon tax will be passed along to buyers of fossil fuels is a crucial question, but the data are scarce. In an important recent review of the literature on carbon pricing incidence, Shang (2021) finds that estimates vary from somewhat less than 100% to even more than the full amount, which can arise when sellers of fossil fuels or carbon-intensive goods have market power. For simplicity, we will assume in this chapter and the analysis in Chapter 8 that cost pass-through is exactly 100%, recognizing this remains a point of uncertainty, one that will differ from product to product and place to place.

7 It is important to emphasize that this diagram's sole purpose is to convey a logical argument. It has no empirical meaning: there are no units on either axis, and even if we had a few data points to plot we would have no basis for drawing an entire demand curve. Figure 6.1 is not a depiction of how the world works, but it helps us think through aspects of the puzzle.

8 Weitzman's (1974) formulation assumes that the pollutant's *flow* creates social costs, but in the case of climate change the culprit is the *stock*. This difference is analyzed by Karp and Traeger (2018), who show, under a set of assumptions, that it provides further grounds for preferring quantity to price regulation. It should be mentioned that Weitzman cast his analysis within the framework of welfare economics, which is criticized in the Appendix to this book. He would not have endorsed the qualitative interpretation I give it.

9 This sets the elasticity of energy demand with respect to energy price at –0.5, applying the concept of elasticities introduced in the previous chapter. Real-world price elasticities of energy demand, of course, will differ according to the specific energy product involved, the prevailing economic circumstances, and the time horizon over which demand is measured. (Short-run changes in demand will be less than long-run, when consumers have more options to alter their energy needs.) This is an extremely practical issue in many business and policy contexts, and the literature estimating these elasticities is massive. As of this writing, the most recent comprehensive overview was provided by three Spanish economists, Xavier Labandeira, José Maria Labeaga and Xiral López-Otero (2017). They examined 1,010 long-run price elasticity estimates from 428 studies and performed various tests to identify patterns. I found two results particularly convincing. First, when they used various methods to group together comparable demand contexts, such as "electricity," "heating oil," "residential demand" and "developing country demand," for fourteen of these fifteen (overlapping) groups, the average price elasticity was between –0.35 and –0.65. Second, the subset of prior estimates (503) that drew on panel data had an average elasticity of –0.52. Panel data, which track the same individuals or similar entities as prices change over time, provide the most reliable basis for such estimates.

So: we can use a long-run price elasticity of demand for energy of –0.5 as a rule of thumb, provided we recognize it is surrounded by a band of uncertainty, and there is no reason to expect the value to remain constant across different circumstances. (This latter point is why I am doubtful that formal meta-analysis, which assumes there is a single "thing" that all individual studies are trying to measure, is appropriate in this context.)

10 Recall the argument in the previous chapter that, by assuming constant elasticity of substitution in production and consumption, economists are simply extrapolating from a narrow range of past experience to the entire potential increase in fossil energy prices and corresponding decreases in demand. Incidentally, the demand curve pictured in this chapter is presented as linear to simplify the discussion. If it were an extrapolation from a particular elasticity estimate, as is normally the case in economic analysis, it would be a hyperbola.

11 Klein (2014).

12 Economists working in general equilibrium theory have established these results at a high level of mathematical abstraction but have not yet developed workable tools to apply them to practical concerns. See Brock and Durlauf (2001), Durlauf and Young (2001) and Horst and Scheinkman (2006).

13 One analyst estimates that such shifts in infrastructure and behavioral patterns could in themselves achieve 20–50% reductions in carbon emissions from urban transport, exceeding the elasticity-induced reductions envisioned in the IPCC's mitigation pathway models. See Creutzig (2016).

14 True, it overshoots the ultimate price at $Q_2$, but so does the tax approach.

15 Fremstad and Paul (2017) cite estimates ranging from about 1,000 to 2,000 collection points for a hypothetical upstream carbon tax in the United States. It's important to note that this applies to a production-based definition of what constitutes US carbon emissions. A consumption-based approach would also count carbon incorporated in imports that Americans consume and deduct the carbon Americans expended in producing exports. Putting numbers on this embodied carbon is difficult, as Chapter 5 has argued. We will return to this issue in Chapter 7.

16 Individual rationing was proposed by the prominent British journalist and climate change author George Monbiot (2006). As for business, much is made of the importance of eliminating "unnecessary" products in Klein (2014).

17 Economists spend much of their time trying to improve the functioning of markets in which the incentives to provide or ascertain quality are insufficient, like health care and financial services.

18 Löfgren et al. (2015).

19 Ellerman et al. (2016).

20 Löfgren et al. (2015).

21 Löfgren et al. (2015).

22 Branger et al. (2015).

23 Löfgren et al. (2015).

24 Löfgren et al. (2015).

25 Löfgren et al. (2015).

26 Ellerman et al. (2016).

27 Martin et al. (2016).

28 Unless otherwise indicated, data on the California cap-and-trade system are drawn from Burtraw et al. (2021).

29 Cullenward (2014).

30 Schmalensee and Stavins (2015).

31 Borenstein et al. (2014).

32 Santikarn et al. (2020).
33 Santikarn et al. (2020).
34 Parry (2019).
35 Although the CDM uses the term Certified Emission Reduction (CER) to designate credits under its auspices, I will continue to use the vernacular term "offsets."
36 Zhu and Tang (2015).
37 Schiermeier (2011). The original cable can be accessed at https://wikileaks.org/plusd/cables/08MUMBAI340_a.html.
38 Zhu and Tang (2015).
39 UNFCCC (2016a).
40 UNEP (2016).
41 UNFCCC (2016a).
42 Schneider (2011), and Schneider and Kollmuss (2015).
43 Erickson et al. (2014).
44 Bast et al. (2015).
45 IPCC, Working Group I (2014), 502.
46 Bock and Burkhardt (2019).
47 Mazzucato (2013).
48 For a comprehensive discussion of the advantages of limiting warming to $1.5°$ rather than $2°$, see IPCC (2018).
49 IPCC (2018).
50 For an overview of the recent history of this political framing, see Roberts (2019a).

# Chapter 7

1 Gertler et al. (2016).
2 Di Liberto (2015).
3 Reuters (2016).
4 Robine et al. (2008).
5 Russo et al. (2016).
6 Access to cooling is important for reasons beyond protection against heat stress; it also has a vital role to play in food preservation and, as we have seen during the current pandemic, the storage of vaccines and other medical supplies. See Sustainable Energy for All (2018).
7 Auffhammer (2011).
8 Shah et al. (2015). Household data for some countries are available only for earlier years. I used the most recent data available.
9 They did this for both residential and commercial AC, but I am confining myself to the residential sector. Commercial units account for somewhat less than half of residential. More recent estimates of the stock of AC units in a few countries and regions have been published by the International Energy Agency. Their totals are somewhat lower than those I have used, but their methodology, including the years from which their data are drawn, are not specified. See International Energy Agency (2018), especially Table 1.1.
10 Davis and Gertler (2015), Gertler et al. (2016) and Isaac and van Vuuren (2009).
11 See the suggestions for minimizing this trade-off in International Energy Agency and United Nations Environment Programme (2020).
12 International Energy Agency (2014).
13 Baer et al. (2007), Caney (2005), Ghersi et al. (2003), Ringius et al. (2002) and Vanderheiden (2009).
14 IPCC Working Group III (2014).

15 It is interesting that economics textbooks typically introduce the Prisoner's Dilemma model in the context of firms conspiring to establish a cartel, another case in which cooperation (here between the firms) is socially undesirable. In this way the texts can acquit themselves of the responsibility for covering this important topic while holding to the overall perspective that individual self-motivated action and not cooperation is the main basis for economic progress.

16 This is a basic model common to the social sciences and can be found in any introductory textbook in economics or political science, as well as other fields. I can recommend the treatment in my own text (Dorman, 2014), since, in addition to presenting the one-time game, it provides an introduction to the main features of repeated games – and most collective action problems in the real world, like action on climate change, arise repeatedly over time. Two highly influential classics in the literature on repeated Prisoner's Dilemmas are Axelrod (1984) and Ostrom (1990).

17 And if the rider has any doubts, the team's managers and sponsors might not.

18 The Lance Armstrong saga illustrates PD dynamics well. When testing was primarily for show, he chose to use performance drugs even though, as a cancer survivor, he should have been especially sensitized to the risks. Winning an unprecedented seven Tours de France apparently counted for more. This in turn put pressure on his teammates and competitors to dope as well. Only when testing was taken more seriously were his titles taken away – and serious testing with harsh consequences is a means to enforce cooperation on everyone, overcoming the incentives of the PD.

19 Trump attempted to repeal this plan, but Biden has reaffirmed it.

20 Extinction Rebellion (n.d.).

21 Lavelle (2020).

22 Victor (2011). The concept was subsequently taken up in a narrower fashion by William Nordhaus (2015).

23 See their website at http://aosis.org/.

24 For two recent elaborations of this argument, see Bierbrauer et al. (2021) and Jakob (2021).

25 Those familiar with game theory will recognize that the preceding paragraphs draw on the theory of indefinitely repeated games with a multiplicity of parties and perfectly divisible provision of public goods.

26 A proposal similar to this one has been made by Nordborg (2021).

27 World Bank (2018).

28 Revenues increase with increasing carbon prices if (the absolute value of) the overall elasticity is less than one, which, as we have seen, it is. But this pattern could be broken if the global economy tips into a different equilibrium, as discussed in Chapter 5. Meanwhile, if rebates are returned by governments at the individual level, there will also be transfers within developing countries, perhaps quite substantial. See Brenner et al. (2007).

29 Porter (2015), and Roberts and Weikmans (2015).

30 The false claims of donor countries are shocking even for those, like myself, largely inured to the routine dishonesty that rules international politics. To pick one example among many, rich countries make profitable loans at market rates and repayment terms to developing countries for ostensibly climate-related purposes and then chalk up the principle to assistance. For the dismaying details, see Hattle et al. (2021). Earlier reports that document the failure of signatories to live up to their climate finance pledges include Adaptation Watch (2015) and Ives (2018).

31 Adaptation Watch (2015) reprises its earlier evidence.

32 UN (2021).

33 UN Development Program (2021).

34 Leading Group (2021).
35 Atkinson (2006).
36 UNITAID (2016).
37 Atun et al. (2017).
38 Leading Group (2011).
39 Shaxson (2011), and Zucman (2015).
40 For a different but similarly motivated model of global funding for poverty alleviation, see De Schutter and Sepúlveda (2012). They estimate the cost of a safety net for all who need it at 2–6% of world GDP.
41 Olmer et al. (2017). This is based on a greenhouse equivalence between carbon dioxide and other gases over 20-year horizon. I am reluctant to accept any particular system of equivalences for reasons explained in Chapter 3.
42 Lo (2013), Shadbolt (2015) and Almendral (2021).
43 Calculations of the carbon content of traded goods are based on input–output matrices that in theory reflect all the direct and indirect contributions intermediate and final products make in their mutual production. As discussed in Chapter 3, however, there are far too many such products to be specified individually, nor can temporal and regional differences in their content and production methods be represented. Models must be highly aggregated, and different modelers choose different aggregations.
44 If France's consumption footprint is 40% more than its production footprint, the latter is about 29% ($1 \div 1.4$) less than the former. The same calculation is applied to China.
45 Mann (2011), Walton and Rockoff (2013) and Wright (1990).
46 Weber et al. (2019).
47 We saw in the previous chapter how this argument justified a substantial distribution of free carbon permits under the EU ETS.
48 For an overview of the literature up to that point, see Condon and Ignaciuk (2013).
49 Here is one example, drawn from Sakai and Barrett (2016). WTO rules require that tariffs intended to equalize regulatory impacts between countries be based on the best available technology (BAT) of the country imposing the tariff. Suppose, for instance, the United States imposes a carbon tax on a Korean refrigerator in a future in which carbon prices are higher in the United States than in Korea. In principle, the amount of the tax should depend on the amount of carbon emitted in manufacturing the refrigerator. But what if US producers are able to make refrigerators in a way that generates fewer emissions than the Koreans? In that case, applying a tariff on the basis of Korean emissions would actually give an unfair advantage to their US competitors, or so the WTO has determined. Instead, the carbon emitted by the lowest-emission producers in the United States should be the basis for the tariff. Applying the BAT principle across the board would clearly reduce the impact of a carbon tariff, perhaps substantially.
50 Böhringer et al. (2014).

# Chapter 8

1 Congress.gov (2021).
2 The arguments are outlined in Kramer (2012); see also NBAA (2012). Eventually, in 2016 the International Civil Aviation Organization, representing the world's major airlines, agreed to a scheme for offsetting approximately a third of the emissions generated by air travel. As of this writing the criteria for what constitutes an offset have not been released; in any case the scheme appears to be weak even in relation to

the Clean Development Mechanism and similar systems discussed in Chapter 6. See Carbon Market Watch (2017).

3 Meltzer (2012), and Schuetze (2012).

4 Under normal circumstances the value of an enterprise should not be less than what it could sell its assets for on the market. It may – in fact, should – be greater insofar as these assets are more productive inside the firm than outside it. The relationship between the second measure of value, which is assessed by the stock market, and the first, the replacement value of the stock of assets, is referred to as Tobin's $q$, named for the Nobel-winning economist James Tobin.

5 One widely accepted definition appeared in a report by the Generation Foundation (2013): an asset is stranded if it "loses economic value well ahead of its anticipated useful life, whether that is a result of changes in legislation, regulation, market forces, disruptive innovation, societal norms, or environmental shocks" (21). The concept of stranded assets has migrated to other policy arenas – for instance, international trade as in Krugman (2018).

6 See Carbon Tracker and Grantham Research Institute on Climate Change and the Environment (2013). Other studies that have looked at the potential for stranded fossil fuel assets include Advisory Scientific Committee (2016), Battiston et al. (2017), McGlade and Ekins (2015) and Scholten et al. (2017). A dissenting view is offered by Yergin and Pravettoni (2016), who believe any transition away from fossil fuels will take place so slowly, over a period of decades, that most existing carbon energy investments will be fully amortized. In other words, they expect the alligators to win. Incidentally, Caldecott (2017) claims the first published work on stranded fossil fuel assets was by Krause, Bach and Koomey, originally in a Dutch government report in 1989 and reprinted as Krause et al. (1992).

7 McKibben (2012).

8 Carney (2015).

9 Advisory Scientific Committee (2016), Battiston et al. (2017), Blackrock Investment Institute (2016), Buhr (2017), Schoenmaker and Van Tilburg (2016) and Scholten et al. (2017).

10 Advisory Scientific Committee (2016), Battiston et al. (2017), Buhr (2017), Fulton and Weber (2015) and Schoenmaker and Van Tilburg (2016). Incidentally, systemic risk to the financial system derives from the likelihood that carbon-related assets will move simultaneously in the same direction as a result of climate policy change. If it were believed that a substantial portion of financial institution portfolios, for instance, in the renewable energy sector, would appreciate as a result of such a change to offset the portion that falls in value, the risk would not be regarded as systemic. None of the research cited above considers whether there is a sufficient presence of such offsetting assets; the implicit assumption, which I believe to be reasonable, is that there isn't.

11 The tendency to overlook demand also applies to corporate reporting on the risks of climate change itself; firms tend to consider impacts primarily on their own operations, occasionally on their suppliers and seldom on their customers. See Goldstein et al. (2019). From the standpoint of elementary economic theory, the most important effect an unanticipated pricing change can have on asset values derives from the shutdown decision – the choice of an owner of whether to end operations at a facility rather than just cut them back a bit. The dividing line occurs where the revenues from continued operation are no longer sufficient to cover the variable costs (costs that depend on the extent of operations). This depends greatly on demand, of course. An additional wrinkle, not covered in introductory textbooks, is that firms can often make further investments that adjust their cost structure in the face of altered

demand, but this in turn depends on the nature of the capital stock, which brings us back to the two factors mentioned here.

12 The instant response of asset values to new information is the basis of "event analysis," a type of economic study that uses such fluctuations to implicitly price the events that triggered them. There is a large literature exemplifying this approach, but one recent example is relevant to the topic of this book, the effect – or better, noneffect – of the election of Donald Trump on the values of fossil-fuel dependent assets. As we vividly remember, the outcome of the 2016 election was a surprise, which is to say it embodied new information about what the politics of the next four years would be like. And share prices in a few sectors of the economy *did* jump within hours of the vote as a result: of the thirty industries examined in a Harvard Kennedy School study, two increased by more than 4%: steel and, the big winner, coal (10%). The coal bounce is not surprising, since it was the one sector targeted by Obama's Clean Power Plan, and most people (rightly) expected Trump to try to reverse these regulations. What should also be observed, however, are the many dogs that didn't bark. Petroleum and natural gas nudged ahead by just under 2%, but chemicals, electrical equipment and transportation barely moved at all. Autos and trucking, along with utilities, actually fell somewhat; analysts had expected them to do better under Clinton than Trump. What is interesting for our purposes is that, except for coal the impact of Trump's election on the value of industries likely to be negatively affected, perhaps severely, by stringent carbon action barely registered a blip. The judgment of the markets was that the policy of ignoring or minimizing the climate threat was bipartisan. Neither Obama nor Hillary Clinton gave them any reason to think otherwise. See Ramelli et al. (2018).

13 This is the approach employed in Battiston et al. (2017) and Buhr (2017). A slightly more inclusive approach was used by the International Renewable Energy Association (IRENA, 2017), which was cited by Tooze (2019). IRENA envisions a carbon budget of 880 Gt $CO_2$ over the period 2015–2050, similar to the one we have proposed in this book. Under one scenario – now purely fictional, alas – mitigation efforts began in earnest in 2015; under the other action is delayed until 2030. The headline number is that, under the delayed scenario, total stranded assets, fossil fuel and otherwise, rise to $20 trillion, about 8% of current global investment. How do they get this? Their total comes from four sources: stranded fossil fuel assets themselves, stranded investments in the power sector (like boilers and turbines for converting fossil energy to electricity), equipment used in industries that burn these fuels, and fixed investments in residential and commercial real estate, such as gas appliances and insufficiently insulating building materials. They compute the portion of these investments that will need to be abandoned ahead of their projected economic life if serious mitigation efforts take place. (But not too serious! Their mitigation scenario allows for carbon emissions in 2050 to still be 40% of their current level, with carbon removal picking up the slack.) It turns out that somewhat over half of the projected stranded assets arise in the building sector, while fossil fuels account for about two-thirds of the rest. This exercise, in my opinion, generates a serious underestimation: (1) It does not incorporate demand. Investments in their study are written off only because of the mechanics of the mitigation scenario: the replacement of some assets by others to get to carbon stabilization require it. But no consideration is given to the risk that assets will become unproductive because they can't earn sufficient revenues to justify their operation. (2) Valuation is based on book value, not market value. (3) The scope is very narrow, considering only assets directly involved in direct energy production or, in the case of buildings, use. No change in the overall structure of the economy or its component markets is taken into account

beyond this. That so much of the scope for asset write-downs is excluded, and yet the outcome is an 8% loss of invested capital, suggests that my rough estimate of 20% of the capital stock is not out of line.

14 Dorman (2020b).

15 See (2018), Chapter 2, 81. My 2050 carbon price represents the top end of the range cited in this report. The IPCC authors caution that their estimates come with a downward bias, however, since some models are unable to meet warming targets at *any* price. Note that the estimates of greatest interest are labeled "Low 2C"; they stabilize at an atmospheric carbon concentration, 450 ppm, believed to give us a two-thirds chance of keeping warming under 2°C. It should be remembered from our discussion in Chapter 5, however, that most such scenarios incorporate speculative technologies that allow overshooting the carbon target with subsequent carbon removal.

16 Yahoo Finance (n.d.).

17 Is it possible global increases in income might mitigate the demand response to higher ticket prices? Perhaps, but (1) global income itself will suffer at least temporarily from a rapid transition away from fossil energy, and (2) in an effective carbon policy fossil fuel prices result from a gap between demand and a restricted supply, so factors like greater income that increase demand also further increase prices.

18 Fidelity Sectors & Industries Overview (March 2020). Note that prices recorded at the beginning of March 2020 are depressed from earlier levels due to market fears regarding the novel coronavirus.

19 Aerodynamic Advisory and Teal Group (2018).

20 Deloitte (2018).

21 Aerodynamic Advisory and Teal Group (2018).

22 World Bank (2021).

23 IRENA (2017).

24 Carney (2015), Diaz-Rainey et al. (2017), Griffin et al. (2015), Scholten et al. (2017), Sen and von Schickfus (2017), Silver (2016) and Stenek (2014).

25 Government response to the pandemic raises another possibility, that in the event of a significant strengthening of carbon policy owners of capital at risk would be bailed out. It is not difficult to imagine scenarios in which trillions of dollars in transfers to affected industries would be defended as forestalling a financial collapse or cushioning the employment impacts on their workforce.

26 For the original study, see Brulle (2021). Some details of my analysis: (1) I left out the political sector ("conservative movement") and tabulated only economic interests, although it is likely conservative organizations are themselves funded and otherwise influenced by businesses. (2) I treated "General Business Interests," like the National Association of Manufacturers, as non–fossil fuel, since this category exists to advance the broad interest of business rather than sectoral objectives that might pit one set of members against another. (3) Since three of the 26 organizations in "Other Corporate Interests" were engaged in cement, I apportioned 3/26 of this sector's composition to fossil fuels. (4) Since 30 of the 48 organizations in "Coal/Steel/Rail" were in coal mining, I apportioned 5/8 of this sector's composition to fossil fuels. No attempt was made to scale participation according to the extent of financial commitment, since only organizational affiliation was examined by Brulle. Note that 13 organizations in "Coal/Steel/Rail" were railroads, compared with five in steel: rail's connection to coal is on the demand side, as coal is the largest single purchaser of rail freight services.

27 For details on the components of the Oregon plan, see Roberts (2019b).

28 Davis (2019).

29 See Ferguson et al. (2016, 2017, 2019, 2020).

30 Gilens and Page (2014).

31 The two chief rebuttals to Gilens and Page were Enns (2015) and Bashir (2015). For rebuttals to the rebuttals, see Gilens (2015, 2016).

32 It is interesting that none of the academic disputants has commented on this. Bashir's paper made a glaring mistake in its treatment of collinearity (the entanglement just referred to), and while he was corrected by Gilens, Gilens also missed the instability issue. Collinearity among independent variables increases the sensitivity of findings to the specifics, and sometimes the minutiae, of model design.

33 Bowman (2020). This was drawn from his PhD dissertation.

34 Elsässer et al. (2018).

35 Page et al. (2013).

36 Antonio Gramsci was an Italian Marxist imprisoned in 1926 by Mussolini for his radical activism. He died behind bars, but his writings were smuggled out and became influential among political theorists. By hegemony, Gramsci had in mind the ability of the rich to set the terms throughout the culture for describing and thinking about social and political matters, a power that might also be contested under some circumstances. See Gramsci (2000).

37 I am old enough to remember *The Un-Politics of Air Pollution* by Matthew Crenson (1971), which I read shortly after it was published. Crenson told the story of Gary, Indiana, and how its horrific pollution problems were shielded from public debate during the 1950s. The short explanation is that business, political and media elites were in enough agreement on the benefits of allowing the city to be enshrouded in noxious fumes for the benefit of steel production that the issue was never given an airing (so to speak). The book made a particular impression on me because, not long before I read it, I had been stranded outside Gary while hitchhiking. For a few hours I had to struggle to breathe the acrid air Gary residents coped with day in and out.

38 I also argued that the curve will probably shift to the left at some point as interlocking adjustments begin to take hold, but even in that case it remains a curve and still slopes up to the left.

39 If the energy companies were publicly owned, this would funnel revenues into the general government budget, so the higher carbon prices would function exactly as a sales tax, but applied to the percentage of carbon in the goods we buy rather than their final sales price.

40 International Energy Agency (2020). Of course, 2020 was an exceptional year for carbon emissions and just about everything else.

41 Bear in mind we are also sidestepping methane and other non-$CO_2$ gases, as discussed in Chapter 3. Including them in a hybrid budget framework would increase initial equivalent emissions in the United States and the corresponding revenue collected at each level of the carbon price.

42 In economics the study of this problem is referred to as tax incidence analysis.

43 The basis for this rather strong position can be found in the review by Shang (2021).

44 Perhaps the most prominent study that incorporates differential income effects into its estimates of the net household burden of carbon pricing is Goulder et al. (2019). It is predicated on the type of computable general equilibrium analysis criticized in Chapter 2 and the Appendix, and it doesn't take into account the shutdown concerns discussed in Chapter 5 and again in this chapter.

45 There has been a small flood of research on this topic over the last two decades with results that vary by the country being analyzed, the type of hypothetical carbon policy instrument deployed and, above all, the choices of the modelers. For an overview, see Ohlendorf et al. (2018). A particularly consequential choice is what

variable to use for household income. Many economists are attached to the notion that individuals at each moment know what their year-to-year income will be until they die and therefore make "optimal" consumption choices in each period based on this forecast. If you believe that, you will want to use a household's consumption, not its income, as the denominator against which to measure carbon payments. (Consumption reflects their "permanent," not transient, income.) This eliminates the main reason for regressivity, the falling share of consumption in income as income rises. I find the lifetime income story implausible in the extreme and ignore research derived from it. On the other hand, some studies adjusting household income for the size and composition (children versus adults) of households demonstrate greater regressivity than the simple, unadjusted figures I use in this chapter. For an example, see Grainger and Kolstad (2010). Finally, an entirely different approach is taken in Horowitz et al. (2017); their baseline model assumes the *entire* burden of price increases for carbon-intensive goods is borne by suppliers, not consumers, apportioned to labor and capital incomes in these sectors, an extreme version of the modeling assumptions noted earlier of Goulder et al. (2019). I find this approach, based on an a priori assumption that lifetime spending equals lifetime income for all households, to be highly implausible.

In a recent overview of carbon pricing research, Shang (2021) finds that most studies using developed country data find household effects, at least in consumption, to be regressive. The evidence in developing countries is more equivocal, however, due to the lack of access to electricity suffered by many low-income households. There the question of progressivity/regressivity remains unresolved, although the review points out that differential electrical access should fall over time. For an earlier summary of the evidence that comes to a similar conclusion, see Wang et al. (2016).

46 This is not the place for a detailed critique of utility as employed in economics; for an example of a utility-based approach to the distribution of carbon revenues, see Burtraw et al. (2008).

47 Barnes (2006).

48 See their website at https://pfd.alaska.gov/.

49 The same logic, that regressive impacts of carbon pricing need to be offset by progressive redistribution of revenues, applies at the international level just as urgently, if not more so. Cutting back on fossil fuels and raising the cost of essentials like fertilizer and transportation will, unless offset in some manner, make food more expensive and therefore increase hunger and food insecurity for millions of the world's most vulnerable people, farmers and urban dwellers alike. The solution, which parallels the argument made in a domestic context, is to return enough of the carbon revenues to these same people so they can continue to meet their needs. That could be achieved by the international revenue sharing mechanism described in the previous chapter. For the problem, but not the solution, see Hasegawa et al. (2018).

50 Those familiar with the work of Henry George may detect a similarity between this view and George's "single tax" agenda. For instance, see Collier (1979).

51 For example, see Saez et al. (2012).

52 Gravelle and Marples (2014).

53 Their roster of advanced economies actually numbers 40, but I excluded six because they are either too small or not independent countries: Andorra, Hong Kong, Macao, Malta, Puerto Rico, San Marino.

54 The historical reasons for this combination of low taxes and high growth are specific to these countries. After a difficult post-1989 period of reorganization, the transition from Communism accelerated economic growth in Eastern Europe while also discrediting the public sector and undermining its ability to collect taxes. East Asian

economies during this period largely adopted growth strategies predicated on persistent trade surpluses, one aspect of which is suppression of domestic spending, private and public.

55 I do not claim that these two simple scatter plots should be regarded as decisive evidence. They are sensitive to choices about which countries to include in the sample, the metrics selected to represent economic performance, the starting and ending dates for the time series, and above all the absence of more sophisticated modeling approaches. I am making the less ambitious claim that strong beliefs about the direct, depressive effect of taxation on economic efficiency should be supported by clear *prima facie* evidence—which they aren't. It is still possible to argue for a more complex, mediated relationship between taxes and economic performance, of course, on the basis of more elaborate modeling, but in that case what constitutes evidence will be conditional on the choices modelers make.

56 Fremstad and Paul (2017) conduct simulations for two tax offsetting mechanisms and come to the same conclusion.

57 See, for instance, the argument voiced in Dandy (2016). Dandy was attacking an initiative in Washington State that would have instituted a carbon tax, with most of the money recycled through tax cuts. Intense opposition from social justice groups helped defeat this proposal. Incidentally, those who suffer most from higher energy costs may not always show up in the conventional oppression rankings. Elderly people, even those above the very bottom of the economic ladder, may try to skimp on winter heating when prices rise, but this puts them at greater risk of dying from diseases exacerbated by low temperatures; see Chirakijja et al. (2019).

58 This point is made strongly in Cronin et al. (2019).

59 This is a complicated issue. If many individuals decide separately to use rebate money for mass transit, this will generate a market that transit providers may try to supply through expanded service. Whether this market-driven approach to creating new transit options is as effective as ex ante pooling of funds to finance public transit development can be determined only on a case-by-case basis.

60 Dorman (n.d.).

61 This brings to mind a fascinating metaphor. A viscous liquid has irregularly shaped particles suspended in its fluid that cause resistance to flow. An example is traditional ketchup, largely made up of tomato particles suspended in flavored water. Before this product was reengineered to reduce its viscosity, it was difficult to pour from a bottle because the particles would obstruct each other. This is why it was helpful to shake the bottle along the pouring axis; this action aligned the particles so they produced less resistance. Political movements that shake up society along a chosen policy axis can also have an aligning effect if the potential support is there, minimizing the drag of all the other issues that would otherwise divert or divide us.

## Appendix

1 Greenstone et al. (2011). The Trump administration disbanded the working group and cut the official estimate of the SCC, primarily by excluding all costs to parties beyond the borders of the United States. This intervention was not regarded as legitimate by most economists, and in the analysis that follows I will assume the "real" SCC estimate remains the one produced in 2011 or as potentially adjusted by mainstream academic researchers. For the Trump approach, see Plumer (2018). A proposal for reconvening the SCC working group and updating its estimates to incorporate more recent advances in data and modeling is accessibly presented in Carleton and Greenstone (2021).

2 Carleton and Greenstone (2021) now recommend a 2% discount rate on the grounds that returns in the capital markets have fallen substantially in the past decade. This would have the effect of increasing the SCC so that its 2020 value would be $125 in 2020 currency.

3 There has been considerable debate over this requirement. For one view, which documents its implementation beginning in 1981, see Rose-Ackerman (2011).

4 Carleton and Greenstone (2021).

5 All of these proposals are complicated by the additional consideration, according to standard economic theory, that should be given to the change in the effect that wealth will have on human well-being over time. Two assumptions are usually made, that real per capita wealth will rise at something like its historic rate into the indefinite future, and that as this wealth increases its unit effect on well-being decreases. Consider this thought experiment: suppose that there are two sorts of people, poor and nonpoor, and that economic gains mean far more to the first than the second. Suppose also that the percentage of poor people in the world is substantially higher today than it will be many years into the future. Then there is a disadvantage in postponing income gains over this period: they would be valued more highly today than down the road. Similarly, reductions in wealth in the future should be weighted less compared with reductions in wealth today. But this is exactly what discount rates do. If you accept the two assumptions above, even a complete refusal to discount the well-being of future generations compared with the current one should still permit a discounting of future economic wealth. For this reason, the intergenerationally egalitarian Stern Report adopted a positive discount rate of 1.5%. See Stern (2006, 2008).

6 When he delivered this locution at a press conference on February 12, 2002, Rumsfeld was being evasive, not profound. For details, see the investigation by Errol Morris (2014) in the *New York Times*.

7 I made some of these bottom-up criticisms in the context of valuing fatal risk in Dorman (1996); this analysis was updated in Dorman and Boden (2021).

8 A condensed version of their work appeared as Colt and Knapp (2016).

9 I am avoiding the entire issue of what economists call "existence values," the utility people get from simply knowing that natural resources or nonhuman animals like fish exist. I regard the standard approach to valuing such things – administering a survey and asking people how much they are willing to pay to be assured there are still fish – as flawed, and so apparently do Colt and Knapp, since they don't use this method or even discuss it. Of course, if no economic value is assigned to the continued existence of fish as such, it will not play a role in the SCC.

10 FAO (2020).

11 See the discussion in Lobell et al. (2011), especially Figure 2. A more recent assessment can be found in Zhao et al. (2017).

12 The notion that prices reflect marginal social benefits in the absence of these and other potential "market failures" is a core hypothesis that can be found in any introductory textbook. In my own it is developed in Dorman (2014), Chapter 6, "Markets and Human Well-Being."

13 If one thought the marginal benefit of x associated with $Q^*$ is unchanged throughout Q, the total benefit would be obtained by projecting a ray from the origin at the slope observed at $Q^*$. The height of this ray would still indicate the total benefit, so in this case the marginal and total benefits would correspond perfectly. It should be obvious there is no reason to expect the total benefit curve to be linear, however. In practice it is common, as discussed in Chapter 2, to apply a multiplier or exponential to the

303 / Notes to pages 267–274

marginal estimation method to account for "nonlinearities" – e.g., Nordhaus (2017b) – but this is also entirely ad hoc and arbitrary.

14  It is possible to specify pairs of B curves that share precisely the same set of structural parameters such that a correspondence can be established between marginal and total costs, but there is no reason to expect the real world to obey these restrictions. Stern came to the same conclusion: "Our standard cost-benefit analysis (CBA) tools ... are largely marginal methods, providing tools for analysis of big changes in, say, one or two markets as a result of a program. But when we are considering major strategic decisions for the world as a whole, with huge dynamic uncertainties and feedbacks, the potential contribution of an approach to decision making based on marginal methods is very limited. Rational decision making has to go back to the first principles from which the marginal methods of CBA are derived. This is not at all to use a different theory. On the contrary, it is to maintain the theory and to avoid a gross misapplication of the special (i.e., marginal) case." See Stern (2008), 11–12. Of course, other arguments presented in this book call into question the larger theory Stern seeks to adhere to by avoiding the marginalist trap.

15  See Weitzman (2009, 2011, 2014). Weitzman centered his discussion of fat-tail possibilities on the role of uncertainty (lack of data) rather than power law distributions. He counterposes the normal distribution to a t-distribution with few degrees of freedom.

16  IPCC (2014), 79.

17  Brock and Xepapadeas (2015). The same conclusion was drawn in Koomey (2013) and more recently in Stern and Stiglitz (2021).

# REFERENCES

Ackerman, Frank. 2014. Richard Tol on Climate Policy: A Critical View of an Overview. Synapse Energy Economics Working Paper.

Adaptation Watch. 2015. *Toward Implementation: The 2017 Adaptation Watch Report.* Accessed at https://static1.squarespace.com/static/56410412e4b09d10c39ce64f/t/5a007300ec212d8b1992399f/1509978912514/AdaptationWatch2017+-+Toward+Implementation.pdf.

Adler, Ben. 2016. Are Plastic-Bag Bans Good for the Climate? Grist, June 2. Accessed at http://grist.org/climate-energy/are-plastic-bag-bans-good-for-the-climate/.

Advisory Scientific Committee (ASC). 2016. Too Late, Too Sudden: Transition to a Low-Carbon Economy and Systemic Risk. Report No. 6 of the Advisory Scientific Committee of the European Systemic Risk Board, Frankfurt.

Aerodynamic Advisory and Teal Group. 2018. The Global Aerospace Industry: Size and Country Rankings. Accessed at https://aerodynamicadvisory.com/wp-content/uploads/2018/07/AeroDynamic-Teal_Global-Aerospace-Industry_16July2018.pdf.

Agnew, Meaghan. 2014. The Sharing Economy Has Gone Big. Like, Ridge Tiller Big. *Modern Farmer*, November 4.

Allen, Craig D., Alison K. Macalady, Haroun Chenchouni, Dominique Bachelet, Nate McDowell, Michel Vennetier, Thomas Kitzberger, Andreas Rigling, David D. Breshears, E. H. (Ted) Hogg, Patrick Gonzalez, Rod Fensham, Zhen Zhang, Jorge Castro, Natalia Demidova, Jong-Hwan Lim, Gillian Allard, Steven W. Running, Akkin Semerci and Neil Cobb. 2010. A Global Overview of Drought and Heat-Induced Tree Mortality Reveals Emerging Climate Change Risks for Forests. *Forest Ecology and Management* 259(4): 660–684.

Allen, Myles, Jan S. Fuglestvedt, Keith P. Shine, Andy Reisinger, Raymond T.
Pierrehumbert and Piers M. Forster. 2016. New Use of Global Warming
Potentials to Compare Cumulative and Short-Lived Climate Pollutants.
*Nature Climate Change* 6(8): 773–776.

Allen, Myles R., Keith P. Shine, Jan S. Fuglestvedt, Richard J. Millar, Michelle
Cain, David J. Frame and Adrian H. Macey. 2018. A Solution to the
Misrepresentations of $CO_2$-Equivalent Emissions of Short-Lived Climate
Pollutants under Ambitious Mitigation. *Climate and Atmospheric Science* 1: 16.

Almendral, Aurora. 2021. Can Massive Cargo Ships Use Wind to Go Green?
*New York Times*, August 24.

Anadón, José D., Osvaldo E. Sala and Fernando T. Maestre. 2014. Climate
Change Will Increase Savannas at the Expense of Forests and Treeless
Vegetation in Tropical and Subtropical Americas. *Journal of Ecology* 102:
1363–1373.

Anderegg, William R. L., Anna T. Trugman, Grayson Badgley, Christa M.
Anderson, Ann Bartuska, Philippe Ciais, Danny Cullenward, Christopher B.
Field, Jeremy Freeman, Scott J. Goetz, Jeffrey A. Hicke, Deborah Huntzinger,
Robert B. Jackson, John Nickerson, Stephen Pacala and James T. Randerson.
2020. Climate-Driven Risks to the Climate Mitigation Potential of Forests.
*Science* 368(6497): 1327.

Anderson, Kevin, and Glen Peters. 2016. The Trouble with Negative Emissions.
*Science* 354(6309): 182–183.

Archer, David. 2007. Methane Hydrate Stability and Anthropogenic Climate
Change. *Biogeosciences* 4(4): 521–544.

Ariely, Dan. 2008. *Predictably Irrational: The Hidden Forces That Shape Our
Decisions*. New York: HarperCollins.

Atkinson, Rob, Netra Chhetri, Joshua Freed, Isabel Galiana, Christopher Green,
Steven Hayward, Jesse Jenkins, Elizabeth Malone, Ted Nordhaus, Roger
Pielke Jr., Gwyn Prins, Steve Rayner, Daniel Sarewitz and Michael
Shellenberger. 2011. *Climate Pragmatism: Innovation, Resilience and No
Regrets*. Toronto: Hartwell Group.

Atkinson, Tony. 2006. Funding the Millennium Development Goals: A Challenge
for Global Public Finance. *European Review* 14(4): 555–564.

Atun, Rifat, Sachin Silva and Felicia M Knaul. 2017. Innovative Financing
Instruments for Global Health 2002–15: A Systematic Analysis. *The Lancet* 5:
e720–e726.

Auffhammer, Maximilian. 2011. The Relationship between Air Conditioning
Adoption and Temperature. Report prepared for US EPA. Accessed at https://
yosemite.epa.gov/ee/epa/eerm.nsf/vwAN/EE-0573-01.pdf/$file/EE-0573-01
.pdf.

Axelrod, Robert. 1984. *The Evolution of Cooperation*. New York: Basic Books.

Aze, T., P. N. Pearson, A. J. Dickson, M. P. S. Badger, P. R. Bown, R. D. Pancost, S. J. Gibbs, B. T. Huber, M. J. Leng, A. L. Coe, A. S. Cohen and G. L. Foster. 2014. Extreme Warming of Tropical Waters during the Paleocene–Eocene Thermal Maximum. *Geology* 42(9): 739–742.

Baer, Paul, Tom Athanasiou and Sivan Kartha. 2007. The Right to Development in a Climate Constrained World: The Greenhouse Development Rights Framework. Accessed at www.ecoequity.org/docs/TheGDRsFramework.pdf.

Ballinger, Benjamin, Diego Schmeda-Lopez, Benjamin Kefford, Brett Parkinson, Martin Stringer, Chris Greig and Simon Smart. 2020. The Vulnerability of Electric-Vehicle and Wind-Turbine Supply Chains to the Supply of Rare-Earth Elements in a 2-Degree Scenario. *Sustainable Production and Consumption* 22: 68–76.

Barnes, Burton V., Donald R. Zak, Shirley R. Denton and Stephen H. Spurr. 1998. *Forest Ecology*. Hoboken, NJ: Wiley.

Barnes, Peter. 2006. *Capitalism 3.0: A Guide to Reclaiming the Commons*. Oakland, CA: Berrett-Koehler Publishers.

Barnosky, Anthony D., Nicholas Matzke, Susumu Tomiya, Guinevere O. U. Wogan, Brian Swartz, Tiago B. Quental, Charles Marshall, Jenny L. McGuire, Emily L. Lindsey, Kaitlin C. Maguire, Ben Mersey and Elizabeth A. Ferrer. 2011. Has the Earth's Sixth Mass Extinction Already Arrived? *Nature* 471 (7336): 51–57.

Bashir, Omar S. 2015. Testing Inferences about American Politics: A Review of the "Oligarchy" Result. *Research and Politics* 2(4). 1–7

Bast, Elizabeth, Alex Doukas, Sam Pickard, Laurie van der Burg and Shelagh Whitley. 2015. Empty Promises: G20 Subsidies to Oil, Gas and Coal Production. Oil Change International and the Overseas Development Institute. Accessed at www.odi.org/publications/.

Bataille, Chris, Max Åhman, Karsten Neuhoff, Lars J. Nilsson, Manfred Fischedick, Stefan Lechtenböhmer, Baltazar Solano-Rodriquez, Amandine Denis-Ryan, Seton Stiebert, Henri Waisman, Oliver Sartor and Shahrzad Rahbar. 2018. A Review of Technology and Policy Deep Decarbonization Pathway Options. *Journal of Cleaner Production* 187: 960–973.

Battiston, Stefano, Antoine Mandel, Irene Monasterolo, Franziska Schütze and Gabriele Visentin. 2017. A Climate Stress-Test of the Financial System. *Nature Climate Change* 7: 283–288.

Beerling, David J., and Dana L. Royer. 2011. Convergent Cenozoic $CO_2$ History. *Nature Geoscience* 4: 418–420.

Benveniste, Hélène, Olivier Boucher, Céline Guivarch, Hervé Le Treut and Patrick Criqui. 2017. Impacts of Nationally Determined Contributions on 2030 Global Greenhouse Gas Emissions: Uncertainty Analysis and Distribution of Emissions. *Environmental Research Letters* 13(1): 1–10.

Berner, Robert A. 2003. The Long-Term Carbon Cycle, Fossil Fuels and Atmospheric Composition. *Nature* 426: 323–326.

Beveridge, Ross, and Kristine Kern. 2013. The "Energiewende" in Germany: Background, Development and Future Challenges. *Renewable Energy Law and Policy Review* 4(1): 3–12.

Bierbrauer, Felix, Gabriel Felbermayr, Axel Ockenfels, Klaus M. Schmidt and Jens Südekum. 2021. A $CO_2$-Border Adjustment Mechanism as a Building Block of a Climate Club. Kiel Institute for the World Economy Policy Brief No. 151.

Blackrock Investment Institute. 2016. Adapting Portfolios to Climate Change: Implications and Strategies for All Investors. Accessed at www.blackrock.com/us/individual/literature/whitepaper/bii-climate-change-2016-us.pdf.

Blyth, Mark. 2013. *Austerity: The History of a Dangerous Idea.* Oxford: Oxford University Press.

Bock, Lisa, and Ulrike Burkhardt. 2019. Contrail Cirrus Radiative Forcing for Future Air Traffic. *Atmospheric Chemistry and Physics* 19(12): 8163–8174.

Böhringer, Christoph, André Müller and Jan Schneider. 2014. Carbon Tariffs Revisited. Harvard Kennedy School Discussion Paper 14-64.

Borenstein, Severin, James Bushnell, Frank A. Wolak, and Matthew Zaragoza-Watkins. 2014. Report of the Market Simulation Group on Competitive Supply/Demand Balance in the California Allowance Market and the Potential for Market Manipulation. Accessed at www.arb.ca.gov/cc/capandtrade/simulationgroup/msg_final_v25.pdf.

Boswell, Ray, and Timothy S. Collett. 2011. Current Perspectives on Gas Hydrate Resources. *Energy & Environmental Science* 4(4): 1206–1215.

Bowman, Jarron. 2020. Do the Affluent Override Average Americans? Measuring Policy Disagreement and Unequal Influence. *Social Science Quarterly* 101(3): 1018–1037.

Boyce, James. 2004. Green and Brown? Globalization and the Environment. *Oxford Review of Economic Policy.* 20(1): 105–128.

Boyce, James. 2019. *The Case for Carbon Dividends.* Cambridge (UK): Polity Press.

Boyce, James K., and Raymond S. Bradley. 2018. 3.5°C in 2100? Political Economy Research Institute Commentary, July. Accessed at www.peri.umass.edu/images/boycebradleyFinal_2018.pdf.

Boysen, Lena R., Wolfgang Lucht, Dieter Gerten, Vera Heck, Timothy M. Lenton and Hans Joachim Schellnhuber. 2017. The Limits to Global-Warming Mitigation by Terrestrial Carbon Removal. *Earth's Future* 5(5): 463–474.

Branger, Frédéric, Jean-Pierre Ponssard, Oliver Sartor and Misato Sato. 2015. EU ETS, Free Allocations and Activity Level Thresholds: The Devil Lies in the Detail. CESifo Working Paper No. 5394.

Brenner, Mark, Matthew Riddle and James K. Boyce. 2007. A Chinese Sky Trust? Distributional Impacts of Carbon Charges and Revenue Recycling in China. *Energy Policy* 35(3): 1771–1784.

Brinkhuis, Henk, Stefan Schouten, Margaret E. Collinson, Appy Sluijs, Jaap S. Sinninghe Damsté, Gerald R. Dickens, Matthew Huber, Thomas M. Cronin, Jonaotaro Onodera, Kozo Takahashi, Jonathan P. Bujak, Ruediger Stein, Johan van der Burgh, James S. Eldrett, Ian C. Harding, André F. Lotter, Francesca Sangiorgi, Han van Konijnenburg-van Cittert, Jan W. de Leeuw, Jens Matthiessen, Jan Backman, Kathryn Moran and the Expedition 302 Scientists. 2006. A Massive Input of Coarse-Grained Siliciclastics in the Pyrenean Basin during the PETM: The Missing Ingredient in a Coeval Abrupt Change in Hydrological Regime. *Nature* 441(1): 606–609.

British Petroleum. 2019. *BP Statistical Review of World Energy*. Accessed at www.bp.com/content/dam/bp/business-sites/en/global/corporate/pdfs/energy-economics/statistical-review/bp-stats-review-2019-full-report.pdf.

Brock, William A., and Steven N. Durlauf. 2001. Discrete Choice with Social Interactions. *The Review of Economic Studies* 68(2): 235–260.

Brock, William A., and Anastasios Xepapadeas. 2015. Modeling Coupled Climate, Ecosystems, and Economic Systems. Fondazione Eni Enrico Mattei Working Paper No. 66.

Brown, Patricia Leigh. 2015. These Public Libraries Are for Snowshoes and Ukuleles. *New York Times*, September 15.

Brulle, Robert J. 2021. Networks of Opposition: A Structural Analysis of U.S. Climate Change Countermovement Coalitions 1989–2015. *Sociological Inquiry* 91(3): 603–624.

Budinis, Sara, Niall Mac Dowell, Samuel Krevor, Tim Dixon, Jasmin Kemper and Adam Hawkes. 2017. Can Carbon Capture and Storage Unlock "Unburnable Carbon"? *Energy Procedia*, no. 114: 7504–7515.

Buhr, Bob. 2017. Assessing the Sources of Stranded Asset Risk: A Proposed Framework. *Journal of Sustainable Finance & Investment* 7(1): 37–53.

Burke, Marshall, and Kyle Emerick. 2016. Adaptation to Climate Change: Evidence from US Agriculture. *American Economic Journal: Economic Policy* 8(3): 106–140.

Burtraw, Dallas, Ann Carlson, Danny Cullenward, Meredith Fowlie and Jennifer Kropke. 2021. 2020 Annual Report of the Independent Emissions Market Advisory Committee. California Environmental Protection Agency.

Burtraw, Dallas, Rich Sweeney and Margaret Walls. 2008. The Incidence of U.S. Climate Policy: Where You Stand Depends on Where You Sit. Resources for the Future Discussion Paper No. 08-28.

Caldecott, Ben. 2017. Introduction to Special Issue: Stranded Assets and the Environment. *Journal of Sustainable Finance & Investment* 7(1): 1–13.

Campbell, Olivia. 2016. How to Talk about Climate Change So Anyone Will Listen. *The Cut.* Accessed at www.thecut.com/2016/11/how-to-talk-about-climate-change-so-anyone-will-listen.html.

Caney, Simon. 2005. Cosmopolitan Justice, Responsibility, and Global Climate Change. *Leiden Journal of International Law* 18(4): 747–775.

Carbon Market Watch. 2017. Visibility Unlimited: Transparency of the New Aviation Carbon Market. Accessed at https://carbonmarketwatch.org/wp/wp-content/uploads/2017/11/Policy-brief-1.pdf.

Carbon Tracker and Grantham Research Institute on Climate Change and the Environment. 2013. *Unburnable Carbon 2013: Wasted Capital and Stranded Assets.* Accessed at http://carbontracker.live.kiln.digital/Unburnable-Carbon-2-Web-Version.pdf.

Carleton, Tamma, and Michael Greenstone. 2021. Updating the United States Government's Social Cost of Carbon. Energy Policy Institute at the University of Chicago Working Paper No. 2021-04.

Carney, Mark. 2015. Breaking the Tragedy of the Horizon: Climate Change and Financial Stability. Speech delivered at Lloyd's of London, September 29. Accessed at www.bis.org/review/r151009a.pdf.

Carozza, David A., Lawrence A. Mysak and Gavin A. Schmidt. 2011. Methane and Environmental Change during the Paleocene-Eocene Thermal Maximum (PETM): Modeling the PETM Onset as a Two-Stage Event. *Geophysical Research Letters* 38(5): L05702.

Carvalhais, Nuno, Matthias Forkel, Myroslava Khomik, Jessica Bellarby, Martin Jung, Mirco Migliavacca, Mingquan Mu, Sassan Saatchi, Maurizio Santoro, Martin Thurner, Ulrich Weber, Bernhard Ahrens, Christian Beer, Alessandro Cescatti, James T. Randerson and Markus Reichstein. 2014. Global Covariation of Carbon Turnover Times with Climate in Terrestrial Ecosystems. *Nature* 514(7521): 213–217.

Chaney, Thomas. 2018. The Gravity Equation in International Trade: An Explanation. *Journal of Political Economy* 126(1): 150–177.

Chen, Chen, and Massimo Tavoni. 2013. Direct Air Capture of $CO_2$ and Climate Stabilization: A Model Based Assessment. *Climatic Change* 118(1): 59–72.

Chirakijja, Janjala, Seema Jayachandran and Pinchuan Ong. 2019. Inexpensive Heating Reduces Winter Mortality. NBER Working Paper No. 25681.

Cho, Renee. 2020. Plastic, Paper or Cotton: Which Shopping Bag Is Best? State of the Planet (Earth Institute, Columbia University), April 30. Accessed at https://blogs.ei.columbia.edu/2020/04/30/plastic-paper-cotton-bags/.

Clarke, Leon, Kejun Jiang, Keigo Akimoto, Mustafa Babiker, Geoffrey Blanford, Karen Fisher-Vanden, Jean-Charles Hourcade, Volker Krey, Elmar Kriegler,

Andreas Löschel, David McCollum, Sergey Paltsev, Steven Rose, Priyadarshi R. Shukla, Massimo Tavoni, Bob van der Zwaan and Detlef P. van Vuuren. 2014. Assessing Transformation Pathways. In *IPCC Working Group III. Climate Change 2014: Mitigation of Climate Change. Contribution of Working Group III to the Fifth Assessment Report of the Intergovernmental Panel on Climate Change*. Cambridge: Cambridge University Press.

Climate Leadership Council. 2019. The Four Pillars of Our Carbon Dividend Plan. Accessed at https://clcouncil.org/our-plan/.

Cohen, Gail, João Tovar Jalles, Prakash Loungani and Ricardo Marto. 2018. The Long-Run Decoupling of Emissions and Output: Evidence from the Largest Emitters. International Monetary Fund Working Paper No. 18/56.

Collaborative Labelling and Appliance Standards Programme (CLASP). 2020. Environmentally Harmful Dumping of Inefficient and Obsolete Air Conditioners in Africa. Accessed at https://storage.googleapis.com/clasp-siteattachments/Annexes-Room-AC-Market-Profiles-for-Ten-African-Countries.pdf.

Collier, Charles. 1979. Henry George's System of Political Economy. *History of Political Economy* 11(1): 64–93.

Colt, Stephen G., and Gunnar P. Knapp. 2016. Economic Effects of an Ocean Acidification Catastrophe. *American Economic Review: Papers and Proceedings* 106(5): 615–619.

Condon, Madison, and Ada Ignaciuk. 2013. Border Carbon Adjustment and International Trade. OECD Trade and Environment Working Papers 2013/06.

Covert, Thomas, Michael Greenstone and Christopher R. Knittel. 2016. Will We Ever Stop Using Fossil Fuels? *Journal of Economic Perspectives* 30(1): 117–138.

Crenson, Matthew A. 1971. *The Un-Politics of Air Pollution: A Study of Non-Decisionmaking in the Cities*. Baltimore: Johns Hopkins University Press.

Creutzig, Felix. 2016. Evolving Narratives of Low-Carbon Futures in Transportation. *Transport Reviews* 36(3): 341–360.

Cronin, Julie Anne, Don Fullerton and Steven E. Sexton. 2019. Vertical and Horizontal Redistributions from a Carbon Tax and Rebate. *Journal of the Association of Environmental and Resource Economists* 6(S1): S169–S208.

Cullenward, Danny. 2014. How California's Carbon Market Actually Works. *Bulletin of the Atomic Scientists* 70(5): 35–44.

Daly, Herman. 1973. *Toward a Steady-State Economy*. New York: W. H. Freeman & Co.

Daly, Herman, and Joshua Farley. 2003. *Ecological Economics: Principles and Applications*. Washington, DC: Island Press.

Dandy, Ellicott. 2016. Why I-732 Is a False Promise: Climate Justice Requires Putting Money Where Your Mouth Is. Front and Centered. Accessed at http://

frontandcentered.org/why-i-732-is-a-false-promise-climate-justice-requires-putting-money-where-your-mouth-is/.

Data for Progress. n.d. "Green New Deal: Candidate Scorecards." Accessed at www.dataforprogress.org/gnd-candidates.

Davis, Kimberley T., Solomon Z. Dobrowski, Philip E. Higuera, Zachary A. Holden, Thomas T. Veblen, Monica T. Rother, Sean A. Parks, Anna Sala and Marco P. Maneta. 2019. Wildfires and Climate Change Push Low-Elevation Forests across a Critical Climate Threshold for Tree Regeneration. *PNAS* 116 (13): 6193–6198.

Davis, Lucas W., and Paul J. Gertler. 2015. Contribution of Air Conditioning Adoption to Future Energy Use under Global Warming. *Proceedings of the National Academy of Sciences* 112(19): 5962–5967.

Davis, Rob. 2019. Polluters Hit by Oregon Climate Bill Gave Big. Koch Industries Was One of the Biggest. *The Oregonian Live.* June 29. Accessed at https://expo.oregonlive.com/news/g66l-2019/06/885b66848a3905/polluters-hit-by-oregon-climate-bill-gave-big-koch-industries-was-one-of-the-biggest.html.

Dawson, M. R., Robert M. West, W. Langston and J. H. Hutchison. 1976. Paleogene Terrestrial Vertebrates: Northernmost Occurrence, Ellesmere Island, Canada. *Science* 192: 781–782.

Dawson, M. R., Robert M. West, P. Raemakers and J. H. Hutchison. 1975. New Evidence on the Paleobiology of the Paleogene Eureka Sound Formation, Arctic Canada. *Arctic* 28: 110–116.

De Schutter, Olivier, and Magdalena Sepúlveda. 2012. Underwriting the Poor: A Global Fund for Social Protection. United Nations, Office of the High Commissioner for Human Rights. Briefing Note 07.

Dean, Joshua F., Jack J. Middelburg, Thomas Röckmann, Rien Aerts, Luke G. Blauw, Matthias Egger, Mike S. M. Jetten, Anniek E. E. de Jong, Ove H. Meisel, Olivia Rasigraf, Caroline P. Slomp, Michiel H. in't Zandt and A. J. Dolman. 2018. Methane Feedbacks to the Global Climate System in a Warmer World. *Reviews of Geophysics* 56(1): 207–250.

Deep Decarbonization Pathways Project. 2015. *Pathways to Deep Decarbonization: 2015 Report.* New York: SDSN–IDDRI.

Deloitte. 2018. Global Aerospace and Defense Industry Financial Performance Study. Accessed at www2.deloitte.com/us/en/pages/manufacturing/articles/gx-mnfg-aerospace-and-defense-financial-performance.html.

Delucchi, M. A., C. Yang, A. F. Burke, J. M. Ogden, K. Kurani, J. Kessler and D. Sperling. 2013. An Assessment of Electric Vehicles: Technology, Infrastructure Requirements, Greenhouse-Gas Emissions, Petroleum Use, Material Use, Lifetime Cost, Consumer Acceptance and Policy Initiatives. *Philosophical Transactions of the Royal Society A* 372: 20120325.

Dessens, Olivier, Gabrial Anandarajah and Ajay Gambhir. 2016. Limiting Global Warming to 2°C: What Do the Latest Mitigation Studies Tell Us about Costs, Technologies and Other Impacts? *Energy Strategy Reviews* 13–14: 67–76.

Dewey, John. 1954. *The Public and Its Problems*. Athens, OH: Swallow Press.

Dewey, John. 1999. *Individualism Old and New*. Amherst, NY: Prometheus Books.

Di, Pengfei, Dong Feng, Jun Tao and Duofu Chen. 2020. Using Time-Series Videos to Quantify Methane Bubbles Flux from Natural Cold Seeps in the South China Sea. *Minerals* 10(3): 2016.

Di Liberto, Tom. 2015. India Heat Wave Kills Thousands. NOAA Climate.gov, June 9. Accessed at www.climate.gov/news-features/event-tracker/india-heat-wave-kills-thousands.

Diaz-Rainey, Ivan, Becky Robertson and Charlie Wilson. 2017. Stranded Research? Leading Finance Journals Are Silent on Climate Change. *Climatic Change* 143: 243–260.

Dickens, Gerald. 2011. Down the Rabbit Hole: Toward Appropriate Discussion of Methane Release from Gas Hydrate Systems during the Paleocene–Eocene Thermal Maximum and Other Past Hyperthermal Events. *Climate of the Past* 7(3): 831–846.

Diffenbaugh, Noah S., Deepti Singh, Justin S. Mankina, Daniel E. Horton, Daniel L. Swain, Danielle Touma, Allison Charland, Yunjie Liu, Matz Haugen, Michael Tsiang and Bala Rajaratnam. 2017. Quantifying the Influence of Global Warming on Unprecedented Extreme Climate Events. *PNAS* 114(19): 4881–4886.

Dimitropoulos, Alexandros, Walid Oueslati and Christina Sintek. 2018. The Rebound Effect in Road Transport: A Meta-Analysis of Empirical Studies. *Energy Economics* 75: 163–179.

Dorman, Peter. 1996. *Markets and Mortality: Economics, Dangerous Work and the Value of Human Life*. Cambridge: Cambridge University Press.

Dorman, Peter. 2014. *Microeconomics: A Fresh Start*. Heidelberg: Springer.

Dorman, Peter. 2015. Why Averting Climate Catastrophe Requires Setting Carbon Budgets, not Targets. Scholars Strategy Network. Accessed at www.scholarsstrategynetwork.org/brief/why-averting-climate-catastrophe-requires-setting-carbon-budgets-not-targets.

Dorman, Peter. 2016a. The Climate Movement Needs to Get Radical, but What Does That Mean? A Delayed Review of *This Changes Everything: Capitalism vs the Climate* by Naomi Klein. Nonsite. Accessed at http://nonsite.org/editorial/the-climate-movement-needs-to-get-radical-but-what-does-that-mean.

Dorman, Peter. 2016b. The Coordinated Activity Theory of the Firm. SSRN Paper No. 3152090.

Dorman, Peter. 2018. Climate Change and Capitalism: It's about Capital, Not Markets. Presented at the 50th Anniversary Conference of the Union for Radical Political Economics, Amherst. MA.

Dorman, Peter. 2020a. The Climate Crisis and the Green New Deal: The Issue Is the Issue after All. *Challenge* 63(4): 219–233.

Dorman, Peter. 2020b. Stranded Assets beyond the Energy Sector. Unpublished manuscript.

Dorman, Peter. n.d. A Citizens' Approach to Carbon Equity: Voting on Rebates and Collective Investments. Scholars Strategy Network. Accessed at https://scholars.org/page/citizens%E2%80%99-approach-carbon-equity-voting-rebates-and-collective-investments.

Dorman, Peter, and Leslie I. Boden. 2021. Risk without Reward: The Myth of Wage Compensation for Hazardous Work. Economic Policy Institute. Accessed at www.epi.org/unequalpower/publications/risk-without-reward-the-myth-of-wage-compensation-for-hazardous-work/.

Durlauf, Steven N., and H. Peyton Young. 2001. The New Social Economics. In *Social Dynamics*, ed. Steven N. Durlauf and H. Peyton Young. Washington, DC: Brookings Institution Press, pp. 1–14.

Dyke, James, Robert Watson and Wolfgang Knorr. 2021. Climate Scientists: Concept of Net Zero Is a Dangerous Trap. The Conversation. April 22. Accessed at https://theconversation.com/climate-scientists-concept-of-net-zero-is-a-dangerous-trap-157368.

Eberle, Jaelyn J., and David R. Greenwood. 2012. Life at the Top of the Greenhouse Eocene World: A Review of the Eocene Flora and Vertebrate Fauna from Canada's High Arctic. *Geological Society of America Bulletin* 124(1–2): 3–23.

Eberle, Jaelyn J., and Malcolm C. McKenna. 2007. The Indefatigable Mary R. Dawson: Arctic Pioneer. *Bulletin of Carnegie Museum of Natural History* 39: 7–16.

Edenhofer, Ottmar, Ramón Pichs-Madruga, Youba Sokona, Shardul Agrawala, Igor Alexeyevich Bashmakov, Gabriel Blanco, John Broome, Thomas Bruckner, Steffen Brunner, Mercedes Bustamante, Leon Clarke, Felix Creutzig, Shobhakar Dhakal, Navroz K. Dubash, Patrick Eickemeier, Ellie Farahani, Manfred Fischedick, Marc Fleurbaey, Reyer Gerlagh, Luis Gómez-Echeverri, Sujata Gupta, Jochen Harnisch, Kejun Jiang, Susanne Kadner, Sivan Kartha, Stephan Klasen, Charles Kolstad, Volker Krey, Howard Kunreuther, Oswaldo Lucon, Omar Masera, Jan Minx, Yacob Mulugetta, Anthony Patt, Nijavalli H. Ravindranath, Keywan Riahi, Joyashree Roy, Roberto Schaeffer, Steffen Schlömer, Karen Seto, Kristin Seyboth, Ralph Sims, Jim Skea, Pete Smith, Eswaran Somanathan, Robert Stavins, Christoph von Stechow, Thomas Sterner, Taishi Sugiyama, Sangwon Suh, Kevin Chika

Urama, Diana Ürge-Vorsatz, David G. Victor, Dadi Zhou, Ji Zou and Timm Zwickel. 2014. Summary for Policymakers. In IPCC Working Group III. 2014. In *Climate Change 2014: Mitigation of Climate Change. Contribution of Working Group III to the Fifth Assessment Report of the Intergovernmental Panel on Climate Change.* Cambridge: Cambridge University Press.

Edmonds, James, Patrick Luckow, Katherine Calvin, Marshall Wise, Jim Dooley, Page Kyle, Son H. Kim, Pralit Patel and Leon Clarke. 2013. Can Radiative Forcing Be Limited to 2.6 $Wm^{-2}$ without Negative Emissions from Bioenergy and $CO_2$ Capture and Storage? *Climatic Change* 118(1): 29–43.

Elgin, Ben. 2020. The Money That Grows on Trees. Bloomberg Green, 3, Winter.

Ellerman, A. Denny, Claudio Marcantonini and Aleksandar Zaklan. 2016. The European Union Emissions Trading System: Ten Years and Counting. *Review of Environmental Economics and Policy* 10(1): 89–107.

Elsässer, Lea, Svenja Hense and Armin Schäfer. 2018. Government of the People, by the Elite, for the Rich: Unequal Responsiveness in an Unlikely Case. Max Planck Institute for the Study of Societies Discussion Paper No. 18/5.

Emanuel, Kerry. 2017. Assessing the Present and Future Probability of Hurricane Harvey's Rainfall. *PNAS* 114(48): 12681–12684.

Enns, Peter K. 2015. Relative Policy Support and Coincidental Representation. *Perspectives on Politics* 13(4): 1053–1064.

EPA. 2016. EPA Fact Sheet: Social Cost of Carbon. Accessed at https://19january2017snapshot.epa.gov/climatechange/social-cost-carbon-fact-sheet_.html.

Erickson, Peter, Michael Lazarus and Randall Spalding-Fecher. 2014. Net Climate Change Mitigation of the Clean Development Mechanism. *Energy Policy* 72: 146–154.

Estes, Richard, and J. Howard Hutchison. 1980. Eocene Lower Vertebrates from Ellesmere Island, Canadian Arctic Archipelago. *Palaeogeography, Palaeoclimatology, Palaeoecology* 30: 325–347.

Eurofound. 2016. *Working Time Developments in the 21st Century: Work Duration and Its Regulation in the EU.* Luxembourg: Publications Office of the European Union.

European Commission. 2020. European Commission Energy Dataset, February 2018 update. Accessed at https://ec.europa.eu/energy/en/data-analysis/country.

European Institute on Economics and the Environment. n.d. WITCH. Accessed at www.witchmodel.org/.

Evergreen State College. 2015. FY 14-15 Greenhouse Gas Emissions Inventory. Accessed at www.evergreen.edu/sustainability/docs/TESC2014-15GHGReport.pdf.

Extinction Rebellion. n.d. Our Demands. Accessed at https://extinctionrebellion .uk/the-truth/demands/.

FAO. 2020. *The State of the World Fisheries and Aquaculture: Sustainability in Action*. Rome: FAO.

Farand, Chloé, and Megan Darby. 2020. Xi Jinping: China Will Aim for Carbon Neutrality by 2060. *Climate Home News*. September 22. Accessed at www .climatechangenews.com/2020/09/22/xi-jinping-china-will-achieve-carbon-neutrality-2060/.

Farquharson, Louise M., Vladimir E. Romanovsky, William L. Cable, Donald A. Walker, Steven V. Kokelj and Dmitry Nicolsky. 2019. Climate Change Drives Widespread and Rapid Thermokarst Development in Very Cold Permafrost in the Canadian High Arctic. *Geophysical Research Letters* 46(12): 6681–6689.

Ferguson, Thomas, Paul Jorgensen and Jie Chen. 2016. How Money Drives US Congressional Elections. Institute for New Economic Thinking Working Paper No. 48.

Ferguson, Thomas, Paul Jorgensen and Jie Chen. 2017. Fifty Shades of Green: High Finance, Political Money, and the U.S. Congress. Roosevelt Institute. Accessed at https://rooseveltinstitute.org/wp-content/uploads/2017/05/RI-Fifty-Shades-of-Green-201705.pdf.

Ferguson, Thomas, Paul Jorgensen and Jie Chen. 2019. How Money Drives US Congressional Elections: Linear Models of Money and Outcomes. *Structural Change and Economic Dynamics*. Accessed at www.sciencedirect.com/ science/article/abs/pii/S0954349X19302012.

Ferguson, Thomas, Paul Jorgensen and Jie Chen. 2020. How Much Can the U.S. Congress Resist Political Money? A Quantitative Assessment. Institute for New Economic Thinking Working Paper No. 109.

Fidelity Sectors & Industries Overview. March 2020. Accessed at https:// eresearch.fidelity.com/eresearch/markets_sectors/sectors/sectors_in_market .jhtml.

Field, Christopher B., and Katharine J. Mach. 2017. Rightsizing Carbon Dioxide Removal. *Science* 356(6339): 706–707.

Fletcher, Sara E. Mikaloff, and Hinrich Schaefer. 2019. Rising Methane: A New Climate Challenge. *Science* 364(6444): 932–933.

Forster, Piers M., Harriet I. Forster, Mat J. Evans, Matthew J. Gidden, Chris D. Jones, Christoph A. Keller, Robin D. Lamboll, Corinne Le Quéré, Joeri Rogelj, Deborah Rosen, Carl-Friedrich Schleussner, Thomas B. Richardson, Christopher J. Smith and Steven T. Turnock. 2020. Current and Future Global Climate Impacts Resulting from COVID-19. *Nature Climate Change* 10: 913–919.

Foster, John Bellamy, and Richard York. 2011. *The Ecological Rift: Capitalism's War on the Earth*. New York: Monthly Review Press.

Fremstad, Anders, and Mark Paul. 2017. A Distributional Analysis of a Carbon Tax and Dividend in the United States. University of Massachusetts Political Economy Research Institute, Working Paper No. 434.

Friedman, Lisa. 2020. A Trillion Trees: How One Idea Triumphed over Trump's Climate Denialism. *New York Times*, February 13, p. A1.

Fulton, Mark, and Christopher Weber. 2015. Carbon Asset Risk: Discussion Framework. WRI/UNEP. Accessed at www.unepfi.org/fileadmin/documents/carbon_asset_risk.pdf.

Fuss, Sabine, Josep G. Canadell, Glen P. Peters, Massimo Tavoni, Robbie M. Andrew, Philippe Ciais, Robert B. Jackson, Chris D. Jones, Florian Kraxner, Nebosja Nakicenovic, Corinne Le Quéré, Michael R. Raupach, Ayyoob Sharifi, Pete Smith and Yoshiki Yamagata. 2014. Betting on Negative Emissions. *Nature Climate Change* 4(10): 850–853.

Fuss, Sabine, William F. Lamb, Max W. Callaghan, Jérôme Hilaire, Felix Creutzig, Thorben Amann, Tim Beringer, Wagner de Oliveira Garcia, Jens Hartmann, Tarun Khanna, Gunnar Luderer, Gregory F. Nemet, Joeri Rogelj, Pete Smith, José Luis Vicente Vicente, Jennifer Wilcox, Maria del Mar Zamora Dominguez and Jan C. Minx. 2018. Negative Emissions – Part 2: Costs, Potentials and Side Effects. *Environmental Research Letters* 13(6): 063002.

Fuss, Sabine, Wolf Heinrich Reuter, Jana Szolgayová and Michael Obersteiner. 2013. Optimal Mitigation Strategies with Negative Emission Technologies and Carbon Sinks under Uncertainty. *Climatic Change* 118(1): 73–87.

Galiana, Isabel. 2014. Benefits and Costs of the Climate Change Targets for the Post-2015 Development Agenda. Copenhagen Consensus Center. Accessed at www.copenhagenconsensus.com/sites/default/files/climate_change_assessment_-_galiana_0.pdf.

Gambhir, Ajay, Laurent Drouet, David McCollum, Tamaryn Napp, Dan Bernie, Adam Hawkes, Oliver Fricko, Petr Havlik, Keywan Riahi, Valentina Bosetti and Jason Lowe. 2017. Assessing the Feasibility of Global Long-Term Mitigation Scenarios. *Energies* 10: 89.

Gehlera, Alexander, Philip D. Gingerich and Andreas Pack. 2016. Temperature and Atmospheric $CO_2$ Concentration Estimates through the PETM Using Triple Oxygen Isotope Analysis of Mammalian Bioapatite. *PNAS* 113(28): 7739–7744.

Gelman, Andrew. 2014. A Whole Fleet of Gremlins: Looking More Carefully at Richard Tol's Twice-Corrected Paper, "The Economic Effects of Climate Change." Statistical Modeling, Causal Inference, and Social Science. Accessed at http://andrewgelman.com/2014/05/27/whole-fleet-gremlins-looking-carefully-richard-tols-twice-corrected-paper-economic-effects-climate-change/.

Generation Foundation. 2013. Stranded Carbon Assets. Accessed at www.genfound.org/media/1374/pdf-generation-foundation-stranded-carbon-assets-v1.pdf.

Georgescu-Roegen, Nicholas. 1971. *The Entropy Law and the Economic Process*. Cambridge, MA: Harvard University Press.

Gertler, Paul, Orie Shelef, Catherine Wolfram and Alan Fuchs. 2016. The Demand for Energy-Using Assets among the World's Rising Middle Classes. *American Economic Review* 106(6): 1366–1401.

Ghersi, Frédéric, Jean-Charles Hourcade and Patrick Criqui. 2003. Viable Responses to the Equity-Responsibility Dilemma: A Consequentialist View. *Climate Policy* 3(S1): S115–S133.

Gigerenzer, Gerd. 2010. *Rationality for Mortals: How People Cope with Uncertainty*. Oxford: Oxford University Press.

Gilens, Martin. 2015. The Insufficiency of "Democracy by Coincidence": A Response to Peter K. Enns. *Perspectives on Politics* 13(4): 1065–1071.

Gilens, Martin. 2016. Simulating Representation: The Devil's in the Detail. *Research and Politics* 3(2): 1–3.

Gilens, Martin, and Benjamin I. Page. 2014. Testing Theories of American Politics: Elites, Interest Groups, and Average Citizens. *Perspectives on Politics* 12(3): 564–581.

Gillenwater, Michael, Xi Lu and Miriam Fischlein. 2014. Additionality of Wind Energy Investments in the U.S. Voluntary Green Power Market. *Renewable Energy* 63: 452–457.

Global Carbon Project. 2021. The Global Carbon Project's Fossil $CO_2$ Emissions Dataset. Accessed at https://zenodo.org/record/5569235#.YZCWwmCIa5e.

GNDE. n.d. The Green New Deal for Europe: A Blueprint for Europe's Just Transition. Accessed at https://report.gndforeurope.com/.

Goldstein, Allie, Will R. Turner, Jillian Gladstone and David G. Hole. 2019. The Private Sector's Climate Change Risk and Adaptation Blind Spots. *Nature Climate Change* 9(1): 18–25.

Goodwin, Philip. 2019. Quantifying the Terrestrial Carbon Feedback to Anthropogenic Carbon Emission. *Earth's Future* 7(12): 1417–1433.

Goulder, Lawrence, Marc Hafstead, GyuRim Kim and Xianling Long. 2019. Impacts of a Carbon Tax across US Household Income Groups: What Are the Equity-Efficiency Trade-Offs? *Journal of Public Economics* 175(C): 44–64.

Government of India, Ministry of Home Affairs. 2016. 2011 Census of India. Accessed at www.censusindia.gov.in/2011census/hh-series/hh01.html.

Government of Pakistan, Statistics Division. 2013. Household Integrated Economic Survey. Accessed at www.pbs.gov.pk/sites/default/files/pslm/publications/hies11_12/Complete_report.pdf.

Graff Zivin, Joshua S., Matthew J. Kotchen and Erin T. Mansur. 2014. Spatial and Temporal Heterogeneity of Marginal Emissions: Implications for Electric Cars and Other Electricity-Shifting Policies. *Journal of Economic Behavior and Organization* 107: 248–268.

Grainger, Corbett A., and Charles D. Kolstad. 2010. Who Pays a Price on Carbon? *Environmental and Resource Economics* 46: 359–376.

Gramsci, Antonio. 2000. *The Antonio Gramsci Reader: Selected Writings 1916–1935*, ed. David Forgacs and Eric J. Hobsbawm. New York: New York University Press.

Grant, Neil, Adam Hawkes, Shivika Mittal and Ajay Gambhir. 2021. Confronting Mitigation Deterrence in Low-Carbon Scenarios. *Environmental Research Letters* 16(6): 064099.

Gravelle, Jane G., and Donald J. Marples. 2014. Tax Rates and Economic Growth. Congressional Research Service. Accessed at www.crs.gov.

Greenstone, Michael, Elizabeth Kopits and Maryann Wolverton. 2011. Estimating the Social Cost of Carbon for Use in U.S. Federal Rulemakings: A Summary and Interpretation. MIT Department of Economics Working Paper No. 11-04.

Griffin, Paul A., Amy Myers Jaffe, David H. Lont and Rosa Dominguez-Faus. 2015. Science and the Stock Market: Investors' Recognition of Unburnable Carbon. *Energy Economics* 52(A): 1–12.

Hake, Jürgen-Friedrich, Wolfgang Fischer, Sandra Venghaus and Christoph Weckenbrock. 2015. The German Energiewende: History and Status Quo. *Energy* 92(3): 532–546.

Hasegawa, Tomoko, Shinichiro Fujimori, Petr Havlík, Hugo Valin, Benjamin Leon Bodirsky, Jonathan C. Doelman, Thomas Fellmann, Page Kyle, Jason F. L. Koopman, Hermann Lotze-Campen, Daniel Mason-D'Croz, Yuki Ochi, Ignacio Pérez Domínguez, Elke Stehfest, Timothy B. Sulser, Andrzej Tabeau, Kiyoshi Takahashi, Jun'ya Takakura, Hans van Meijl, Willem-Jan van Zeist, Keith Wiebe and Peter Witzke. 2018. Risk of Increased Food Insecurity under Stringent Global Climate Change Mitigation Policy. *Nature Climate Change* 8(8): 699–703.

Hattle, Andrew, Christopher Roy, Hans Peter Dejgaard, John Nordbo and Bart Weijs. 2021. Climate Adaptation Finance: Fact or Fiction? CARE Denmark and CARE Netherlands. Accessed at www.care-international.org/files/files/CARE_Climate_Adaptation_Finance_Fact_or_Fiction.pdf.

Haupt, Lyanda Lynn. 2011. *Crow Planet: Essential Wisdom from the Urban Wilderness*. Boston: Back Bay Books.

Hauri, Claudine, Tobias Friedrich and Axel Timmermann. 2016. Abrupt Onset and Prolongation of Aragonite Undersaturation Events in the Southern Ocean. *Nature Climate Change* 6(2): 172–176.

Hawkins, Troy R., Bhawna Singh, Guillaume Majeau-Bettez and Anders Hammer Strømman. 2013. Comparative Environmental Life Cycle Assessment of Conventional and Electric Vehicles. *Journal of Industrial Ecology* 17(1): 53–64.

Heal, Geoffrey. 2020. Economic Aspects of the Energy Transition. NBER Working Paper No. 27766.

Hirota, Marina, Milena Holmgren, Egbert H. Van Nes and Marten Scheffer. 2011. Global Resilience of Tropical Forest and Savanna to Critical Transitions. *Science* 334: 232–235.

Hong, B. D., and E. R. Slatick. 1994. Carbon Dioxide Emission Factors for Coal. Quarterly Coal Report, January–April. Accessed at www.eia.gov/coal/production/quarterly/co2_article/co2.html.

Hönisch, Bärbel, Andy Ridgwell, Daniela N. Schmidt, Ellen Thomas, Samantha J. Gibbs, Appy Sluijs, Richard Zeebe, Lee Kump, Rowan C. Martindale, Sarah E. Greene, Wolfgang Kiessling, Justin Ries, James C. Zachos, Dana L. Royer, Stephen Barker, Thomas M. Marchitto Jr., Ryan Moyer, Carles Pelejero, Patrizia Ziveri, Gavin L. Foster and Branwen Williams. 2012. The Geological Record of Ocean Acidification. *Science* 335: 1058–1063.

Horowitz, John, Julie-Anne Cronin, Hannah Hawkins, Laura Konda and Alex Yuskavage. 2017. Methodology for Analyzing a Carbon Tax. US Department of the Treasury, Office of Tax Analysis Working Paper No. 115.

Horst, Ulrich, and Jose Scheinkman. 2006. Equilibria in Systems of Social Interactions. *Journal of Economic Theory* 130: 44–77.

Hubau, Wannes, Oliver Lawrence Philips, Simon Lewis, Hans Beeckman and 102 coauthors. 2020. Asynchronous Carbon Sink Saturation in African and Amazonian Tropical Forests. *Nature* 579(7797): 80–87.

Huybrechts, Philippe, Heiko Goelzer, I. Janssens, Emmanuelle Driesschaert, Thierry Fichefet, Hugues Goosse and Marie-France Loutre. 2011. Response of the Greenland and Antarctic Ice Sheets to Multi-Millennial Greenhouse Warming in the Earth System Model of Intermediate Complexity LOVECLIM. *Surveys in Geophysics* 32(4–5): 397–416.

ICF Resources. 2021. Accessed at www.icf.com/resources?type=reports-and-research.

Im, Eun-Soon, Jeremy S. Pal and Elfatih A. B. Eltahir. 2017. Deadly Heat Waves Projected in the Densely Populated Agricultural Regions of South Asia. *Science Advances* 3(8): e1603322.

IMF. 2021. *World Economic Outlook Database, October 2021.* Accessed at www.imf.org/en/Publications/WEO/weo-database/2021/October.

Inglis, Gordon N., Fran Bragg, Natalie Burls, David Evans, Gavin L. Foster, Matt Huber, Daniel J. Lunt, Nicholas Siler, Sebastian Steinig, Richard Wilkinson, Eleni Anagnostou, Margot Cramwinckel, Christopher J. Hollis, Richard D. Pancost and Jessica E. Tierney. 2020. Global Mean Surface Temperature and Climate Sensitivity of the EECO, PETM and Latest Paleocene. Preprint submitted to Climate of the Past. Accessed at https://cp.copernicus.org/preprints/cp-2019-167/.

International Atomic Energy Association. 2017. International Status and
Prospects for Nuclear Power 2017. Accessed at www.iaea.org/About/Policy/
GC/GC61/GC61InfDocuments/English/gc61inf-8_en.pdf.

International Energy Agency. 2014. *Africa Energy Outlook: A Focus on Energy
Prospects in Sub-Saharan Africa*. Paris: IEA.

International Energy Agency. 2018. The Future of Cooling Opportunities for
Energy Efficient Air Conditioning. Accessed at www.iea.org/publications/
freepublications/publication/The_Future_of_Cooling.pdf.

International Energy Agency. 2020. Global $CO_2$ Emissions in 2019. Accessed at
www.iea.org/articles/global-co2-emissions-in-2019.

International Energy Agency and United Nations Environment Programme.
2020. Cooling Emissions and Policy Synthesis Report: Benefits of Cooling
Efficiency and the Kigali Amendment. Accessed at https://webstore.iea.org/
cooling-emissions-and-policy-synthesis-report.

International Institute for Applied Systems Analysis. 2021. SSP Public Database
Version 2.0. Accessed at https://tntcat.iiasa.ac.at.

International Maritime Organization. 2014. Third IMO Greenhouse Gas Study
2014. Accessed at www.imo.org/en/OurWork/Environment/
PollutionPrevention/AirPollution/Documents/Third%20Greenhouse%20Gas
%20Study/GHG3%20Executive%20Summary%20and%20Report.pdf.

IPCC. 2014. *Climate Change 2014 Synthesis Report*. Geneva: IPCC.

IPCC. 2018. *Global Warming of 1.5°C (Special Report)*. Accessed at www.ipcc
.ch/report/sr15/.

IPCC. 2019. *Special Report on Climate Change, Desertification, Land
Degradation, Sustainable Land Management, Food Security, and Greenhouse
Gas Fluxes in Terrestrial Ecosystems*.

IPCC, Working Group I. 2013. *Climate Change: The Physical Science Basis*.
Cambridge: Cambridge University Press.

IPCC, Working Group I. 2021. Climate Change: The Physical Science Basis.
Accessed at www.ipcc.ch/report/ar6/wg1/#FullReport.

IPCC, Working Group II. 2014. *Climate Change 2014: Impacts, Adaptation, and
Vulnerability*. Cambridge: Cambridge University Press.

IPCC, Working Group III. 2014. *Climate Change 2014: Mitigation of Climate
Change. Contribution of Working Group III to the Fifth Assessment Report of
the Intergovernmental Panel on Climate Change*. Cambridge: Cambridge
University Press.

IRENA. 2017. Stranded Assets and Renewables: Accelerated Renewable Energy
Uptake and What It Means for Asset Stranding in Energy, Industry, and
Property. Accessed at www.irena.org/-/media/Files/IRENA/Agency/
Publication/2017/Jul/IRENA_REmap_Stranded_assets_and_renewables_
2017.pdf.

Isaac, Morna, and Detlef P. van Vuuren. 2009. Modeling Global Residential Sector Energy Demand for Heating and Air Conditioning in the Context of Climate Change. *Energy Policy* 37(2): 507–521.

Ives, Mike. 2018. Rich Nations Vowed Billions for Climate Change. Poor Countries Are Waiting. *New York Times*, September 9.

Jackson, Tim. 2009. *Prosperity without Growth: Economics for a Finite Planet*. London: Routledge.

Jacobs, David. 2012. The German Energiewende: History, Targets, Policies and Challenges. *Renewable Energy Law and Policy Review* 3(4): 223–233.

Jakob, Michael. 2021. Primer: Why Carbon Leakage Matters and What Can Be Done against It. *One Earth* 4(5): 609–614.

Jones, Chris D., Thomas L. Frölicher, Charles Koven, Andrew H. MacDougall, H. Damon Matthews, Kirsten Zickfeld, Joeri Rogelj, Katarzyna B. Tokarska, Nathan P. Gillett, Tatiana Ilyina, Malte Meinshausen, Nadine Mengis, Roland Séférian, Michael Eby and Friedrich A. Burger. 2019. The Zero Emissions Commitment Model Intercomparison Project (ZECMIP) Contribution to C4MIP: Quantifying Committed Climate Changes Following Zero Carbon Emissions. *Geoscientific Model Development* 12: 4375–4385.

Joppa, Lucas. 2020. Progress on Our Goal to Be Carbon Negative by 2030. Microsoft on the Issues, July 21. Accessed at https://blogs.microsoft.com/on-the-issues/2020/07/21/carbon-negative-transform-to-net-zero/.

Kahneman, Daniel. 2011. *Thinking, Fast and Slow*. New York: Farrar, Straus and Giroux.

Kallis, Giorgos, and Sam Bliss. 2019. Post-Environmentalism: Origins and Evolution of a Strange Idea. *Journal of Political Ecology* 26: 466–485.

Kanter, David R., Stephen M. Ogle and Wilfried Winiwarter. 2020. Building on Paris: Integrating Nitrous Oxide Mitigation into Future Climate Policy. *Current Opinion in Environmental Sustainability* 47: 1–6.

Karp, Larry, and Christian Traeger. 2018. Prices versus Quantities Reassessed. CESifo Working Paper 7331.

Kermani, Amir, and Yueran Ma. 2020. Asset Specificity of Non-Financial Firms. NBER Working Paper No. 27642.

Klein, Naomi. 2014. *This Changes Everything: Capitalism vs. the Climate*. New York: Simon & Schuster.

Klemettinen, Timo. 2007. Overview of Music Education in Finland. Presented at the Symposium on Music Education in Finland, New York University, January 31. Accessed at www.artistshousemusic.org/videos/overview+of+music+education+in+finland.

Knoll, Andrew H. 2015. *Life on a Young Planet: The First Three Billion Years of Evolution on Earth*. Princeton, NJ: Princeton University Press.

Kolbert, Elizabeth. 2014. *The Sixth Extinction: An Unnatural History*. New York: Henry Holt and Co.

Koomey, Jonathan. 2013. Moving beyond Benefit–Cost Analysis of Climate Change. *Environmental Research Letters* 8(4): 041005.

Kossin, James P., Kerry A. Emanuel and Suzana J. Camargo. 2016. Past and Projected Changes in Western North Pacific Tropical Cyclone Exposure. *Journal of Climate* 29: 5725–5739.

Kramer, Andrew E. 2012. 23 Nations Fight European Airline Emissions Law. *New York Times*, February 23, B9.

Krause, Florentin, Wilfrid Bach and Jonathan Koomey. 1992. *Energy Policy in the Greenhouse*. New York: Wiley.

Krey, Volker, Gunnar Luderer, Leon Clarke and Elmar Kriegler. 2014. Getting from Here to There: Energy Technology Transformation Pathways in the EMF27 Scenarios. *Climatic Change* 123(3–4): 369–382.

Kriegler, Elmar, Ottmar Edenhofer, Lena Reuster, Gunnar Luderer and David Klein. 2013. Is Atmospheric Carbon Dioxide Removal a Game Changer for Climate Change Mitigation? *Climatic Change* 118(1): 45–57.

Krugman, Paul. 2018. Trade Wars, Stranded Assets, and the Stock Market (Wonkish). *New York Times*, April 4.

Labandeira, Xavier, José M. Labeaga and Xiral López-Otero. 2017. A Meta-Analysis on the Price Elasticity of Energy Demand. *Energy Policy* 102: 549–568.

Lashof, Dan. 2015. Our Clean Energy Economy. Accessed at https:// nextgenpolicy.org/blog/our-clean-energy-economy/.

Lavelle, Marianne. 2020. Biden's Appointment of John Kerry as Climate Envoy Sends a "Signal to the World," Advocates Say. *Inside Climate News*, November 24. Accessed at https://insideclimatenews.org/news/24112020/ biden-kerry-climate-envoy-cabinet-picks-paris-agreement/.

Lavoie, Don. 1985. *Rivalry and Central Planning: The Socialist Calculation Debate Reconsidered*. Cambridge: Cambridge University Press.

Leading Group. 2011. How Can We Implement Today a Multilateral and Multi-Jurisdictional Tax on Financial Transactions? Accessed at www.leadinggroup .org/IMG/pdf/Rapport_TTF_ANG_oct_2011_bis.pdf.

Leading Group. 2021. The Leading Group on Innovative Financing for Development. Accessed at www.leadinggroup.org/rubrique69.html.

Lee, Ronald. 2003. The Demographic Transition: Three Centuries of Fundamental Change. *Journal of Economic Perspectives* 17(4): 167–190.

Leiser, David, and Ronen Aroch. 2009. Lay Understanding of Macroeconomic Causation: The Good-Begets-Good Heuristic. *Applied Psychology* 58(3): 370–384.

Lenton, Timothy M., Johan Rockström, Owen Gaffney, Stefan Rahmstorf, Katherine Richardson, Will Steffen and Hans Joachim Schellnhuber. 2019. Climate Tipping Points – Too Risky to Bet Against. *Nature* 575(7784): 592–595.

Liger-Belair, Gérard. 2003. The Science of Bubbly. *Scientific American* 288(1): 80–85.

Lindsey, Rebecca. 2020. Climate Change: Atmospheric Carbon Dioxide. NOAA. Accessed at www.climate.gov/news-features/understanding-climate/climate-change-atmospheric-carbon-dioxide.

Lo, Chris. 2013. Skysails: Bringing Wind Back to Ship Propulsion. *Ship Technology*, December 2. Accessed at www.ship-technology.com/features/feature-skysails-bringing-wind-back-ship-propulsion/.

Lobell, David B., Wolfram Schlenker and Justin Costa-Roberts. 2011. Climate Trends and Global Crop Production since 1980. *Science* 333: 616–620.

Löfgren, Åsa, Dallas Burtraw, Markus Wråke and Anna Malinovskaya. 2015. Architecture of the EU Emissions Trading System in Phase 3 and the Distribution of Allowance Asset Values. Resources for the Future Discussion Paper 15-45.

Lorde, Audre. 2018. *The Master's Tools Will Never Dismantle the Master's House.* New York: Penguin.

Luderer, Gunnar, Christoph Bertram, Katherine Calvin, Enrica De Cian and Elmar Kriegler. 2016. Implications of Weak Near-Term Climate Policies on Long-Term Mitigation Pathways. *Climatic Change* 136(1): 127–140.

MacDougall, Andrew H., Kirsten Zickfeld, Reto Knutti and H. Damon Matthews. 2015. Sensitivity of Carbon Budgets to Permafrost Carbon Feedbacks and Non-$CO_2$ Forcings. *Environmental Research Letters* 10(12): 1–10.

Malone, Patrick, and R. Jeffrey Smith. 2018. Plutonium Is Missing, but the Government Says Nothing. The Center for Public Integrity. Accessed at https://publicintegrity.org/national-security/plutonium-is-missing-but-the-government-says-nothing/.

Mann, Charles C. 2011. *1493: Uncovering the New World Columbus Created.* New York: Alfred A. Knopf.

Martin, Ralf, Mirabelle Muûls and Ulrich J. Wagner. 2016. The Impact of the European Union Emissions Trading Scheme on Regulated Firms: What Is the Evidence after Ten Years? *Review of Environmental Economics and Policy* 10(1): 129–148.

Märtz, Alexandra, Patrick Plötz and Patrick Jochem. 2021. Global Perspective on $CO_2$ Emissions of Electric Vehicles. *Environmental Research Letters* 16(5): 054043.

Masson-Delmotte, Valérie, Panmao Zhai Hans-Otto Pörtner, Debra Roberts Jim Skea, Priyadarshi R. Shukla, Anna Pirani, Wilfran Moufouma-Okia, Clotilde Péan, Roz Pidcock, Sarah Connors, J. B. Robin Matthews, Yang Chen, Xiao Zhou, Melissa I. Gomis Elisabeth Lonnoy, Tom Maycock, Melinda Tignor and Tim Waterfield, eds. 2018. *Global Warming of 1.5°C.* IPCC.

Matthews, H. Damon, Katarzyna B. Tokarska, Joeri Rogelj, Christopher J. Smith, Andrew H. MacDougall, Karsten Haustein, Nadine Mengis, Sebastian

Sippel, Piers M. Forster and Reto Knutti. 2021. An Integrated Approach to Quantifying Uncertainties In the Remaining Carbon Budget. *Communications Earth & Environment* 2: 7.

Matthews, Tom. 2018. Humid Heat and Climate Change. *Progress in Physical Geography* 42(3): 391–405.

Mazzucato, Mariana. 2013. *The Entrepreneurial State: Debunking Public vs. Private Sector Myths.* London: Anthem Press.

McGarry, John. 2016. Clean Energy Economy Drives Job Creation. Accessed at www.climatesolutions.org/bright-future/clean-energy-economy/1466023288-clean-energy-economy-drives-job-creation.

McGlade, Christophe, and Paul Ekins. 2015. The Geographical Distribution of Fossil Fuels Unused When Limiting Global Warming to 2°C. *Nature* 517: 187–190.

McKibben, Bill. 2012. Global Warming's Terrifying New Math. *Rolling Stone*, August 2. Accessed at www.tfl.net/PresentationHandouts/Global%20Warming's%20Terrifying%20New%20Math.pdf.

Meltzer, Joshua P. 2012. Prohibiting Compliance with the EU Emissions Trading Scheme: Why This Is Not a Good Idea. Brookings. Accessed at www.brookings.edu/opinions/prohibiting-compliance-with-the-eu-emissions-trading-scheme-why-this-is-not-a-good-idea/.

Mendelsohn, Robert, William D. Nordhaus and Daigee Shaw. 1994. The Impact of Global Warming on Agriculture: A Ricardian Analysis. *The American Economic Review* 84(4): 753–771.

Mercier, Hugo, and Dan Sperber. 2017. *The Enigma of Reason.* Cambridge, MA: Harvard University Press.

Messenger, Jon. 2018. Working Time and the Future of Work. ILO Future of Work Research Paper Series No. 6.

Metz, Bert, Ogunlade Davidson, Heleen de Coninck, Manuela Loos and Leo Meyer, eds. 2005. *Carbon Capture and Storage* (IPCC Technical Report). Cambridge: Cambridge University Press.

Microsoft. 2020. Corporate Social Responsibility Report. Accessed at www.microsoft.com/en-us/corporate-responsibility.

Microsoft News Center. 2019. Microsoft Expands Clean Energy, Connectivity Investments in Washington State with Chelan Public Utility District. April 12. Accessed at https://news.microsoft.com/2019/04/12/microsoft-expands-clean-energy-connectivity-investments-in-washington-state-with-chelan-public-utility-district/.

Monbiot, George. 2006. Here's the Plan. *The Guardian*, October 31. Accessed at www.monbiot.com/2006/10/31/heres-the-plan/.

Morris, Errol. 2014. The Certainty of Donald Rumsfeld (Part 1). *New York Times*, March 25.

Myers, Samuel S., Antonella Zanobetti, Itai Kloog, Peter Huybers, Andrew D. B. Leakey, Arnold J. Bloom, Eli Carlisle, Lee H. Dietterich, Glenn Fitzgerald, Toshihiro Hasegawa, N. Michele Holbrook, Randall L. Nelson, Michael J. Ottman, Victor Raboy, Hidemitsu Sakai, Karla A. Sartor, Joel Schwartz, Saman Seneweera, Michael Tausz and Yasuhiro Usui. 2014. Increasing $CO_2$ Threatens Human Nutrition. *Nature* 510: 139–143.

Naafs, B. David, Megan Rohrssen, Gordon N. Inglis, Outi Lähteenoja, Sarah J. Feakins, Margaret E. Collinson, Elizabeth M. Kennedy, P. K. Singh, M. P. Singh, Dan J. Lunt and Richard D. Pancost. 2018. High Temperatures in the Terrestrial Mid-Latitudes during the Early Palaeogene. *Nature Geoscience* 11(10): 766–771.

Natali, Susan M., John P. Holdren, Brendan M. Rogers, Rachael Treharne, Philip B. Duffy, Rafe Pomerance and Erin MacDonald. 2021. Permafrost Carbon Feedbacks Threaten Global Climate Goals. *PNAS* 118(21): e2100163118.

National Academies of Sciences. 2021. *Reflecting Sunlight: Recommendations for Solar Geoengineering Research and Research Governance*. Washington, DC: National Academies Press.

National Academy of Sciences. 2015. *Climate Intervention: Carbon Dioxide Removal and Reliable Sequestration*. Washington, DC: National Academies Press.

National Academy of Sciences. 2018. *Negative Emissions Technologies and Reliable Sequestration: A Research Agenda*. Washington, DC: National Academies Press.

National Oceanographic and Atmospheric Administration. 2019. *Arctic Report Card 2019*. Accessed at https://arctic.noaa.gov/Report-Card/Report-Card-2019.

NBAA. 2012. Coalition Calls on Clinton, LaHood to Take Further Action in Opposition to EU-ETS. Accessed at https://nbaa.org/press-releases/coalition-calls-on-clinton-lahood-to-take-further-action-in-opposition-to-eu-ets/.

Nelson, Gerald C., Hugo Valin, Ronald D. Sands, Petr Havlík, Helal Ahammad, Delphine Deryng, Joshua Elliott, Shinichiro Fujimori, Tomoko Hasegawa, Edwina Heyhoe, Page Kyle, Martin Von Lampe, Hermann Lotze-Campen, Daniel Mason d'Croz, Hans van Meijl, Dominique van der Mensbrugghe, Christoph Müller, Alexander Popp, Richard Robertson, Sherman Robinson, Erwin Schmid, Christoph Schmitz, Andrzej Tabeau and Dirk Willenbockel. 2014a. Climate Change Effects on Agriculture: Economic Responses to Biophysical Shocks. *PNAS* 111(9): 3274–3279.

Nelson, Gerald C., Dominique van der Mensbrugghe, Helal Ahammad, Elodie Blanc, Katherine Calvin, Tomoko Hasegawa, Petr Havlik, Edwina Heyhoe, Page Kyle, Hermann Lotze-Campen, Martin von Lampe, Daniel Mason d' Croz, Hans van Meijl, Christoph Müller, John Reilly, Richard Robertson, Ronald D. Sands, Christoph Schmitz, Andrzej Tabeau, Kiyoshi Takahashi,

Hugo Valin and Dirk Willenbockel. 2014b. Agriculture and Climate Change in Global Scenarios: Why Don't the Models Agree. *Agricultural Economics* 45: 85–101.

Nimgaonkar, Vivek. 2015. The Energiewende Paradox: Rising German Emissions Despite an Emphasis on Renewable Energy Policy. Penn Wharton Public Policy Initiative, November 17. Accessed at https://publicpolicy .wharton.upenn.edu/live/news/1056-the-energiewende-paradox-rising-german-emissions.

Nisbet, Matthew C. n.d. Study Finds That Fear Won't Don't Do It: Why Most Efforts at Climate Change Communication Might Actually Backfire. Big Think. Accessed at http://bigthink.com/age-of-engagement/study-finds-that-fear-wont-don't-do-it-why-most-efforts-at-climate-change-communication-might-actually-backfire.

Nordborg, Henrik. 2021. Global Climate Compensation: An Action Plan to Prevent Catastrophic Climate Change. Accessed at https://nordborg.ch/wp-content/uploads/2021/01/Global-Climate-Compensation.pdf.

Nordelöf, Anders, Maarten Messagie, Anne-Marie Tillman, Maria Ljunggren Söderman and Joeri Van Mierlo. 2014. Environmental Impacts of Hybrid, Plug-In Hybrid, and Battery Electric Vehicles: What Can We Learn from Life Cycle Assessment? *The International Journal of Life Cycle Assessment* 19(11): 1866–1890.

Nordhaus, William. 2013. *The Climate Casino: Risk, Uncertainty, and Economics for a Warming World.* New Haven, CT: Yale University Press.

Nordhaus, William. 2015. Climate Clubs: Overcoming Free-Riding in International Climate Policy. *American Economic Review* 105(4): 1339–1370.

Nordhaus, William D. 2017a. Revisiting the Social Cost of Carbon. *PNAS* 114(7): 1518–1523.

Nordhaus, William D. 2017b. Evolution of Assessments of the Economics of Global Warming: Changes in the DICE Model, 1992–2017. NBER Working Paper 23319.

Norway, Office of the Auditor General. 2017–2018. Investigation of Norway's International Climate and Forest Initiative. Document 3:10. Accessed at www .riksrevisjonen.no/globalassets/reports/en-2017-2018/ norwayinternationalclimateandforestinitiative.pdf.

OECD. 2016. OECD Family Database. Accessed at www.oecd.org/els/family/ database.htm.

OECD. 2021. OECD.Stat. Accessed at http://stats.oecd.org/.

Ohlendorf, Nils, Michael Jakob, Jan Christoph Minx, Carsten Schröder and Jan Christoph Steckel. 2018. Distributional Impacts of Climate Mitigation Policies: A Meta-Analysis. German Institute for Economic Research (DIW Berlin) Discussion Paper No. 1776.

Olmer, Naya, Bryan Comer, Biswajoy Roy, Xiaoli Mao and Dan Rutherford. 2017. *Greenhouse Gas Emissions from Global Shipping, 2013–2015*. Washington, DC: International Council on Clean Transportation.

O'Neill, Brian C., Timothy R. Carter, Kristie Ebi, Paula A. Harrison, Eric Kemp-Benedict, Kasper Kok, Elmar Kriegler, Benjamin L. Preston, Keywan Riahi, Jana Sillmann, Bas J. van Ruijven, Detlef van Vuuren, David Carlisle, Cecilia Conde, Jan Fuglestvedt, Carole Green, Tomoko Hasegawa, Julia Leininger, Seth Monteith and Ramon Pichs-Madruga. 2020. Achievements and Needs for the Climate Change Scenario Framework. *Nature Climate Change* 10(12): 1074–1084.

Open Secrets. 2020. Microsoft Corp, Summary. Accessed at www.opensecrets .org/political-action-committees-pacs/microsoft-corp/C00227546/summary/ 2020.

Ostrom, Elinor. 1990. *Governing the Commons: The Evolution of Institutions for Collective Action*. Cambridge: Cambridge University Press.

Pagani, M., M. Huber and B. Sageman. 2014. Greenhouse Climates. In *Treatise on Geochemistry, Vol. 6: The Atmosphere – History*, 2nd ed., ed. James Farquhar. Amsterdam: Elsevier, pp. 281–304.

Page, Benjamin I., Larry M. Bartels and Jason Seawright. 2013. Democracy and the Policy Preferences of Wealthy Americans. *Perspectives on Politics* 11(1): 51–73.

Pal, Jeremy S., and Elfatih A. B. Eltahir. 2016. Future Temperature in Southwest Asia Projected to Exceed a Threshold for Human Adaptability. *Nature Climate Change* 6: 197–200.

Palmer, Lisa. 2016. How Rising $CO_2$ Levels May Contribute to Die Off of Bees. *Environment 360*, May 10.

Parry, Ian. 2019. Putting a Price on Pollution. *Finance & Development* 56(4): 16–19.

Parry, Ian, Chandara Veung and Dirk Heine. 2014. How Much Carbon Pricing Is in Countries' Own Interests? The Critical Role of Co-Benefits. IMF Working Paper 14/174.

Pearce, Fred. 2020. Why Clouds Are the Key to New Troubling Projections on Warming. Yale Environment 360. Accessed at https://e360.yale.edu/features/ why-clouds-are-the-key-to-new-troubling-projections-on-warming.

Pencavel, John. 2018. *Diminishing Returns at Work*. Oxford: Oxford University Press.

Penney, Veronica. 2020. Think You're Making Good Climate Choices? Take This Mini-Quiz. *New York Times*, August 30.

Peters, Glen P., Jan C. Minx, Christopher L. Weber, and Ottmar Edenhofer. 2011. Growth in Emission Transfers via International Trade from 1990 to 2008. *Proceedings of the National Academy of Sciences* 108(21): 8903–8908.

Petrenko, Vasilii V., Andrew M. Smith, Hinrich Schaefer, Katja Riedel, Edward Brook, Daniel Baggenstos, Christina Harth, Quan Hua, Christo Buizert, Adrian Schilt, Xavier Fain, Logan Mitchell, Thomas Bauska, Anais Orsi, Ray F. Weiss and Jeffrey P. Severinghaus. 2018. Minimal Geological Methane Emissions during the Younger Dryas–Preboreal Abrupt Warming Event. *Nature* 548(7668): 443–446.

Phadke, Amol, Umed Paliwal, Nikit Abhyankar, Taylor McNair, Ben Paulos, David Wooley and Ric O'Connell. 2020. *2035: Plummeting Solar, Wind, and Battery Costs Can Accelerate Our Clean Electricity Future.* Goldman School of Public Policy, University of California Berkeley. Accessed at www.2035report.com/.

Pistone, Kristina, Ian Eisenman and Veerabhadran Ramanathan. 2019. Radiative Heating of an Ice-Free Arctic Ocean. *Geophysical Research Letters* 46(13): 7474–7480.

Plumer, Brad. 2018. Trump Put a Low Cost on Carbon Emissions. Here's Why It Matters. *New York Times*, August 23.

Porter, Eduardo. 2015. Getting to $100 Billion in Climate Change Aid. *New York Times*, September 30, B1.

Prieger, James E., and Jonathan Kulick. 2018. Cigarette Taxes and Illicit Trade in Europe. *Economic Inquiry* 56(3): 1706–1723.

Rackley, Stephen A. 2017. *Carbon Capture and Storage*, 2nd ed. Oxford: Butterworth-Heinemann.

Rae, James W. B., Yi Ge Zhang, Xiaoqing Liu, Gavin L. Foster, Heather M. Stoll and Ross D. M. Whiteford. 2021. Atmospheric $CO_2$ over the Past 66 Million Years from Marine Archives. *Annual Review of Earth and Planetary Sciences* 14(6): 599–631.

Rahmstorf, Stefan, Jason E. Box, Georg Feulner, Michael E. Mann, Alexander Robinson, Scott Rutherford and Erik J. Schaffernicht. 2015. Exceptional Twentieth-Century Slowdown in Atlantic Ocean Overturning Circulation. *Nature Climate Change* 5(5): 475–480.

Ramelli, Stefano, Alexander F. Wagner, Richard J. Zeckhauser and Alexandre Ziegler. 2018. Stock Price Rewards to Climate Saints and Sinners: Evidence from the Trump Election. Harvard Kennedy School Faculty Research Working Paper No. 18-037.

Rashid, Harunur, Leonid Polyak and Ellen Mosley-Thompson, eds. 2011. *Abrupt Climate Change: Mechanisms, Patterns, and Impacts.* Washington, DC: American Geophysical Union.

Raymond, Colin, Tom Matthews and Radley M. Horton. 2020. The Emergence of Heat and Humidity Too Severe for Human Tolerance. *Science Advances* 6 (19): 1838.

Raymond, Crystal L., David L. Peterson and Regina M. Rochefort, eds. 2014. Climate Change Vulnerability and Adaptation in the North Cascades Region,

Washington. US Department of Agriculture, Forest Service, Pacific Northwest Research Station. General Technical Report No. PNW-GTR-892.

Retraction Watch. 2015. Retraction Watch. Second Correx for Controversial Paper on the Financial Benefits of Climate Change. Accessed at http://retractionwatch.com/2015/07/22/second-correction-for-controversial-paper-on-economic-gains-of-climate-change/.

Reuters. 2016. India Braces for More Heat after Temperatures Break Records. May 23. Accessed at http://news.trust.org/item/20160523105746-434l9/?source=spotlight.

Riahi, Elmar Kriegler, Nils Johnson, Christoph Bertram, Michel den Elzen, Jiyong Eom, Michiel Schaeffer, Jae Edmonds, Morna Isaac, Volker Krey, Thomas Longden, Gunnar Luderer, Aurélie Méjean, David L. McCollum, Silvana Mima, Hal Turton, Detlef P. van Vuuren, Kenichi Wada and Ottmar Edenhofer. 2015. Locked into Copenhagen Pledges: Implications of Short-Term Emission Targets for the Cost and Feasibility of Long-Term Climate Goals. *Technological Forecasting and Social Change* 90(A): 8–23.

Riahi, Keywan, Detlef P. van Vuuren, Elmar Kriegler, Jae Edmonds, Brian C. O'Neill, Shinichiro Fujimori, Nico Bauer, Katherine Calvin, Rob Dellink, Oliver Fricko, Wolfgang Lutz, Alexander Popp, Jesus Crespo Cuaresma, Samir KC, Marian Leimbach, Leiwen Jiang, Tom Kram, Shilpa Rao, Johannes Emmerling, Kristie Ebi, Tomoko Hasegawa, Petr Havlik, Florian Humpenöder, Lara Aleluia Da Silva, Steve Smith, Elke Stehfest, Valentina Bosetti, Jiyong Eom, David Gernaat, Toshihiko Masui, Joeri Rogelj, Jessica Strefler, Laurent Drouet, Volker Krey, Gunnar Luderer, Mathijs Harmsen, Kiyoshi Takahashi, Lavinia Baumstark, Jonathan C. Doelman, Mikiko Kainuma, Zbigniew Klimont, Giacomo Marangoni, Hermann Lotze-Campen, Michael Obersteiner, Andrzej Tabeau and Massimo Tavoni. 2017. The Shared Socioeconomic Pathways and Their Energy, Land Use, and Greenhouse Gas Emissions Implications: An Overview. *Global Environmental Change* 42: 153–168.

Ricke, Katharine L., and Ken Caldeira. 2014. Maximum Warming Occurs about One Decade after a Carbon Dioxide Emission. *Environmental Research Letters* 9(12): 124002.

Riley, James C. 2001. *Rising Life Expectancy: A Global History*. Cambridge: Cambridge University Press.

Ringius, Lasse, Asbjørn Torvanger and Arild Underdal. 2002. Burden Sharing and Fairness Principles in International Climate Policy. *International Environmental Agreements* 2: 1–22.

Ripple, William J., Christopher Wolf, Thomas M. Newsome, Mauro Galetti, Mohammed Alamgir, Eileen Crist, Mahmoud I. Mahmoud, William F. Laurance, and 15,364 scientist signatories from 184 countries. 2017. World

Scientists' Warning to Humanity: A Second Notice. *BioScience* 67(12): 1026–1028.

Roberts, David. 2019a. The Green New Deal, Explained. *Vox*, February 23. Accessed at www.vox.com/energy-and-environment/2018/12/21/18144138/green-new-deal-alexandria-ocasio-cortez.

Roberts, David. 2019b. Oregon Is Poised to Set a Cap on Greenhouse Gas Emissions. That's a Huge Deal. *Vox*. June 5. Accessed at www.vox.com/energy-and-environment/2019/6/5/18650155/climate-change-oregon-carbon-cap-trade-california.

Roberts, Timmons, and Romain Weikmans. 2015. Is the "$100 Billion by 2020 Goal" from Copenhagen Being Met!? A Dispatch from the Paris Climate Conference. Brookings PlanetPolicy, December 4. Accessed at www.brookings.edu/blog/planetpolicy/2015/12/04/is-the-100-billion-by-2020-goal-from-copenhagen-being-met-a-dispatch-from-the-paris-climate-conference/.

Robine, Jean-Marie, Siu Lan K. Cheung, Sophie Le Roy, Herman Van Oyen, Clare Griffiths, Jean-Pierre Michel and François Richard Herrmann. 2008. Death Toll Exceeded 70,000 in Europe during the Summer of 2003. *Comptes Rendus Biologies* 331(2): 171–178.

Rogelj, Joeri, Piers M. Forster, Elmar Kriegler, Christopher J. Smith and Roland Séférian. 2019. Estimating and Tracking the Remaining Carbon Budget for Stringent Climate Targets. *Nature* 571: 335–342.

Rogelj, Joeri, Oliver Fricko, Malte Meinshausen, Volker Krey, Johanna J. J. Zilliacus and Keywan Riahi. 2017. Understanding the Origin of Paris Agreement Emission Uncertainties. *Nature Communications* 8: 1–12.

Rogelj, Joeri, Andy Reisinger, David L. McCollum, Reto Knutti, Keywan Riahi and Malte Meinshausen. 2015. Mitigation Choices Impact Carbon Budget Size Compatible with Low Temperature Goals. *Environmental Research Letters* 10(7): 2–10.

Röhl, Ursula, Thomas Westerhold, Timothy J. Bralower and James C. Zach. 2007. On the duration of the Paleocene–Eocene thermal maximum (PETM). *Geochemistry, Geophysics, Geosystems* 8(12): Q12002.

Rose-Ackerman, Susan. 2011. Putting Cost–Benefit Analysis in Its Place: Rethinking Regulatory Review. Yale Law School Faculty Scholarship Series, Paper 4156.

Roth, Steve. n.d. Why Economists Don't Know How to Think about Wealth (or Profits). Evonomics. Accessed at http://evonomics.com/economists-don't-know-think-wealth-profits/.

Royer, Dana. 2014. Atmospheric $CO_2$ and $O_2$ during the Phanerozoic: Tools, Patterns, and Impacts. In *Treatise on Geochemistry, Vol. 1–16*, 2nd ed., ed. Karl Turekian and Heinrich Holland. Amsterdam: Elsevier, pp. 251–267.

Rudmin, Maxim, Andrew P. Roberts, Chorng-Shern Hong, Aleksey Mazurov, Olesya Savinova, Aleksey Ruban, Roman Kashapov and Maxim Veklich.

2018. Ferrimagnetic Iron Sulfide Formation and Methane Venting across the Paleocene–Eocene Thermal Maximum in Shallow Marine Sediments, Ancient West Siberian Sea. *Geochemistry, Geophysics, Geosystems* 19(1): 21–42.

Ruppel, Carolyn D., and John D. Kessler. 2018. The Interaction of Climate Change and Methane Hydrates. *Review of Geophysics* 55(1): 126–168.

Russo, Simone, Andrea F. Marchese, J. Sillmann and Giuseppina Immé. 2016. When Will Unusual Heat Waves Become Normal in a Warming Africa? *Environmental Research Letters* 11(5): 054016.

Sadasivam, Naveena. 2015. Economy Would Gain Two Million New Jobs in Low-Carbon Transition, Study Says. Accessed at https://insideclimatenews .org/news/18112015/low-carbon-economy-may-create-2-million-jobs-study-finds-clean-energy.

Saez, Emmanuel, Joel Slemrod and Seth H. Giertz. 2012. The Elasticity of Taxable Income with Respect to Marginal Tax Rates: A Critical Review. *Journal of Economic Literature* 50(1): 3–50.

Sagoff, Mark. 1988. *The Economy of the Earth: Philosophy, Law, and the Environment.* Cambridge: Cambridge University Press.

Sakai, Marco, and John Barrett. 2016. Border Carbon Adjustments: Addressing Emissions Embodied in Trade. *Energy Policy.* 92: 102–110.

Santikarn, Marissa, Angela Naneu Churie Kallhauge, Suneira Rana, Daniel Besley and Joseph Pryor. 2020. *State and Trends of Carbon Pricing 2020.* Washington, DC: World Bank.

Scammell, Rosie. 2015. Pope Francis Recruits Naomi Klein in Climate Change Battle. *The Guardian,* June 27. Accessed at www.theguardian.com/world/ 2015/jun/28/pope-climate-change-naomi-klein.

Schendler, Auden, and Michael Toffel. 2011. The Factor Environmental Ratings Miss. *MIT Sloan Management Review* 53(1): 17–18.

Schiermeier, Quirin. 2011. Clean-Energy Credits Tarnished. *Nature* 477: 517–518.

Schipper, Lee. 2000. On the Rebound: The Interaction of Energy Efficiency, Energy Use and Economic Activity. An Introduction. *Energy Policy* 28(6–7): 351–353.

Schleussner, Carl-Friedrich, Alexander Nauels, Michiel Schaeffer, William Hare and Joeri Rogelj. 2019. Inconsistencies When Applying Novel Metrics for Emissions Accounting to the Paris Agreement. *Environmental Research Letters* 14(12): 124055.

Schmalensee, Richard, and Robert N. Stavins. 2015. Lessons Learned from Three Decades of Experience with Cap-and-Trade. Kennedy School of Government Research Working Paper No. 15-069.

Schneider, Lambert Richard. 2011. Perverse Incentives under the CDM: An Evaluation of HFC-23 Destruction Projects. *Climate Policy* 11(2): 851–864.

Schneider, Lambert, and Anja Kollmuss. 2015. Perverse Effects of Carbon Markets on HFC-23 and SF$_6$ Abatement Projects in Russia. *Nature Climate Change* 5: 1061–1063.

Schneider, Stephen. 1996. *Laboratory Earth: The Planetary Gamble We Can't Afford to Lose*. New York: Basic Books.

Schneider, Tapio, Colleen M. Kaul and Kyle G. Pressel. 2019. Possible Climate Transitions from Breakup of Stratocumulus Decks under Greenhouse Warming. *Nature Geoscience* 12(3): 163–167.

Schoenmaker, Dirk, and Rens Van Tilburg. 2016. What Role for Financial Supervisors in Addressing Environmental Risks? *Comparative Economic Studies* 58(3): 317–334.

Scholten, Rebecca, Tineke Lambooy, Remko Renes and Wim Bartels. 2017. Accounting for Future Generations. Does the IFRS Framework Sufficiently Encourage Energy Companies to Reflect on Climate Change in the Valuation of Their Production Assets, Taking into Account the New Initiative of the Task Force on Climate-Related Financial Disclosures? An Exploratory Qualitative Comparative Case Study Approach. Presented at 29th SASE Annual Meeting, Lyon. Available at https://ssrn.com/abstract=2995630 or http://dx.doi.org/10.2139/ssrn.2995630.

Schröder, Enno, and Servaas Storm. 2018. Economic Growth and Carbon Emissions: The Road to "Hothouse Earth" Is Paved with Good Intentions. Institute for New Economic Thinking Working Paper No. 84.

Schuetze, Christopher F. 2012. U.S. Fight against E.U. Airline Emissions Plan Heats Up. *International Herald Tribune*, August 6. Accessed at https://rendezvous.blogs.nytimes.com/2012/08/06/u-s-fight-against-european-airline-emissions-plan-heats-up/.

Searchinger, Tim, and Ralph Heimlich. 2015. Avoiding Bioenergy Competition for Food Crops and Land. Working Paper, Installment 9 of Creating a Sustainable Food Future. Washington, DC: World Resources Institute.

Sen, Suphi, and Marie-Theres von Schickfus. 2017. Will Assets Be Stranded or Bailed Out? Expectations of Investors in the Face of Climate Policy. ifo Working Paper No. 238.

Seo, S. Niggol. 2015. Fatalities of Neglect: Adapt to More Intense Hurricanes under Global Warming? *International Journal of Climatology* 35(12): 3505–3514.

Shabecoff, Philip. 1988. Global Warming Has Begun, Expert Tells Senate. *New York Times*, June 24.

Shadbolt, Peter. 2015. "Vindskip" Cargo Ship Uses Its Hull as a Giant Sail. CNN. January 16. Accessed at www.cnn.com/2015/01/16/tech/vindskip-wind-powered-container-ship/index.html.

Shah, Nihar, Max Wei, Virginie Letschert and Amol Phadke. 2015. Benefits of Leapfrogging to Superefficiency and Low Global Warming Potential

Refrigerants in Room Air Conditioning. Lawrence Berkeley National Laboratory. Accessed at https://eta-publications.lbl.gov/sites/default/files/lbnl-1003671.pdf.

Shang, Baoping. 2021. The Poverty and Distributional Impacts of Carbon Pricing: Channels and Policy Implications. IMF Working Paper No. 21/172.

Sharmina, Maria, Oreane Y. Edelenbosch, Charlie Wilson, Rachel Freeman, David Gernaat, Paul Gilbert, Alice Larkin, Emma Littleton, Michael Traut, Detlef P. van Vuuren, Naomi Vaughan, F. Ruth Wood and Corinne Le Quéré. 2021. Decarbonising the Critical Sectors of Aviation, Shipping, Road Freight and Industry to Limit Warming to 1.5–2°C. *Climate Policy* 21(4): 455–474.

Shaxson, Nicholas. 2011. *Treasure Islands: Uncovering the Damage of Offshore Banking and Tax Havens*. New York: St. Martin's Press.

Shellenberger, Michael, and Ted Nordhaus. 2004. The Death of Environmentalism: Global Warming Politics in a Post-Environmental World. Report to the Environmental Grantmakers Association. Accessed at https://grist.org/article/doe-reprint/.

Silver, Nicholas. 2016. Blindness to Risk: Why Institutional Investors Ignore the Risk of Stranded Assets. *Journal of Sustainable Finance & Investment* 7(1): 1–15.

Sluijs, A., G. J. Bowen, H. Brinkhuis, L. J. Lourens and E. Thomas. 2007. The Palaeocene–Eocene Thermal Maximum Super Greenhouse: Biotic and Geochemical Signatures, Age Models and Mechanisms of Global Change. In *Deep-Time Perspectives on Climate Change: Marrying the Signal from Computer Models and Biological Proxies*, ed. M. Williams, A. M. Haywood, F. J. Gregory and D. N. Schmidt. London: Micropalaeontological Society, Special Publications, pp. 323–349.

Smil, Vaclav. 1994. *Energy in World History*. Boulder, CO: Westview Press.

Smith, Brad. 2020. Microsoft Will Be Carbon Negative by 2030. Microsoft on the Issues, January 16. Accessed at https://blogs.microsoft.com/blog/2020/01/16/microsoft-will-be-carbon-negative-by-2030/.

Smith, Noah. 2014a. The Most Damning Critique of DSGE. Accessed at http://noahpinionblog.blogspot.com/2014/01/the-most-damning-critique-of-dsge.html;

Smith, Noah. 2014b. The Equation at the Core of Modern Macro. Accessed at http://noahpinionblog.blogspot.com/2014/01/the-equation-at-core-of-modern-macro.html.

Smith, Noah. 2016. Economists Give Up on Milton Friedman's Biggest Idea. *Bloomberg Review*. Accessed at www.bloomberg.com/view/articles/2016-07-26/economists-give-up-on-milton-friedman-s-biggest-idea.

Smith, Pete, Steven J. Davis, Felix Creutzig, Sabine Fuss, Jan Minx, Benoit Gabrielle, Etsushi Kato, Robert B. Jackson, Annette Cowie, Elmar Kriegler, Detlef P. van Vuuren, Joeri Rogelj, Philippe Ciais, Jennifer Milne, Josep G.

Canadell, David McCollum, Glen Peters, Robbie Andrew, Volker Krey,
Gyami Shrestha, Pierre Friedlingstein, Thomas Gasser, Arnulf Grübler,
Wolfgang K. Heidug, Matthias Jonas, Chris D. Jones, Florian Kraxner, Emma
Littleton, Jason Lowe, José Roberto Moreira, Nebojsa Nakicenovic, Michael
Obersteiner, Anand Patwardhana, Mathis Rogner, Ed Rubin, Ayyoob Sharifi,
Asbjørn Torvanger, Yoshiki Yamagata, Jae Edmonds and Cho Yongsung.
2016. Biophysical and Economic Limits to Negative $CO_2$ Emissions. *Nature
Climate Change* 6(1): 42–50.

Snover, A. K., G. S. Mauger, L. C. Whitely Binder, M. Krosby and I. Tohver.
2013. Climate Change Impacts and Adaptation in Washington State:
Technical Summaries for Decision Makers. State of Knowledge Report
Prepared for the Washington State Department of Ecology. Climate Impacts
Group, University of Washington, Seattle.

Sobel, Dava. 1995. *Longitude: The True Story of a Lone Genius Who Solved the
Greatest Scientific Problem of His Time.* New York: Walker & Co.

Song, Lisa, and Paula Moura. 2019. An (Even More) Inconvenient Truth: Why
Carbon Credits for Forest Preservation May Be Worse than Nothing.
ProPublica. May 22. Accessed at https://features.propublica.org/brazil-
carbon-offsets/inconvenient-truth-carbon-credits-don't-work-deforestation-
redd-acre-cambodia/.

Song, Lisa, and James Temple. 2021. A Nonprofit Promised to Preserve Wildlife.
Then It Made Millions Claiming It Could Cut Down Trees. ProPublica. May
10. Accessed at www.propublica.org/article/a-nonprofit-promised-to-
preserve-wildlife-then-it-made-millions-claiming-it-could-cut-down-trees.

Sparrow, Katy J., John D. Kessler, John R. Southon, Fenix Garcia-Tigreros,
Kathryn M. Schreiner, Carolyn D. Ruppel, John B. Miller, Scott J. Lehman
and Xiaomei Xu. 2018. Limited Contribution of Ancient Methane to Surface
Waters of the U.S. Beaufort Sea Shelf. *Science Advances* 4(1): eaao4842.

Staver, A. Carla, Sally Archibald and Simon A. Levin. 2011. The Global Extent
and Determinants of Savanna and Forest as Alternative Biome States. *Science*
334: 230–232.

Steele, Michael A., and John L. Koprowski. 2003. *North American Tree
Squirrels.* Washington, DC: Smithsonian Books.

Steffen, Will, Johan Rockström, Katherine Richardson, Timothy M. Lenton, Carl
Folke, Diana Liverman, Colin P. Summerhayes, Anthony D. Barnosky, Sarah
E. Cornell, Michel Crucifix, Jonathan F. Donges, Ingo Fetzer, Steven J. Lade,
Marten Scheffer, Ricarda Winkelmann and Hans Joachim Schellnhuber. 2018.
Trajectories of the Earth System in the Anthropocene. *PNAS* 115(33):
8252–8259.

Stenek, Vladimir. 2014. Carbon Bubbles and Stranded Assets. *Development in a
Changing Climate.* Accessed at http://blogs.worldbank.org/climatechange/
carbon-bubbles-stranded-assets.

Stern, Nicholas. 2006. *Stern Review on the Economics of Climate Change.* Cambridge: Cambridge University Press.

Stern, Nicholas. 2008. The Economics of Climate Change: Richard T. Ely Lecture. *American Economic Review: Papers & Proceedings* 98(2): 1–37.

Stern, Nicholas, and Joseph Stiglitz. 2021. The Social Cost of Carbon, Risk, Distribution, Market Failures: An Alternative Approach. NBER Working Paper No. 28472.

Storey, Michael, Robert A. Duncan and Carl C. Swisher III. 2007. Paleocene–Eocene Thermal Maximum and the Opening of the Northeast Atlantic. *Science* 316(5824): 587–589.

Stork, Nigel E. 2010. Re-assessing Current Extinction Rates. *Biodiversity and Conservation* 19(2): 357–371.

Struzik, Ed. 2020. The Age of Megafires: The World Hits a Climate Tipping Point. Yale Environment 360, September 17. Accessed at https://e360.yale .edu/features/the-age-of-megafires-the-world-hits-a-climate-tipping-point#:~: text=Indeed%2C%20just%20as%20global%20warming,a%20new%20era %20of%20megafires.

Stutzer, Alois, and Bruno S. Frey. 2008. Stress That Doesn't Pay: The Commuting Paradox. *The Scandinavian Journal of Economics* 110(2): 339–366.

Suc, Jean-Pierre, Séverine Fauquette, Speranta-Maria Popescu and Cécile Robin. 2020. Subtropical Mangrove and Evergreen Forest Reveal Paleogene Terrestrial Climate and Physiography at the North Pole. *Palaeogeography, Palaeoclimatology, Palaeoecology* 551: Article 109755.

Sustainable Energy for All. 2018. Chilling Prospects: Providing Sustainable Cooling for All. Accessed at www.seforall.org/sites/default/files/SEforALL_ CoolingForAll-Report_0.pdf.

Tavoni, Massimo, and Robert Socolow. 2013. Modeling Meets Science and Technology: An Introduction to a Special Issue on Negative Emissions. *Climatic Change* 118(1): 1–14.

Tavoni, Massimo, and Richard S. J. Tol. 2010. Counting Only the Hits? The Risk of Underestimating the Costs of Stringent Climate Policy. *Climatic Change* 100(3–4): 769–778.

Thailand, National Statistical Office. n.d. Executive Summary: The 2010 Population and Housing Census. Accessed at http://popcensus.nso.go.th/ upload/census-report-6-4-54-en.pdf.

Tokarska, Katarzyna B., Martin B. Stolpe, Sebastian Sippel, Erich M. Fischer, Christopher J. Smith, Flavio Lehner and Reto Knutti. 2020. Past Warming Trend Constrains Future Warming in CMIP6 Models. *Science Advances* 6(12): 9549.

Tooze, Adam. 2019. Why Central Banks Need to Step Up on Global Warming. *Foreign Policy*, July 20. Accessed at https://foreignpolicy.com/2019/07/20/ why-central-banks-need-to-step-up-on-global-warming/.

Townsend, Solitaire. 2017. We Should Replace Angry Climate Porn with a Positive Message. Positive.News. Accessed at www.positive.news/2017/perspective/29995/replace-angry-climate-porn-positive-message/.

Trenberth, Kevin E., Aiguo Dai, Gerard van der Schrier, Philip D. Jones, Jonathan Barichivich, Keith R. Briffa and Justin Sheffield. 2014. Global Warming and Changes in Drought. *Nature Climate Change* 4(1): 17–22.

Turetsky, Merritt R., Benjamin W. Abbott, Miriam C. Jones, Katey Walter Anthony, David Olefeldt, Edward A. G. Schuur, Charles Koven, A. David McGuire, Guido Grosse, Peter Kuhry, Gustaf Hugelius, David M. Lawrence, Carolyn Gibson and A. Britta K. Sannel. 2019. Permafrost Collapse Is Accelerating Carbon Release. *Nature* 569(7754): 32–34.

UN. 2021. We Can End Poverty. Accessed at www.un.org/millenniumgoals/.

UN Department of Economic and Social Affairs. 2016. Demographic Yearbook. Accessed at http://unstats.un.org/unsd/demographic/products/dyb/dyb_Household/dyb_household.htm.

UN Development Program. 2021. The SDGS in Action. Accessed at www.undp.org/content/undp/en/home/sustainable-development-goals.html.

UNEP. 2016. The Montreal Protocol on Substances That Deplete the Ozone Layer. Accessed at http://ozone.unep.org/en/treaties-and-decisions/montreal-protocol-substances-deplete-ozone-layer.

UNFCCC. 2016a. CDM Project Activities. Accessed at http://cdm.unfccc.int/Statistics/Public/CDMinsights/index.html.

UNFCCC. 2016b. Synthesis Report on the Aggregate Effect of Intended Nationally Determined Contributions. Accessed at http://unfccc.int/focus/indc_portal/items/9240.php.

UNITAID. 2016. Innovative Financing. Accessed at www.unitaid.eu/en/how/innovative-financing.

University of New Hampshire. 2016. Campus Carbon Calculator v. 6.5 Users Guide. Accessed at www.sustainableunh.unh.edu/sites/sustainableunh.unh.edu/files/images/v6.5_Users_Guide.pdf.

UN-REDD. 2016. Seventh Consolidated Annual Progress Report of the UN-REDD Programme Fund. Accessed at www.unredd.net/documents/programme-progress-reports-785/2015-programme-progress-reports/2015-annual-report.html.

UN-REDD Programme. 2021. Accessed at www.un-redd.org/.

US Bureau of Economic Analysis. 2020. Integrated Macroeconomic Accounts for the United States. Accessed at www.bea.gov/data/special-topics/integrated-macroeconomic-accounts.

US Bureau of Labor Statistics. 2016. Occupational Employment Statistics. Accessed at www.bls.gov/oes/current/naics4_212100.htm.

US Congress. 2019. Text of H. Res. 109. Accessed at www.congress.gov/bill/116th-congress/house-resolution/109/text.

US Congress. 2021. S.1956: European Union Emissions Trading Scheme Prohibition Act of 2011. Accessed at www.congress.gov/bill/112th-congress/ senate-bill/1956/actions.

US Department of Justice, Office of Legal Policy. 2012. Prison Rape Elimination Act Regulatory Impact Analysis. Docket No. OAG-131, RIN 1105-AB34.

US Energy Information Agency. 2020. Today in Energy. Accessed at www.eia .gov/todayinenergy/detail.php?id=21912.

US Environmental Protection Administration. n.d. Mortality Risk Valuation. Accessed at www.epa.gov/environmental-economics/mortality-risk-valuation#difference.

US EPA. 2021. Atmospheric Concentrations of Greenhouse Gases. Accessed at https://cfpub.epa.gov/roe/indicator.cfm?i=24.

US White House. 2021. Fact Sheet: President Biden Sets 2030 Greenhouse Gas Pollution Reduction Target Aimed at Creating Good-Paying Union Jobs and Securing U.S. Leadership on Clean Energy Technologies. April 22. Accessed at www.whitehouse.gov/briefing-room/statements-releases/2021/04/22/fact-sheet-president-biden-sets-2030-greenhouse-gas-pollution-reduction-target-aimed-at-creating-good-paying-union-jobs-and-securing-u-s-leadership-on-clean-energy-technologies/.

Valley, John W., Aaron J. Cavosie, Takayuki Ushikubo, David A. Reinhard, Daniel F. Lawrence, David J. Larson, Peter H. Clifton, Thomas F. Kelly, Simon A. Wilde, Desmond E. Moser and Michael J. Spicuzza. 2014. Hadean Age for a Post-Magma-Ocean Zircon Confirmed by Atom-Probe Tomography. *Nature Geoscience* 7: 219–223.

van der Zwaan, Bob, Hilke Rösler, Tom Kober, Tino Aboumahboub, Kate V. Calvin, David E. H. J. Gernaat, Giacomo Marangoni and David McCollum. 2013. A Cross-Model Comparison of Global Long-Term Technology Diffusion under a 2°C Climate Change Control Target. *Climate Change Economics* 4(4): 1–24.

van Vuuren, Detlef P., Sebastiaan Deetman, Jasper van Vliet, Maarten van den Berg, Bas J. van Ruijven and Barbara Koelbl. 2013. The Role of Negative $CO_2$ Emissions for Reaching 2°C: Insights from Integrated Assessment Modeling. *Climatic Change* 118(1): 15–27.

van Vuuren, Detlef P., Elke Stehfest, Michel G. J. den Elzen, Tom Kram, Jasper van Vliet, Sebastiaan Deetman, Morna Isaac, Kees Klein Goldewijk, Andries Hof, Angelica Mendoza Beltran, Rineke Oostenrijk and Bas van Ruijven. 2011. RCP2.6: Exploring the Possibility to Keep Global Mean Temperature Increase below 2°C. *Climatic Change* 109(1): 95–116.

van Vuuren, Detlef P., Heleen van Soest, Keywan Riahi, Leon Clarke, Volker Krey, Elmar Kriegler, Joeri Rogelj, Michiel Schaeffer and Massimo Tavoni. 2016. Carbon Budgets and Energy Transition Pathways. *Environmental Research Letters* 11(7): 1–12.

Vanderheiden, Steve. 2009. *Atmospheric Justice: A Political Theory of Climate Change*. Oxford: Oxford University Press.

Victor, David G. 2011. *Global Warming Gridlock: Creating More Effective Strategies for Protecting the Planet*. Cambridge: Cambridge University Press.

von Hirschhausen, Christian. 2014. The German "Energiewende": An Introduction. *Economics of Energy & Environmental Policy* 3(2): 1–12.

Wallace, Tim, and Krishna Karra. 2020. The True Colors of America's Political Spectrum Are Gray and Green. *New York Times*, September 2.

Walton, Gary M., and Hugh Rockoff. 2013. *History of the American Economy*. Mason, OH: South-Western Publishing.

Wang, Qian, Klaus Hubacek, Kuishuang Feng, Yi-Ming Wei and Qiao-Mei Liang. 2016. Distributional Effects of Carbon Taxation. *Applied Energy* 184(C): 1123–1131.

Weber, Sylvain, Reyer Gerlagh, Nicole A. Mathys and Daniel Moran. 2019. $CO_2$ Embedded in Trade: Trends and Fossil Fuel Drivers. CESifo Working Paper No. 7562.

Weitzman, Martin. 1974. Prices vs. Quantities. *Review of Economic Studies* 41(4): 477–491.

Weitzman, Martin L. 2009. On Modeling and Interpreting the Economics of Climate Change. *Review of Economics and Statistics* 91(1): 1–19.

Weitzman, Martin L. 2011. Fat-Tailed Uncertainty in the Economics of Catastrophic Climate Change. *Review of Environmental Economics and Policy* 5(2): 275–292.

Weitzman, Martin L. 2014. Fat Tails and the Social Cost of Carbon. *American Economic Review: Papers & Proceedings* 104(5): 544–546.

Westbrook, Robert B. 1993. *John Dewey and American Democracy*. Ithaca, NY: Cornell University Press.

Westerhold, Thomas, Ursula Röhl, Heather K. McCarren and James C. Zachos. 2009. Latest on the Absolute Age of the Paleocene–Eocene Thermal Maximum (PETM): New Insights from Exact Stratigraphic Position of Key Ash Layers +19 and −17. *Earth and Planetary Science Letters* 287: 412–419.

Williams, Michael. 2000. Dark Ages and Dark Areas: Global Deforestation in the Deep Past. *Journal of Historical Geography* 26(1): 28–46.

Williams, Michael. 2003. *Deforesting the Earth: From Prehistory to Global Crisis*. Chicago: University of Chicago Press.

Williams, Richard G., Vassil Roussenov, Thomas L. Frölicher and Philip Goodwin. 2017. Drivers of Continued Surface Warming after Cessation of Carbon Emissions. *Geophysical Research Letters* 44(20): 10633–10642.

Williams, Roberton C., III, Hal Gordon, Dallas Burtraw, Jared C. Carbone and Richard D. Morgenstern. 2015. The Initial Incidence of a Carbon Tax across Income Groups. *National Tax Journal* 68(1): 195–214.

Wing, Allison A., Kerry Emanuel and Susan Solomon. 2015. On the Factors Affecting Trends and Variability in Tropical Cyclone Potential Intensity. *Geophysical Research Letters* 42: 8669–8677.

World Bank. 2010. *Cities and Climate Change: An Urgent Agenda.* New York: World Bank.

World Bank. 2012. Turn Down the Heat: Why a 4°C Warmer World Must Be Avoided. Accessed at http://documents.worldbank.org/curated/en/865571468149107611/pdf/NonAsciiFileNameo.pdf.

World Bank. 2018. World Bank Country and Lending Groups. Accessed at https://datahelpdesk.worldbank.org/knowledgebase/articles/906519.

World Bank. 2021. World Development Indicators Accessed at http://databank.worldbank.org/data/reports.aspx?source=world-development-indicators.

World Resources Institute and World Business Council for Sustainable Development. 2020. Greenhouse Gas Protocol Standards. Accessed at https://ghgprotocol.org/standards.

WorldoMeter. 2021. Accessed at www.worldometers.info/world-population/world-population-by-year/.

Wright, Gavin. 1990. The Origins of American Industrial Success, 1879–1940. *The American Economic Review* 80(4): 651–668.

Wunderling, Nico, Jonathan F. Donges, Jürgen Kurths and Ricarda Winkelmann. 2021. Interacting Tipping Elements Increase Risk of Climate Domino Effects under Global Warming. *Earth System Dynamics* 12: 601–619.

Yahoo Finance. n.d. Accessed at https://finance.yahoo.com/.

Yao, Weiqi, Adina Paytan and Ulrich G. Wortmann. 2018. Large-Scale Ocean Deoxygenation during the Paleocene–Eocene Thermal Maximum. *Science* 361(6404): 804–806.

Yergin, Daniel, and Elena Pravettoni. 2016. Do Investments in Oil and Gas Constitute "Systemic Risk"? IHS Energy Strategic Report. Accessed at https://cdn.ihs.com/www/pdf/SystemicRisk-report.pdf.

Zamora, Daniel, and Michael C. Behrent, eds. 2015. *Foucault and Neoliberalism.* Cambridge: Polity.

Zelinka, Mark D., Timothy A. Myers, Daniel T. McCoy, Stephen Po-Chedley, Peter M. Caldwell, Paulo Ceppi, Stephen A. Klein and Karl E. Taylor. 2019. Causes of Higher Climate Sensitivity in CMIP6 Models. *Geophysical Research Letters* 12(2): 85782.

Zhao, Chuang, Bing Liu, Shilong Piao, Xuhui Wang, David B. Lobell, Yao Huang, Mengtian Huang, Yitong Yao, Simona Bassu, Philippe Ciais, Jean-Louis Durand, Joshua Elliott, Frank Ewert, Ivan A. Janssens, Tao Li, Erda Lin, Qiang Liu, Pierre Martre, Christoph Müller, Shushi Peng, Josep Peñuelas, Alex C. Ruane, Daniel Wallach, Tao Wang, Donghai Wu, Zhuo Liu, Yan Zhu, Zaichun Zhu and Senthold Asseng. 2017. Temperature Increase Reduces

Global Yields of Major Crops in Four Independent Estimates. *PNAS* 114(35): 9326–9331.

Zhu, Jinshan, and Yingkai Tang. 2015. The Design Flaw of the Displacement Principle of Clean Development Mechanism: The Neglect of Electricity Shortage. *European Journal of Law and Economics* 40: 367–391.

Zickfeld, Kirsten, and Tyler Herrington. 2015. The Time Lag between a Carbon Dioxide Emission and Maximum Warming Increases with the Size of the Emission. *Environmental Research Letters* 10(3): 1001.

Zucman, Gabriel. 2015. *The Hidden Wealth of Nations: The Scourge of Tax Havens*. Chicago: University of Chicago Press.

# INDEX